Alan St

58.4

AN 49396N

Invitation To Self-Management, first published 1989 by Dab Hand Press, 90 Long Drive, Ruislip, Middlesex HA4 OHP.

British Library Cataloguing in Publication Data

Stanton, Alan
Invitation to self-management.
1. Organisations. Teams. Management
I. Title
658.4'02

ISBN 0 9513862 0 4

Copies available by post from Dab Hand Press
Trade Distribution to Bookshops through Turnaround Distribution Co-operative, 27 Horsell Road, London N5 1XL, telephone 01-609-7836.

Typesetting and production by Karia Communications Ltd
Cover Design by Ben Edgell

Printed and bound in Great Britain by
Biddles Ltd, Guildford and King's Lynn

To Zena and Rachel
Who gave up their
Sitting-room table.

Contents

Newcastle FSU Staff and Management Committee Members Quoted

NAME	JOB	STARTED	LEFT
Newcastle FSU workers			
Parveen AKHTAR	Groupworker	Nov 1983	—
Blanche CALLAN	Part-time Secretary	Apr 1975	—
Pam CARTER	Student Unit Supervisor	Jan 1980	Sept 1980
"	Student Unit Supervisor	Oct 1982	Sept 1984
Anne DAVIES	Social Worker	Jan 1985	May 1986
Shirley DEVLIN	Childcare Worker Women's Workshops	Dec 1981	Sept 1984
Ernie DOBSON	Community Worker	Sept 1979	—
Shirley FORSTER	Social Worker	Oct 1979	May 1985
"	Part-time Social Worker	Aug 1986	Dec 1986
Alison HARKER	Social Worker	Jan 1975	Dec 1979
Lin HARWOOD	Groupworker	Jan 1979	June 1983
Chris JOHNSON	Community Worker	Sept 1978	Nov 1983
Evelyn RAE	Part-time Secretary	June 1972	—
Ali RHIND	Women's Workshop Worker	Nov 1981	Sept 1984
Angela SEWELL	Student Unit Supervisor	Oct 1984	Oct 1987
Joan SMITH	Groupworker	Nov 1974	Nov 1977
"	Unit Organiser	Nov 1977	Aug 1983
Carol TATE	Cleaner	Mar 1972	—
Sally WALKER	Women's Workshop Worker	May 1982	Apr 1984
Yvonne WATERS	Secretary	Feb 1978	—
Lilian WHITE	Social Worker	Sept 1980	Aug 1986
Elliot YABANTU	Community Worker	Feb 1984	—

Other staff mentioned: Donna AKHTAR (translator and groupworker) and Jean MOWBERRY (book-keeper) were both sessional workers. Val CHAPMAN, was a temporary social worker 1983/4. Brenda WHITE worked part-time at the independent Pool Girls' Club from November 1982 to August 1985, and then as a volunteer while she was on a youth and community work course.

Unit Management Committee:

Tony BOYD		1982	Nov	1985
Ian BYNOE	Mar	1984	Nov	1985
Margaret CHILES	Dec	1981		—
Monica ELLIOT	Dec	1981	Oct	1984
Pam FLYNN	Dec	1981	Oct	1984
Tom HAMMILL	June	1976	Nov	1985
Alan JACKSON	Dec	1981	July	1985
Shahin ORSBORN	Mar	1984	Nov	1985
Peter STONE	Mar	1975	Nov	1984

Introduction

This book will change the way you feel and think about your workplace.

At first glance, maybe that seems unlikely. For, at its heart, this is a story of one small team, running a social work and community work agency in a poor part of a small city. And even by the time it was printed, most of the people described had moved on.

But don't be deceived. Underlying their story are the same issues and problems you face at work and, more importantly, exploring them will show why and how your workplace can change.

★

The team, Newcastle-upon-Tyne Family Service Unit (FSU), never saw themselves as special, and certainly not as a model for others. They wondered: "Why should there ever have been any fuss about it?" insisting that how they worked was "ordinary and mundane". But fuss there was, in August 1984, when the staff and local management committee of the Unit rattled the parent organisation — National FSU — by formally applying to work *collectively*. The shock waves were all the greater because Newcastle Unit insisted they *had already* been working democratically within a hierarchical shell.

This is the first study with such a collective team in Britain. It gives a picture of the Unit before and after its shift to formal self-management, concentrating on the working relationships among a group of colleagues. My aim was to go under the skin of a group who deliberately set out to work and learn together.

If you take a quick riffle through the pages, you'll notice several more unusual features. One is that a hefty chunk of the book is the views of Unit staff, management committee, users, students, and colleagues in other agencies. At their own request, they give their real names, and have all agreed to their words being used. The team also approved the final draft. So you are reading comments and ideas which they owned and wished to share.

A second likely surprise is that, while I'm writing on *teamwork*, you'll find next to nothing about 'how to do it'. This is not a cookbook of tested recipes; it contains no techniques or exercises; no suggested structures. Indeed, I strongly doubt that such 'how' approaches can succeed unless they also examine the 'why' and 'what' of working together.

For staff in hierarchies, the 'why' of this book will be clear once they realise that I am focussing on the *processes* of working collectively. My argument is that collective teams — especially those, like Newcastle FSU, within a hierarchical agency — offer us important lessons. And such lessons gain in urgency each time an official report criticises a lack of agency co-ordination. Sadly, in most organisations, effective teamworking is far more praised than practiced.

Not that we need outside reports. The problems and constrictions of conventional workplaces are usually obvious to those who work there. All too frequently, tasks are fragmented and individualised. Staff spend energy on survival, rather than giving their best. People's experience and skills may be left untapped and undeveloped, and there is defensiveness, distrust and cynicism. The culture encourages complaints about others — 'them', 'the hierarchy', 'my staff' — but guarded and indirect, rarely forthright and open.

But of course, that isn't the whole picture. In numerous organisations, committed and enthusiastic workers do set out to pool their skills, support each other's work, and learn together to improve their service to users. As at Newcastle, healthy and effective teamworking takes root. But then, the issue is finding ways to build on this. For regularly, a collaborative staff group is ignored and dismantled at the first restructuring. How often do we realise what we've lost only when it's gone?

In either setting — the individualised office or the informally collaborative team — the experience of collective teamwork offers a fruitful option. It is valuable precisely because it comes out of *intentional* experiments in joint working; members set out to shape their own history, changing their own working relations and the way they relate to users.

★

It is important to acknowledge one reason why this experience has rarely been drawn on. For many outsiders, working collectively is far from "ordinary and mundane". On the contrary, it's frequently invested with a heady blend of hopes and fears; impossibly high expectations, or deep scepticism and suspicion. Both inhibit people exploring their potential for co-operation.

Saying that collective teams offer fresh possibilities, I'm not writing a simple success story. And there is no happy ever after. At Newcastle Unit, as for other groups, teaming up was as difficult and painful as in your own office or agency. They didn't 'solve' the problems of teamworking, and aren't condescendingly offering a 'right' way to follow. So you'll read about their messes and muddles, as well as the solid achievements; the weaknesses alongside the strengths.

Because I'm not idealising collective working, I hope readers who already work in a co-op or collective haven't begun to feel smug. For you will find many of the ideas here distinctly unsettling, and some of the criticisms will sting. In particular, this book is impatient with groups who assume that working collectively means only the adoption of a particular structure and set of ground rules. Phrases like 'We are a collective' and 'We work as a co-op' are sometimes intoned like a mantra. Instead of actively exploring the processes of working together, these labels can cover up a mishmash of poor practice and unco-operative staff relations. In the worst cases, formally collective teams can lend themselves to individuals who indulge their egos, refusing to face the realities of sharing skills and power.

So if you work collectively, the book is for you as well. You will find me and the Newcastle team committed critics who say what your best friends need to tell you, as well as offering positive suggestions.

★

Where are agency users in all this? Though we will explore the Unit's working mainly from the team's perspective, that includes a discussion of the pattern of its services. Collective working makes its own contribution to issues of how a team's work is chosen and by whom.

In addition, this book has something vital to say about the *qualitative* link between a collaborative work group and the service an organisation provides. When Newcastle Family Service Unit talked about trying to be a democratic team, they didn't just mean staff running things. Self-management, they argued, was part of their overall aim of enabling the *participation* and *empowerment* of users. They insisted that an agency wishing to work more equally with users, respecting and empowering them, must itself adopt forms of organisation which strengthen the same relations among its workers.

This has implications for people outside public agencies who set out to change them. How can users, members of community groups, and even politicians aim to change public agencies, making them more open and responsive? One answer is that we need to understand and work towards a collaborative organisational culture.

★

Outline of the Book

Part I, *Teaming Up*, starts by explaining how the Newcastle team and I came to meet; and sketches the City, the Unit, and the research. Then we trace their history. Why did a 'democratic team' seem a natural and obvious step in Newcastle, but a radical and nearly unacceptable departure elsewhere in FSU? To answer, we move away from the agency to explore some of the writing on social services teams. Why is genuine teamwork so elusive?

Returning to Newcastle, we look at the relationships — working and personal — among members. Who worked there, and what sort of people were they? How closed and closeknit are collective teams? What is it like to 'come in' — as a new member or outsider? Such teams can often seem unruly and even downright rude. Why is this, and what sort of working relations are they aiming at?

Part II, *Working Together*, outlines the Unit's work. We find out why their secretaries opted out of self-management. Then, how did the team choose new work? We examine the myth that agencies have a choice between 'reactive' and 'proactive' approaches. FSU's alternative *interactive* approach is illustrated by its changing services for black people.

What of the influence of local authority funding on the pattern of work? British grant aided agencies are usually classified as 'voluntary' sector, in contrast to 'statutory' organisations run by local and central government. I suggest the relationship is better understood as one of 'purchase of service'.

Next we discuss two challenges to Newcastle Unit's division of labour. The first, influenced by systems ideas, suggests a greater pooling and integration of work. This is followed by a look at writing on collectives. Had the Unit failed to be a 'real collective' in the sense sometimes used by socialist and feminist members of groups elsewhere?

Part III, *Common Judgement* tackles the criticism that collective working takes far too much time. How true is this, and how should we judge the meetings and decision-making process, not just in collective teams, but in all agencies?

Part IV, *Common Wealth*, sees teams generating and managing common assets. Teamwork, it's argued, is as much about mutual learning as working together. But then what about members' different levels of skill and experience, differing ambitions and plans? And how do we extend co-learning outside a workgroup: to students; or users? Collective working suggests a challenge to ideas of 'the body of knowledge', as well as identifying a practitioners' knowledge separate from professionalism.

A different kind of common wealth is a team's use of its building. Can groups begin to make their own geography as well as their own history? We analyse the tensions involved in opening up an agency's space — among workers, and toward the outside, whether users or colleagues.

Part V, *Sharing Power*, tackles central questions of power and control. How do co-operative and collective groups discipline members in the absence of a boss? Have they an unfair 'community justice'?

Feminist approaches to power sharing influenced Newcastle as well as other collective teams, and these are discussed within the wider context of gender in social services agencies.

Finally, we take the ideas and tentative conclusions reached so far, and examine the Unit's attempts at community participation and control. I suggest that we can learn something about making community control a reality in a range of forums where 'lay' people and practitioners are involved together in the management of public resources.

★

A last word about timing. The 'story' told here mainly takes place before 1986. Two years on may seem like a bad time to publish a book on collective teamwork. The Newcastle Unit itself is not only a different team, but struggling to survive public expenditure cuts. And the picture is similar elsewhere, as collaborative agencies of all kinds fall victim to an increasingly closed political climate.

Yet, it is always easier to postpone such changes. Somehow the day when we have a bit more time and a few more resources never seems to come. It also needs saying that the issues of democratic working and empowerment become *more*, not less important when under attack. Even if we can't always defend what people have gained, we can record, analyse and use their experiences and difficulties as the seeds for a different way of doing things in the future.

PART I

TEAMING UP

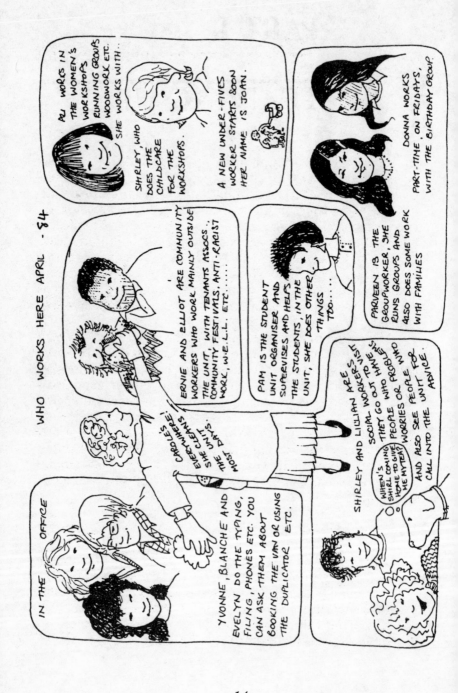

AL WORKS IN THE WOMEN'S WORKSHOPS RUNNING GROUPS WOODWORK ETC... SHE WORKS WITH...

SHIRLEY, WHO DOES THE CHILDCARE FOR THE WORKSHOPS.

A NEW UNDER-FIVES WORKER STARTS SOON HER NAME IS JOAN.

DONNA WORKS PART-TIME ON FRIDAYS, WITH THE BIRTHDAY GROUP.

ERNIE AND ELLIOT ARE COMMUNITY WORKERS WHO WORK MAINLY OUTSIDE THE UNIT, WITH TENANTS ASSOCS., COMMUNITY FESTIVALS, ANTI-RACIST WORK, W.E.L.L. ETC.......

CAROLE! EVER CLEANS THE UNIT SHE DOES THE DAYS MOST DAYS.

PAM IS THE STUDENT UNIT ORGANISER AND SUPERVISES AND HELPS THE STUDENTS, IN THE UNIT, SHE DOES OTHER THINGS TOO.....

PARVEEN IS THE GROUPWORKER, SHE RUNS GROUPS AND ALSO DOES SOME WORK WITH FAMILIES

IN THE OFFICE

YVONNE, BLANCHE AND EVELYN DO THE TYPING, FILING, PHONES ETC. YOU CAN ASK THEM ABOUT BOOKING THE VAN OR USING THE DUPLICATOR ETC.

SHIRLEY AND LILLIAN ARE SOCIAL WORKERS THEY GO OUT TO PEOPLE WHO HAVE PROBLEMS OR WORRIES AND ALSO SEE PEOPLE WHO CALL INTO THE UNIT FOR ADVICE.

WHEN'S SHIRL COMING HOME TO GIVE ME MY TEA?

One

Scene Setting

In August 1983 I had a phonecall from Janet Williams, then an assistant director of the national charity, *Family Service Units*. One of Janet's responsibilities was the Unit in Newcastle-upon-Tyne. She and Tim Cook, then FSU's director, invited me to their London head office. They wanted to discuss a formal proposal made by Newcastle Unit — that the team be allowed to work *collectively*. Janet and Tim approached me as someone researching with collective teams. It was the third year I'd been visiting and writing about agencies as varied as law and advice centres, social work offices and residential homes.

Here's the picture they gave of Newcastle Unit. A small staff group — then nine full-time and six part-time workers - had slowly grown more collaborative. The person in charge locally, was Joan Smith, Unit Organiser (UO). As 'boss', Joan had been more than willing to share management tasks. When in 1982, she'd taken six months sabbatical leave, the other staff divided up her work. On her return much of this joint management was left intact, and over the next year the share-out continued. In August 1983 Joan left, and most of the team (and its local management committee) were asking to self-manage.

I found Tim and Janet taking the proposal very seriously.

Tim Cook: The first time that the possibility of Newcastle wishing to operate collective (i.e. without a U.O.) I was quickly aware that personally, I was actually quite interested in it. Leaving to one side that it was in FSU. And I think Janet would say, jointly we were quite excited intellectually by the idea.

But they knew it wasn't this straightforward. They couldn't just "leave to one side" that it was within FSU, since it was far from a local matter. Partly, this was because FSU is a network of local Units — all the others with a Unit Organiser. (Some also have a senior social worker.) But the main issue was that the agency is legally constituted-as a single national charity with a director and assistant directors, and a National Council as its overall governing body.

> *Janet Williams*: Tim thought it important that the
> implications of the proposal for the whole organisation
> were fully understood.

About Family Service Units

A brief note for readers unfamiliar with FSU. Family Service Units was formed in 1948 as a non-profit company. There were (1988) twenty-three local Units round the country, plus a small head office. In total the agency had some 270 paid staff.[1] Local Units have always worked in poorer city areas. Their original brief was to help families on an individual basis, but later many developed group and community work. Now each Unit has its own distinct approach, with a mixture of different work and particular projects.[2]

Both FSU nationally and local Units, take on social policy issues as well. The agency publishes books and pamphlets, and makes submissions to local and central government bodies. In the two years preceding Newcastle's proposal, Tim Cook served on the Barclay Committee on social work,[3] for which FSU commissioned research.[4] Tim also chaired a committee on Clients' Rights, for the National Council of Voluntary Organisations;[5] and FSU published its own discussion paper on the topic.[6]

Another feature of the agency was a network of groupings across Units. In 1984/5, there was a Women's Development group, a Family Therapy group, and a Social Policy group, each drawing staff from different levels.

Within the national network, each Unit has considerable autonomy. "For most practical purposes", wrote one Unit Organiser, "FSU is a free association of largely autonomous and individualistic local agencies, each with its own management committee"[7]. Even so, Newcastle's proposal *was*, constitutionally, a matter for the agency as a whole. Tim Cook therefore referred it to the formal machinery — the National Management Committee and the National Council, FSU's governing body.[8]

Maybe it seems strange that I'm talking about self-management inside an organisation with a director, assistant directors, and National Council, not to mention each Unit's local management committee. Some people confine the term 'collective' to a small number of agencies which, like co-ops, are formally autonomous. But this is really to banish collective teamwork to the margin, treating it as an exotic specimen which can't thrive in everyday workplaces.

The exciting thing for me, listening to Tim and Janet, was the chance of learning how a collective team could grow within a larger organisation. What would happen when it became formally self-managing? Was it possible for me to research with the team; describing the process of collective working inside the staff group, and in relation to its users, to the management committee, and the national network?

Tim and Janet were interested, as were Newcastle staff when I met them two months later.

The Issue Debated

FSU's National Council and Management Committee weren't the only ones debating Newcastle's proposal. Self-management was bound up with other issues: trade union pressure for standard conditions of service[9]; tensions between the centre and semi-autonomous local Units.[10] The Unit Organisers discussed the implications for their individual position, and strength as a formal group within the agency.

With all this happening, Tim Cook argued that only a legitimate formal decision, finally from National Council, could settle the basis for change and set bounds round it. For about six months the organisation seemed more or less evenly divided on the issue. It was a period of irritation and anger, with feelings often running high. There was a lot of argument about the potential benefits and dangers of "joint staff management" (as Newcastle Unit were calling it).

The Unit lobbied for support within the organisation, and then formally presented its case. Tim recommended against — out of a concern for the rest of FSU rather than doubts about the scheme as such.[11] In February 1984 the National Council decided, by a narrow margin, to agree in principle to Newcastle's scheme.

"Let's Give It Our Backing"

Once the go-ahead came, Tim thought the scheme should be supported and learned from.

> *Tim Cook*: Right, let's give it our backing. Let's be big enough to eat our words, as it were, and give it our blessing and really go for it.

Formal recognition meant the Newcastle team could plan ahead, settle down to stability and get on with their work. The rest of the agency seems to have taken a similar view. What had been a major talking point rapidly went off the boil.[12]

> *Janet Williams*: There haven't been the waves, the repercussions. *Not* a word.

Another consequence of approval was that the agency's rules and procedures needed modifying. Given the existing rules, for one Unit to work collectively had been raised as a difficult anomaly. In fact, procedures covering discipline, grievances, and Newcastle's representation at various meetings outside, were adapted without trouble, once the principle of a collective team had been approved.

This illustrates one way in which Newcastle's membership of a larger organisation makes its experience important. It would be far less interesting if the Unit *had* been an independent group, or had to leave FSU.

National Council's decision meant research could go ahead. Though I visited the Unit twice before the final agreement, it wasn't until April 1984 that this study could properly begin.

Out to Elswick

Visitors' Newcastle rarely fails to impress. Here's a city announced by its river and distinctive bridges, and immediately presenting wide main shopping streets, monuments, and castle. A clean, cheap and efficient metro train speeds you to the Scandinavian-designed Civic Centre, or to leafy Edwardian Jesmond (reputedly inhabited by professionals, business-people, and staff from the University) and on to the coast and Victorian Whitley Bay.

You reach the Family Service Unit in the opposite direction, heading west, parallel with the River Tyne for about a mile. The city centre bustle changes to quiet streets and small local shops. While in town, graffiti on the metro were quickly scrubbed off, here "No Pakis" on the wall of the brewery stays daubed for months. At eight-thirty in the morning you can see the queue for yesterday's bread and cakes; half price at the 'seconds' shop. In the early evening a row of men on a bench wait for the working men's club to open up.

The Unit is in a part of town called Elswick. Its building is a large old house, next door to a pretty park, and near the top of one of the many streets that drop towards the river. Looking down the steep banks towards the quiet Tyne, over rows of 1960's Council houses, it's hard to imagine this area as once the centre of Newcastle's industrial wealth. Yet a hundred years ago it was:

> The most important centre in the world for the manufacture of ships, arms and locomotives.[13]

The West End of Newcastle can't be separated from this history. Its mines, shipyards, and engineering works have shaped the area's culture; its politics and class patterns — even the layout of the streets. The city — with its proverbial coal — grew rapidly in the industrial revolution, and the products of the factories of the West End 'made' many famous names. This was where Stephenson's *Rocket* was built, as were Armstrong's guns. Going back only seventy years, in the First World War the Armstrong-Whitworth "Elswick factory had built a third of Britain's total production of guns, 47 warships, more than 1000 aeroplanes, 14.5 million shells and 21 million cartridge cases".[14]

Now most of that industry has gone. The water and tracts of land alongside it are empty. A sign of the times was Vickers' proposal to build a riverside leisure centre.

"Brasilia of the Old World"

Other things have changed. Elswick had long been over-crowded and poor. In the 1960's, an ambitious slum clearance programme demolished huge swathes of the area, and virtually the whole of southern Elswick and neighbouring Benwell was rebuilt.[15] Jon Davies, who lived in the area, wrote a scathing account of this redevelopment, arguing that little sensitivity was shown to local people, especially the most powerless. With sarcasm, he quotes T.Dan Smith, then leader of the City Council, dreaming of Newcastle as "the Brasilia of the Old World". That dream, argues Davies, was: "an all-out effort to abolish the past and manufacture the future".[16]

On the other hand, the City avoided some of the worst mistakes of towns elsewhere. The new homes were mostly low-rise, many with small gardens. And action had been needed; some of the old blocks were notorious, they were so appalling.

The dislocation of families and communities caused by the redevelopment was partly what led to FSU being invited to the area in 1968. Many local people still regret the way communities were broken up. This, for instance, was the view of Joyce Robinson, who ran a pensioners drop-in centre down the road from the Unit.

> *Joyce Robinson*: Once this area was pulled down it was a bus-ride to go and see my grandmother that I'd seen every day. Because she was just chucked out of this area and sent to Long Benton, and we moved to Scotswood. And it's a world away, you know. It's all wrong.

Patterns Then and Now

I'm not saying that, either in employment or housing, there was some past golden age with jobs, homes, and grandparents-round-the- corner for everyone. As a local community project wrote:

> Working class families of West Newcastle have consistently over the years experienced a pattern of poor housing and bad amenities, insecurity of work, high unemployment and low wages.[17]

Below are some brief statistics about the area around the Unit at the time of this study. They're taken from Newcastle City Council publications, and reflect the pattern of inner city decline we might expect — especially in a northern town previously dominated by the old heavy industries. But perhaps the fact that we *have* come to expect such dismal figures blunts our response to them? Somehow the people themselves may slip through the tables and percentages.[18]

For there have been positive changes too — often because local people fought for change. And FSU has supported them -whether in campaigning against slum properties and damp, or by rolling up their sleeves to help with street parties and Festivals. The latter are not frills — or something uncontroversial to stick in an Annual Report. Locals are rightly proud of Elswick Park and its swimming pool. A day there at Elswick festival isn't just fun, but one way of saying that people's lives are more than the sum of their problems.

FSU's Area During the Research - Some Figures

Newcastle FSU's work was focussed mainly on the two West End wards of West City and Elswick. Within this patch of about four square miles live some 7000 people. Both City Council and national statistics show all the problems of an 'old' inner city area.[19] When this study began in 1984, West City ward had a male unemployment rate estimated at 42.7%. Elswick's was the second highest in Newcastle at 40.5%. Between 1979 and 1984 long term unemployment in the city trebled. The City Council's *Social Audit* in 1984, said that "about one third of children in Newcastle inner city will have one or both parents unemployed". Among young people in Newcastle overall unemployment was then 52%.

West City had one of the highest rates of overcrowded housing. It had a higher proportion of children (especially under-fives) than the city as a whole, and the lowest rate for children staying at school after sixteen. Elswick had similar features, the census data also showing one of the highest proportions of ethnic minorities, with about one-in-ten of its population in families originating in Pakistan or Bangladesh.

For the city at large, the Social Audit estimated that "40% of Newcastle's population is dependent on some kind of State benefit, excluding child benefit and housing benefit". It presented a pessimistic view of the future, recording a reduction in the quality of life "particularly marked among the unemployed and those on lower incomes". It noted the causal link between high unemployment and worsening physical health, referring to the experience of Health and Social Services for evidence of depression, marital tensions, and financial problems, all leading to heavier demands for Council help.

A Labour controlled local authority, Newcastle City Council was not regarded as left-wing. It kept within Government spending limits till 1985/86. In opposing Government cuts, it argued, for example, that housing rehabilitation and repairs were "inadequate to maintain the quality of the existing housing stock" and that, especially for people in the public sector, living conditions were deteriorating.

Participatory Research

Let me outline how I did this study. It meant finding out about the city, the local area and the agency, as well as talking with people, and reading the documents available. In the Unit itself I went to meetings, study days, group supervision, and a number of other gatherings. Staff and users put up with me being around the place, interviewing, interrupting, joining in the lunchtime chatting, or asking people to hunt up old reports.

This book draws on my contact with Newcastle FSU between November 1983 and July 1988. But the main interviews and discussions were between April 1984 and November 1985. So people's views are (unless stated) from that period.

As I begin to quote what people said, there's an unconventional side to the research which needs mentioning. From the beginning, FSU and I agreed on a *participatory research* approach. In brief, this means research *with* people, inviting them to become, as far as possible, co-workers and co-investigators in the project.[20]

One aspect of this was that all interviews were loosely structured and open-ended. I asked people to raise questions and themes they found important. So, it was an *inter-view*,[21] not just their comments on questions *I* had decided on. All taped interviews and group discussions were transcribed verbatim and then returned, to be edited or altered, as the person or people interviewed chose.[22] At each stage of writing, drafts were circulated to workers at the Unit who discussed and commented on them. Those who left were also given this opportunity.[23] Staff, management committee members, and the other contributors, were asked to read and comment on the final draft. So you are reading a book that Newcastle FSU judged worth owning.

Of course, a large part of the book is my own observations and views — which sometimes contradict those of staff and others quoted. Not that there was a single Unit 'line'. Readers will find themselves listening to a medley of voices, reflecting the range of views and perceptions I found.

Let me stress that these questions aren't merely technical problems for researchers. Nor is it simply that a collaborative process is the right way to learn with and about collective and collaborative teams. There's an important larger issue. A participatory model is essential if social investigation is to lead to citizens' knowledge, rather than people's data becoming experts' property. As we'll see, at Newcastle such an approach seemed closely in tune with how Unit staff tried to work with each other and their users.

A Package of Changes

Well, there I was. In and out of FSU during the day; at people's homes in the evenings; asking them how the Unit operated, and about changes in its practice and philosophy. How did they see collective working, its strengths and weaknesses? Were there differences for users or new workers? Members of staff and the management committee described the daily work; told me about meetings; and discussed policy. I heard the views of some of the users, of former staff, and workers in other agencies. Discussion might lead back to the past; or to hopes and fears for the future. People compared the Unit with other workplaces; they told me about their experiences and their values. And, of course, there were the worries and questions, the gossip, and jokes.

Very quickly, I found that neither workers nor management committee members saw their collective working as something new and separate. Instead, they put it in the context of a number of other changes at the Unit, going back several years. Indeed, they viewed the joint management scheme as formalising a coherent 'package' of developments which had already occurred.

The next chapter sketches these changes. They included the team taking on the planning and review of work; group discussion and supervision of staff's daily workloads; and the deliberate distribution of the Unit Organiser's 'management' tasks. This was linked to a shift in the work they did —for instance developing community and group work, and reducing their catchment area.

Management Structure Must Reflect The Work

However, Unit workers gave an even more fundamental reason for self-management. Working collectively, they insisted, was logical and necessary *given the way they wanted to work with users*. The Unit's proposal to National Council included this statement:

> [Joint management] is consistent with our way of working with people in the community. In all our work with individuals and with groups, we encourage people to become independent, skilled and responsible for their own actions. We also encourage people in the community to support each other rather than to rely on Unit staff for support. It is therefore important to have a management structure which reflects these beliefs.

What was this link — this logical consistency? Here's Chris Johnson, one of the Unit's community workers.

> *Chris Johnson*: What we kept saying so strongly to the management committee and to FSU nationally: that you can't on one level give power to clients and then not follow that through. Joint staff management is a logical outcome of what you're saying the working policies are going to be with people in the community — the social work clients. There's a real feeling of ideological contradiction in having a really hierarchical staff management structure internally in an organisation, and then talking about giving the people we're working with more power over their lives.

In other words, they weren't advocating workers' self-management as an end in itself, but as the consequence of the aim underlying all their work: the empowerment of users. Of course, many social services agencies, including national FSU, talk about empowering clients, raising their self-esteem and confidence, and helping them realise their capabilities. However, when Newcastle Unit spelled out such aims, they went a crucial step further.[24]

They claimed that trying to empower users will actually be *undermined* if an agency's own internal social relations are undemocratic. Agencies which deny power and responsibility to workers, and which prevent the development of *their* skills, interdependence and mutual support, will inhibit or even work against such an approach to its users.[25]

This argument applies to more than social services agencies and the 'helping' professions. It suggests there is a good or bad 'fit' between the structures of any agency, the social relations among its workers, and the quality of services to users.[26] There have been similar conclusions drawn in service settings elsewhere. Doctors, for example, have observed how patient care is affected by the type of regime in a hospital.[27] But Newcastle FSU were not aiming at good care or even improved therapy. They were after democratic self-management — by users of their own lives, and by workers of their workplace.

Not everyone at the unit advocated such an explicit theory. In fact, it was less worked-out theory than a broad understanding — stronger and clearer for some people than others. In the next chapter we can see this understanding emerging, by going back several years and tracing the changes I've mentioned.

Events Outlined In Chapter Two

1968   National Family Service Units sets up Newcastle-Upon-Tyne Unit by invitation of the City Council, which asks for work with 'problem families' in the West End of Newcastle.

1973   Unit casework post changed to community worker. Student Unit set up with post of organiser.

1974   Groupwork organiser (Joan Smith) appointed.

1975   January: Study day looks at the implications of group and community work 'multi-disciplines'.
July: Study day proposes smaller catchment area and more integrated working.
August: Newcastle's director of Social Services agrees in principle to the proposed changes. Meeting with Bishop Auckland Unit to discuss Unitary approach.

1976   Small area survey to set new boundaries.
November: Unit clothing store closed. Friends of FSU (a group of volunteers running the store) decides to disband.
Staff from FSU attend meetings with workers from other Newcastle agencies, about the work of Paulo Freire.

1977   Formal switch to smaller area.
Dorothy Whittaker, Prof. of Social Work University of York, acts as Unit Consultant.
Rex Halliwell resigns as director of national FSU, Tim Cook appointed director. Joan Smith appointed Newcastle Unit Organiser.
National FSU calls for development plan from each Unit. Newcastle workers present a policy statement to the local management committee, and this later forms the basis of the Unit's development plan submitted to national FSU. Three management committee members highly critical of staff plan, but fail to persuade a majority of the committee.

1978   Tensions and disarray among staff team.

1979   Building reorganised; reception room equipped.

1980   Study days lead to delegation and sharing of many Unit Organiser's tasks.
Staff team becomes more collaborative; all staff involved in hiring.
Feminist perspectives become explicit in Unit's work and approach.

1981   Second area Survey. October: Preparations for Joan Smith's sabbatical leave.

1982   April-October Joan on sabbatical.

1983   June: Lin Harwood leaves.
August: Joan Smith leaves.
September: Newcastle Unit asks FSU National Council to approve joint staff management.

Two

History

Shirley Forster: When people ask us about, 'Why are you now organised as a collective?' we always say, 'Well, it was a natural development out of the way the Unit was going'. It wasn't a theoretical idea about management that we then tried to apply. It came as other sorts of work developed. So first of all the history, and maybe you'll see from this the threads of how it came together.

Way back in 1979, workers began supervising, supporting, advising each other, drawing from each other's knowledge and skills rather than leaving this to the Unit Organiser. As this developed we found we had a greater pool of imagination, ideas and enthusiasm between us than one person could possibly provide. — Unit Annual Report 1983/4

This chapter isn't *the* history of the Unit, but traces the threads Shirley Forster mentioned. I'll begin earlier than 1979 because, while the experience of the 1984 staff group took them back five years, change started well before then. This was clear when talking to former workers, to users, and colleagues in other agencies; as well as from old Unit records. (Which, incidentally, the staff who applied to self-manage hadn't read.)

Saying there were *interlinked* changes doesn't mean that joint management was somehow the last step in an inevitable sequence. Nor was there was ever any grand plan to move towards collective working. Like Shirley, Joan Smith recalled an "evolutionary process", that "started from a point that was unrecognised as leading to a collective".

They saw a family of ideas and developments, and it's that continuing kinship which is significant, rather than how one thing followed another. For this reason the story here has

27

important implications for people in agencies elsewhere. It's far more than how one team developed; Newcastle Unit 'doing it their way'.

Work with Families

Newcastle FSU was set up in September 1968. Its original brief from the City Council was what the agency had traditionally done elsewhere — intensive family casework often over a long period, focussing on families with multiple problems. Here's the view of Peter Stone, formerly an assistant director of Newcastle Social Services, and a member of the Unit's management committee.

> *Peter*: The history of it is that the FSU was invited to come to Newcastle by the City Council. That's how the deal was set up. The City wanted, specifically, intensive casework with families at that time. Because that was what was 'in' and that was the kind of Unit that was created. It was also, though, an expression of the stirrings of a wish to work with voluntary organisations.

Shirley Forster also remembered the Unit's early days. In 1972, she'd been a volunteer after leaving school (returning eight years later as a social worker).

> *Shirley*: The style of the work then was that you had your own little caseload. And what you did with it — however effective or good the workers were — it was a bit of a mystery what they actually got up to with their 'own' families.

A mystery to each other, that is, since the Unit Organiser supervised everyone separately. But important changes were underway.

> *Shirley*: They shifted from a completely casework service into providing a bit of community work.

Community Work and Groupwork

Community work grew out of one worker's casework with families living in Elswick Street flats. She realised it made more sense to see the flats as the problem, rather than the families. In 1973 her post was formally altered to community work. The Unit had also developed some groupwork — mainly with mothers and children, and as an adjunct to casework. In 1974 Joan Smith was appointed groupwork organiser, and they phased out the use of volunteers to run groups.

These appointments implied questions about the Unit's initial brief. Though casework was still the major area of work, having separate approaches was seen as a serious tension within the staff group and, as we'll see, by management committee members. They felt the Unit had simply added extra 'methods' without becoming a multi-disciplinary team. Staff wrote papers for study days in 1975, asking: "Is Unit to provide a service to a small group of families or to a whole neighbourhood?" The community worker wrote:

We have become much more aware of the pressure
both the immediate and wider environment has on
families, and many social workers feel they cannot significantly help families unless these outside pressures
can be altered.

Integrating Work in a Smaller Area

A linked issue was their catchment area which then included much of the city's West End. As a result, many users lived some distance away — three and four miles for some families. Staff suggested a smaller area. After all, they were a very small team. By concentrating on one patch, they hope to offer realistic help with "internal problems" like poor relationships and lack of self-esteem, as well as "external" ones such as poor housing, poverty, and lack of amenities.

Joan Smith remembered this as a time of growing self-criticism about staff's separation from each other and parallel working.

Joan: Staff beginning to say how ridiculous it was that we weren't working with each other. We were all employed at the same place, going about our work without any recourse to any other work that was going on at all. There was a long process of internal discussion which began to evolve as a decision to work in a smaller area, and to try to link the different methods of work together, so that we could become community based.

Workers called for better co-ordinated and therefore more efficient services. One wrote:

I think we must move away from the concept of a casework agency and *really* see ourselves as offering help to problem families and meeting areas of need in different ways and by different methods. I think we must learn to share our knowledge more and take more interest in each other and each other's work.

Other staff were more critical, challenging the terms 'client' and 'problem family' and the dependency of users. Alison Harker, who came as a social worker in 1975, was plunged into this debate.

Alison: The traditional method of working was very high dependency. So the families were encouraged to become incredibly dependent on the Unit and the Unit workers. That was really in direct contravention to the style of community work that was going on.

The community work dimension led to questions about all the work, including material aid like second-hand clothing. Evelyn Rae had joined as a secretary in 1972.

Evelyn: The staff changed yet again, and they didn't agree with giving clothes and material gifts. You know, they were relying on us for clothes, and we didn't want them to rely on us for their material needs. Well, the people I knew loved the clothing store.

So, change wasn't just new methods developed to tackle old problems, but a rethinking of how those problems came to be defined and taken on as Unit work. "Did the Unit have its own longterm aims?" asked a worker at a 1975 study day. If so, "Does longterm mean propping up the family until the kids have grown up?" A paper rejected this.

> The vast majority, if not all our families are disadvantaged; victims of inadequate discriminating housing policies and educational system, with poor job prospects and insufficient money. What do we do to 'help'? Keep them as helped, always on the receiving end and encouraging dependency, perpetuating their sense of their own inadequacy by always placing them in a recipient role.

Later that year, they discussed their thinking with Newcastle's director and assistant director of Social Services. The director, Brian Roycroft, saw the shift towards community work and a smaller geographical area as logical developments for FSU. A reduced area was formally agreed by the City the following year. New boundaries were set after Unit staff and students had undertaken a survey, which included statistical information and the views of local people, groups, and agencies. Now there was to be a "more community orientated approach" and a "more unified team" which would "better integrate the skills and resources that we have".

A Working Philosophy

The Unit's developing practice reflected what staff had learned from their work. Just as clearly, how they put this understanding together was influenced by ideas and values — like the community work perspective, and its challenge to traditional ways of working. Another influence is shown by words like 'integrate' and 'unified'.

To explain — social work at this time showed considerable interest in ideas borrowed from 'systems theory'. These seemed to offer a way of bridging the old and new work 'methods', the latter rapidly emerging in large local authority departments as well as grant-aided agencies like FSU. The general notion was to avoid homing in on the 'client', looking instead at how families, groups, or agencies affect each other in overlapping networks.[1]

During 1975, Newcastle took part in a workshop on 'integrated methods' with Bradford and Leeds Units. Bishop Auckland FSU in County Durham, their nearest neighbours, were even more influential. When the two Units met that year, Newcastle were especially interested in their stress on community work, and determination to value the strengths of local people as well as help with their problems.[2]

Following reduction of Newcastle's catchment area, most of the team were involved in group and community work projects. But they never developed a unified package, and one worker left who wanted this to happen.

> *Joan Smith*: We were lumbered with phrases like 'integrated methods' and 'the Unitary approach' and people having their own interpretation and understanding of what that meant.

Joan explained how Unit workers linked different work and learned from each other. Her description remained as true during 1984/86.

> *Joan*: Majoring in the skills which you'd received or trained in, and which you felt happy and comfortable with, but wanting to develop other skills as well... You know, if their skills were as a community worker then those skills could actually inform groupwork and inform casework.

Paulo Freire

Another strong set of ideas was evident at this time. During 1976 several staff from the Unit joined community workers from other Newcastle agencies to discuss the writing of the Brazilian educator Paulo Freire.[3]

> *Alison Harker*: I had struggled through things like *Pedagogy of the Oppressed* for years. With a certain amount of success; it's awfully hard going.

I'm not presenting Freire as Newcastle's guru. His books, though still in the Unit's tiny library, mostly go unread. The staff who bought them never got together and said:

> *Joan Smith*: Now, how will this apply to the Unit? Or even in our discussions about the Unit philosophy we never actually said, 'Now, as Paulo Freire would see it..'

Even so, at a crucial time in the Unit's development some of the workers came to these ideas with excitement. Freire helped them formulate and extend their own thinking.

> *Joan*: We did not produce a 'programme' out of those meetings, but it's very likely that on an individual level our attitudes and approaches to people were influenced by Freire.

It was also more than this, because Freire's ideas offer a way of understanding the Unit's later development. I'll be referring again to his work, so here's a brief sketch.

Freire writes on education, not social or community work as such, though there are strong links with the latter in his practice, which centred on literacy programmes (in Latin America and later in Africa). He asks, not how we teach people to read, but how learning to read can become a means of liberation. How can a professional — usually a paid worker from outside an area — develop a liberatory practice with the people who live there? Freire argues a set of essential do's and don'ts. At the heart of these is respect for the knowledge and experience of the people worked with, and the meanings they give to their lives.

The outside worker is not there to fill them up with her or his knowledge. That's just more oppression. Instead there must be dialogue, so the relationship becomes one of co-learners and co-teachers. In such a dialogue, users of services are co-subjects, not the objects of the expert or professional. The work is therefore 'with' people, not 'on' them. This doesn't ignore the expertise or commitment of an outside practitioner. But the substance of the dialogue which takes place is built on the themes and problems of people in the area. Its aim is their knowledge; for them to speak their voice; and ultimately their empowerment.

Freire argues that the means used to achieve this must reflect the ends. For example, he insists it isn't enough for the worker genuinely to intend working towards people's empowerment — she or he must not mislead or manipulate them. Steering people towards a goal chosen by the worker, but hidden from them, is not dialogue but 'domestication'.

Some of Freire's influence can be seen in Joan Smith's book,[4] *Growing Together*, which follows the Unit's work with one family. Apart from describing relationships between staff and users, the study is remarkable for the family's own participation in the book. Joan checked out with family members, what she had written, enabling them to challenge and change her version of events.

Consolidating the Changes

From 1976, the Unit wound down work in other parts of the West End and took on new work — especially about poor housing. They tended to work in pairs or small groups — a feature noted by Dorothy Whittaker, Professor of Social Work at York, who acted as Unit consultant in 1977 and 1978. Existing groupwork changed as well.

> *Alison Harker*: Rather than having things like mothers' groups or groups for kids of a certain age, for example, the type of groupwork which started to happen was much more to do with family groups and linking up family groups. So families who had been through the groups themselves then became involved with other family groups.

Another way of bridging people's work was through supervision. Staff had been individually supervised by the Unit Organiser. Finding one Unit Organiser 'abrasive', fieldworkers met without him. After he left, those meetings evolved into a measure of group discussion, operating together with paired and individual supervision.

Policies Presented

In 1976, the Unit nailed its new colours to the mast, with a "Change" document, included in a statement for national FSU the following year. The Unit, they wrote, "will move away from a pattern of work characterised by the separation of groupwork, casework, and community work". However, while describing the work as "integrated", staff insisted on a philosophical, not simply a functional unity.

> This alteration in our style of work has involved formulating a philosophy which has only lately become clear. It began from a rejection of the idea that people with problems are somehow 'to blame' or 'at fault' and need to be individually treated. In fact we recognised that many people have the same problems, not of their own making, but because of certain societal arrangements. As a result, people, communities, areas, are labelled as 'deprived', and they are deprived, of the basic entitlement of dignity. This also means they are deprived of choice, opportunity and power. We regard these as very basic deprivations.
>
> It is difficult to clarify where deprivation of these rights constitutes injustice, and this is further complicated by the fact that those suffering these deprivations allow themselves to be deprived and perhaps do not recognise what is taking place. This is perhaps the ultimate injustice brought about by the historical development of deprivation.
>
> This philosophy calls for a more unified approach. The strong emphasis on individual work with families, were it to continue as before would, we feel, merely compound the view that certain people have problems all of which are to do solely with them and have no wider implications. If we believe this we are deceiving ourselves, and our families, and society as a whole. Moreover we are allowing an unjust view to continue, and we are not being of real service to anyone. On the contrary we are propagating misconceptions.

Among wider implications, was a need for the Unit to tackle issues of social policy.

> Recognising that some of the distress we meet goes be-
> yond the local situation and is inextricably bound up
> with national issues, we are committed to involvement in
> social policy issues.

Quoting this at length, I'm not saying new workers have simply sailed on under the same flag ever since. The reality is more complicated and more interesting. But listening and talking to workers, I encountered ideas similar to those Dorothy Whittaker heard eight years earlier. Both groups of staff insisted on the importance of goals which valued users' independence, and of work which brought them more power over their lives.

> *Dorothy Whittaker*: To me it was striking how frequently
> such end-goals as the following came up: experiences of
> having choices and being able to make choices and deci-
> sions on one's own behalf; identifying *own* purposes and
> taking effective action towards them; increasing and
> maintaining levels of dignity, pride and self-confidence;
> establishing support systems within the neighbourhoods
> so that the residents became progressively less depen-
> dent on professional helpers; and the like. (Consultancy
> report April 1977)

Meanwhile... Elsewhere in FSU

Newcastle wasn't alone in its developments. In FSU general-ly, family casework had been the predominant approach, at least till the late sixties. This was now challenged by a number of Units who had introduced group and community work.

The years 1976/1977 were crucial for the agency, as this shifting practice became the subject of a fierce debate. Rex Halliwell, then director, was asked for a five year develop-ment plan, and wrote a document broadly endorsing FSU's traditional model of work with families. His plan was sharply criticised, particularly at national conference, and Halliwell resigned. (To be succeeded by Tim Cook.)

Each Unit, and National Office staff, were then asked to formulate their own development plans. There was a long and searching look at what FSU was doing and how it did it. Newcastle's plan went to National Council in September 1977. It reflected all the changes: in work done; restructuring of consultation and supervision; and in the Unit's philosophy.

Conflict With Committee Members

Conflict at national level was mirrored in Newcastle. Members of the local management committee disapproved of the way things had been going. Their disagreement - simmering for some time - now boiled over.

> *Joan Smith*: As it was obvious that it was going to be quite a radical change in the way the Unit was operating, people now felt more able or forced to speak their opposition.

Three leading committee members, including the secretary and chairperson, wrote a carefully argued criticism attacking both the Unit's development plan and the changes it reflected. They stated their support for "the traditional FSU service to disadvantaged families". Expansion into group and community work, they said, "has yet to prove its worth", and "We would question how much of this community work is directly relevant to FSU's brief".

They disapproved of the ending of material aid to families, especially shutting down the second-hand clothing room. This had been run by a group of volunteers called 'Friends of FSU', who then disbanded. Jennifer Roddick, a former member of the group told me how upset they'd been.

> *Jennifer*: Yes, very upset. Because they felt that it was the wrong way to do things. But again, in those days we were not aware of the value of group work. Group work to us was a new thing and we felt, 'That isn't what we thought the FSU was all about when we first came and got involved in it'.

The committee members in disagreement were not only doubtful about new ways of working. They also objected to the development plan's "statement of purpose", which said:

> FSU is concerned with people who have no voice, who
> are powerless in many aspects of their lives. All FSU's
> functioning, present and future should be aimed at
> working with people towards changing this situation.
> This is how the Unit would see the purpose of the
> organisation. We would see this as being the basis
> of all the types of work carried out by the organisation.

The dissenting members were deeply sceptical. They dismissed the philosophy put forward as "undefined... The aims
are not converted into a practical basis on which to work".
They thought staff unreasonable and impracticable in expecting to work with families towards independence. In their
view:

> FSU is concerned with deprived people who have not
> been able to cope with the complexities of modern life,
> who are perhaps never going to find a 'voice' of their
> own.

But the staff stood firm, gaining support from a majority of
the committee. The criticism was withdrawn. Of course, looking back from a 'winners' perspective, we can overlook some
perfectly valid concerns. It *is* easier flying a grand flag, than
spelling out what goes on beneath it. And maybe this danger
is greater, as phrases about 'working towards people's dignity
and self-confidence' join the conventional wisdom of social
and community work; just as 'participative' and 'democratic'
have sidled into the rhetoric of many agencies.

Strains and Stresses

The dispute with members of the committee shows that developments were neither tidy nor inexorable. In 1978, Dorothy
Whittaker was again consultant, and found a feeling of weari-
ness. She wondered "how much the long struggle of the staff
against the committee might have had a unifying effect, and
obscured real differences which have existed for some time".
Dorothy saw serious strains inside the staff group, as people
who'd fought for change were:

...exhausted by prolonged efforts over the last several years to talk, reconcile, identify positions etc etc. They do not have the energy to continue this effort with new people. The new members of staff, who have not, of course, participated in earlier discussions have no way of knowing when they are treading over old ground or when they are raising hackles by bringing up what appear to them to be straightforward issues.

There was substantial turnover. Some workers left after several years for new jobs or to get qualified. Others came and went. Pam Carter, (who joined in September 1980) then worked in the nearby Crudas Park Social Services team, where she was liaison senior with the Unit.

Pam: They had a lot of really bad employment problems. Since 1980 things have been relatively stable staffwise. Very stable in most of the jobs. But before that they had quite a lot of times when people came for short periods and didn't stay long.

Opening Up the Unit Building

1978/79 saw a further marked change. They reorganised the layout and use of the building, opening it up to users. The big old house which has always been their base, hadn't seemed welcoming.

Pam Carter: The Unit was a terrible place. Really sort of cold. That was my impression. Very shabby.

Alison Harker recalled an incident which, for her, symbolised how closed the building had been. During 1977, local children broke in repeatedly. Several parents, furious with their kids, brought them to a meeting.

Alison: It felt that when the kids came into the building they'd never been there. Well, they had been there before; loads of times! They'd had a great time. But, like, it wasn't their building.

The team made a determined effort to alter this. In 1979 a visitor — whether user, or colleague from another agency — would be taken into a comfortable sitting room on the first floor — a large, welcoming space at the centre of the place.

> *Joan Smith*: Eventually we got some decent carpet, and one of the members of the committee gave us a settee, and we scrounged or bought furniture from other places.
>   Yes, that was part of the process, really. An area that should be used and could be used by everyone: people who worked at the Unit and people who came; other workers from other agencies who came; and people from the area who came in. That was a place where anyone could meet. We had to use our discretion as to whether whatever developed in there was work that should be done in private to preserve confidentiality, or something that could usefully be done in the sitting room.

As well as making space for the sitting room, staff rearranged the rest of the building. Separate rooms for the student unit and its supervisor had disappeared some time before. Now they even had a phase when:

> *Joan*: most people decided that they didn't want *a* desk or *a* place that was theirs; a filing cabinet that was theirs.

In fact, staff gradually began sitting in the same places. And Joan never formally relinquished the tiny UO's office, although this was always used by other staff as well.
   The Unit's use of its space is explored in chapter fourteen. Readers who know other Family Service Units may be puzzled to find this raised, since informality is usually seen as a normal feature of FSU's approach. This includes working, "from an ordinary house in an ordinary street".[5] So let me underline the importance of Newcastle's changes. In several ways, rearranging space signalled where they were heading.
   One aim was more open working among the staff team; explicitly moving away from private space for privatised work. This needed the recognition of space as a flexible *com-*

mon resource. There was, as Joan Smith put it, "a breakthrough from having territory that was yours". Just as vital was their intention to open up to users.

> *Shirley Forster*: That felt more welcoming. You weren't, sort of, sat in the secretaries' office waiting for a social worker to take you somewhere else. If your person wasn't in, the person you needed to see, you put the kettle on, have a coffee and so on.

Of course, there's a connection between openness among colleagues and openness to users. A team which wants to reduce its barriers — casting off its shell — needs a greater degree of trust and mutual sharing and support — it needs a stronger internal skeleton.

The Collaborative Team

All this time, there had been Unit Organisers. (Joan Smith from 1977) So mutual sḷaring grew within a formal framework of 'line management'. From 1980, there was a transition towards a team of equals, with study days leading to many of Joan's tasks being delegated or shared. Both Janet Williams and Blanche Callan used the word "democratic" to describe this. (Blanche joined in 1975 as a half-time secretary.)

> *Blanche*: Joan was the Unit Organiser. But as time went on, it was sort of a big change. They started really then trying to change to democratic. Only it wasn't actually said as that. Joan took a more active part — apart from being a boss — in the Unit. It was a lot more informal.
> But the first couple of years I was here, Joan was definitely the boss. Then it seemed to change. And they didn't want hierarchy. She seemed to be in line with that.

> *Janet*: These decisions [at the study days] enabled a considerable move forward in the democratic approach to the management of the Unit and have resulted in considerable benefits to staff, the work, and Joan personally.[6]

Joan took on more direct work with users, like running groups. Though she was still an important and central person, management tasks gradually became much more a team responsibility. Crucially, her position as link person diminished.

> *Ernie Dobson*: Originally when I first came here [1979] Joan would disappear for a week or three days. And you would simply know that "Joan's gone to UO's" [meeting]. But by the time she left we were working with her on preparing what issues were coming up. And looking at what things came up, and the struggle she had in the group. She got to a situation where she could not identify with other UOs saying how isolated they were, and what a lot of hassles they had with their staff. She didn't feel she was in that kind of position.

Another of the UO's jobs had been liaison with and attending the local management committee. For Shirley Forster, committee meetings back in 1979 had been:

> An occasion for the UO to put on a posh frock and for the secretaries to rush out buttering scones and buying cakes. And these all went down to the room downstairs which the cleaner was ordered to tidy up specially.

Tom Hammill then chaired the committee.

> *Tom*: One saw a pattern developing, changing. For instance, who would be the representative at committee meetings. In the old days it was the Unit Organiser and *only* the Unit Organiser. Other members of staff were allowed in if one wanted to to see them. And never spoke unless asked questions.

Now other staff went to meetings — and spoke up.

> *Peter Stone*: Joan Smith would sometimes say, "I'm not taking the lead on this. Someone else in the group is handling it". And that might be an administrative matter, it might not.

Later on, staff's involvement with and understanding of the committee was followed by active recruitment of new members.

Hiring And Firing

Legally, FSU staff are hired and employed by the national agency. However, local committees play a large part in the actual process. So plainly, a Unit Organiser who is the main or only link with the committee exercises a strong influence on hiring policy. At Newcastle, though a management sub-committee interviewed and recommended candidates, by 1980 staff as well as committee members were interviewing applicants, with some users informally included.[7]

> *Shirley Forster*: They [staff] all had a look at me and decided what they thought. I was also introduced to some people who were users of the Unit. They didn't formally interview me, but they met me and met the other applicants for the job, and their comments were fed into the staff group.

Ernie Dobson recalled a round of interviews when the other workers, in effect, overruled Joan. Becoming a collaborative team was more than just support and sharing.

> *Ernie*: The rest of the staff group were beginning to flex our muscles a bit. [laughing] We'd just interviewed for a new worker... We as a staff group interviewed candidates, and an interviewing panel interviewed candidates. It was my turn to do a dirty job, and I had to go out and tell Joan that we didn't like any of the candidates. Which she found quite hard to take. We'd had a discussion as a staff group. Which she wasn't part of because she'd been in on the formal interviews.
> I feel on reflection, it's probably about — again without it being overtly stated — we were in a sense attempting to take more power over. I remember that as quite a crucial period. Because we were quite united about that. Joan and the rest of us had our differences that day. But we coped with it, you know. She wasn't as pissed off the next day.

Staff participation in hiring meant more control over the team as a group. Ernie mentioned they'd been criticised "for employing people like ourselves". But he and other workers questioned how far a team should be prepared to take all-comers. Didn't they need some common values? This was Joan's view.

> *Joan Smith*: It's more crucial to get someone with the right attitude towards people we're supposedly helping, than all the best qualifications and degrees. That sometimes has been quite an area of difficulty. Because it's hard to put into words. And we got into uncomfortable discussions with people on the committee about, 'You're choosing people on the basis of whether they will fit in with the staff group'. Sometimes maybe we denied that a bit. But in fact that's right.

Tom Hammill suggested that teamworking requires at least one basic similarity among staff.

> *Tom*: People who are sympathetic to this way of operating; for whom it's part of the attraction of the work. So I think perhaps stability and continuity will be maintained in that way.

From a different standpoint, staff recruitment had considerably widened. If 'people like us' means a community work or social work qualification, then hiring Lilian White was a radical departure — continued in other ways. Lilian, born and brought up in Elswick, became a nurse — first in general nursing and then psychiatric. Like other members of her family she had been active in the local community.[8]

> *Shirley Forster*: We decided we were gonna value one sort of experience more highly than the traditional CQSW [social work qualifying] certificate. We were gonna value training in another profession, local knowledge, and a particular sort of personality over and above somebody who came with years of social service experience and certificate. That was the first of many battles which we were to have out with national office and our own committee, as part of changing the staff group. Lilian was in fact appointed after a battle, but

on inferior salary until she proved [to national FSU]
she could do the job.

Till 1988, the Unit hadn't fired anyone, though workers had
failed to have their appointment confirmed after six months
probation.

> *Lin Harwood*: Well, [staff member] beat his girlfriend
> up. I mean, that was awful. Because his six-month thing
> was up, it was a resign-or-get-the-sack job. And of
> course, we all knew about all this. And FSU being the
> place it is, and having a commitment to not ignoring
> things like wife abuse, women getting beaten; and not
> wishing to have one rule for clients and another for
> everyone else, Joan had a word with him. Oh, yeah.
> People have been squeezed out before.

As we'll see, Lin (formerly groupworker) was herself squeezed
out, following a long, raw dispute among the team. But by then
[1983] it wasn't Joan having "a word" but the whole staff group
involved.

In 1980, the team, on average fifteen years younger than
Joan Smith, contained a range of skills, experience and qualification which made traditional 'vertical' supervision increasingly difficult. A peer group becomes more likely when there are
real peers. This contrasted sharply with FSU in the early and
mid seventies when fieldworkers tended to be much younger
and were often untrained.

More equal relations within the team extended to the formal periodic assessments which FSU requires for all staff.
Rather than something separate between Joan and the individual, assessments became the responsibility of fieldworkers
as a group.

A Feminist Team

From 1980 onwards, among the ideas and values influencing
the Unit was a deepening feminist current.

> *Pam Carter*: It became much more feminist... Either
> people had been involved in the Women's Movement,
> or if they hadn't they were sympathetic to it or

interested in it. The Unit as a whole had quite a lot of arguments and discussions. That's when we got into doing group work with women.

I think people who disagreed with it basically got out. [Two workers] were both blokes who weren't sympathetic, and basically they just got out. In a very hostile way.

FSU was one of the first agencies in Newcastle with workshops for women and, in the Pool Girls' Club, youth work aimed specifically at girls.

Brenda White: Well, when we first started it was a big thing. Girls' work was new and everybody was keen and interested. I know that a lot of people are still keen and interested, but women who have left have gone off and started their own girls' group. And it's gone from there.

Working with women was one sign of change, but it went deeper. Staff with a feminist perspective brought ideas and experience that fitted and complemented the Unit's earlier practice and philosophy. Many feminist approaches to organisation stress the kind of non-hierarchical collective working that was developing.[9]

'Interregnum'

To write the book *Growing Together*, Joan Smith was given sabbatical leave — from April to October 1982. Other Units have times 'between' two Organisers, or when a UO is absent. FSU nationally prefers to use the revealing word 'interregnum', for which the agency had a standard procedure. Responsibility is passed *upwards* — to the assistant director and the chairperson of the local management committee. But Newcastle did it differently.

Planning for her sabbatical began in October 1981. All the tasks and responsibilities held by Joan were allocated to specific members of the team and were taken up by them in stages over the preceding months. During the period of her sabbatical, fieldwork staff managed the Unit as a joint team, with different individuals responsible for different tasks. The staff found this a workable experience, which facilitated the development of new ways and ideas. (Joint Management Proposal)

Joan and the other staff compiled a list of UO jobs to be done. It's an odd list.[10] Though they needed to reduce her work to small do-able tasks, still, it was almost entirely administration. So there's a lot about getting the post; buying coffee, and washing dishes after committee meetings. Joan notes that "Janet Williams doesn't need to be fetched and carried from the station" for Management Committee meetings, "but she does need to be fed". There are instructions about the building; and on case reviews and agendas. There's also a word of caution.

Other agencies, outsiders, need a 'boss' person to refer to. There have been many instances of this recently.

The only listed work which wouldn't be part of the job of a good secretary, related to case reviews and staff assessments, where the UO had a formal procedural role. Then there was "informal supervision and support". It marked the change that had taken place, when Joan wrote:

It doesn't seem appropriate to 'delegate' this responsibility to anyone. If it isn't shared and mutual, does it have any meaning?

Responsibilities then, were handed 'downwards'. We can see, even at this point, how joint staff management was not the same as being 'leaderless', a term often used to describe other teams 'between leaders'. And clearly, at least in retrospect, this was a trial period, giving both workers and committee the experience and confidence of self-management. It was a chance "to learn from our mistakes", as the Unit said later to National Council. Peter Stone (longest serving member of the committee) saw the whole period leading up to Joan's sabbatical as:

Peter: A sort of familiarisation period for all of us when different roles were tried out by the staff. In the sense that they opted to act in a non-hierarchical way, even when there was the hierarchical position of the Unit Organiser there.

Tom Hammill, another 'veteran', agreed.

Tom: It turned out to have been a dry run. And it was very thoroughly prepared for, and I was involved in that. Staff and committee had really gone into it in considerable detail and taken it very seriously. There was quite a bit of apprehension around by the staff at that time. And management committee took that on board. They saw the value of Joan's work and recognised that she needed to have the time to write it up, and wouldn't get it otherwise. The management committee were involved in the whole of that process. There was a great deal of sharing out went on at that time about who would do what, how, and about snags that might come up.

The six months wasn't all plain sailing. For one thing, there was the worry about outsiders wanting a 'boss person'.

Joan: The fact that there was a Unit Organiser at the Newcastle Unit denied or gave the wrong impression to the outside world of the way the Unit was being run. And that was a tension and a problem that we were aware of for quite a long time.

Then, as Tom mentioned, there had been anxiety among the staff.

Lilian White: I must admit, I remember thinking at that time, 'Oh, my God, it's going to be disastrous. Help!' But everybody seemed to be really confident about covering while Joan was away. And we did it, and it was okay. It worked fine. We covered the job she normally did. Obviously the people who felt more able and more confident took over the types of skills they thought they could carry through. So we shared it out in order of the individual skills people had, and the confidence they had to carry through certain jobs.

So Joan was away for six month. We got on really well. There were some concerns from outside about 'Who do we contact when things go wrong, or we're unhappy with something?' So we stuck up named people who would be responsible for certain areas of the work. Particularly for Social Services [Department].

Not everyone saw things so positively.

Lin Harwood: Well, what happened was Joan went on sabbatical and we were all supposed to share Joan's jobs out between us.

Now, if a job didn't get done, Chris [Johnson] did it. My thing about that is: leave it undone. Bring it to a meeting and have a group thing about, 'This job was not done'. Don't go and bloody do it. I wouldn't do that. It's like being a mother, you know. If my kids don't do something I'm not gonna run behind them. So there was a whole thing about Chris took more and more on. And she was the unofficial Unit Organiser. Outside people saw her like that.

Chris Johnson: Well, I don't know. I think at times that was the myth rather than the reality. I did take on some of those things, that's true. I did carry some of that responsibility. I think probably one of the things that happens in any collective situation, is that at some times some people are feeling more responsible than others for the actual success of the operation. And that's perhaps inevitable. But to see me as, in some cases, a surrogate Unit Organiser really undervalues what some other people did in that time.

I think one of the things is that different people take up different roles in different times. At that stage some people felt much less happy about taking on some of the Unit Organiser tasks than I did. If you look now [July 1984] those people actually now feel happier taking on a much wider range of tasks than they did a few years ago. And one of the important things about working as a joint staff management group is that it gives people time to grow and learn new skills and take on new areas of responsibility.

Joan's Return

Behind Lin and Chris' disagreement lie crucial issues of formal and informal power. So it's interesting that Lin made the reverse criticism of Joan: that she didn't properly exercise the formal power she was given.

> *Lin Harwood*: Joan never ran the show. Although she was the Unit Organiser, she never directed things in that sense of the word. It was kind of laissez-faire management. Do you know what I mean? You don't have the right to be alienated, because she wasn't doing anything. But nor could you have anything else.

By the time Joan returned, two things had happened. Joan herself had decided to quit. Being away made her realise how her interests were changing. She wanted, for instance, to give far more time to the Peace Movement. She left the following August (1983). The second change was that other staff had begun to feel comfortable about running the Unit jointly.

> *Lilian*: When Joan came back it was really strange. It seemed as though there wasn't a niche for her to get back into again. It was really difficult. We were doing all her jobs. I remember a lot of resistance to people handing them back over again.

> *Shirley*: We wanted to give her all the shitty stuff back.

> *Lilian*: All the jobs we didn't like doing. That's right.

> *Shirley*: She said, 'Nick-off, I'm not having this. I want to do a nice job. You've got nice jobs'.

Joan did resume a share of 'UO's work', but spent more time on direct work with users. Still, she wasn't simply one of the team. Lin was right to insist that Joan's power extended beyond the list of formal management tasks: the D-I-Y Unit Organiser kit used for the sabbatical. She had power as a person, as a skilled experienced worker, and as the staff member who still carried the Unit Organiser title. Without putting it as strongly as Lin, other staff echoed her view about the weakness of having someone who is, but isn't, the boss. As long as Joan was technically UO, other workers felt they'd had an escape clause — a way out from responsibility.

Looking back on this period, they saw how the 'positive' aspects of co-operative work — sharing skills and knowledge, supporting colleagues — were far better developed than the harder 'negatives' — a need to review and control other people's work. That meant using and owning the group's power, for example, to sanction someone. Chris Johnson, who left before joint management was agreed, thought this "the biggest challenge to collective working generally".

> *Chris*: Once you've no longer got the bad guy to do the management, how do you actually do it?

Lin's Leaving

All these issues surfaced during the dispute leading to Lin Harwood's resignation. Lin had been a central member of the team, working at FSU four years, the first three of which were happy and productive. Like any similar falling out, her resignation left scars and fractured friendships.[11]

As groupworker, Lin had been instrumental in setting up or helping to run several successful projects, especially the Women's Workshops, and a Holiday Group where local parents raised funds and organised holidays. The workshops, which she and Sally Walker piloted, got three years funding from the Department of Health and Social Security (DHSS), including money for extra staff.[12] Lin then transferred a major part of her workload, and didn't afterwards find a role which satisfied either her or other workers.

> *Sally Walker*: What happened after that, was there wasn't any other clear areas of work developing for her. She tried to get other people to support her in finding more work to do, and that wasn't forthcoming. She got lost in what she was meant to be doing.

As we've seen, Lin criticised the Unit's management. She preferred a more traditional model of supervision, where each worker has an individual supervisor. This went hand-in-hand with her growing interest in Family Therapy, something the rest of the team weren't in tune with. Lin finally left in June 1983, following a series of increasingly bitter meetings where it seemed impossible to resolve things. Though people saw the issues and experienced the dispute in different ways, everyone had found the tensions seeping into all their work.

> *Lilian White*: No matter how much you tried or what you put into something like that, when it came to discussion around that time it was completely negative and unproductive. And it came there was really bad feelings about it all.

The trouble began during Joan's sabbatical and continued when she returned. Staff thought Joan's ambiguous position hadn't helped.

> *Pam Carter*: My kind of analysis of what happened, is that it occurred during the period when Joan was still the nominal leader, but wasn't actually in charge. Lin was more uncomfortable with that kind of conflict, uncertainty, than other people.

Ernie Dobson stressed that it happened, "by and large when we were moving towards the system of management we've got, but didn't have at the time". It was not then a collectively working team, but "one going through a transition". One lesson, said Ernie, was the need for very clear rules and procedures — including a grievance procedure that worked. Had there been collective working:

> *Ernie*: I would have felt, like I would feel about anything now [1985], I would have felt more responsibility for making sure it was sorted. Not that I didn't feel that at the time. I also hope we would have clearer systems and mechanisms for dealing with it.

During the dispute, Lin did use the agency's grievance procedure, but found it didn't actually do the job. It resolved nothing. Partly, the Unit had had no practice. But more significantly, the procedure was anomalous: an informally democratic team had to trundle out machinery designed for a different sort of work group.

Pam Flynn: When the grievance procedure was launched in that particular case it was defective.

Pam, who joined the management committee in 1981, later proposed new procedures for joint management, which recognised the new balance of power. She understood that form should follow function — the rules and procedures of an organisation ought to fit the realities of its operation. She also made the realistic assumption that working collectively won't guarantee harmony. Conflict being normal and inevitable, you anticipate a big bust-up sooner or later, and try and devise ways to come through it.[13]

Some staff drew different lessons. For them, events with Lin were evidence of the team's failure to solve its problems and, in failing, causing hurt and pain. That was how the secretaries remembered it.

Yvonne Waters: I'll be quite honest. Sometimes when the tension was so great I made excuses and didn't go. [laughing] I said, 'I've got too much work. I'm waiting for the accountant'. Which I was. But I could've gone and come out [of the meeting]. But the atmosphere was so electrifying, I thought, 'Oh, I can't stand it'. It upset me. I don't like people fighting; I get all agitated.

Blanche Callan: It upset quite a lot of other people as well. Reduced them to tears.

Women's Workshop staff were caught up in this backlash. Ali Rhind (fulltime) and Sally Walker had both been good friends with Lin. Now they found themselves on opposite sides, with Sally feeling deeply that the team had not given Lin the support nor honest criticism she was due.

Self-Management

Early in 1983, Joan Smith announced her decision to leave that August. She'd thought of staying longer.

Joan: To have seen it develop a bit further. Certainly seen it through the period of negotiating with the National Committee. But I was also eager to get on and do other things.

From then on, the joint management proposal was no surprise.[14] But nor was it surprising when the team applying to self-manage were the full-time fieldworkers.

The episode with Lin had coloured the views of people like Sally Walker and Shirley Devlin (Under-fives worker in the Women's Workshops), who wrote a statement opposing joint management. It was also signed by the secretaries and Carol Tate, the cleaner. Describing themselves as "on the periphery of the staff group", they asked how part-time workers would take a full part in a collective team. They queried other issues: pay; accountability; time taken to reach decisions; and the problem that some people are more at home in a group than others — especially in meetings.

In fact, part-timers were never excluded, though the team was slow to bring them in. The secretaries were explicitly invited to be part of self-management (with higher salaries discussed[15]), but their views were firm.

> *Yvonne Waters*: We have said we're not — at this
> particular time — part of the joint management. We
> made that clear from the very beginning.

> *Blanche Callan*: Because of the extra responsibility
> involved; it's the kind of responsibility that I don't
> want. And that's why I haven't become part of it.

Even among the full time fieldwork staff, not everyone was automatically confident it would work.[16] Despite the very gradual transition, and the "dry run", some were cautious or downright doubtful — in particular Shirley Forster and Lilian White.

> *Lilian*: I know it had been a gradual transition, and
> we'd been moving towards working collectively. But it
> was still a shock when the actual suggestion came. A
> fear of the unknown. There were quite a few meetings
> at the early stages. I felt that I was dragging my heels
> and being pushed faster than I wanted to go. It was
> something about seeing a boss as a safeguard. Even
> though Joan hadn't fulfilled that function for a helluva
> long time. Also it was after Lin left. There wasn't much
> trust around, and it was a question of rebuilding that.

For me it was an emotional thing rather than the practical working it out. The reluctance was what was going on inside my guts rather than inside my head.

People drew on their own history as well as the Unit's. Lilian looked back on "the very strong hierarchy of nursing" and "what it's like to be the last in the chain, the line of people that's kicked if things go wrong at the top". Whereas Ernie Dobson had been used to the opposite, working for a Neighbourhood Council in London where, as he said, "that workplace, the whole thing was entirely controlled by local people".

★

We've come to Autumn 1983. Newcastle's proposal was moving through the national machinery, the outcome still finely balanced. As we saw, the Unit referred to their history in support of joint management, arguing a pattern of interconnected changes. The sketch here supports such a view, and not only as a winners' history, either. It's true that what Shirley Forster called "a natural development" could also be seen as the logic of hindsight. But, in fact, people with critical or dissenting views confirmed what had happened by the very clarity of their opposition. This includes some who had changed their minds — often starting with negative or at least mixed feelings.

When Newcastle workers thought back over the changes, the most common image was of cycles. Ernie Dobson mentioned how debates on basic issues — like the relationship between community work and casework — tended to recur at two year intervals. Chris Johnson and Pam Carter recalled phases when the team became more insular; times when they'd debated values. Chris felt that setting up joint management had meant a period of introspection. Joan agreed.

Joan Smith: Where you put your energy or what demands your energy is cyclical, I think. There are times when you have energy to get out there and develop the work. Then something happens and all your energies seem to be going internally — into the Unit. Then it goes up again. But I think it's a sort of

spiral progression towards something, rather than a very
clear progression.
　　And it's always felt to be frustrating, a bit of a
nuisance, when we're in this phase of having to put
our energies into sorting things out internally.
That energies ought to be going into work. And
yet both are required somehow.

But national FSU did not see joint management as a logical
progression — natural, spiral or otherwise. For them, it posed
all sorts of problems. As we'll see in the next two chapters, this
wasn't just an internal wrangle in one agency. The doubts
raised elsewhere in FSU go to the heart of a number of issues
about teams and teamworking.

An excerpt from Joan Smith's book, *Growing Together: Innovatory Work With a Whole Family*

I try to encourage Helen to take much of the necessary action herself, making contact with people on her own behalf rather than continually acting as advocate for her. We have spent many hours talking about this as it was clearly contrary to Helen's expectations of the way I would operate. It seems that on the whole, her requests to many of the welfare agencies have met with the immediate giving or promise of material aid which would ease the current problem, or a direct "No" — both of which Helen would accept without question.

It would be easier for us in the Unit to say, "Leave it to me, I will tap whatever resources are known to me to get you what you need, whether it's housing, money, clothing, work or whatever. I know the system. I can make the contacts. I can express your needs and plead your case articulately". My own experience in social work has taught me that, without doubt, such a style of intervention is less time-consuming and often has the desired result. Yet what does it do to the Helens of this country? By holding on to whatever knowledge and access to information I have, I am making sure that my position remains powerful. Even though I may be using that power for the 'benefit' of Helen, every time I use my power in such a way I confirm Helen in her powerlessness. I am actually creating that very dependence on me which could lead to the description or 'labelling' of her as inadequate, poor manager, or scrounger. It seems to me that the last state such a style of intervention would achieve is that of Helen's independence.

Working with Helen is not easy. It is almost impossible to avoid feeling depressed about her situation and very hard indeed to enable her to express any feelings about anything. Her passive acceptance is a hindrance to the progress of the work as she would be prepared to give up trying to solve any problem at the first setback. Her self-image is so low that she expects to fail.

Three

Arguments for Change

I asked Tim Cook about Newcastle Unit's arguments. Did he see the changes there as linked together, especially with how they wanted to work with users? In retrospect, Tim was ready to understand the logic of it, but wondered, had they actually developed like that?

> *Tim Cook*: I can totally understand their position. In that sense I agree. The difficulty is, that presupposes a whole lot of jumps which I don't think I would have made at the time. I can see now with hindsight that's how they were developing it. Firstly they aren't the only Unit to have been working on these lines. Obviously FSU generally are trying to be more equal with clients. And some Units operate with much more delegated responsibility from the Unit Organisers and so on.
>
> So that Janet and I, the first time we heard the proposal, in a very deep gut level it didn't come as a bolt out of the blue. Whereas in some other Units it might have done. But it didn't have the kind of logical coherence to it that the Unit either had itself, or came to present to us.

Such differences in perception were a sore point between the Unit and other parts of FSU. Newcastle staff liked and trusted Tim, and he had expressed confidence in both the originality and quality of their work.

> *Tim*: Newcastle had a reputation of trailblazing. One of the first into community work; first certainly into race issues; and a lot of the women's issues.
>
> At no time was I ever concerned about the quality of their work or their integrity as individuals. That was

58

not an issue at all, as far as I was concerned, because
it's of the highest.

So Newcastle couldn't understand why he played safe,
recommending against their proposal, because of (in his
words) "the concerns and anxieties within the organisation".
They were baffled that national FSU appeared not to
recognise what they had become, and how this fitted into all
the other changes that had been welcomed. Did National Management Committee see it as just an administrative arrangement that would need unscrambling? If so, what of the whole
blend of practice and principle underlying the Unit's day to
day work and team functioning? Since, over the years, FSU
had been complimentary about Newcastle's omelette, how
were they expecting the eggs to be put back into their shells?

More Equal With Clients

A further reason Newcastle workers felt let down was hinted
at in Tim Cook's remark about "trying to be more equal with
clients". In 1982, as part of a wider debate about clients' rights,
national FSU published *Family Involvement in the Social Work
Process*. Trying to move from statements of principle to practical change, it argued for considerably more honesty and clarity with users; giving them more information; and inviting
their participation in reviews and case conferences. The following year Tim chaired an NCVO Working Party on clients'
rights.[1]
    Newcastle saw these initiatives as very much in tune with
their own approach. The Unit had tried unsuccessfully to
bring users onto the local management committee.[2] Families
were invited to case conferences. But deeper than this, was a
feeling that their overall philosophy was entirely consistent
with how the agency *nationally* said it wanted to work. To reject self-management seemed to imply that national FSU
wasn't living up to its stated principles.
    When I first met Janet and Tim, communication between
them and Newcastle was strained. They felt a "moral tone" in
the Unit's letters and messages, with the 'rightness' of self-
management coming through. Plainly, there's something of
this in Chris Johnson's challenge in chapter one, asking how
FSU could speak about client's rights and advocate users hav-

ing power, but "then not follow that through". Ernie Dobson talked of the Unit's way of working as "just good practice", and Lilian White saw it as a common philosophy.

> *Lilian*: The philosophy we use throughout the Unit as well. It is very similar throughout all the work we do. Whichever sort of work would feel there'd be the same attitudes, the same approach.

At one level, it *is* a moral issue — an argument that if work towards empowerment is right for users, then the same principle should apply in relations among staff. Newcastle can be taken as appealing for fairness and consistency. Democracy is 'a good thing' whether for users or workers.

The Logic of Empowerment

However, this falls short of the framework I sketched at the end of chapter one, about the 'fit' between how an agency wishes or chooses to work with users, and staff relations and structures. Having seen how Newcastle developed its ideas over several years, we can understand their crucial step beyond a consistency of principle to make the further link. Because once principled choices were made about working with users in this way, certain practical choices had to follow about how the Unit worked and was managed.

The key idea here is that the direct work of an agency with its users — for Newcastle FSU, the visits to families, meetings with community groups, groupwork sessions, and so on — can't be considered separately from how the agency runs; how the staff work together.

Because social relations among workers colour and shape and change the relationships between the agency and its users.

In chapter one, I presented this negatively. Closed, controlling, hierarchical staff relations will undermine attempts to work openly, equally, and in ways that respect users rights. If relations among staff don't (or aren't allowed to) change, then the likelihood is that services will slowly be recast into the old moulds. At best, improvements occur despite what goes on in the office, which leads to individual workers viewing their agency or work group as unsupportive, unhelpful, and operating against what the worker tries to achieve.[3]

In contrast, achieving positive goals requires these influences to be reversed. Empowered workers can more effectively work towards empowering users. Colleagues who are honest and clear with each other are supported in approaching users with honesty and clarity. This does not mean that reversing the process is mechanical and automatic. Nor is it easy. Sure, we can agree in principle that workers should not mislead and manipulate users. But isn't it all too simple to justify such action 'in their best interests'? As we'll discuss later, work which empowers other people requires acknowledging your own power and the power of your group.

Their insistence on the logic of empowerment was Newcastle's major challenge to the rest of FSU. But the challenge applies as forcefully elsewhere — to any agency aiming for users' rights, empowerment, and participation.

Further Reasons for Joint Management

I've dwelt on one aspect of the case for joint management because of its wider importance. But it wasn't the only reason given. The Unit also stressed the scheme's local nature. If not quite time honoured, it was (they hinted) at least something of a tradition in Elswick. Their written proposal spoke too, of "the growing numbers of staff with considerable work experience", and they advocated a collective team approach to maximise the use of these diverse skills.

> We have found in practice that [self-management]
> enables the maximum development of the skills and
> potential of each member of staff. The considerable
> 'practice skills' of experienced workers are not lost to
> people in the community when they take on
> management responsibilities.

Lilian and Ernie elaborated during a Unit discussion.

> *Ernie Dobson*: Somehow even before Joan left and be-
> fore changing the structure, there was some kind of
> philosophy here about making the best use of workers'
> potential, respecting each other as equals. And then

sharing out management tasks. And from time to time having discussions about general policy issues which affected all our work. Somehow having that attitude to each other and working in that way contributes to the quality of our work, in that our work is more thought out, and some of the attitudes we have to each other spin off into the way we do our work with the people we work with.

And because of the way we're structured makes us make better decisions about our work. But it's more than saying 'two heads are better than one'. It's beyond that somehow.

I can see that look on people's faces. Somebody help me out. Come on. Somebody say, 'Yes, I know what you're talking about'!

Lilian White: Yes, I'm getting into it now. It's something to do with the whole range of skills that staff group has, and how we lend to each other. There's always things that you can pool. It's rare that you come to a Unit meeting without hearing something that you could try if you're stuck.

Management Committee Views

On the management committee, both Ian Bynoe and Margaret Chiles mentioned the links between collective working and the approach to users. Ian was the only member who'd previously worked in a collective — a Law Centre. Margaret had been a City Councillor and remained active in local affairs. For her, the main question was whether a collective team was accountable to local people, especially users.

Other committee members gave more practical reasons for self-management. They all agreed that collective working was part of the sequence of developments at the Unit, and many of them were irritated by the apparent inability of the rest of FSU to understand this. Tom Hammill, for instance, who taught social policy at Newcastle University, had been a member of the committee since 1976, and chaired it prior to Alan Jackson.

Tom: The question of change to Joint Staff Management I felt was, in a way, formalising something that had been going on anyhow. I was very impressed with the way in which the Unit was operating in those two or three years before Joan went. I felt it was a period of considerable stability.

I thought it was very well planned and prepared for. The staff had a tremendous incentive. They wanted this to succeed, right? They wanted to work in the way they're working now. It wasn't an idea that suddenly arose from nowhere. It had developed over a longish period of time and rose to fruition when they were faced with a replacement for Joan.

Confidence among committee members hadn't prevented worries and questions about joint management. Still, they voted unanimously to support the scheme. They all agreed on three other points. First, no committee member championed collective working as an overriding *principle* in isolation. Second, and quite plainly, all of them saw it as substantially *achieved*. It was "formalising something that had been going on anyhow". Last, while nobody ruled out the option of having a Unit Organiser, that was no longer the axiomatic starting point for discussion. The context had shifted, so that a self-managing staff team had become the *new status quo*. This last point deserves particular attention.

Why, I asked Ian Bynoe, hadn't they simply looked round for a Unit Organiser prepared to work as Joan had? He'd heard a similar suggestion when supporting joint management at National Management Committee.

Ian: It was stressed that that was *history*. That Joan had left; that Joan wasn't there. That these were reports as to what was happening *now*.

Pam Flynn also felt that the Unit had its system worked out. Her own job was then in Newcastle's Adult Education Outreach Project, and she was strongly sceptical about collective working.

Pam Flynn: I like hierarchies, I'm afraid. I mean, I only like them when they work well. But I do tend to like structures. And to be suspicious of wimping about in great angst-ridden meetings.

She thought national FSU correct to raise queries, but that they had been dealt with, even if Unit practice remained to be fully tested. Pam couldn't see why they needed one person as manager. "It's like: do you put your eggs in this basket or that basket?". Her main feeling was irritation with national FSU.

> *Pam Flynn*: Why has this taken so bloody long to sort out? That's been my attitude. You know, it's driven me potty going to and fro. And people in London have no idea what happens in Newcastle.

Peter Stone, too, was "quite sure that there's a satisfactory structure there", though he wasn't advocating collective working for his own workplace. (He'd represented Newcastle Social Services since 1975)

> *Peter*: I don't have to be an enthusiast about the principle to be a supporter of it. But I think smaller groups of people do genuinely need to find their own way of working together. Even within hierarchies people need to find their own way of operating the hierarchies.
>
> And that group, whatever the validity of the conclusions it had reached, had spent a long time reaching conclusions to which the group felt committed. And I think it would have needed a real rolling back of the carpet to impose any other system. I would have been concerned about the realities of recruiting anybody to come. I mean, who would you have found? Did you need a gauleiter? Did you need a conciliator? Did you need a superperson? I just don't think it would have been easy.

As I said, the chief issue for Margaret Chiles was accountability of a democratic team to its users. Which went beyond self-management as such, and certainly was not about having a Unit Organiser.

> *Margaret*: I don't think having the Unit Organiser makes any difference.

Ian Bynoe pointed up the change in perspective. Speaking on the Unit's behalf at National Management Committee, he'd felt as though he was talking a different language to many of the other people there.

> *Ian*: Certain members, I felt, considered the proposal was wildly 'Left'. They must have done. They wanted the 'boss' and they couldn't perceive of an organisation without one. But, 'It was amazing! All that was going on in Newcastle! All these things. We're surprised that you find time for staff management', they said.
>
> They couldn't see the point we were making. That it liberates resources and it raises the morale, and it raises the degree of commitment. It raises all sorts of thresholds which traditional hierarchies stifle.
>
> And one person who's going up the ladder, perhaps at the right time and in the right place gets the job... A Unit Organiser would be employed on their strengths and weaknesses, and they wouldn't be rejected if they had a weakness. Well, their weakness could stifle and inhibit the whole growth of a Unit. Whereas bringing everybody into the planning and into the thinking behind the policy and priorities, and ways of working, frees all those resources, spreads the load.[4]

The Disappearing Boss

Hearing the views of Newcastle workers and committee members, one topic was signally absent. Nobody was talking about *leadership*. Now, most writing and a lot of discussion of team-working merges into an examination of leadership as a concept, and the role of the leader. It's assumed to be all one and the same thing, although such an assumption is rarely justified.

Another Family Service Unit, East London, illustrates what I mean. For a year, 1972/73, they had no Unit Organiser, and chose to self-manage. (The usual FSU practice is for another worker to be Acting Organiser.) Marcia Tondel and Dave Holder, two of the staff, wrote about the experience, sketching the gradual move towards a "peer-group team".[5] They spelled out why this meant the team taking responsibility. The UO who left had been committed to joint decision-making and shared work. But, as long as he was still there, "We wanted to be independent as a peer-group team, but still wanted the comfort of having a leader".

During their year of self-management, East London found that many outsiders: "seemed to manifest a belief that a legitimate organisation structure is hierarchical... When our UO left, a few agencies and individuals even expected us to be closing the Unit!" It's not unusual for collective and co-operative teams to be discussed or approached in this way. The belief that hierarchy is natural and obvious makes it hard for people to understand teams and individuals who don't share it.

At Newcastle, (as in East London) the team wanted authority to self-manage. No one denied the need to manage as such. The vital point is that moving beyond hierarchy is not synonymous with being anti-authority.[6] Neither Newcastle staff nor its local committee were asking to work as a 'leaderless group', nor simply arguing against a boss.[7] They just weren't discussing the issues within this framework at all.

Yet this was exactly how many people elsewhere in FSU saw Newcastle's proposal. For instance, in Tim Cook's eyes it meant, "to operate collective, ie. without a Unit Organiser." And Tim's comment was six months after National Council had given Newcastle the go-ahead. The Council itself never positively endorsed joint staff management, but agreed that "in principle Units did not need to have a Unit Organiser".

Unit Organisers and the Paradox of Joan Smith

As a group, the Unit Organisers were apparently unable to see beyond the edge of the same frame. A UO's working party on Unit Management reported in 1983, and attributed tremendous importance to the team leader.

> The position of the Unit Organiser provides the opportunity to develop a personal style of leadership and make a very individual contribution to the nature and services of the Unit within the context of a number of other factors; the needs of the client group and Local Committee of Management, and the requirements of the funding authority. The value which FSU places on staff participation in professional policy and decision making means

that the UO needs to provide creative leadership whilst encouraging all members of the team to share fully in the responsible development of Unit policy and practice. The 'Lynch pin' position of the Unit Organiser in the leadership of the team, and in relation to staff, committee, clients, the National Organisation, the funding authority and other agencies may be experienced as a creative tension, but may also raise issues of isolation and insecurity.

A majority of UO's opposed Newcastle's proposal, translating it (as we might expect) into "the issue of running a Unit without a UO". Their opposition strongly influenced Tim Cook.

Tim: In the light of a heated and difficult discussion at the UO's meeting in the Lake District, at that time the balance seemed to me that it was right to oppose it.

This wasn't the whole picture. The UO's were a diverse bunch of people and even on major issues, tended to split. Within their group the majority against Newcastle's proposal was only three.[8] Among the minority were those who offered support to the Unit and to Joan Smith.

Joan: They are the ones who are already quite involved with their own staff group; who see themselves as an important part of the machinery for the Unit, but not necessarily the essential fuel to keep the whole thing going.

But the majority view was argued at National Management Committee and National Council. There, vital questions about the quality of team working were raised, only to imply that the answer was to keep the Unit Organiser. (E.g. problems of group collusion, and response in an emergency.) UO representatives drew attention to the "critical overview role, and the unrecognised areas of leadership, with Joan Smith paradoxically being a prime example of this". The UO's had mixed feelings about Joan in other ways.

Janet Williams: She occupied quite a significant position in the UO's group, and in the organisation.

She'd represented them [the UO's] at National Council
meetings for quite a long time and done it very well,
and was a much respected person, and very much
liked.

Even so, some UO's were annoyed that, as they saw it, Joan
hadn't kept them informed of Newcastle's development. Joan
accepted their criticism in part, agreeing that, by providing a
designated "boss person", perhaps a wrong impression had
been given. After all, other Units had also changed their way
of working. They too had developed neighbourhood and
community work, groupwork, and special projects. UO's elsewhere had encouraged 'collegiate' teams, with other staff joining in planning and review of work, and sharing management
tasks. Sometimes this was matched by group supervision. So
the real paradox was Joan's opinion:

> *Joan*: It did seem pretty obvious that that sort of
> hierarchical role would have to disappear altogether in
> the end.

The point here is not to establish who did and said what, but
to illustrate that there were sharply distinct conceptions of
what a 'team' was and how it should run. Joan believed some
of the other Organisers saw her as threatening their own position.

> *Joan*: [They] saw me, in a whole range of ways, as
> being incompetent or irresponsible, and making unfair
> demands. Not taking my responsibilities seriously. Not
> really understanding what the Unit Organiser's job is;
> how complex it is. Not having the skills or the authori-
> ty to demand, to steer the whole thing, to be in control.

She recalled discussion groups at the UO's meetings where
she had talked about Newcastle becoming a democratic team.

> *Joan*: I actually did talk quite a lot about it, and I
> think if people didn't hear, that's a case of putting
> their own interpretation on the sort of things I was
> describing. I was talking about *democracy* and in my
> own mind having a fair amount of power sharing and

individual autonomy and personal responsibility of the
various members of staff in the Unit. And sharing of
responsibilities which were normally regarded as being
the Unit Organiser's (like supervision, and things like
that). Then, talking about that would be heard and
received according to the hearer's perceptions and
understandings of the words used.

Again, the question isn't about setting the record straight, but
exploring the different frameworks people use, especially in
what is meant or understood by a democratic team.

A Democratic Team

> *Tim Cook*: Somebody did — somewhere at a meeting
> — say, 'Well, to save all this aggro why don't they just
> have someone who's called the UO except they're paid
> the same as everyone else? But it'll just save a lot of
> hassle.' I knew Newcastle would never buy it. Well, I
> would have been very surprised. Because that's not in
> keeping with what I see as their proper level of
> honesty.

The Unit Organisers' representatives made a similar
suggestion at National Management Committee. "The Newcastle Unit's objectives", they said, "could be achieved within
the existing structure as it had with a UO". Hadn't Joan
achieved just this? And didn't other Units run democratically? Underlying that view are some important ideas about
teams, as I said, fused together with notions about leadership.
In brief, the assumption is made that different sorts of teams
are actually variations on a single theme. You may ring the
changes on management or leadership *style*, but underneath
there's a common fixed basis — a structure with taken for
granted rules about how a work group is, and should be,
organised.

Newcastle workers understood how confusing this was.
As we'll see in the next chapter, its a confusion which permeates much of the thinking and writing about teams in social
services work.

"The Buck Doesn't

Stop With You"

Shirley Forster: I think there's a lot of confusion that people talk about. Which is the difference between being in a democratic team that's led by somebody, and being a democratic team. Lots and lots of people are confused about that and don't understand there's a tremendous difference. The idea of a democratic team which has an appointed leader who is, at the end of the day, the boss, that's a very different situation.

And I think it has effects on Unit Organisers. However democratic their teams are, how come if they've got a funding application to write they don't feel able to delegate it to somebody? How come they're so essential they can't be spared from their post? Maybe some of them not coming to the [Unit Organisers'] meeting is around saying, 'I am so important; my team will fall apart without me. 'Cause actually they're not as capable as me'.

And what we've found is that's not true. That there's nobody here who's indispensable. We'll miss people when they leave, and really miss their skills. But holes are filled up; the show doesn't fall apart. I think we've stopped having the fantasy that it will fall apart if somebody leaves.

Ernie Dobson: I think there's also the attitude of staff towards the Unit Organiser as well. That kind of democratic hierarchical situation, I think we went through that experience with Joan. It was that you can only go so far, even when the Unit Organiser is willing to co-operate. And even when you want to share tasks and kind of muck-in, there's still deep down a feeling that the buck doesn't stop with you, but it stops at somebody else; it stops at the Unit Organiser. You might not be conscious of it. But they end up being the people who've still got to be aware and thinking about everything that's going on. They still feel the

70

responsibility. They can't truly delegate or share things. Because they feel it, and to some extent expect it.

Shirley Forster: Oh, we used to give it to Joan, didn't we? She used to end up saying, 'Don't give me that shit. We're sharing this'.

Lilian White: That's right. Quite a lot of the time.

Four

Thinking About Teams

In this chapter I want to widen out the discussion about teams and teamwork, particularly in social service agencies. Why do outsiders repeatedly misperceive and misinterpret collective working? To answer, we need to explore some of the assumptions shaping people's beliefs about organisations, leading them to assume there is one sort of "legitimate organisation structure".

As FSU is our starting point, I'll introduce research and writing about fieldwork teams in personal social services. Readers unfamiliar with this needn't worry - they'll soon recognise all the issues.

Teams in Social Services Work

Newcastle City Council followed the usual pattern for an English Authority. Its Social Services department employed fieldwork staff based in local area offices, and it also grant-aided a small number of agencies (like FSU) to provide specific services. In Britain, the vast majority of social services teams are found within local authorities.

This common pattern arose from the 1968 Seebohm Committee and subsequent legislation.[1] Social Service departments with area teams were central to Seebohm's recommendations. They were to offer an integrated service, bringing together different specialisms in accessible local offices. At the time, there was an expectation that the new departments would promote co-operation and open communication among staff, as a means of making services flexible and adaptable.[2]

In 1982, the Barclay Committee reported on field social work.[3] It reviewed local teams, and again saw them as a way of providing efficient and co-ordinated services. However, the majority Barclay Report concluded that the potential for a responsive community orientated service — part of the Seebohm philosophy — hadn't been fulfilled. So Barclay proposed 'community social work', one model being 'patch' teams, based in a limited geographical area and closely involved with local people and local networks.

Many local authorities have introduced such schemes; sometimes involving comprehensive re-organisation. In Newcastle, though the City's social services teams were organised in small areas, there was no overall move to a community social work approach. However, Newcastle FSU's own reorganisation in 1977 clearly foreshadowed these ideas, when it substantially reduced its catchment area, and aimed at integrating different methods and sharing skills and experience. The Unit believed (like the Seebohm and Barclay Committees) that the potential for teamwork is greatest when staff share premises and work in the same local area, often with a common group of users.

Naive Questions

Before this chapter begins to read like a dull summary of the recent history of British social services, let me pause and ask some apparently naive questions. Why should teamwork have been such an issue? Did it really need weighty, government sponsored reports to propose co-ordination of different skills; or deliberate on how workers might support and supervise each other? If work groups do not collaborate like this, why call them teams at all?

The answer is discouraging. In the personal social services, loud and sustained calls for better teamworking are a signal of its *absence*.[4] Plenty of work groups are designated as 'teams'. The word is so much "soaked in positive values"[5] that it's used for practically any arrangement where staff are even notionally grouped together. But despite at least twenty years with an explicit goal of integrated teamwork, in practice, work groups usually turn out to collaborate very little.[6]

This pessimistic picture is confirmed by three research studies. In the first, Carole Satyamurti looked at one social services department during and after the reorganisation recommended by Seebohm. She found that:

Social workers worked on the basis of individual responsibility for individual clients. Their work was therefore privatised, at times to the point of possessiveness.[7]

Satyamurti's remedy was "the development of more shared models of work", which she viewed as "a precondition for other changes".[8] She wanted meetings to become a means of sharing and analysing workers' experience, and of improving decisions. Different specialist skills within a team would be available if clients could relate to the whole team rather than a single worker, practicing 'privately'.

A later study examined social services teams throughout Britain. Olive Stevenson and Phyllida Parsloe's research was a major project, covering thirty-five area teams in ten separate local authorities. They too found very little group or shared work. Nor, in the main, did field staff function as groups to decide policy.

The majority of team members went about their 'case work' as individuals... Some workers managed to build a psychological wall around themselves and their work.[9]

Another 'wall' seemed to divide workers from senior management - "the hierarchy". Stevenson and Parsloe quote this typical view:

We have the capacity to generate energy between ourselves and this is not happening. Everybody is having to cope on their own and they are building up barriers around themselves for protection.[10]

Parsloe suggested that teams fall on a continuum — ranging from 'individualist' to 'collective'.[11] In general, they found teams far closer to the former. In such an individualist type, superiors allocate work, usually casework. Individual practice seems to inhibit new methods, especially in areas like groupwork. Joint working is discouraged, and the whole team is unlikely to collaborate on common projects. There are few meetings and little learning together. Workers don't share their experience and views of local problems, resources and developments, and this hinders their response to community need. Stevenson and Parsloe found some teams where the existence of specialists became an excuse for not building a common understanding.

> One community worker told us that she considered her presence allowed the rest of the team to ignore the demands of a community work approach and retreat without guilt into their 'one-to-one casework'.[12]

In favour of the individualist team, Parsloe noted that it often produces individual work of high quality. Conversely, it can lead to overdependence on the leader, on whom workers may deposit their feelings. Members may be "kept at a rather infantile and dependent level".[13]

The findings of subsequent research by Jim Black and others, were just as bleak.[14] They compared three social services offices, two in rural areas and one urban, and found work individualised, with marked antagonism to "the hierarchy".[15] Staff were neither responding flexibly to users, nor pooling skills to enhance services. Instead, they tended to define clients' needs in ways that fitted the (individual) help on offer. Again, the researchers proposed more efficient team working as one remedy.

Radical and Socialist Critiques

In chapter two, we saw how Newcastle Unit also wanted teamwork as a means of integrating their skills. It was inefficient, said Joan Smith, "going about our work without recourse to any other work that was going on at all". However, there was another reason for the changes they made — new ideas and values for how they wanted to work with users.

Writing on social services contains this second strand, especially in a number of radical and socialist critiques. So, in calling for more teamwork, there has been an overlap of views. Voices on the Left have advocated "working as collectively as possible, both in terms of the quality of the practice and to ensure political support".[16] "The creation of a real team approach to welfare work" has been seen as "progressive practice"[17]; as "prefiguring the future"[18]; and "creating new social relations which challenge the traditional boundaries between clients and workers".[19]

Unfortunately, these warm endorsements[20] rarely accompany detailed descriptions of actual examples. There are very few accounts of teamworking from a socialist or radical perspective.[21] In a curious way, despite challenging orthodox ideas about working together, such writing serves to strengthen a pessimistic view about what is possible. The socialist "real team" appears largely an aim, or perhaps only a hope.

We might conclude that there is no mystery about why people assume one kind of "legitimate organisation structure" — because that's what there is. What predominates in practice is the hierarchical department with its individualist offices, and staff who build psychological walls round their desks. But, actually, this is only part of the explanation.

The Invisible Team

Ask yourself why you're now reading an account of Newcastle's collective teamwork. It wasn't because they had been successfully collaborating. No, the event that led to this study was the Unit's proposal for a formal change in management. Joan Smith's departure forced them to come out of the closet.

Not all teams choose or are pushed into being this open. Some think twice before going public on their self-management and, in many fields, they keep prudently quiet. At Newcastle, at least on paper, it seemed from the outside that nothing much had altered till Joan went. Collective teamwork was somehow 'invisible', and they were able to pass in the straight world of one-team-one-boss.

I said before that people often find it hard to understand collective working because they carry certain ingrained ideas about organisation structure. I'll now go further to say that hierarchical thinking can so shape and influence us that we *fail* to see collective teamwork when it does develop.[22] It somehow doesn't exist until one day it announces: Please see what we have become.[23]

Technical and Managerial

The dominance of this way of thinking becomes plain if we look at what usually happens when people with power to initiate change, set out detailed recommendations. Take the Seebohm and Barclay Committees. Though both had wide-ranging discussions about teams, their practical proposals were narrow and limited, centering on formal structures and designated roles.

A more recent example was a review by Bath University of the Borough of Brent's Social Services department. Bath's report highlighted, in an extreme form, the fragmentation and lack of co-ordination found by research elsewhere. It was a "department in deep distress", where rumour had replaced open communication.[24] Yet these poor social relations were ignored by the researchers' proposals, which boiled down to the usual administrative rejigging and creation of new managerial posts.[25]

So often, when they move from discussion to action, reformers seem to find themselves stuck with one set of organisational tools.[26] This *technical/managerial* approach takes either a team or a department to be simply an arrangement of staff with defined roles and tasks. It's technical, because achieving aims like collaborative teamwork is seen as a technical problem. Indeed, teams themselves are viewed as tools to produce the measurable objectives of efficiency and effectiveness. Telling colleagues about your work is 'feedback'; going into someone else's office 'interface'.

The approach is managerial, because it assumes that structures and procedures, appropriately engineered and efficiently managed, will ensure proper functioning. Within this framework, changing an organisation requires setting new objectives and getting the 'right' roles and lines of command. Praise teams, but pass the job descriptions. Since control is assumed to be top-down, structures are inevitably hierarchical. Typically, accountability is to those who control or own, through line managers. Change entails administrators redrawing organisational charts and moving staff around.

However, this approach presents a fundamental difficulty. And it's this: describing a structure or prescribing a model based on its assumptions, still gives no answer to the 'naive questions' I put before. For, despite all the committees, research and various restructurings, the goal of teamworking seems as elusive as ever. The technical/managerial approach cannot tell us why some groups end up pooling and sharing, communicating and trusting, and not others. It simply doesn't address some of the central questions about teamwork.

Take Me to Your Leader

Or, as I suggested in the last chapter, it tries to answer them by referring to the *style* of the leader.[27] So a major feature of the technical/managerial approach is the great weight it places on positions like manager and team leader. If not the crucial "lynchpin" suggested by the FSU's Unit Organisers, they are at least "Linking Pins"[28] — people who overlap and connect parts of an organisation.

The trouble is, instead of explaining different kinds of teams, notions of leadership and role of the leader crowd out exploration of teamwork altogether. It's not surprising if a major source of misunderstanding about Newcastle's self-management was the idea elsewhere in FSU that this meant being 'leaderless'. Within the technical/managerial framework, not having a leader looks like *the* substantive difference in collective working.

Similar ideas coloured the discussion of social services teams mentioned above. Stevenson and Parsloe believe: "it is difficult to exaggerate the influence of the team leader on the team.[29] The Barclay Committee, recommending neighbourhood 'patch' teams for community social work, stressed the "key management role" of team leader; envisaging "an entrepreneurial figure" to develop and help "his" staff, and to bargain for resources for "his" team.[30]

But, if we reflect for a moment, we'll realise that this has very little to do with teamwork as collaboration and co-operation. In fact, it's more like a replica, at manager level, of the solo individualist working of fieldstaff. Managers who talk about 'my team' as though they own it, become "entrepreneurs" who develop psychological walls round their 'business'. That's a recipe for just the sort of isolation and insecurity that FSU Unit Organisers spoke of, and which workers at Newcastle learned of from Joan, and later from Lilian.[31]

In any case, it isn't necessary to consider a particular style of manager to realise we've slid from talking about the role and function of a team leader, to describing the personal *qualities* of that person: 'who' rather than 'how'. And from there, it's a short hop to thinking that the simplest way to change an organisation or team is to promote, appoint, or even 'headhunt' the right boss. Like a fading football club, the quest is: find the manager who'll work the magic.[32]

Far from bringing us any nearer to understanding team-work, we are left with a view that organisations contain two elements. One is a basic structure, technically prescribed. Complementing this is the second element — different management styles due largely to the personality and talents of the leader.

A Managerial Dilemma

The options on offer are thereby reduced to two: altering structures, or changing leaders. So we can see why organisations go through recurring cycles. Either a reorganisation — large or small scale — is underway, shuffling the pieces around; or the 'wrong' people are being paid off and the 'right' people brought in.

But either-or restricts the range of questions people can put. Are they querying the structure and its rules and roles? Or criticising personnel? As long as Joan Smith remained Newcastle Unit Organiser, the other UO's were in just this cleft stick. If the team's functioning was seen to *belong* to Joan's personal style and creative leadership, how were they to question the development of collaborative working? It would have seemed either like a personal attack on her, or a challenge to each UO's right to manage their own team.

Janet Williams was stuck in the same tramlines when she did Joan Smith's formal assessment in 1980. Although the "democratic style of management in the Unit" looms large in Janet's report, it still had to be discussed as part of the UO role. There was no provision for accepting the real logic of "democratic" — and make the running of the team as such, a legitimate and proper subject for scrutiny.[33]

Let me say plainly that what happened was not a failure by FSU, but illustrates a general point. For any agency concerned with teamwork, these aspects of the technical/managerial approach are not just unhelpful but *disabling*. They mean that provided a particular manager is competent, the standard of individual work in their team is okay, and there are no disasters, an agency will not assess or examine teamworking separately from what it views as an achievement, feature, or failure of the team manager. When (as with Joan Smith) a manager or team leader's reputation is sound, there seems even less need to judge the weaknesses and strengths (individual and collective) of the rest of 'their' staff in contributing to the team's running.

The Team as 'Collection'

For some readers, what I've written may seem unfairly balanced. After all, aren't there alternative approaches to teamwork — group dynamics, for example? And haven't many writers on social services teams explicitly supported the development of co-operative and collective ways of working?

These and (no doubt) other comments would be accurate. So let me explain that I haven't set out to review the wide range of writing on teams. My aim was to suggest what it is about current practice and thinking on organisations, that so often shapes and limits people's understanding of collective running.

Now, it's quite true that we're very rarely asked to swallow full-strength technical managerialism.[34] Even so, it has a habit of seeping into and becoming the dominant flavour in all sorts of recipes for teamwork. To give an example, some writers on social services teams use sporting metaphors to describe different sorts of teams. An individualist group is compared to an athletics team — people with unique skills, 'playing' separately. Collective teamwork is seen as closer to, say, a football side.[35]

At first glance, this looks attractive. It suggests that there *are* alternatives to the way most people now work — including a collaborative model. And if the reality of co-operation 'on the field' was explored, we'd have a different and potentially very useful framework. Unfortunately that isn't the case. It turns out to be only a neat way of tabulating an *arithmetical* view of teamwork — eg. football teams have 11 players; tennis teams 1+1+1+1+1. Team building is tackled as if it meant the *collection* of specific quantities and qualities of individuals.

Other versions of this idea are more sophisticated, but share the assumption that teams are essentially variations within the same basic hierarchical structure.[36] They may talk about work groups as networks; or as selections of personality types — "plants" and "completers"[37] — but this just offers classification in place of understanding. They don't and can't explain *why* groups do or don't run collaboratively. People together are still seen as component assemblies.

The Nature of Teams

Perhaps this seems unkind. Certainly, the other major approach to teamwork is organic rather than mechanical: encouraging and nurturing those aspects of work groups which by their nature grow to interdependence and co-operation. What we can loosely call a group dynamics approach asks about the *nature* of teams, drawing from social psychology.[38] A work group is assumed to mirror other kinds of groups, for instance in its stages of development and internal dynamics.

While a review of this writing is beyond the scope of this book, nevertheless, it will be plain that both I and the Newcastle team borrowed from such theories. For example, Sally Walker saw the dispute with Lin as 'scapegoating'.[39] The Unit Organisers' group raised related issues, like the danger of collusion. I mentioned cyclical patterns, as the team went through phases of internal questioning, followed by renewed energy in developing the work outside. The idea here is not that events are mechanically determined, but that it's as well to remember how things have their 'seasons', and that not all productive activity is immediately obvious.

The important question, though, is whether a group dynamics approach provides an escape from technical/managerial thinking. I want to suggest that, in many cases, the two are not true alternatives, but serve to *complement* each other. Let me give an example.

Consider the theoretical division adopted by many writers on organisations, who split a team's functioning in two. On one side are the tasks of a work group — what it does and how it does it. On the other, comes the supporting, maintaining work that enables the practical 'business' to take place — a group's internal dynamics and relationships. In this form there aren't phases of work so much as separate spheres — one labelled 'task' or 'production', the other 'maintenance' or 'socioemotional' aspects.[40]

But what this does is to pull apart the personal and the organisational. We have divided up something which people at work experience as a whole. It may be tidy analysis, but it makes for bloodless description — and another way in which a workplace stops being recognisable to the staff there. More worryingly, if members of a team or agency adopt the same distinction they make one-sided interpretations of the problems they face.

So, in Carole Satyamurti's research, she found social workers with "a siege perspective",[41] keeping clients at a distance as a way of controlling their own fears. Instead of coming together to change the situation — the organisation of their work, or perhaps the resources available — they used the team as a means of getting *sympathy*. As Satyamurti put it, the work group helped people "to deal with the *experience* of the problem rather than with the problem itself".[42]

Let me make it clear that I am not dismissing the insights offered by a group dynamics approach, but questioning how far it actually challenges prevailing technical/managerial ideas. The strength of writers like Satyamurti and Parsloe is in blending the personal and organisational. They discuss teamwork, not as boxes and lines, but a process where people's work and internal relations ought to come together.

I said earlier that there are few descriptions of collectively working teams in personal social services. However, one helpful account is Phyllida Parsloe's picture of the team she *didn't* meet. Suppose that a collective rather than an individualist team became a "legitimate organisation structure", what would be its strengths and weaknesses?

A collective team, thought Parsloe, would show the opposite in each respect.[43] Staff might share work, which could centre on groups and neighbourhoods as well as individuals and families. The team would recognise, encourage, and make resources available for members' interests and skills with different users or user groups. Other shared aspects would include: group supervision; involvement of the whole team in hiring; and regular meetings for management, training, and allocation of work — with the chair rotated.

She suggested that a collective approach was needed to develop community based work. "The team as a whole and its individual members may have links with local groups and with volunteers, and their premises may be used by members of the community". This type of team: "will give considerable weight to the existence of potential clients as well as those already known to them". They could: "use their group cohesion as a safe base from which to move out into the community and open themselves up to members of the public".

Parsloe also set out some of the difficulties. Group cohesion might act as a barrier: "Some teams seem to act as if their task is to man the barricades". A collective team, "demands work and discipline and can only be reached over a long period during which conflicts are resolved". She pointed out too, that the habit of co-operation is not something our socialisation prepares us for. It needs "the ability to adapt one's pace to that of others and to substitute collective success for individual achievement".

Collective teams are also posed a question - one which came up in different ways at Newcastle. What has an individual worker to gain from collective working? There may be good policy reasons for collaboration, and good ideological reasons as well. But the team of individuals, comments Parsloe, "offers the social worker the pleasure of planning their work and using whatever social work methods they wish without interference from others".[13]

This matches each of the research studies, which show fieldwork staff defending their individual "professional" freedom against what they saw as encroachment by departmental management. It's not hard to see how the untested (for them) potential of teamwork would be less attractive than each worker's limited but real autonomy as a practitioner.

So can staff, who see apparently good reasons to hold onto a pattern of individualised work, be persuaded to explore or even consider the possibility of working collectively? Are there collective ways of keeping the pleasures of work while dealing with the worries that an enlarged group responsibility seems to threaten? One reason for looking at Newcastle's experience is to see how far the personal and the organisational can be brought together — not just in a theoretical model — but in daily practice.

Naming Names

People come and go; organisations remain. But readers know now why this book isn't just about the structures and procedures of Newcastle Family Service Unit. Still, why quote Lilian and Joan and Ernie and the rest, using their real names? Haven't they all moved on — whether to new jobs, or in their ideas and experience? One reason is because this participatory study includes these particular people discussing the issues as they saw them, as well as my interpretations and discussions with them.

It's also to avoid making teamwork impersonal; separating the 'functions' and 'systems' of an agency from the emotions and affections that people bring with them or build with each other. They are persons not personnel. Writing about organisations will be useful to practitioners when it stops distancing lived experience in the attempt to measure and categorise it.

This matches Newcastle Unit's understanding of the need for relations among workers to fit those with users. To work with users, respecting them as people who bring their own feelings and meanings, isn't to deny the task in hand, nor the rules and powers constraining a worker within an agency.

Five

Colleagues & Relations

I wonder what sort of picture readers have of the Newcastle team. Does the description so far, with the people introduced, give an idea of what it was like to visit or even work there? This chapter offers some snapshots from varying angles: by colleagues coming into the team from outside; new staff; some of the students; and one of FSU's assistant directors.

Sometimes, people decide such a team isn't for them, having the notion (or perhaps experience) of collective groups as like-minded people, with an intensity of relationships not suiting everyone. Is such intensity inevitable? And, in other ways, does collective working rely on a narrow range of team members? Answering this at Newcastle, I'll look again at hiring, and how closeknit or closed the team was.

Since I've argued that existing frameworks for analysing teams have serious drawbacks, I'll introduce some alternative ideas based on *reference* — people referring to one another as peers. The chapter ends with a brief sketch of what we might call collective working relations — what Newcastle staff were aiming for when they talked about a change in "their attitude to each other" and "supervising, supporting, advising each other, drawing from each other's knowledge and skills".

A Commitment to Sharing

In chapter three, we saw the team looking for new workers who could share their approach to users. Staff who came and stayed, were also those who accepted collective working and, from joint staff management onward, this became Unit policy. Neither of these required a social work background or qualification. The team included workers qualified in other ways. Ali Rhind and Sally Walker, for instance, had community arts experience, while Lilian White had been a nurse.

Once collective working is established, it's sometimes said that a group risks becoming exclusive. Suppose that, given the chance, many more people would choose to work collectively. Would they be chosen? Phyllida Parsloe implies that, for a collective team in social services, the pool of potential staff might be narrow.

> To work in such a team when it is fully developed demands both an ideological commitment to sharing and the personal skills and confidence to put this into practice.[1]

Teams in other fields echo her view. For example, a Californian legal collective insisted that new members:

> have to share the same basic assumptions as far as politics goes and they have to be willing to accept the collective way of doing things.[2]

Describing Newcastle, I've tended to concentrate on similarities among the staff; their shared values and growing cohesion. Pam Carter's description after 1980 seems to support the view of a narrowly based team.

> *Pam*: There was a sort of group of people of similar age, similar political beliefs — not party political. And once they became established with very little movement, then things really took off.

Tom Hammill, on the management committee, saw the advantages of hiring people who wanted to work collectively, but wondered if this would override other criteria. Might it prevent the choice of staff who were: "the best people for giving the skill and service that the community needs, or because they're people who in some way can bring in fresh ideas — maybe not in tune with existing ideas?"

In fact, the policy that new workers must accept self-management wasn't used to exclude applicants without experience of collective working. All the same, it was essential to have a *core* of staff who were experienced — both as practitioners and in running the Unit. The apparent paradox is that the more a team shares and deepens its skills as practitioners *and* in self-management, the easier it becomes to take on new staff who break the existing mould. New workers with varied experience and qualifications can then have support (available and offered) by those:

> *Chris Johnson*: who felt happy enough and confident enough to do that supporting at any one time.

How Wide a Net?

There's still an issue of who fits in, something any team has to consider. A Unit Organiser elsewhere, wrote that cohesion was essential for small teams and that all Family Service Units had to strike a balance between skills and personalities.[3] But this begs the question of how many staff work solo — a point made by Pam Carter, who spent five years in a local authority social services office.

> *Pam*: I think that social services teams can accommodate a much greater spectrum of personalities and interests comfortably, than a team like ours can — by ignoring each other.

FSU did extend its spectrum, with both staff and management committee pushing for this. Alan Jackson, committee chair till 1985, wanted to see more staff with a working class background.

> *Alan Jackson*: Rather than middle class trendies coming in from the Jesmonds and Sandyfords of this world to say, 'This is what should be happening'.

Alan strongly supported the recruitment of Lilian White, and later of Parveen Akhtar and Elliot Yabantu, two of the Unit's first black workers. For these and other appointments they deliberately widened their net when publicising job vacancies.

> *Chris Johnson*: If you look at how we got Lilian, it was very much on the grapevine. And that's a whole issue of who applies for jobs, you know. That you might see an advert and never actually feel confident enough to

apply because you don't feel you fit the criteria. I mean, we sort of went to her and said, 'Please apply'. And if you're serious about encouraging people who aren't middle class too, you've also got to look at that. How do you actually get them in?

Intensity of Relationships

Applicants can be put off by more than adverts. Outsiders sometimes fear (and sometimes hope) that joining a collective team entails close personal friendships. There are strong hints from inside collectives that intimate and intense relationships mark this way of working. "Plants die here from the heavy vibes" was another comment from the Californian legal collective.[4]

At Newcastle, there were and had been team members who were close friends outside. But it wasn't the main feature of the team's relations, and needs qualifying even for those who were friends. Friendship and work could pull in different directions[5] — the clearest example was the aftermath of the dispute with Lin Harwood.

Other aspects of people's personal lives discouraged a team of friends. Some staff lived outside the city. Even those within walking distance had commitments which distanced them.

> *Yvonne Waters*: Well, we've all got families to see to. You can't just put them off.

> *Ernie Dobson*: On the whole people have social networks; other people have other social networks.

At the Unit, there were the usual office celebrations — drinks to toast new babies, and leaving parties for old staff. Users and committee members often came — as they did to the annual general meetings which turned into socials. Day by day, the main chance for workers to get together was lunchtime around the kettle in the reception room. Sandwiches were fetched from the bakers' shop up the street, or with luck there might be pakoras left over from the *Milan* group. The importance of eating together was stressed by Ali, who would have liked staff relations to have been closer.

Ali Rhind: I feel as though I've nagged quite a lot about, you know, we make a coffee room or we get a machine upstairs, or we decide to all go to the pub.

In general, workers weren't intimate or closeknit. Their relations were middle-distance ones; neither aloof nor intense. A balance was found where staff were ready to respect and make space for each others' personal feelings and lives, but without work being taken over by them. If blending the personal and organisational is one thread in the texture of collective working, at FSU it didn't entail everyone becoming friends or each member of the team liking all the others. It was a blend, not integration.

One response is to say that collective working *ought* to be more intimate, even 'familial', and often is. Certainly, some research, particularly from the United States, supports this view.[6] So, it may be surprising when I suggest that FSU came much closer to the present pattern among collective teams in Britain. There are two reasons for this, first relating to the research studies and the second, to people's expectations of 'the personal' in teams.

Much of the writing which describes intense personal ties inside collective teams, was based on groups during the 1970's. Workers then were very often young, unattached, and perhaps in their first really demanding job. Intensity of staff relationships went together with commitment to the work. In this, British and United States experience ran parallel.[7]

But, at least in Britain, this phase came to an end. As workers got older and had more private life outside, the job became less all-consuming. They didn't want to work the very long hours which allowed them to put in a more than full day, and then meet other members of the team in the pub.[8] I'm suggesting, therefore that, unlike similar teams within hierarchies, the picture outsiders have of relationships within collective teams, was painted at *one stage* of their development.

In addition, expectations of close and 'familial' relationships are strengthened by the fact that members do aim for more equal relationships, and respecting colleagues as people. But outsiders often misunderstand what this means. A common misapprehension is that people working co-operatively or collectively have no barriers between them. It's all or nothing — as if there were no middle ground between the distance of fellow employees and the intimacy of friends. But this muddles kin and kith — when collective peers are the latter; *not* relatives, but people nearby who we can call on to co-operate when we need extra help.[9] So opening the door to 'the personal' need not mean the end of all social distance.

The FSU staff were neither a clique nor a club.[10] They mostly enjoyed working together and were close enough to use each other's homes for study days. Workers were also happy leading separate lives outside work, and in this very similar to many other teams who work collectively.

Joining In

Parveen Akhtar became the groupworker at the end of 1983. She was then the youngest team member; a quiet person, diffident about the skills she could offer. It took a year for her to begin feeling confident and relaxed.

> *Parveen*: I was new and just getting used to the Unit. I wasn't familiar with anything at all. A lot of times I think when people are working in a collective group, they take it for granted that you, sort of, just come in and tune in.

Parveen is from the West End's Pakistani community, and previously worked with Newcastle Community Relations Council. Her brief at FSU included work with both white and Asian users, though the main demand came from the Asian communities, especially families referred (and often referring themselves) with individual problems rather than for groupwork.

> *Parveen*: It's a lot of satisfaction, in the sense that I was able to help people; to provide a service which wasn't being provided by other agencies.

She took part in the 'Family Discussion Group' which reviewed casework, and did substantial co-work with other staff. For instance, she and Donna Akhtar (no relation) jointly ran 'the Birthday Group' for Asian women with babies (later, the 'Milan' group).

> *Parveen*: I feel I've had a tremendous amount of support from the other workers in the Unit to run this group.

Elliot Yabantu became community worker early in 1984, and at 51, was the oldest fieldworker. Before coming to Newcastle he'd worked in community education. Elliot is a refugee from South Africa. Speaking slowly and thoughtfully, he makes it plain where he stands, what he believes in.

> *Elliot*: I'm very strong on issues of justice. It's probably the basis on which I work. I would like to see fairness. So that's why I never want, really, my views to prevail.

I asked his opinion of collective working, as someone used to formal hierarchies based on institutional racism in South Africa, and then considerable personal autonomy in his work in Liverpool. Had he been persuaded by Newcastle's system? He laughed.

> *Elliot*: Well, I don't think it's necessarily being persuaded. I mean, the way I've worked myself in a supervisory capacity, I've always involved my staff (if I may use that expression) in decision-making. Looking at the problems and letting people have their say rather than me imposing my views.
>
> I was told at the interview; they said they were working towards forming a collective. I had no objections, though I had never worked in a collective before. I was quite curious to know.

During Elliot's first six months, his family were still in Lancashire — made harder by community work's unsocial hours. At his first assessment (after six months) other workers criticised his lack of participation in Unit management — including sometimes missing team meetings. They also acknowledged their own failure to support him properly, and a more formal support group was set up.

Students

Parveen and Elliot could gradually get used to collective
work, but the same wasn't true for everyone. At any one time,
the Unit usually had three or four social work and community work students on placement. How did they feel about FSU?
I've stressed how even the word 'collective' can conjure up a
range of expectations, some idealistic and some fearful.

> *Pam Carter*: Students have often said to me when
> they've been here about two weeks, 'I was terrified'.
> And what happens is they go back and give (presuma-
> bly) positive information to other students.

The majority of students I spoke to, liked the Unit.[11] "Very
supportive" was a frequent comment. "You're allowed
weaknesses here as well as strengths", said someone else.
Though nobody doubted that FSU would be capable of failing someone on placement. A final year student told me the
Unit suited her. In particular, she felt her views were listened
to. Though she also said:

> If this is a first placement I think it could be a fright-
> ening situation. Because a lot is left to your motivation.
> It would be easy to sit back and just, you know, be lost
> and unhappy.

Another found herself justifying FSU's collective working at
her college.

> I've had to get a lot of stick from other students saying,
> 'What do you mean it's non-hierarchical? It can't be!
> You're just pie-in-the-sky. There must be some'. Or
> they have to dig around for instances where people
> haven't discussed everything with everyone else.

One student drew on her experience as a user.

> As an ex-client, not of this place but social services, I
> would have much preferred to have been treated
> honestly, as I think most of the clients here are.

There were negative opinions. Two men looked and sounded miserable each time I met them. One woman simply said she'd rather have a boss. It seemed that the Unit could be an unhappy and frustrating place if someone expected and preferred a highly structured hierarchical set-up. Pam Carter mentioned another problem.

> *Pam*: Some of the students have said they find it easier in social services to ask someone sitting next to them for advice about something that's happening. They tend to feel inhibited about that in the Unit. Or some of them do — obviously not all students are the same. But the less confident students would find that very difficult. Because the norm is, you're supposed to ask somebody to make time with you to meet.

As we'll see shortly, this question of taking the initiative is very important. It was expressly mentioned by Sarah Banks, a student who was complimentary about FSU, comparing it with her previous placement in a rigid local authority hierarchy.

> *Sarah Banks*: They do actually draw you in and treat you more as an equal than you would be treated in, for instance, social services. Maybe it's a personal thing. I think, if as a student you feel you want to be part of it, then there's openings for you to push yourself in. Maybe you have to make a bit of an effort. I think from the start I just felt the whole atmosphere here was very friendly and equal.

It would be easy to interpret Sarah's experience as the difference between an informal voluntary organisation, and a local authority or state agency with statutory responsibilities. But this misses the point: the team were not just friendly, but set out to be democratic. Sarah enjoyed being treated more equally.

> *Sarah*: To come and find that everything was more open — you didn't have to bow and be deferential to anybody — was very refreshing, and also much more in tune with my own philosophy of how people should work.

Informal and Equal?

Till now, we've had impressions from — at least temporary — insiders. Did colleagues outside see it as informal and equal? Actually, some of them made a point of remarking on it — with disapproval. One health visitor, in particular, would have preferred what she saw as a more professional and distanced approach.

> *Pam Carter*: You get a range of people who say, 'This building isn't informal and welcoming enough', to other people who are very suspicious 'cause it's even as informal as it was. The image is very different depending where people stand.

One image of 'informal' might imply that rules are relaxed in a creative way; another, that the agency's service was downright sloppy. So it was interesting when, in May 1984, FSU's National Council met in Newcastle.

> *Tim Cook*: The nice thing about that visit was people whom I knew had been concerned or opposed to [joint management] at qualitatively different levels were properly, suitably impressed with what they saw.

I attended that National Council meeting and had the same impression. Members seemed to feel that maybe Newcastle wasn't so different. What had some Council members imagined? Tim Cook wasn't sure of their expectations (or in some cases, fantasies). He thought perhaps, a suspicion that no work was being done — with blazing posters and political flags flying instead.

In fact, they found the Unit well organised, with a lot of challenging work going on. If something was due to efficient public relations, Council members didn't only see what they were meant to. The evening before, at a public meeting of the Church of England's Commission on the Inner Cities, one member heard Shirley Forster speaking from the floor about the problems of the West End.

Janet Williams

These were, as I said, snapshots of the Unit. However there was one colleague who visited regularly, and whose knowledge went back six years. Assistant directors in FSU had an ambiguous position. They weren't formally line managers, yet were the main link between the director and individual Units. Janet Williams had been assistant director responsible for Newcastle since 1979, coming at least every other month for management committee meetings. Her specific duties included advising UO's and local committees, and ensuring staff assessments. She took part in hiring as 'the employer', and in any grievance and disciplinary procedures.

I asked Janet how she'd found the changes at Newcastle over the years. She mentioned something which outside agencies can find disquieting about a collective team — when there's no formal hierarchy, you may be unsure who to speak to.

> *Janet*: It has become routine now [1984] for the team to be clear about who their liaison person is. Now, there was a time when the changeover was going on (even while Joan was still there and for some time after she left), when I think they went through this phase of rather, 'This is how we organise ourselves; the rest of the world's gonna have to fit around us. If somebody rings up we'll put them onto the relevant person.' Rather than ensuring that people are aware who the relevant person is.
>
> It's a very discomfiting thing when you have to be, sort of, shoved from pillar to post. Or you're afraid you're gonna be shoved from pillar to post. Lines of communication in that respect are much more clearly worked out now. I know who's the person who should have done something, or should have organised somebody else to do something.

Most callers at an agency are less concerned about who-does-what in general, than how their own request is dealt with. Janet understood why the Unit's internal changes affected links with National Office, but that didn't prevent it being initially disconcerting.

Workers in collective teams elsewhere often attribute this kind of complaint to irritation with, or opposition to self-management as such. They interpret it as an attempt by outsiders to insist on hierarchy.[12] Sometimes this may be true. Janet was quite clear that she could not relate to the Unit simply as an experienced, helpful senior colleague.

> *Janet*: That doesn't recognise the full extent of my role. It ignores or plays down the role I have as assistant director.

But there's another essential aspect. When we call at a hierarchical office we can guess roughly how it runs and what we're expected to do.[13] But faced with a collective team, people may be baffled rather than hostile or critical. Who *is* it polite to talk to? Who is supposed to speak to you? For someone not used to them, collective teams can seem rude and offhand.

> *Janet*: I think what I experienced when I first went there (that was six years ago) was that they were just very off-hand. And took no trouble at all to make me feel comfortable. Well, you'd be brought in; you'd be sat down in the reception room and just left to deal with whoever might be there.
>
> But now, I know, I recognise most of the people. You know, the clients and people from the other projects and that kind of thing. But it took me a couple of years, I should think, before I really found that at all comfortable.

Janet's early visits coincided with the Unit reorganising its building and opening up the reception room as "a place where anyone could meet". This idea, of deliberately mixing callers as a way of breaking down barricades, is found in other accounts of collective teams. The aim is creating neutral space where even senior personnel of social services agencies are treated like anyone else, and where people can meet (and be met by) all kinds of visitors.[14]

Well, barriers aren't removed so simply. As in the discussion of 'teams', it's not enough to assemble individuals in the same space at the same time, hoping they'll mix together naturally. Janet Williams felt uncomfortable, and saw staff as ill-mannered to someone:

> *Janet*: When they do actually occupy a, sort of, recognised position in the same organisation. It's discomfiting to just have the door open and be pointed in the direction of where you should go and left to get on with it.

And plainly she had a point. As would any visitor — recognised position or not. Shouldn't callers be put at their ease? What about users, left with an uncomfortable stranger off the London train?

Reference and Deference

People sometimes apologise for talking about these small niceties of behaviour, in case they seem petty. By focussing on them, I'm not suggesting that everything is a matter of manners, or that for agencies to run smoothly and comfortably, everyone should know their place. But I am saying that it's often in the *etiquette* of collective working that outsiders first see and feel its change to equality of status. For they rarely 'see' changing philosophies or even altered structures. Maybe the annual report states 'How We Are Organised' or 'What We Believe'. But most callers 'read' an agency through their small interpersonal dealings with it. However, if people are responding to surface manners, how does that help us understand collective working relations more generally?

Well, think back over the comments made about Newcastle. Within the apparently conflicting impressions people formed, there turns out to be a pattern. Moreover, its a pattern found in other collective teams. Sarah Banks caught its essence when she remarked that, in an egalitarian team, "you don't have to bow and be deferential".

Let me spell this out. In organisational life everywhere, rules of behaviour reflect and interact with the values and structures of an agency. Within a hierarchy, conventions of polite behaviour are unlikely to be neutral; either openly or implicitly, they assume hierarchical authority. So we find, not simply rules for smooth running, but sets of interpersonal rituals which mark and also confirm people's unequal status.[15] By contrast, groups setting out to achieve equality of status, move away from this etiquette of deference. We then see different and changing conventions based on *reference*.

> *Janet Williams*: It's easy and it's straightforward and it's sorted out. I know who the person who deals with the committee is. It's partly them having got themselves sorted out. And I think maybe it's partly their having acknowledged other people's need for clarity about these things. I've also got accustomed to not dealing with the one person about everything, or most things.

Janet illustrates how new terms or rules of reference are required for the overall who-does-what, as well as in daily contacts. They will apply both to the 'courtesies' offered outsiders and to workers' relations with each other. The team needs to set these new conventions, and then make them clear (better still, transparent) to people outside. In addition, outsiders have to expect and get used to the new customs.

Egalitarian Manners

Though there are snags. Eventually, perhaps "it's easy and it's straightforward". But the new rules don't come immediately, nor will they be fully worked out. Neither will the process happen by itself. Some hard work is involved, especially when it comes to links with other agencies. 'Sorting' takes goodwill, inside and outside teams, which is sometimes missing.

One problem, I've suggested, is many people's discomfort and unfamiliarity with egalitarian manners. There are new things to learn and, for a time, you don't know 'where you stand'. But resistance to reference is also a matter of power relations. Ignoring or avoiding the conventions and courtesies of existing power relations is often a way of protesting against them. So, although members of collective teams often see themselves as *responding* to attempts from outside to impose deference, in practice the process works both ways. Some outsiders are being asked to forgo the privileges of power and status.

This is part of a long tradition, whereby egalitarian groups set out to contest conventions which reflect social distance and serve to keep people in their places. After all, 'courtesy' originally meant the manners of the court. Let's take some examples where people have introduced new terms of reference.

For many years, Quakers avoided titles implying rank (Sir, Mr), instead referring to each other as 'Thee' and 'Thou'. Though this eventually marked the equality of members, it began as a "gesture of social protest", and was seen as a threat. "Thee and thine will (if they can) expel Mine and Thine, dissolving all property into confusion".[16]

Similar new conventions have been established quite recently, first as a protest and then an expression of change in social relations. For instance, in France and Germany, younger people commonly use the familiar 'you' form.[17] In English, adopting the feminist 'Ms.' and avoiding gender-specific nouns (e.g. 'chairman') is part of a systematic strategy for altering language practice. Language becomes both a symbol and a tool in a power struggle.[18]

I am not suggesting that we transform power relations simply by altering manners. Nor that first-names make you a peer. A firm can train reception staff in friendly 'customer relations', without altering its hierarchy. Similarly, a social services office can foster a warm, welcoming image by getting new carpets, some potted plants, and a polite receptionist to greet callers. This may even suggest that some forms of interpersonal behaviour are more like rituals and ceremonials — 'Your obedient servant', or 'Have a nice day'.

But while power relations don't *determine* other sorts of social relations, there is an interaction "between the distribution of substantive rights and power in a society and the distribution of conversational courtesies".[19] We only realise how 'substantive' are some apparently 'ceremonial' rituals when someone forgets or ignores them — like a member of a collective team.

In other words, we recognise the interaction most vividly when there is a 'bad fit' between manners on the one hand, and status and power on the other. The polite smile slips. Understanding this helps us explore the process I referred to before — whereby there is a fit between social relations within a team, and relations with users. Without such a fit, there is strain and possibly conflict; the different patterns will work against each other. Hierarchical power, for instance, and a hierarchical way of organising within a work group will seep through into encounters with users.

Three Stages

Earlier, I mentioned a pattern in the changes at Newcastle. But it wasn't simply a shift from deference to reference. The sequence implied by the Quakers and other examples, suggests three, rather than two stages. At first, existing rules of deference are the norm. The second stage is characterised by *opposition* to these rules. It's followed by a third stage marked by the development of a new set of principles and practice which stands on its own.

We frequently find a corresponding sequence in the development of collective teams. Hierarchy is succeeded by anti-hierarchy, then moving to fully collective working with agreed rules of reference. In the second, *oppositional* stage it's likely that members of a collective team may be rude and offhand. They'll sometimes make a point of not applying conventional manners which enable those with higher status and more power to feel at ease — naturally, at the expense of the less powerful, who feel inhibited and uncomfortable. The more lateral conventions of the third stage are still developing.[20]

In practice, the sequence will rarely be as tidy as this. But if we return to Janet Williams' description, the three stages aren't hard to find. Early on, Janet's main lines of communication were through Joan Smith. She and Joan had known each other when they were both Unit Organisers. When coming to Newcastle, Janet stayed in Joan's home.

> *Janet*: I liked her; I still do. I still keep in touch with her.

In the second stage it seemed, from Janet's point of view, as if there weren't rules. Here were an *unruly* team who:

> *Janet*: Went through this phase... the rest of the world's gonna have to fit around us.

Eventually, there were new procedures, and a new etiquette of who to refer to and how to set about it. The new procedures

were increasingly explicit, so people outside might weigh them
up and see advantages.

> *Janet*: They hand me around, and that works fine. I'm
> perfectly happy and comfortable with that. Either
> somebody rings, or I ring and say I'll be needing a bed.
> I know them all informally in the sort of way that I
> knew Joan. Partly because they've been around that
> much longer. As time's gone by I know that much more
> about their work; their interests; the whole person.

Being Assertive

The three stage pattern was a recurring one at Newcastle, and
in the development of other collective teams. We'll recognise
it from chapter three, where I talked about a team moving beyond anti-hierarchy. What, elsewhere in FSU, was seen as opposition to a leader — and perhaps an *attack* on the existing
structures — was regarded in Newcastle as commonsense support for the new, third stage, status quo.

Notice, I'm not saying everybody will be "perfectly happy
and comfortable" with the new rules and courtesies. But the
nature of their particular discomfort will tell us a lot about reference. Consider Pam Carter's comment about students finding it hard to ask someone for advice. "The norm is you're supposed to ask somebody to make time with you". In other
words, you *refer* to other staff rather than defer to supervisors
of higher status. Instead of respecting status differences and
waiting till you're told, you have "to push yourself in" (as Sarah Banks said). But if 'good manners' imply ranking, then
Newcastle's norm would be bad manners elsewhere. For some
students, this posed a problem.

> *Pam Carter*: They would never feel assertive enough to
> — [laughing] — actually say to somebody like Shirley,
> 'Would you mind arranging a meeting with me'.

In short, even at the third stage, difficulties are common when
outsiders come into contact with collective teams, and don't
understand the new rules of reference. Sometimes, bringing
hazy or unrealistic expectations, they mistake them for the absence of rules altogether (and therefore permission to behave

as they choose). Or they may see them as an attack on their own taken for granted rules of deference.

The framework I've suggested indicates how such problems might be eased. Outsiders who appreciate the changes taking place, can adapt their behaviour, in particular avoiding the mistake that without hierarchy there are no rules. They can help a team working collectively to do the same. As Janet Williams' experience showed, an approach to the person 'in charge' can be reframed as a request for someone with clearly designated responsibility. Collective teams, meanwhile, can find out how they are seen from outside. And they can ask themselves whether they are really disputing deference, or failing to agree and explicitly set out their points of reference.

Collective Working Relations

Clearly, the discussion so far is incomplete. Collective working relations may not require a team of friends, but it's more than egalitarian manners and arranging for who-does-what to be apparent to outsiders. So, what sort of relationships are people aiming at when they work collectively and co-operatively as peers, rather than as individuals, or hierarchically? What's different about co-workers *referring* to each other?[21] To go back to an earlier question, what should a newcomer expect from such a team as it tries to balance and blend its tasks, with respect for colleagues as people?

I'll end with a brief summary of what such work relations might look like; the direction that an individual joining a collective team could expect things to take. It draws on many of the themes mentioned before, as well as looking forward to later chapters.

Here, I'm not presenting FSU as a team which had 'arrived' at fully developed collective working. These are aims, not a list of achievements. No doubt, some readers will say this is how many agencies aim to work with *users*. In which case, how often are the same criteria applied to relations among staff? For the Newcastle team it was essential that the two went together.

★

Becoming peers in a collective team means that workers take responsibility for their own actions and their own power, rather than looking for an 'other' to blame or be 'in charge'. People are expected to speak for themselves rather than for others. It needs workers to develop assertiveness, standing their ground. You make proposals which involve demands on colleagues and on the group as a whole — and do this plainly rather than through 'games' or other ways that are hidden. Other staff have to be ready to listen to new ideas and proposals, or criticisms of the old ways of doing things. People should be prepared to give clear responses; to negotiate, or maybe say a clear 'No'.

Clarity and honesty extends to honesty about what people can and can't do — their abilities and competence. Offering to share skills first needs acknowledging the skills and strengths people have, and others may not. Workers' skills, experience and personal qualities need building on. The other side to this is giving and inviting clear criticism, and accepting that colleagues can and should review the team's work as a whole. A team is a group of co-learners as well as co-workers.

Such a pattern of relationships implies a trust and confidence that won't come at once. Conflicts within a team will make some staff doubt if it can be built at all. I've stressed the positive aspects, and many people will see the negatives first. Moving out into the open, making yourself and your work more vulnerable to colleagues, is potentially risky. People play games because they expect a pay-off. Moaning about things in a corner seems a lot safer than complaining directly and trying to get change.

It's important to say too, that a workplace isn't a therapy group, meeting for a limited period in a self-contained setting. Feelings of stress, frustration and anger come from the work as well as from each other. There are issues of priorities, competence, and quality of service to users, that override how people might like to treat colleagues.

From notes given to students on placement.

Views about social work: That we should influence policy as well as do individual work.

That 'professionalism' equals openness and honesty.

Handing over power to consumers as much as possible —enabling people to 'speak for themselves'. Using language which is accessible to as many people as possible, avoid jargon.

PART II

WORKING
TOGETHER

Part II of the book groups together several topics under the
theme of *work done*. Though I said that working collectively is
much more than simple co-ordination,[1] that doesn't mean
losing sight of day to day tasks. So chapter six briefly sketches
Newcastle FSU's work during my contact with them. I'll then
return to the issue of the secretaries — paradoxically a
hierarchical bit of a collective team.

Chapter seven explores how and why the Unit's work
changed. As we've seen, effective teamwork has been advocated as a means of achieving flexible, responsive services to
meet changing needs. But then, whose needs are met, and
whose views influence and shape the development of services? Does the choice belong to the agency and its staff, or to
users and potential users? I'll ask these questions about the
most marked shift in FSU's pattern of work during 1983-85,
towards Asian people.

Chapter eight takes a broad look at grant-aid, asking how
far a 'voluntary' agency can or should choose its own pattern
of work, if its largest paying customer wants something else.

Discussing each of these topics, I'll be proposing a central idea — that the aim of a collective team should not be autonomy, but an *interactive dialogue*. There should be give and
take; push and pull; debate and negotiation among workers
users and funders, and with colleagues in other agencies. The
last two chapters in Part II compare this approach with two
other models of collaborative teamwork. Chapter nine looks
again at ideas for 'integrated' and 'unitary' working in social
services. Chapter ten draws from writing and research about
collectives as a way of organising a formally egalitarian
workplace.

Six

The Pattern of Work

The drawing *Who Works Here* (in chapter one) was sketched by Ali Rhind in 1983. It went in the annual report and on the reception room wall, as a picture of staff and their work. Later it was redrawn as a jigsaw — *How FSU Fits Together* — updated with new 'pieces'.

By 1985, new staff included Anne Davies, social worker, and Angela Sewell, student unit organiser replacing Pam Carter. Jean Mowberry worked part-time on the accounts. With the end of funding for the Women's Workshops, Ali Rhind had left, as had Sally Walker and Shirley Devlin. Many of the workshops moved to West End Leisure and Learning (W.E.L.L). Those remaining became part of the workload of other staff, with help from sessional workers and students.[2]

Earlier I mentioned Brenda White, part-time worker at the Pool Girls' Club. Let me explain that, while Brenda had a small office at FSU, the Club was held in the Elswick swimming pool building. Brenda wasn't on the Unit's staff, as the Club was independent and separately funded. However, Pool Girls had originally been set up by FSU, and there were still strong links. Students helped run it, and Shirley Forster was on its management committee, supervising Brenda.

Despite a good deal of this mingling, most of the Unit's daily work with users was specialised. Among the fulltime fieldwork staff there were the divisions of casework, community work, and groupwork.

The social workers and students had caseloads — families and individuals who would say that so-and-so was 'their' social worker. The box (inset) is from a 1983 leaflet. As we saw, the pattern had shifted over the years, especially away from their early brief to work with, "what used to be called multi-problem families" as Peter Stone put it. This was partly Unit policy — its philosophy of trying to work with users in a

SOCIAL WORK

There are two social workers at the Unit. They offer help and support to families with problems. These may be due to bad housing, not having much money, debts, ill health, problems at school etc., which may have led to a lot of bad feeling in the family. We can't get rid of all these things, but we may be able to help a family sort out at least some of them.

How can we help? Every family is different and so are their problems but here are some of the ways we might help.

Regular meetings with all the family: a Unit worker can sit down with the whole family to help them to sort things out together and try to see things from each other's point of view.

Meetings with parents: Parents often carry the strains, worries and problems of a growing family and often find they don't have the time to sit and talk to each other about themselves and their worries. We can help you to sort things out together and to take a look at how you can help your family get on better.

What you should do if you think social workers could help you

Call in or ring to make an appointment. Then we can decide together whether the help we can give you is what you want and whether you want to commit yourself to seeing us again.

Help for just one person: We are willing to offer help if you have a need to talk to someone alone.

Finding the right person to help: e.g., working out if a solicitor or doctor would be the best person and finding one you could talk to easily, working out what to say to write to D.H.S.S., or Housing, etc.

PLEASE NOTE: Many people think that social workers only take children into care. We do this too, very, very, occasionally - but we believe that the best people to help children are nearly always their parents and so we make sure parents get as much help as possible to look after their children the way they want to.

Your affairs are kept private

We won't talk to anyone outside the Unit about your affairs without your say so, unless there is an emergency or something very serious has happened.

As soon as the problem is sorted out to your satisfaction we will stop meeting. (If we felt something very serious was happening and that you should continue to see a social worker, we would tell you what this was.)

different way. But it reflected changes outside too. For instance, in Elswick there were then fewer children being referred to Social Services.

Even so, during my contact, the social workers were doing family work of considerable seriousness and complexity. At different times, they were involved with children in Care, and with non-accidental injury; and marital problems. To their central skills they'd added others, such as Lilian White's interest in play therapy. Staff gave advice, and dealt with welfare rights.

The Unit discussed community work in 1984, describing their approach as: "Finding out what issues most concern people in the area, and helping local people to achieve their needs and interests through working together in groups". (Inset are two examples from a leaflet for users) They added that it could well involve city-wide or even national level work. The interests of racial minorities was mentioned as a special focus.

In previous years Chris Johnson and Ernie Dobson had been the community workers. Chris was involved in helping local women set up a cleaning co-op, and forming several housing co-ops. They'd helped local parents organising against the closure of a school. During 1984, when Elliot Yabantu took Chris' place, work included residents' and tenants' groups, West End Leisure and Learning, the Community Festival, a local studies group, and Elswick Park and Pool Committee. Most of groups they worked with had themselves approached the Unit for help.

Elswick Park and Pool

We've been working with local people who came together last year to form a Management Committee for the Park and Pool. They help decide what goes on in the Park and work hard for particular events such as the Festival day and the playscheme. They can also raise with the Manager any problems or complaints from people who use the Park and Pool.

Elswick and Benwell Festival

We worked with people from all over West City, Elswick and Benwell to make 1982 a memorable year for local festival. After months of hard work and with money from the Priority Area Teams and the City's Festival Committee, July's events included films, discos, a play, garden fete, pie and pea supper, and a visit to the Sikh temple. The festival ended with a very enjoyable day in Elswick Park.

Groupwork had included the Women's Workshops, and Parveen Akhtar continued working with some of these after funding ceased. The 'Birthday Group', for example, began with a focus on ante- and post-natal care, and informal health education. It grew naturally into *The Milan* [Forum] *Group* for Asian women. Parveen's workload became wider, for very soon after she came to the Unit, Asian families were increasingly referred, or referred themselves directly to her. So the distinction between casework and groupwork was blurred.

One other work area was what they called Social Policy. An example was when Newcastle City Council invited community and grant-aided groups to comment on its 'Green Paper' proposals for policies towards ethnic minorities, and Parveen and Elliot wrote a response. Other Unit staff prepared comments on a Green Paper on women.

The Secretaries

By 1985 the three secretaries were still sharing their piece of 'jigsaw', but outside joint management. Yvonne Waters was fulltime; Blanche Callan and Evelyn Rae both part-time. Before talking about their decision to opt out, let me outline their work. Typing and reception was a major part of their day. They worked on the Unit accounts; looked after the telephones and filing; kept tabs on staff; and occasionally helped users to operate the duplicator and photocopier. Blanche designed leaflets and reports.

The two adjoining rooms for reception and admin, were the building's 'centre'. While the secretaries had less contact with users than fieldwork staff, they were still a vital part of the 'skin' of the Unit — something made plain by George Cross, local activist and frequent user of FSU.

> *George Cross*: They're always helpful if you want any advice or want to know where people are. You've got a good system for that.

It was — literally — a key position. They opened the front door, locked and unlocked rooms for meetings, and looked after keys for the Unit van (on constant loan to community groups). For phone callers and visitors they *were* the reception. And, like admin staff in many offices, they functioned as informal information holders. Everyone approached them — users as well as staff — for advice, help, or two minutes chat. Students quickly found the secretaries were the shortest route into the daily business of the place.

> *Marie Hannah* (student): Their knowledge of the building, whereabouts of certain files, etc, was of great help to me, and I would have been lost without it.

> *Evelyn Rae*: We show them around, and keep their office procedure going as best as possible.

> *Yvonne Waters*: And of course, you see, the three of us have been here quite a lot of years. So that a lot of the families we can go back and tell them — give them the gen right back on the families.

Shirley Forster thought this work was not properly acknowledged.

> *Shirley*: They also enjoy — one of their not very recognised roles is that they play a tremendous amount in supporting students and talking to students. We were having a giggle about what they do; like giving the students verbal profiles of the staff. 'Don't take any notice of Shirley, she's always like that'.

Blanche Callan caught another aspect of this relationship with students.

> *Blanche*: We aren't a competition for them. They can be ordinary with us. Whereas they feel as if they have to perform out there.

"Out there" meant with fieldwork staff, who would be involved in formal assessment of the student's placement. So students could gravitate to the secretaries, for information and to get their bearings, without feeling they were being judged. Perhaps the secretaries' room was safe territory because they too were not peers within the Unit?

Opting Out of Joint Management

Why weren't the secretaries part of self-management? It was a
question often asked.

> *Elliot Yabantu*: The other day I was at West End
> Resource Centre and somebody said to me, 'Well,
> how's FSU? How are you getting on?' I said, 'Alright,
> I'm quite happy; it's a relaxed atmosphere'.
>   She said, 'Well, you're supposed to be working as
> a collective. But from what we hear, the secretaries are
> cut off from the rest of the staff'.

Originally the secretaries decided to stay out of joint management for six months but, four years later, hadn't changed their
minds. Despite this, their feelings about working at the Unit
confirmed changes in personal relations described by other
staff. This was especially clear when they thought back over
several years.

> *Evelyn Rae*: Certainly the workers are easier to get
> along with now [1984] than they were. Well, they're
> just friendlier. They tell you more things, you know.
> There was a time when we didn't know anything
> personal about them at all. I mean, they would never
> ever discuss their personal lives. We didn't discuss ours
> with them either.
>   They would be sympathetic if they thought I was
> having trouble. I'm sure they would, the staff now, the
> present staff would. But I think they're more likely to
> notice than they would've years ago. They just took no
> notice of you at all.

All three assured me they trusted other staff to consider their
interests.

> *Blanche Callan*: Because we're not part of the staff
> management, doesn't mean to say that the rest of the
> staff aren't going to be considering us as well, when
> they're talking about the future of the Unit.

At one point, they even poked gentle fun at the whole notion of the collective team, by circulating a map of the filing system and signing it, "Y.E.B. Secretarial Democratic Joint Staff Management Collective". They said, very firmly, that they did not want the extra responsibilities connected with managing the Unit. Neither did they welcome going to meetings — recalling only too well the 'electrifying' meetings about Lin's work. Sally Walker thought this was an important factor. She added:

> *Sally Walker*: I think what's happened with the
> secretaries is that they've opted out. And there's been
> very clear statements they don't want to go to
> meetings; they don't want to identify with the
> collective. They just want to get on with their job.

From Unit records, recollections of former staff, and the secretaries themselves, it seems that for some years the three women hadn't been included in the thinking and planning about changes in Unit philosophy. Largely, they had been expected to 'get on with their job'. So they weren't carried along with the rest of the staff group, for example, in ideas about empowering users and trying to work with them in different ways.

In 1983, when the Unit asked to self-manage, Sally Walker and Shirley Devlin (both part-time in the Women's Workshops) wrote a 'Response to Democratic Management in FSU', criticising the proposal. They described themselves as "on the periphery of the staff group", making "observations from outside rather than from direct involvement in the day to day running of the Unit". The secretaries signed this criticism, though they were less 'outside' than Sally and Shirley. The Women's Workshops were expected to run as a semi-independent project, in a way that administration staff could hardly function in a small team. It makes more sense to see the secretaries as *under* the staff group, particularly as they chose to be managed by it.

Below The Staff

The secretaries' position, then, resembled what we might expect in a hierarchical office — or at least one with a benign boss. It's a position often criticised for keeping women in a subordinate role; where 'professional' staff take decisions, and support staff carry the routine 'maintenance' work. So criticism from outside was understandable. Some insiders felt much the same. On the Unit management committee, for example, Ian Bynoe thought that, without the secretaries as a full part of the staff group, "it wasn't desperately collective really". Not only was there a national hierarchy and a local management committee, but:

> *Ian*: Then, believe it or not, below the staff (if one could say that), or in a different department from the staff management team and not involved in staff management, there's another group, a support staff group.

Elliot Yabantu agreed.

> *Elliot*: I will be much happier with the secretarial staff being actually involved in the decision-making process, rather than expect us to take decisions and give instructions to them.

During 1983 the Unit discussed using the extra money from the Unit Organiser's salary, to top up the secretaries pay. But when they opted out of joint management this came off the agenda, except as something for longterm change[3].

Subsequently, the formal proposal for joint management included a "supervision/support group" for the secretaries, with "accountability to the Unit team through a liaison person". This, broadly, was the framework adopted throughout the team and not surprisingly, reflected what I've called 'rules of reference'. The idea was for specific people to make themselves available to the secretaries on a regular basis. Again, not surprisingly, it worked badly. The secretaries were used to and expected rules of deference. Meetings didn't always happen, and the liaison staff found themselves stuck uncomfortably between the two groups — sometimes as carriers of complaints in both directions. Shirley Forster later took on the job and found conflicting expectations of what the liaison meetings were for.

Shirley: They hate having (or say they hate having) meetings. So when I first took that job on I agreed with them that we'd only meet as and when there was anything to discuss. I realised that as soon as I called a meeting they'd all panic because they'd think they were in trouble.[4]

To make the link work, the staff group had to shift from a peer relationship to one of line management.

Shirley Forster: I've set up with them a series of meetings that are going to be regular, to discuss stuff from the Unit meeting. But it'll also be like a forum for us to — what am I trying to do? — get them to have a much clearer relationship with us. Also much more clear discussion between the groups about: What work do they want to take on? What do they need from the management team to be able to do that work? Are the demands we're making unfair?

It also meant that I actually worked up the nerve to say the very hard things like, 'We are going to manage you. And that means that at the end of the day we may end up telling you to do something even if you don't like it'.

With this tougher line went Shirley's determination to get recognition for the wider work the secretaries did. She knew how easily admin becomes invisible when it's done well and smoothly; only getting other staff's attention when things start going wrong. Shirley felt that some of their work was undervalued — like helping users to type or duplicate when community groups came to use the Unit's equipment. I mentioned the stress Shirley gave to their relationship with students. That kind of informal support is easily overlooked, or even dismissed as gossip — the traditional description for the talk of less important people.[5]

Shirley: They do it in a very supportive interested way with students. But we just — it's just like gossiping in the office. Nobody recognises it's a valuable job. I'd like to see a way of raising the status of all that. And they do lots and lots of informal support to the staff. If you go out and you have a horrible visit and want somebody to moan to, you actually moan to them. It quite often feels that they're not working and you're not working when you're doing it. But it ought to be; that's valuable.

Holding Back

The team didn't stop hoping the secretaries would eventually join in, though they speculated that this might need a change of staff first. Yvonne, Evelyn and Blanche hadn't taken jobs in a democratic team, and their expectations in previous workplaces and from most of their years with FSU had been of hierarchy.

Wanting them in wasn't just a matter of feeling uncomfortable, nor even of principle. (Though both played a part.) In the last chapter, I outlined the kind of working relations the team were aiming for as part of an open dialogue within a peer group. It's plain that if one person, or a small group, aren't fully involved then there's a waste. What people contribute to the team, and the development of their own potential is, at least partly blocked. So what the team gives to users is that much less and that much poorer.

Opting out meant holding back. The secretaries tended to present a joint view even when there were strong undercurrents of disagreement among them.

Evelyn Rae: The three of us are usually in agreement when we say something. [Laughing] We never depart from each other.

Pam Carter felt that, despite dissatisfaction with the secretaries' position among both staff and committee members, it had become:

Pam: More of a taken-for-granted flaw in the system, rather than something there's any genuine debate about. Reading your account now [January 1987] really makes me realise just how much the staff group were asking the secretaries to join in on the staff's terms rather than on their own terms.

Seven

Choosing Work

Lilian White: Local people coming and saying, 'We perceive, or we've got this need for a local residents' association, or for casework'.

When it comes to choosing work, what difference does it make to have a team run collectively? I mentioned the expectation — or at least hope — that it would develop new community based work; and by having a more open relationship to users and potential users, meet their needs more flexibly.

In recent years, social services agencies have been much criticised for their choice of which needs to meet. More exactly, it's said that often, they *don't* choose, but are 'demand led', reacting almost passively to requests by users.[1] Critics have suggested a conflict between *responding* and, at the same time, trying to *innovate*. A 'reactive' approach is compared unfavourably with the alternative of investigating need and initiating new ventures. In the ugly and unnecessary jargon, this is labelled 'proactive'.

The use of jargon is important. It lends a ring of technical rigour to what is really a question of values. For one person's dynamic proactivity may well be someone's else's insensitive intrusion. On top of that, the pairing somehow converts responsiveness — hardly a bad thing — into an apparent negative. When people use such terms, it sheds light on the pattern of their thinking. So what are they really saying about the relationship between service providers and users?

I skirted this issue before. One archetype of the proactive social services worker is, of course, the entrepreneurial manager. Given the kind of thinking about teams discussed in chapter four, the pattern of a team's work is often attributed to the personality and 'leadership style' of a particular manager. I suggested that some of this thinking could be found within FSU. Both Tim Cook and Janet Williams saw creativity and sparkle growing out of people's personal qualities and enthusiasms.

> *Janet*: Units tend to come and go in their fortunes. If one's been around for a while it's possible to see that a Unit will have a phase (often not more than three or four years) when there's a particularly potent staff group producing new ideas; lots of energy; maybe a particular ability to get money; or two or three people who are very good at writing or running workshops, or whatever; people who have abilities and interests above and beyond the usual run. And then a significant person leaves.
>
> Or a number of people are collected around a Unit Organiser. That happens sometimes. There's somebody who collects a number of like-minded people around themselves, and then they leave and the Unit's fortunes change again. They don't necessarily decline; they may just be adopting a rather different profile for a time.

From this viewpoint, change comes mainly from individuals. And, if all Units are in this ebb and flow, then working collectively can be seen as just one more new initiative among many others.

> *Tim Cook*: Indeed, one or two people — old hands in FSU who've now left and heard about Newcastle not wanting to have a UO — said, 'Ah, well, it would be Newcastle.'

However, neither Tim nor Janet proposed that a Unit's choice of work could be divorced from the needs of the area it served. But the argument for proactive teamwork is that it can go beyond services that only respond to requests. Members have the potential to assess social need, and then shape services that go out and meet it. As the Barclay Committee wrote:[2]

> A well organised team, whose members represent a wide range of generalist and specialist skills and knowledge, is far better placed than any individual social worker could be to assess the levels of social need, reach decisions on priorities, and provide any appropriate service — whether to one single client or to a client group.

In this description we'll recognise strong echoes of the two models of teamwork at either end of the spectrum described by Phyllida Parsloe.[3] At one end, the individualist team is seen as reacting to requests from clients and other agencies. In contrast, a collectivist team is imagined pooling its knowledge and skills, and proactively moving out into the community.

It's important to understand that, underlying this picture, is an implicit definition of 'need', as something discoverable, measurable and, for an agency, 'out there' beyond the office door. So, asking whether to be reactive or proactive, presents agencies and individual workers with an either-or choice. You either wait for need to come to you, or go out and meet it; keep your heads down and respond to users as they appear, or harness up your teams and sally forth!

Arriving at Priorities

Let's explore these issues at Newcastle. If we ask who decided work commitments and priorities at the Unit, the answer wouldn't be simple. Take community work, one of the earliest areas to develop away from the original brief, with far-reaching consequences for the rest of their work. In one sense it was a Unit initiative, shaped by ideas and events from outside Elswick. But it also grew out of the casework the Unit was invited to do; a response to the families worked with.

> *Evelyn Rae*: There was one social worker at Elswick Street flats — just along the way. And she worked solely in there; that's the only place she worked. It was more like community work really.

That was in 1972 and '73. Ten years on, community work was far from obviously anchored in this way. When Chris Johnson left in 1983 there were some doubts expressed about the priorities and choices in her work.

> *Alan Jackson*: Perhaps it was unfortunate that Chris Johnson, who'd been in the Unit for a great many years, had developed other links outside the Unit. And it's not a criticism of Chris at all. She was a strong positive member of the group. And has been instrumental in establishing this whole new way of working which I support. But at the same time, I know that she

was involved in other groups that weren't particularly related to Family Service Unit or the area that we cover.

By far the most forthright critic of Chris Johnson's choices was Chris herself.

> *Chris Johnson*: I think there's a question of how priorities are arrived at, even within the staff group. Certainly my feelings from five years working at FSU was that I could do more or less what I wanted. Now, that might be because what I wanted fitted in quite nicely with everybody's priorities. But there was never much challenging of the work.

It needs saying that, although Chris spent time outside the Unit's catchment area, the issues were hardly marginal to local people. They included housing, health, and women's employment.[4]

> *Chris*: Alright, I had worked here a long time. There was the trust that I would get things done; that I was committed; that I did put a lot of work in. Obviously the amount of groups and the amount of results did show that there was somebody fairly competent working fairly hard.

Chris felt the most useful criticism of her work had come from colleagues outside the Unit. And she wanted to see this repeated inside the team.

> *Chris*: Challenging of the choice or challenging of the way in which it was done. Perhaps one example of one time it did happen, which was really good, was in a management committee meeting. We were having a review of work, and were talking about unemployment.
>
> I was talking about the work I was doing with women. Monica [Elliot] who works for the Tenants' Federation and is also a local, was the first person to actually challenge me and say, 'What is this work about? What sort of women are you working with? What kind of jobs are you actually producing? What are they being paid?' These kinds of discussions I

think are really important. It's important that people are critical.

When Elliot Yabantu succeeded Chris, the management committee pushed him to take up more local issues. He rapidly got involved in helping tenants' groups which had approached the Unit. Work with ethnic minority communities and with West End Leisure and Learning fitted in with his own interests, as well as developments in the area. Supposing they had not? "What", I asked Elliot, "if your colleagues as a group wanted you to set priorities and take up work that differs from how you saw the need?"

> *Elliot*: We do, as staff management group, take decisions, policy decisions. If then that kind of instruction — if you like — were based on the policy decision, I would have to observe that, to abide by it. But it would have to be well rationalised. Because we have got to relate what I'm doing as a community worker to what in fact the people in the area want.

Ernie Dobson was less sure that community work priorities could be reviewed in quite this way.

> *Ernie*: I'm not sure to what extent the work is up for grabs, really. Given the variety of methods we use. I think general policy and management of the Unit is. I'm not sure that work ever has been or will be; whether we as a group of social workers, group worker, and community workers, can discuss together where a lot of the priorities are.

But Ernie was not claiming the right to initiate work as he saw fit. Instead, both he and Elliot were looking for forums where their work could be discussed and its direction shaped. Early in 1985 the Unit set up a community work meeting, inviting people from local groups — tenants' associations, W.E.L.L., the Elswick Festival Committee, as well as members of the FSU management committee. Elliot and Ernie described their current work and future plans, and this was 'put up for grabs' by the meeting.

By summer 1985, this group hadn't developed successfully into real criticism and direction to the Unit's community
work. But people who came were beginning to talk widely
about issues and problems in the area.

An Interactive Process

Elliot criticised a draft of this section, saying I'd made the
process seem too neat — as if it was just a matter of sitting
down and democratically asking users what they wanted.

> *Elliot*: My involvement for example on Bentinck Es-
> tate. Would people say, 'We invited this man here'? Or
> have they accepted me because I'm there?
> What I'm saying, in the final analysis there is a
> sense in which we can still say, to an extent, we do
> take decisions on what we perceive to be the need in
> the area. Having picked up information, as Ernie said.
> There isn't a neat kind of final point that is arrived at
> between the people and the workers.

So let me spell out my point. It was not tidy; and they weren't
claiming some sort of linear step by step procedure: investigation — discussion — action. To me, it seemed that they were
trying to develop an *interactive* process. Consistently, the same
question would come up in each area of the Unit's work: how
could they achieve an exchange of views and perspectives
about their work, with users, local people, and staff in other
agencies? The purpose of such a dialogue wasn't to abstract or
extract a neat picture of the 'needs' locally and then construct
services. Instead, needs were thought of as changing and flu-
id; shaped by as well as shaping agency policies.[5]
Let me also stress that this was a developing, not a fully
and consistently worked out process. In the past, the Unit had
made ambivalent use of some of the accepted social services
approaches to assessing need. For instance, a standard tool is
the 'Needs Survey'.[6] The Unit twice made such surveys, once
in 1976 and later in 1981. The survey reports talked of finding
information which would help them match services to needs.
The 1976 survey helped set their reduced catchment area.
It gathered statistical data, but also included the views of other agencies and some users. The 1981 survey was carried out

by Unit Students, using a questionnaire. Both surveys were on a small scale, and Pam Carter, who wrote up the second, admitted that its results fell far short of the aims. She mentioned the constraint that, as FSU, they were then expected "to work with the families with the most severe social problems". Pam also made the point that while local people knew their needs, they weren't usually aware of what options might be available to meet them.

Neither survey was participatory; they didn't involve local people in initiating questions or gathering and interpreting information.[7] On the other hand, users and practitioners taking part had an open-ended invitation to say what they thought the problems and needs of the area were. And giving people such an opportunity is potentially different from the traditional survey approach, since it opens up the chance of changing an agency's agenda.[8]

I don't mean there's some simple formula whereby people are asked what services they need, and this is straightforwardly turned into practice. Nor were the two Newcastle surveys models of instant response. But being prepared to listen, even suggesting that a dialogue ought to take place, is to seek a different kind of relationship between an agency and its users and colleagues. In other words, an interactive process isn't just interaction between professional staff and the data they collect. As the Unit stated in the 1981 survey report:

> If problems, issues and areas of work are identified, no matter how accurately, by statutory or voluntary agencies, the extent to which they can work with the community is limited if that perception is not shared by the local people.

At other times, when the Unit wrote reports, they drew from both government statistics and City publications. Some people felt that more of this kind of knowledge could be used. For instance, Alan Jackson queried how far Unit staff obtained and deployed available statistics.

> *Alan Jackson*: There's all sorts of things could be obtained from the Housing Department that'd be relevant. Because there's been quite a distinct change of housing policy. Partly due to FSU's work, but for other reasons as well. There are issues that are

happening in the area that perhaps we're not picking up. Like, for example, tonight I heard about a survey for 'Keep Newcastle Warm'.

Alan wanted the Unit's links with other agencies to help build, "an overview of what's going on, for example, in the West End of the city; and how we can translate that into some kind of action". He questioned whether existing liaison was sufficient. Unit workers worried about this too. Had they failed to keep some of their bridges in repair? Pam Carter observed that, apart from a strong link with the liaison senior Mike Wardle,[9] there were few informal contacts between FSU and the nearby Crudas Park social services team.

> *Pam*: I think both their team (social services) and the Unit are actually quite insular at times. The Unit has been very inward looking. And that's one of the things I think has got better. We've got less inward looking. But the same would apply to both the health visitors and nursery staff; very few of them pop into the Unit.

She also thought the Unit's community workers lacked contact with agencies such as social services, health centres and schools. Though, of course, they were in regular contact with other groups and individuals in the area, and took part in a number of forums. (Including: the Play Forum; the Elswick Pool Committee; The Festival Committee; a group for black workers; the Council for Voluntary Services.) Let me repeat that these links were not built simply for FSU to 'liaise' or 'coordinate', but so there should be a continuing dialogue.

Interactive or Proactive?

Sceptical readers may wonder if describing the Unit's approach as 'interactive' really amounts to more than a quibble about words. Does it differ, for instance, from what supporters of community social work advocate as a proactive approach of consultation and participation with users and local people? For example, in their study of three social services teams, Jim Black and others, argued that the traditional area team was neither responsive nor innovative.[10]

> Adaptability, whether to local communities, or to the elderly as client group, was not a prime feature of the teams we studied. Their priorities as defined by statute, departmental policy and casework tradition, lay elsewhere in reactive individual policy and casework bounded by available service provision.

They urged an "adaptive" service from local teams who would:

> recognise and accept their accountability to their locality; and develop patterns of working which are seen to be based on an assessment of local needs and conditions.

So, let me explain why this proposal *is* different from how I saw Newcastle tackle the issue.

The argument for proactive social services work calls for departments and agencies to reach out, find, and meet needs. But, actually, this is rather puzzling. It implies that social service professionals and administrators (whether in the 'statutory' or 'voluntary sectors') don't substantially initiate, plan and shape services.[11] But isn't this precisely what does happen — locally by senior staff, and nationally by the academics and administrators who sit on Government committees?

The Seebohm Committee, for instance, saw its recommendations become legislation determining the entire agency structure in England and Wales. That Committee, comment Nick Bolger and others:[12]

> Contained no trade union representative, no representatives of specifically working class organisations; no pressure groups and no client groups. By and large the history of changes in the organisation of social services is a history in which working class organisations have been conspicuous by their absence.

So then, is the argument that *direct service workers* should be more proactive? They regularly tell researchers that too much is 'top down', with not enough responsibility delegated to local teams to develop variation in service.[13] In Newcastle Social Services, local offices seemed to have considerable discretion. Here's Kath Satoris, senior at Clifton Mount office, nearby FSU.

Kath Satoris: With Social Services I don't think you'll get many overall policies out of Newcastle. That they say, 'This will apply for the whole of Newcastle Social Services'. I think probably what you'll get is individual offices like ours trying to formulate their own priorities. Certainly here, with us just being two seniors, we find that relatively easy. We can, sort of, guide things in certain ways here.

I'm not criticising Kath and Clifton Mount workers when I make the obvious point — localised discretion does not in itself ensure a forum for dialogue with users and other local people. Giving a measure of autonomy to individual managers (or even individual staff members) is not the same as building collaborative team working, nor of finding ways to encourage an interactive process with users.

Elsewhere in Britain, ideas for neighbourhood services and decentralisation have been developed as 'patch' and 'community social work'. Thoughtful and committed social service workers have looked to these schemes as a means of making services more flexible and meeting people's needs, not least by offering help before problems become critical. In addition, the schemes often claim to involve users and local people as partners and participants. Do they succeed?

Peter Beresford and Suzy Croft are sceptical, suggesting that many 'successes' are not borne out by independent studies. Users and local people have been widely involved in *providing* services, usually as volunteers or pittance-paid 'good neighbours'. However, most local authorities instituting patch and community social work make little attempt to engage people outside, other than professionals. Certainly, authorities have not fulfilled their promise of involving people as partners at the level of setting priorities and shaping services. Sadly, Beresford and Croft fear the schemes may be more about meeting the needs of the senior administrators and academics who proposed them.[14]

This illustrates a more general point that, examined closely, many of the examples of 'proactive' work are not, after all, about the process of matching services to people's needs. Instead, they turn out to be arguments and claims about the kind of agency and agency structure that will best 'go out' to 'them' and interpret 'their' needs. Will it be a neighbourhood or centralised service? A generalist team or specialised posts? The assumption is always that *we* know what we are doing. Now, how should we go out and get *them* to fit in?

It comes down to this: seeing services as either reactive or proactive only makes sense because users are presented as objects, either of the agency's active intervention, or of its selection and rationing. *Need* itself becomes an object of the agency's activity, somehow separate from users as people with their own meanings and perceptions. Indices are to be collected and compared; a continent of need is out there to be explored and mapped, and priorities become measured according to the consequences for the agency.[15]

The Needs of Black People

What would an alternative, interactive approach be like? Over 1983/86 the biggest change in Newcastle FSU's services was in its response to black people locally. How did these potential users make themselves heard and felt? I hope to show that the Unit was neither imposing its own framework and definitions of their needs on black people, nor simply reacting to users' demands.

> *Naseem Shah*: FSU has achieved positive results in the last couple of years. They have not just employed black people but also incorporated them into the management committee and on to interviewing panels. They have also reached out to the black community, and publish their services in their language.

For a number of years, Naseem was Newcastle Social Services' only black social worker. She joined FSU's management committee in July 1985. I'm not quoting her as expert testimony that they had it 'right' on race. Nor did anyone claim the Unit to be a model of good practice. Despite comparing FSU favourably with her own department, Naseem remained very critical of some aspects. For example, she thought that posts hadn't always been advertised in ways which encouraged black people to apply.

Many people may doubt how far a predominantly white agency can actually change itself and its policies to respond to the needs of black people. Will it, for instance, do any more than adopt a skin game scored on the numbers of black workers or users? Elliot Yabantu expressed his own doubts. He wanted FSU to adopt clear and agreed anti-racist policies, at both local and national level.

> *Elliot*: FSU now sees itself as an equal opportunities organisation. It has put that in writing. And I think with that goes the notion of positive discrimination. Hence people like me have been taken on, though I'm not a social worker, nor in professional terms a community worker.
>
> What does equal opportunity with FSU mean? Is it really part of anti-racism? Or just something people feel a bit guilty, and they want to do a little bit?

During the research these issues were becoming increasingly central — as they were in many other public service agencies. The Unit was extremely positive about Elliot and Parveen joining. It was a time when workers were proud of developing Racism Awareness Training within Newcastle, and the Unit had a local reputation for its anti-racism.[16]

The Newcastle Context

The context for the change in FSU's work was its location in the West End. As a visitor from London, Newcastle surprised me. I've enjoyed working and living in areas with a rich multi-racial mix. But here was a city with little obvious ethnic variety. Not only are Geordies predominantly white, they're often blonde; with faces that remind you of their links — past and present — with Scandinavia.

But follow the line of Hadrian's wall — built by one set of immigrants to keep out another — and a mile or so west, in Elswick, Arthur's Hill and Fenham, things begin to alter. Women wear Kamiz and Dupatta; an old church hall has been converted to a mosque; shopkeepers are often from Bangladesh and Pakistan. In this part of town, black people are more than one-in-ten.[17]

Immigration, from the Picts and Romans onwards, has long been a Newcastle feature. Tyneside as a whole has attracted outsiders, whether as a regional centre, a major industrial city from the last century, or a seaport. In chapter one, I mentioned Jon Davies' book on the redevelopment of the West End in the 1960's. Davies saw how planning blight added to other factors so:

> The houses became cheap and available and thus proved attractive to immigrants of all types, whether white, brown or black, whether from Tyneside, the rest of England, India, Pakistan, or Eastern Europe.[18]

In the 1966 census the Indian and Pakistani population was less than 1% of the City population. In 1981 the figure was 2.4%. Research in Newcastle has shown black people living in private rather than public housing, in older and more overcrowded property than white families. They were also more likely to have elderly relatives living with them.[19]

Saying Asian 'communities', reflects the fact that people tend to group themselves according to a number of differences. Language and religion are the most obvious, with country (often district) of origin being another. Language can be a major problem for recent arrivals, or those living their lives substantially within their own community. Donna Akhtar gave one example: women from rural areas in Bangladesh joining husbands.

Donna Akhtar: The population you've got here in the West End, they mainly come from a certain district in Bangladesh, which is the Sylhet district, and very disadvantaged in Bangladesh itself. And because they wanted to better themselves they've come abroad. This is the sort of people we are dealing with in the West End. They have been disadvantaged from home. And coming here they're facing double disadvantages.

Parveen Akhtar: I remember the West End Resource Centre saying, 'We don't have any Asian people using us at all'. I suggested to them that maybe what they needed to do was to get into the Asian Community Centre; pass information onto them, what they're doing or what they're there for. They never got round to doing that.

> But people referred to them to get some
> information. But they were just in no position to deal
> with them because they just couldn't communicate.

FSU itself might be criticised for taking its own time to learn
about the needs of black people in the area, and altering services accordingly. The 1981 annual report mentioned racism in
the West End as, "a growing obstacle to our work"; rather
than anti-racism as a growing part of the work itself, which is
what it became. Should they have been quicker off the mark?
There were some cautious voices on the management committee.

> *Ian Bynoe*: The black community in the West End is a
> minority of that community. It's quite right to
> concentrate on minorities. But there's also the majority
> — an oppressed minority within Newcastle.

Peter Stone hinted that users' needs don't necessarily match
current staff enthusiasms. He worried that FSU could be ac-
cused of being, "just a dedicated follower of fashion. You
know, like the bits of Asian work that pop up". These 'bits' became a quarter of the casework by the end of 1984, and the annual report made a point of mentioning the criticism.

> There has been criticism regarding FSU giving special
> preference to black people. However, we have agreed
> that we have merely recognised that black people have
> been unfairly and unequally considered in the past. Thus
> positive action is now required to redress this inequality.

> *Parveen Akhtar*: I think the way I've taken the job here
> is this agency itself has sought out people like myself
> to get employment in the area.

The Unit didn't appoint Parveen and Elliot to work solely with
black people. Donna Akhtar's position was slightly different,
as she was specifically hired (as a sessional worker) to interpret for the Birthday Group, which had become entirely Asian
women. However, Donna also interpreted for Unit staff and
students, supporting a policy that both white and black staff
should work with white and black users. The thinking behind

this was, partly, to avoid the danger that 'unqualified' black staff working only with black users could be severely limited in finding another job.

> *Elliot*: The world outside is not FSU. It's the world that demands professionalism — you must have qualification. What I found was the worry among black people in the [national] conference was, 'Well, what would happen if I left FSU with no qualification?'

Just as important, the Unit wanted to act both as an example and a pressure group on other agencies in the city, encouraging them to widen services and include black people. They didn't want other agencies referring black clients solely to the small number of black workers, nor setting up a separate and limited service.

> *Elliot*: In separation there's also suspicion.

The wider Newcastle Council context is important. Until 1987, Newcastle's Housing Department had no staff member speaking any Indian language. The same applied to health visitors in the city. Till 1985, Naseem Shah and Donna Akhtar were the only black workers in Social Services. Donna went from FSU to become an aide at the Crudas Park team. She said how, before working at FSU, she never realised an employer would regard Hindi/Urdu as a valuable asset.

> *Donna*: I never thought, you know, that it's going to help anybody at all. Till I came to FSU and was given this boost that I know all these languages.

I don't want to imply that the City's thinking was static. In 1984, Newcastle Council appointed an Asian woman as research officer, to examine the needs of ethnic minorities. But they also put out a discussion paper which contained the astonishing statement that:

> Newcastle does not face major difficulties or issues because of the presence of ethnic minorities.

FSU was only one of the groups and agencies which pointed out that ethnic minorities themselves faced major difficulties, some of them created, or at least not assisted, by the City Council. [A note from Pam Flynn: "By way of an update, when the City Council moved from a Race Equality Green Paper (consultative) into an Action Plan, which is monitored and updated annually, they did change their attitude."]

There was also some sensitive rethinking at local level. Kath Satoris, at Clifton Mount, saw the local authority following FSU's lead. Several Clifton Mount staff took Urdu classes and lectures on Asian Culture and history. But as Kath felt:

> *Kath Satoris*: Ten percent of our population is Asian and they do not make up 10% of our caseload. They do not make up 10% of our referrals. As they've probably got more needs, they should make up greater than 10%.
>
> It's forced me to look at and say we are a practically all white team. One of the home help organisers originated from the Caribbean, but has lived in England all her life and doesn't particularly work with the black community. We don't give them a very good service. I'm very aware of that. I mean, I think I've perhaps failed to convince the rest of the team of that.

Pulling And Pushing

The drawing, *Making a Molehill out of Mountain*, was in FSU's annual report. Adopting a proactive/reactive way of thinking, we could see it as two separate lists — initiatives 'outwards' and demands 'inwards'. In fact, Unit staff were explicitly trying to illustrate a dialogue — a pulling and pushing. How does this match what actually happened? Let's look first at Elliot's work and then at Parveen's.

After a year at FSU, Elliot had won the respect of many people locally for his energy and commitment. "He's got hisself around a bit", said George Cross. They'd found him "a bit of a stickler for detail", as well as someone who wasn't content to respond passively to what happened. One small instance was the Unit's involvement in setting up summer playschemes at the request of Asian families. At a public meeting, a local youthworker urged that playschemes should be more centralised — naturally, with his own club as the cen-

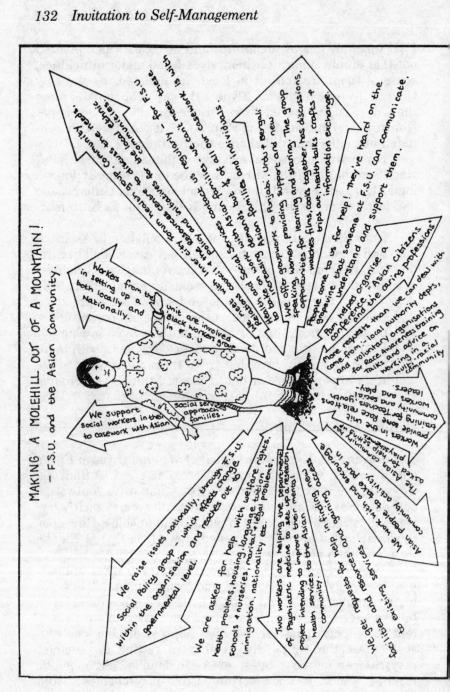

MAKING A MOLEHILL OUT OF A MOUNTAIN!
- F.S.U. and the Asian Community.

tre. Elliot rose to insist, gently but firmly, that many black parents preferred small schemes based on just a few streets. Newcastle he explained, was less safe for black people than white.

Elliot was ready to push his Unit colleagues, spelling out the steps he saw following logically from what they said they wanted. Since they wished more black people to use the Unit, well then, they needed to ask what was preventing it. Was the building accessible and welcoming enough? How should they change the reception people got?[20] The Unit wanted to bring together black and white people sharing a common interest, for instance as tenants or residents. But, continued Elliot, part of the problem was language. So, why stop short at arguing for interpreters in public agencies? What about translation between black and white members of a community group when needed?

Plainly, such ideas were rooted in what Elliot learned in his work. In the same way, other Unit staff began to suggest a number of possibilities for an explicit programme aimed at the the needs of black people. They could encourage black students, and get more black staff. What would effectively influence other agencies, including the University and Polytechnic? Changes were discussed for the Unit itself, ranging from small tasks like translating leaflets, to fundamental questions about the shape of services offered — for white people as well as black.

I mentioned that Parveen Akhtar gradually came to work more and more with Asian users. This was not the Unit's original intention, though it was the assumption of some people outside.

> *Jean Tams*: There's quite a lot of coloured people in the area, and a lot of them's frightened to come out, and things like that. Well, we've got Parveen as well. Parveen's for the Asian community.

Margaret Chiles and Monica Elliot (management committee members) complained about the service given to one user. They'd expected Parveen to do the work, and felt that the person who took it on (a student) couldn't fully communicate with the woman concerned.

> *Margaret Chiles*: I thought, 'This woman desperately needs some sort of social work support, preferably from somebody who speaks Hindi'. So I tried speaking to her on the phone and got out of her permission to ask a social worker to get involved. And I thought, 'Well, FSU would be much better than social services'. Because my experience of social services hadn't been very good. And it was very near FSU. And because they had employed Parveen who spoke Hindi.

Initially, the Unit resisted such calls on Parveen, for the reasons above. But, during her first year, two things altered their views. First, groups which thrived were the workshop groups with Asian women. Other groups were planned and prepared, but just didn't take off. (e.g. a project, jointly with social services, for parents of children in Care.) Second, Parveen found herself deluged with requests for individual work for Asian people, either through other agencies or referring themselves. And not only was she contacted at the Unit; people often stopped her in the street or phoned her home.

For a long while Parveen tried to tackle both lots of work. The groupwork, she saw as her brief from the Unit. At the same time, she helped those people who came to her, sometimes with family problems, but often for information or advice.

> *Parveen*: A lot of the problems that come up won't sometimes fall under the category of casework. There's one-off contact; there's welfare rights.

The pressure on her was discussed at Family Discussion Group — a group supervision meeting for the social workers, groupworker, student unit organiser, and students. For a time, the problem seemed to be helping Parveen cut back on this work. Other staff tried to take on more. The Unit looked for ways to make her original brief plainer to people outside. Parveen herself discussed things with Shahin Orsborn, a management committee member who acted as her consultant.

> *Parveen*: I feel I need to have it recognised that it is an area which does take up time. I think it is an important area, but an issue whether it should be part of my work

and how the Unit should respond to this kind of need.
It also has implications for the development of
groupwork.

Shahin Orsborn: When we did Parveen's assessment
panel that was really important. Because people did
give her amazing support. They were prepared to sit
down and discuss with each other the work and the direction. And yes, initially, there were some difficulties
about her having to do casework when she's been employed as a groupworker. But I feel that's now been
sorted out, really, insofar as her work is taking a kind
of clearer direction anyway.

Shirley Forster wasn't so sure.

Shirley Forster: 'People gave her amazing support'?
Well, I think that was our intention. But in practice it
was a long hard slog for Parveen to get us to understand her view of the casework she did, never mind
support her in it.

Shirley commented, too, on how much other workers learned
of the needs of Asian people through Parveen. In practice,
'sorting out' meant redefining the problem. Originally, people
bringing Parveen their worries had been seen as a problem for
her and for the Unit. Now the perspective shifted, leading to
different questions being asked as well as older ones being
asked more carefully. How could the Unit support Parveen in
taking on this new work, but in a way that didn't let other
agencies off the hook?

Shirley Forster: Black people are coming to the Unit —
mostly they're coming because Parveen is here. White
people have got so many other resources they can tap
up, that on the whole they come to us if they think
we've got the service that they need. Black people
come because there's nowhere else to go.

With referrals from other agencies, FSU sometimes suggested
that Parveen could best be used as a consultant rather than
take on full responsibility for the work. As she explained to the

Family Discussion group, this might be more than just a matter of policy.

> *Parveen*: The family knew me and, with my connections within the community, it was quite a dangerous situation. I was too much at the centre of it. And I'd rather that an English social worker took that case, and I could just give them support.

Another continuing issue was how far to ask existing Asian community organisations to respond. Was the Unit sufficiently aware of the danger of disabling people's own networks?[21] Shahin Orsborne's experience was that networks of black people in Newcastle were not yet very strong. Although there were the religious bodies — temples, mosques and gurudwara.

> *Shahin Orsborne*: They have that. But that doesn't cater for all the black community either — the religious centres. As far as all the Christian centres don't cater for all of the white community. Again, I think [FSU] would be sufficiently aware of all the problems of taking over and doing things for black people. But really it's much more a case of need — meeting and providing provisions that black people can use — yeah?

And, I think, workers at FSU would have added, developing a process that enables those needs to push against and shape the Unit's programme.

> *Shirley Forster*: Your ideal solution — I can't imagine how you'd do it — is to have the people controlling the Unit to be a bunch of local users who are a multiracial group committed to providing services for a multiracial community. So that your push — if you like — for services to be openly available would come from the residents in the community.

"I'm Black All The Time"

(From a Unit discussion of chapter seven.)

Parveen Akhtar: I don't think it was really that sort of pressure. With myself doing that sort of work, it was also a sense of responsibility. If I saw those problems and I was working in this sort of an area, I should be doing something. Or I should be bringing it up in places where other people should be doing something. It's not a case of such a thing as pressure — not in that sense.

Ernie Dobson: Maybe it's not a pressure in the sense of some organised campaign to get you to do something. But what it is, is people actually making demands on your time and you feeling that you ought to respond to those demands. But the other thing that Alan highlights — which I think is right — is that the initial response to that in the Unit was, 'Well, somehow we have to protect Parveen. Parveen's a groupworker; she must have time to do groupwork'.

And then a shift in that thinking to saying that a more appropriate response, in terms of people creating demands and putting pressure on you, is maybe we should change your job.

The thing that could come across a bit stronger for me, is that, okay, working with the black community and doing anti-racist work is something that we've got into within the last two or three years. But I don't see it as a fad, or supplanting something else. I just think it's the way all the agencies in this area ought to be working really. I don't see us providing a specialist service. For me it's about looking at what are the needs of the area and how we need to change. And having a new awareness about that and responding accordingly.

Parveen: I don't think it is a specialism. I think that maybe something that comes across is that it's a specialist provision from this agency. I don't see it that way. I see it as being like the normal work we do. We provide the same sort of service for everybody. I mean, it's like Peter Stone's comment about it being in the fashion to work with the black community at the moment. As a black person I find it difficult to understand comments like that. For me, being black isn't a fashion for the year. I'm black all the time. And issues related to black people are there all the time, and they have been there all the time. Just because we've started working in that sort of area doesn't mean it's fashionable.

NEWCASTLE FAMILY SERVICE UNIT

We are a voluntary organisation offering community work, groupwork and social work services to a small multi-racial neighbourhood. We are looking for two experienced workers to maintain the multi-racial nature of the team. Commitment to anti-racist, anti-sexist and non-hierarchical ways of working is essential. Experience is as important as any formal qualifications.

1. COMMUNITY WORKER (Locum). Salary £7,437-£11,280 (according to experience and qualification) to undertake community work in the area until September 1986, while the current black worker is on training. Experience in community development essential. Local knowledge an advantage. It would be valuable to have knowledge of any of these languages : Punjabi, Bengali (Sylheti), Urdu, Hindi, Cantonese, and to have had personal experience of racism. Job share considered.

2. BENGALI SPEAKING WOMAN WORKER for women's group (part-time 18 hours). Salary £7,437-£11,280 (pro rata = £3,719-£5,640). To run a weekly group for Asian women, and provide home visiting and some casework. (Exempted under Section 7(2)(e) of the Sex Discrimination Act).

Application forms and job description from **Anne Davies, Family Service Unit, Grindon Lodge, Beech Grove Road, Newcastle upon Tyne NE4 6RS. Tel. 091-273 5642.** Closing date: 25th September.

FSU IS AN EQUAL OPPORTUNITY EMPLOYER.

Eight

Grant Aid

The Unit and the Local Authority

There was another very strong 'push' on FSU's choice of work. I called Newcastle City Council the Unit's biggest customer. Unit salaries and running costs were met very substantially by an annual grant from Newcastle's Social Services department — the second largest grant to a 'voluntary' agency by that department.[1] Other funding was contingent on this money.[2]

I've put the term 'voluntary' in quotes for a specific reason. FSU's financial dependence on the City Council is reproduced by thousands of agencies across the country. This places it within a wider debate, usually presented as the relationship between, on one side, *statutory* agencies forming part of local authority or government departments and, on the other, the *voluntary* sector, sometimes described as "outside the State".[3] I suggest treating this distinction extremely warily. Though it appears to offer a helpful and even commonsense way of framing the issues involved, the framework hides a political and ideological judgement, and tends to assume the answers to many of the questions it raises.

In Britain, the label 'voluntary' is used for a huge sweep of bodies. In fact, being non-profit as well as non-statutory are its only common features. The 'sector' is taken to include service providers as well as campaigning organisations; small mutual aid groups dependent on members' subscriptions; and large national charities.

Writing and research in this area distinguishes these different types — especially the last group of agencies, like FSU, funded predominantly by grants.[3] Nevertheless, such organisations still prefer to identify themselves with the voluntary sector as a whole; implying that they remain more akin to groups of volunteers or mutual aid associations.

They're also quite likely to mention their origins and links with charitable and voluntary work, rather than stressing the reality of what they've become — non-profit businesses sometimes employing hundreds of paid staff and with a turnover running into millions of pounds.[4]

In case this seems like an argument over categories, let me point out some of the practical implications. To begin, here's a comment from Kath Satoris, senior at the Clifton Mount office of Social Services, comparing her team with FSU.

> *Kath Satoris*: There's a certain amount of, perhaps if you like, jealousy. That they seem to have time and space that local authority workers don't have. I don't think FSU's unusual in that though. I think we think that of an awful lot of the organisations. You know, you phone up and say, 'Can you take the case?', and they say, 'Sorry, we're full'.
>
> We end up thinking, 'Charming. I wish we could say that'. You know what I mean? That's very much a human response.

Local authority staff often see themselves like this: hemmed in by "demand pressures and subject to various kinds of bureaucratic restraints"[5] which voluntary bodies are assumed not to have. Of course, there *are* important differences. Not least is the local authority's power to cut funding to a grant-aided agency. As advocates of the 'voluntary' sector acknowledge, this can give it more power over the agency's workers than it has over its own staff.[6]

The problem with such comparisons is that, all too often, their outcome is to stereotype both 'sectors'. So, on the one hand, we have an apparently inevitable identification of State agencies as bureaucratic, centralised, and directive.[7] On the other, we're given a picture of innovative, voluntary agencies — your flexible friends, who are, so it's claimed, probably more caring as well.[8] Like Kath Satoris' "very much a human response", attitudes on both sides appear as mirror images. Focussing in this way on the divide, the result has been to narrow research and debate, and discourage fruitful exchange — especially between members of small teams of service workers.

Purchase of Service

Nationally, FSU's structure as a network of local Units makes these issues very clear. Each Unit was separately funded, with most of the money coming from the 'host' authority. Staff were therefore employed by one body (national FSU), and in effect paid by another. Newcastle Unit's fieldwork staff were all paid on the same local authority grade, so pay scales, increments and rises depended finally on the City Council coming up with the cash. Even their building was owned and maintained by the City's Housing Department.

At national level, with no possibility of money being switched from area to area, FSU could not accumulate reserves of a size to enable the financing of a Unit, or even several posts. National Office was itself dependent on government funding.

This is what Ali Rhind faced, as funding for the Women's Workshops was running out. There seemed nowhere to turn except, fruitlessly, writing numerous letters to foundations and charities.

> *Ali*: At the moment [April 1984] the project is set up with money from the DHSS: three years limited funding as an experimental project. I mean, I just feel quite angry. I'm not sure who I feel angry with. You know, you raise these expectations and what the hell next? Surely there must be some provision? If an experiment's successful, well, what's the next step? And there isn't. And I just feel this general anger.[9]

The issue is more than funders reducing grants or ceasing to fund. In broad terms, a grant-aided agency must continually be aware of funders' views on what they're paying for. That means anticipating what might attract money in the future. As a consequence, agencies often paint themselves into a corner as 'experimental' projects.[10] Selling themselves as innovators, they have persuaded many funders of the lure of the new.[11] So foundations and other bodies give grants for 'setting up' and 'seed money' on the shaky assumption that projects will be picked up by major funders like local authorities.

The fact of this dependence makes the tie with the local authority much nearer what's called in the United States, 'purchase of service'. Newcastle FSU's link with the City was not a formal contracting-out of services by a public funding agency. But the strong similarities with this model makes it extremely useful in understanding the relationship.[12]

The link is half-way acknowledged when, for example, a body like the Barclay Committee on social work wrote of a "potential complementarity" between State and grant-aided agencies.[13] FSU was mentioned twice in Barclay's discussion of the voluntary sector. One Unit, working on a local authority housing estate, had created "supportive networks and greater interdependence which has to date *resulted in a reduced referral rate from the estate to the local area social work team*"[my italics]. FSU was also cited as an illustration of:

> agency agreements with voluntary bodies whereby there is a written contract stating clearly what the grant aid is given for, and the type of service that is to be provided in return for the grant aid.

In Newcastle, as Ernie Dobson joked, "there wasn't a campaign in the sixties to have FSU in Elswick". It was the City Council which had invited them in 1968, funding the Unit for work the City wanted done. Since then, their grant had to be approved annually by Newcastle's Social Services Committee. In 1984, FSU wrote a report for the Committee, underlining — as they put it — "the most crucial statements".

What they emphasised were unabashed 'selling points'. The needs of Elswick and its high unemployment were stressed. They listed "numerous tenants, residents and community groups" which FSU had helped set up. They mentioned their involvement in environmental and social problems; self-help groups; employment creation and housing cooperatives; street parties, community festivals and play activities.

As a small organisation, they said, FSU was "able to respond to changes in thinking and policy very quickly". They cited their response to the City's Papers on women and on racial equality; the Unit's work with women and girls; its involvement in "a variety of anti-racist initiatives and ... services to the black community".

The Unit's casework and groupwork, they argued, "reduces the demand on social service workers". They listed work with socially isolated women and one parent families, for whom, self-help groups provided mutual support. They described their "intensive, innovative and imaginative work", which aided "independent functioning", and reduced the risk of Reception into Care.

A Matter of Hats

Anyone used to seeing agencies like FSU as part of the voluntary sector, could interpret what I've written as a critique of grant giving. And superficially it may seem close to the criticism that such bodies are Quangos — quasi autonomous non-governmental organisations, masquerading as 'real' voluntary groups.[14] But that's not what I mean. In fact, it's vital to see that this argument only gains its force from the notion that there are (and ought to be) two *distinct* sectors. The idea that their interdependence is something not quite kosher, only arises if we assume they are separate and different in kind.

If statutory agencies are characterised as bureaucratic and constraining, then we ask only how a voluntary agency can distance the services it provides from the source of its money. A report like FSU's to a local Council is seen, at best as a necessary evil, and at worst as the selling out of the voluntary principle. I want to suggest that it's neither of these, and go on to look, not at what separated the Unit from its funders, but at some of the links and connections — including several which were very positive.

The often considerable overlap between the two 'sectors' is rarely discussed. But FSU presenting its work and the City Council hearing about it, weren't separate, disconnected bodies. And the Unit's formal relationship with its funders was probably similar to other Family Service Units, and to many grant-aided agencies.

For one thing, its management committee had always included local councillors, with places 'in the gift' of the main political parties. Margaret Chiles had been a member of the committee before her election to the City Council.

> *Margaret Chiles*: After I'd been on a year, I was by then
> a councillor. And there was the possibility of my being
> an appointed member by Social Services Committee,
> or continuing as a member as a local person. I was
> happier being just a local person because then I had
> no remit. Because if you're appointed by a committee
> you should really represent their policy. And as I
> didn't very often agree with their policy I didn't want
> to be their representative.

Originally, the City Council had the right to nominate six
members of FSU's management committee, including its
chair and vice-chair. So the disagreements in 1977 about
changes in Unit philosophy and whole way of working were
not just between people who differed on principle, but among
individuals active elsewhere in the political life of the city.
Take the person who then chaired the committee. She was
also chair of the Council's Housing Committee, as well as a
member of one of Newcastle's established political families.[15]
It would have to be a very odd definition of 'the State' which
took such people to be outside it.

> *Peter Stone*: Eventually we did quite formally negotiate
> with the Council that they would reduce their
> nominations to three, and would no longer insist on
> being chairman. At that time there was a councillor
> still in the chair who stayed in the chair because we all
> wanted her to stay. She was a hard worker and she
> took an active part in the FSU's life as a committee
> member.

Peter's comment illustrates something else thing obscured by
a statutory/voluntary division. Officers and councillors from
the funding authority may begin with a brief to control, but
end by getting far more positively involved. Peter Stone
joined the committee representing Brian Roycroft, the director of Social Services, originally a member himself.

> *Peter*: Whilst there is a firm belief among the people
> who aren't involved, that the way to control what other
> organisations are doing, or alternatively to look after
> your own grant investment, is to be a member of the

committee, I just don't believe that. And I haven't for a
long time. Because I've never found that we've got any
control! I think that we get our control from setting up
a structure in which we have to tell each other what
we're doing. I don't mean that we do that very well, but
we do have a structure for doing it. And because once
a year we decide how much we're prepared to pay, and
the organisation decides how much they're prepared to
offer in seeking their grant.

So I don't think we get the control by being members of committees except in some very strange circumstances. I think the other thing that happens is
that if you elect someone, or tell someone to go off and
take part in another organisation, they personally become allied with the interests of that organisation. You
can't keep going to something you've no time for. But
also I think it's one of the things that the local authority can do for the voluntary organisations. I mean, we
do have people with expertise and skills, experience
and judgement. And it's a kind of resource that we can
make available to some extent.

So when I say I've got two hats on, I've only formally got the one that my job role gives me. But in
practice I accept that it's two. One role is to work for
the local authority. But one role is to be a member of
the FSU's management committee and take a personal
part in their debates.

Unit staff had their reservations about Peter — particularly
when they weren't sure which 'hat' he was wearing. But when
it came down to it, they valued his contribution and support.

Despite what Peter Stone said about having little control,
at several crucial points, local authority agreement was
needed for changes at FSU. When they reduced their catchment area and altered services in 1976, Unit records refer to
"agreement reached after consultation". But in reality, Social
Services had to approve the changes. Similarly, everyone in
the Unit — and at national FSU — understood that the City
could have vetoed joint management.

Peter: I didn't feel any great need during the course of
the discussions [about joint management] to raise it in
any formal way internally. But when we were getting to

the point of reaching a decision, then I suggested to the Unit that they should write to us and seek a formal view as to what they were doing. And at that stage I talked about it with the director [of Social Services]. I talked about it with the chairman of the [Social Services] committee — particularly with the chairman of the committee — as to whether it was something that he would want to have a formal discussion about it in committee; and he didn't.

The implied veto has a bearing on whether Newcastle had the option of leaving FSU in order to self-manage. This had been raised nationally; annoying the Unit, who wanted to remain within the agency. A further cause of irritation was the risk that a bid for independence might have resulted in closure. Though some of the Unit staff were not so pessimistic, this was Alan Jackson's view, and it influenced his attitude towards the agency nationally.

> *Alan Jackson*: They are part of the national network and it's important to remain part of that. But the second part is that if we had declared UDI [independence], Jeremy Beecham, leader of Newcastle City Council, would have kicked us into touch. I mean, there's no doubt in my mind whatsoever. We'd have been kicked into touch and that would have been it; the Unit would've been closed.

When it came to writing formally to the City about Joint management, the letter went from Alan, as chair of the management committee, to Peter, as assistant director Community Services. Alan was himself a City Council officer (senior in the fostering section of Social Services) but a committee member at FSU under his private hat. It was, as other research has suggested, that "staff of statutory agencies in an official or semi-official capacity" can provide impetus and energy to grant-aided bodies.[16]

This point is reinforced if we look at the background and experience of Unit workers. Since hiring is one way services are shaped and chosen, it's significant that half the staff team during 1984/85 had a local authority background. (So had more than half the management committee.) When we blinker our view by separating statutory and voluntary *organisations*, we can miss seeing how *people* move from one to another. Over the years, the gain in experience and fresh perspectives from people with these helix careers can offer a considerable amount to any team. This is complementarity in a richer form than it's usually discussed.

Working Links

What of FSU's day to day contacts with 'statutory' agencies? I mentioned Pam Carter's wish for more informal contact with colleagues from other agencies — especially those working with families and individuals. My impression — from talking to staff in some of the local agencies — was of considerable parallel working in the area. Shahin Orsborn, then a deputy head in a community school, painted a similar picture of the education service.

Within social services, the staff concerned with the Unit's community work were Peter Stone and Les Roberts, (who took Peter's committee place at the end of 1984.) They knew of the work being done, though didn't see it as their job to direct it. As local Social Services teams didn't include community workers, this seems to have reduced regular contact with the Unit's. Though Clifton Mount office kept abreast of work affecting them.

> *Kath Satoris*: We're especially interested in the work Elliot's doing in B. Street. Because we're very aware that we visit every other house in B. Street.

Casework referrals went through two liaison seniors — Kath Satoris at Clifton Mount and Mike Wardle at Crudas Park, who regularly met Unit workers. Checking a year's records showed the Unit accepting most referrals.[17]

> *Kath Satoris*: By what criterion do I pass cases to FSU? I think what it tends to be is cases where because we're very full and they live in the appropriate area, so I think I'll ask FSU. It seems vaguely like the type of work they do, that is, it's not an elderly case, or it's not a single person. Or because someone like Pam [Carter]

has contacted me saying, 'I've got three students starting. Have you got any appropriate work for them?
We'll take it on'.

I would find it quite useful if they perhaps took
on more of the traditional FSU families, you know.
I've got a particular family at the moment that I'm
feeling very stuck with — a woman on her own with
kids that seem to be running wild. I think that the type
of detailed, very 'working with the client' work that
FSU do would be very valuable. Yet I very much know
that they're full and couldn't take it on. And I think
they're feeling that they don't particularly want that
sort of case anymore. But I think there is a need for
someone to respond to clients of that type.

Kath stressed that she wasn't line manager to FSU, nor to any
other grant-aided agency. I invited her to pass on to the Unit,
what she called, "odd niggles about things". The main one
was that, "perhaps in terms of their casework, FSU do need to
sell themselves more."

Really Good Reasons for Paying £100,000

Comments about "selling themselves", or "looking after your
own grant investments" recall the issue of purchase of service.
But, I'm not suggesting that FSU were simply employees of
Newcastle City Council in another guise. The relationship, as
I've begun to show, was more complex and, at this point, more
constructive.

Peter Stone: I do think that in organisations like the
local authority, it is important that some people do
deliberately try to step out of the ordinary expectations.
We can roll on, you know, like steam rollers, without
ever thinking about anything. And we tend to do that.
I think we do need to deliberately step aside from it.
And you can only do that if you're prepared to chance
your arm now and then.

I think, in a sense, one of the few really good
reasons for paying £100,000 a year or whatever it is, for
FSU, is to learn something from them.

In case this sounds too good to be true, I'll add that relations with other parts of the local authority weren't always friendly. Quite regularly, FSU was in conflict over one issue or another. Councillors and officers had complained of Unit workers supporting activities and advocating policies critical of the City Council.

> *Joan Smith*: Some councillors were saying that we were being too political and biting the hand that was feeding us, and that sort of cliche.

> *Margaret Chiles*: The powers-that-be had decided that they weren't gonna replace the Housing Action Officer. As a result whole streets just went downhill. There were no facilities; their appearance was dreadful. There were lots of empty houses boarded up and, like, mess everywhere.
>   And a few people got concerned about it. And Ernie got involved. They had regular meetings and it was really good. They organised a big meeting and got out a petition. As a result of that the Council was forced into accepting that they should replace the Housing Action Officer. And that to me was great, because it stimulated a lot of local activity which has continued.

Margaret thought FSU ought to involve itself much more in this kind of work, and she was critical that other local tenants' issues weren't always taken up. She'd referred one tenant's group and been disappointed in the work done. (Unit staff's reasons were not to do with the constraints of local authority funding, but what they saw as the wishes of the local people involved.)
     For Unit workers a lot of this pushing was welcome. It was a feature of networks where different people — including members and officers of the funding authority — would be pushing them, but consider it legitimate for the Unit to push back. It formed part and parcel of the *interactive dialogue* described in the last chapter. Though, on funding there were limits.

> *Ernie Dobson*: There's a limit beyond which we will not go, and the ultimate contradiction is our existence. If

you keep pushing and pushing that's where you end
up. The Unit's not going to the Civic Centre and
saying, "Here's your £100,000 back. Go set up
a Women's Centre, a Black Resource Centre,
and give it to the people of Elswick".

Cartels and Grant Addiction?

Suppose Ernie's example was reversed. What if the City
Council told FSU that it preferred another, maybe more radical way to spend its grant? Instead of the influence of the funding authority on an agency, the issue would be its *power* to determine and insist on specific work and priorities.

Even when survival is not the immediate issue, it's clear
that the pushing power of an organisation like FSU can't compare with a single large funder. Won't this show that grant-
aided agencies have a very definite common interest; that, if
they don't unite, they've nothing to lose but their funds? So,
should they act together — overlooking differences, in size,
aims, philosophy, methods and a host of others? Putting it
another way, the notion of a uniform wide-ranging voluntary
sector may be dubious theory, but, when it comes to cash, it
can seem like practical good sense.

This, broadly speaking, is the implicit rationale for 'um-
brella' voluntary sector institutions such as the National
Council for Voluntary Organisations, and Councils for Social
Service locally. Like OPEC, cartels of independent suppliers
can try to fix terms with large customers, distributing 'orders'
according to agreed formulas, with the minimum interference
in each agency's internal running. Such measures gain in urgency when local authority spending is under threat from central government. If purchase of service does not exist, reduced
public expenditure makes it necessary to invent it.[18]

As a marketing plan, this has many of the strengths and
weaknesses of any cartel. It depends, for example, on whether
individual members are tempted to break ranks, by
undercutting, say, or making separate deals in other ways. A
revealing point is that it doesn't depend on agencies needing
to be "outside the State". On the contrary, their common interest is in *continued* State funding, but on terms which do not
lead to their virtual control by central or local government.[19]

However, this is one strategy only. What others are there? Plainly, any alternative must take account of the political reality of grant-aided agencies, and this often means that breaking away from control by centralised funding can appear impractical if not idealistic.

One suggestion comes from Ken Worpole.[20] He points out that 'grant aid' is actually a tiny part of our own common wealth, spent for collective public purposes. The money doesn't actually come from the Town Hall, but out of rates and taxes. Worpole calls this "ideological laundering", and advocates that what's going on should be made transparent to everyone.

Along similar lines, Owen Kelly offers a sharp analysis of Community Art.[21] He traces the steps taken by community artists in Britain from a loose grouping involved in radical cultural activities, to becoming a sub-division of State funded art. Kelly proposes alternative finance, including fundraising from individuals, and even voluntary tithes.[22] Grant-aid, he argues, should be accepted only with carefully drawn agreements about the work to be done and ways of doing it.

Kelly warns that grant-aid should never reach a proportion of total income which would threaten the entire project if withdrawn. However, many agencies have already gone well past this point. He calls this "grant addiction" and recognises the difficulties of withdrawal. (Local authority grants are often called 'mainline' funding.) So, his proposal may mean short-term sacrifice with no guarantee of longer term benefit. It *is* a lot easier asking a bank manager, than persuading large numbers of the bank's customers that they ought to take a hand in how their money is used.

Though neither of these critiques solves the problems facing agencies like FSU, they do offer fresh thinking. The idea that agencies — State as well as voluntary — are getting and spending *common wealth*, begins to remove some unhelpful conceptual fences. Perhaps we could even dispense with the term 'grant', with its connotations of grace and favour towards deserving causes. If our aim is the collective overview of collectively funded provision, it becomes crystal clear that the basic issue is democratic accountability. And that involves workers, users, and local people — not simply the accountability of one institution to another.

The Allies of a Collective Team

Let's return to Newcastle FSU and its practical options. As long as it is funded by the City Council, FSU must engage in the processes described by Peter Stone. Yet, as I've stressed, the Unit and the local authority, negotiating annually and telling each other what they were doing, were only two formal parts of a larger and continuing interaction that went on at different levels.

Seeing the relationship as a set of ongoing links in this way can be criticised for relying on a large measure of consensus, or at least mutual tolerance, between two agencies. Weren't FSU just very lucky, and for quite a long time? They had sympathetic people in their funding authority, with Council policies which left them room to manoeuvre. Since a dialogue needs at least two parties willing to enter it, in a different town with different local officials, I might have written a far gloomier story — had there been any story to tell.

This is true. But only partly so, since organisations are not structural monoliths. FSU was no more in negotiation with a single 'party' across the table, than the City itself faced a united voluntary sector.

Nor does my argument exclude conflict and the necessity to build alliances and coalitions with which to face it. But choosing allies is not a simple matter of making common cause with other organisations because they also receive grants. That is only one approach, and would mean ignoring — and in some cases swallowing — disagreements on a range of other issues.

I've described how the Unit's networks cut across all kinds of divisions, as long as there were common interests in the work being done, or the principles involved, (eg. the black workers group). When there is conflict, such links and connections become a web of potential alliances and support. The web crosses the statutory/voluntary divide, as it does many others. In the same way, Unit staff were trying to build coalitions and links with users and other local people.

The allies of a collective team will be found among other grant-aided agencies, but also within the local authority, and outside both sorts of agency. Any team trying to work in ways which enable empowerment would be well advised to put traditional categories aside, and make common cause with whoever endorses and supports their principles and practice.

Nine

A Tale of Two Units

Chapters nine and ten continue the theme of common-work, asking whether this was contradicted by Newcastle Unit's division of labour. Did the existence of specialisms and separate work mean it was less of a collective resource for users?[1] Here we'll return to Unitary theory[2] — systems ideas applied to social services. These had been behind some of the criticisms made ten years earlier, about staff working parallel and not sharing skills. Chapter ten considers specialism when the team, "was supposed to be working as a collective".

Visitors were sometimes surprised by Newcastle's specialism and individual working. They assumed joint management would mean more of everybody doing everything. Instead, a hefty slice of the direct work with users was done individually. It was noticeable that separation of work continued even when staff were involved, as local residents, in areas outside their job at the Unit. Both Carol Tate and Parveen Akhtar had taken part in community projects, and Jean Mowberry was a leading member of the group of residents helping to run the Elswick Festival.

On the other hand, shared work wasn't unusual. Two staff — or a staff member and student — might co-work with a family. Groupwork was normally paired. For instance, Ali Rhind and Sally Walker had co-worked in the Women's Workshops; Parveen and Donna Akhtar planned and ran the 'Birthday Group' together. During 1983/84 all social workers and students were involved on a 'Women and Health' project. The community workers came together on particular projects, as well as supervising one another. Parveen also joined Ernie and Elliot on some of the anti-racism, and in contributing to the Unit's responses to the City's policy documents on ethnic minorities. Most important, planning and review was always shared, whether in paired supervision, group discussions, team meetings, or at the occasional study day for the whole team.

But had the team compromised or even undermined their aims and principles by not integrating different work more fully? Let's look at what FSU could have learned from a Unitary model. The obvious place to begin is with a book about Bishop Auckland Unit, which explicitly used this model to explain and analyse its work.[3]

Bishop Auckland Unit

In chapter two, I mentioned the contact between the two Units. Bishop Auckland FSU, about 35 miles south of Newcastle, worked on a local authority housing estate of around 6000 people. It ran from mid-1973 to 1979, when funding stopped. FSU was invited (as to Newcastle) to work with families seen as having multiple problems. Bishop Auckland Unit was also asked to develop some "community spirit", which the local authority and public agencies viewed as sadly lacking.

Dave Holder and Mike Wardle, who wrote about the Unit, were respectively, senior social worker and Unit Organiser. They brought a commitment to teamwork, and to trying out groupwork and community work, as well as casework. They hired staff who were prepared to use at least two of the three 'methods', and the team — which eventually rose to ten — included teachers as well as social services workers.

They started by offering family casework. Shortly afterwards, a needs survey of the area led to proposals for other types of work: with community groups; to set up client groups (eg. of school truants); and trying to bring together some of the agencies in the area. For two years these approaches were seen as distinct, and ran parallel. The same applied to educational work when that was added. Holder and Wardle describe this phase as a "multi-method stage". Despite keeping work in separate compartments, it helped build up staff skills, which were, to some extent, shared in team meetings and six-monthly review days.

After two years, a second "transitional phase" began, when the team became more flexible, particularly in response to casework referrals. The crucial change was in how a 'problem' became defined. Previously, the referring agency and perhaps the Bishop Auckland worker, specified the problem to be tackled. For example, a family referred for casework would be allocated a caseworker. "We were still trapped in a narrow definition of the problem and were still too protective of our professional roles."[4] In the second phase, the team discussed together how a referral could be handled, and might redefine the problem. One alternative would be involving a client in community work. While this change encouraged small group discussions and information sharing among staff, much of the community work was still separated — for example, work on a community newspaper.

The separation, say Holder and Wardle, was resolved in a third "Unitary phase", when the whole team decided what to offer and who would do the work. They allocated and reviewed work by considering it from all available angles, with staff adding their knowledge and point of view. Connections were made between what was happening within a family, in a tenants' group, or in the Housing department.

> It was increasingly difficult to assert, 'I am a caseworker' or, 'I am a community worker'. Rather it was matter of saying: 'In response to this particular issue we require a certain kind of casework, a certain kind of community work. Which of us is best able to provide that service?'[5]

The three stages were signalled by supervision. At first, Mike Wardle alone supervised each worker. Though allocation and closure of cases went to the Unit meeting, Mike's authority prevailed. From the transitional phase on, the Unit regularly reviewed work. Individual supervision (with UO or senior) continued, but the Unit meeting increasingly modified policy and directed workers in individual cases (including the supervisors).

Illustrating these changes, Holder and Wardle discuss an issue raised earlier — the implication that effective teamwork means individual staff losing some professional autonomy. As workers in Bishop Auckland became more accountable to each other, they had to consider the effect of what they did in one area, on the work of team members elsewhere. Why did individuals give up part of their discretion in this way? Their answer was that, working together, people were more effective; their ability to effect change actually increased. Everyone could now contribute to team decision making. Staff were available as a resource to their colleagues, and there was a Unit overview and evaluation.

Holder and Wardle argued that "corporate teamworking", was essential, strengthening integration of work in a number of ways. Information, suggestions, and criticism were offered supportively. Workers shared tasks — like liaison with other agencies, and chairing team meetings, (with the UO 'sitting out'). It became a "mutually accountable team"[6] stressing participation, open communication and shared responsibility.

> For a Unitary approach to work it must be a team effort - we do not believe that the skills needed can be incorporated in one person.[7]

Two Units Compared

Newcastle parallels will be plain, especially in the early years when staff there began to pool experience and skills and relate their overall service to the needs of users. The argument about redefining problems applies equally to Newcastle workers' shifting perception of the needs of Asian users. The two Units also shared an understanding that teamwork is essential in offering a better service. Here, Holder and Wardle have some very helpful things to say about collaborative working, in particular, their perception that individual workers gain more from co-operation than from maintaining control over individual work.

Yet, finally, there were basic differences. Bishop Auckland remained "corporate" rather than developing into a collective team. To Shirley Forster (who'd been a student at Bishop Auckland), Mike Wardle was still "chairman of the board". There was also a marked divergence in the two Units' theories. Newcastle workers never adopted or wanted a Unitary approach. Though, in the mid-seventies, they had talked of integrating work, hardly anyone took this to mean *dissolving* the categories used. As Joan Smith neatly put it, they wanted "to major in" a skill, but be influenced by other things that were going on.

The 1983 Newcastle staff group which asked to self manage, had spent considerable time in sharing and reporting on each other's work. Till they reached a point where, for community and casework in particular:

Pam Carter: It's a comfortable rubbing along sort of relationship.

Ernie Dobson: Longstayers can see fundamental discussions — particularly the relationship between different methods of work — coming up at two year intervals. For some of us, we've heard it all before.

By early 1985, new workers were beginning to ask about the "rubbing along", not necessarily with the idea of blurring different kinds of work, but re-opening questions of how they linked together. However, this sort of challenge is not the same as that explicit in Holder and Wardle's book, since they argued that, "the Unitary approach is inherently a model for organising teamwork".[8] Well, why hadn't Newcastle used this 'inherent' model?

Unitary Theory

The answer requires an outline of Unitary theory. In most standard accounts the theory has four central features. I'll list these, giving some examples from Newcastle's practice to illustrate the kind of interpretation the theory would give. (By the way, I'm not implying that Unit workers used Unitary theory. Here I'm using it on them!)

1 — *Social situations consist of a set of different and overlapping systems.*

What I've said about *interactive* networks can be seen in this way. For instance, there were the overlaps between members of the management committee and officers in the local authority. Another set of links explain some of the tensions felt by Parveen. As a member of staff she belonged to one 'system', and to its subsystem — the Family Discussion group. Outside the Unit was her own ethnic community in the area. Overlapping both, was the group of black workers who met together.

A family can be thought of as a system in itself. But the family is also part of a street, and a neighbourhood. At another level, it belongs to a network of friends and relations. And individual family members may be members of their own systems — such as school, work, church or club.

2 — *Systems influence and act on each other.*

This means that, for example, a family as one system can interact with another — FSU, perhaps, or another agency like the Education or Housing Department. Agencies also interact with one another. It's a major feature of the Unitary model that these interactions — the relationships *between* systems — are as important as what happens inside them. Shirley Forster described one piece of social work which nicely illustrates these points.[9]

She was working with a woman who wanted her daughter home from local authority Care. Shirley approached this in two ways. First, the mother needed help in understanding and altering the things that had gone wrong. So Shirley discussed and got the woman's agreement to a list of tasks aimed at changing how mother and daughter behaved together. (Eg. Shirley advised, "If you say, 'No', mean it. Don't give in when she has a tantrum".)

But, at the same time as altering this 'family system', there were further tasks aimed at changing relations between the family and other agencies. Shirley found some of the residential staff were convinced of "the inadequacy and inability of parents whose kids go into care to do anything". So, at the children's home, the mother had to remember to take her child to the toilet, since previously, "she wet on the floor and upset everyone". She was to play with the girl when visiting, not simply for the child's benefit, but, "to demonstrate your ability to relate to and engage your daughter".

3 — *"Problems are not attributes of people but of social situations."*[10]

In other words, 'the problem' in Shirley's example did not *belong* to the mother nor to the daughter. Partly, it was about how they were together — their relationship. But there was another poor interaction — between them as a family, and the social services staff caring for the child. It will be clear that we've returned to the question of who is evaluating something as a problem, and why.

4 — *Change requires an 'action system' operating on a 'target system'.*

The point here is the need for an alliance of people who set out to get change. Shirley as agency worker, together with the mother, formed an 'action system' aimed at two 'targets' — the daughter and the children's home. On a different issue altogether, FSU, working with other anti-racist groups in Newcastle, could be seen as an 'action system' persuading the City Council to modify its policies on ethnic minorities. As these examples show, an agency's users may be included in the 'action system'. They aren't necessarily 'the target', and it's seldom them alone.

A Bit of History

When Newcastle workers read this chapter in draft, they wondered if it was really needed. Several of them saw Unitary theory as a bit of history — a fashion of the late 1970's. Hadn't debates in social work moved on? We can see this if we think back to the disagreements among Newcastle staff and management committee during 1976/77. One part of that argument was whether staff should have stuck to traditional approaches — trying to change families "who have not been able to cope with the complexities of modern life", as the dissenting management committee members put it. In other words, was it the *family's* problem that needed solving?

Or were the staff right to try and unravel some of these complexities to help the families? If so, there were fresh possibilities — like working with tenants' groups, or trying to bring about change, for instance, in the City's Housing department. It meant that links with other agencies, and those agencies' relations with the families, were just as much a proper target for social work.

Undoubtedly, the legitimacy of such wider intervention has become more acceptable in social services work. The term 'problem family' isn't heard so often. And it's no longer a novelty to come across the idea that problems are defined by the interaction between an agency and a user, or even that an agency itself may pose a problem for its users.[11]

Not all aspects of Unitary theory have become part of the currency of social services work. One reason for interest in systems thinking in the mid-seventies was the growth of community work and groupwork, and their apparent threat to social work as a profession. If "social work began as a collection of specialisms in search of a profession",[12] Unitary theory seemed at the time to offer a professional base. Newcastle Unit's lack of enthusiasm for the theory tallied with their lack of interest in professional status as such. Skills, knowledge and experience were valued; professional status was not. The team also resisted the assumption that there is something called 'social work', which has within it sub-categories known as casework, community work and groupwork.

The Missing Team

Let's return to the Bishop Auckland Unit. While their model of Unitary theory includes the four features above, it will seem that I've left out something vital. *Teamwork* as such, is conspicuously absent. How can this be? After all, given the aim of co-ordinating services and avoiding fragmentation among different specialisms, shouldn't team working be a central characteristic of a Unitary approach? Holder and Wardle certainly thought so. They described a process of team building whereby the whole team became part of the 'action system', pooling knowledge, planning, and carrying out joint strategies, affecting users at a number of different levels.

But this stress on teamwork is not found in the main writing on Unitary theory. In fact the opposite is true. The perspective is almost always that of an individual social worker, with virtually no discussion of even the possibility of a co-operative or collaborative team.[13] One United States writer refers invariably to a sole professional social worker with a "unique style".[14] Agencies have a "profusion of titles and ranks", and the singular status of the social worker is not just emphasised but celebrated.

> His office, it's decor and the trappings of professional insignia lend further credence to his authority and further symbolise his superordinate position.[15]

Not surprisingly, such rules of deference tend towards an action system of one.

Now, I'm not saying Holder and Wardle got it exactly wrong — that Unitary theory is inherently individualistic. It is possible for a whole team to become an action system.[16] Even taking a single worker as starting point, that person, "still has an array of alternative systems with which intervention might be effective".[17] However, the theory fits individual parallel working quite comfortably, and is usually presented that way.

But this raises a difficult question: Which of the "array of alternative systems" is appropriate in a particular situation? Take Shirley Forster's work with the mother and daughter. Was she right to work as she did? Or should Shirley have chosen to work 'on' mother and daughter as the target, perhaps with the staff of the children's home within the action system? Similarly, recall the discussion of priorities in the Unit's community work. Should Chris Johnson have built up links outside the Unit's catchment area? Her view could be interpreted as a perfectly valid systems analysis of the problem.

> *Chris*: A lot of the employment stuff has gone out of the area. The housing co-op stuff went out of the area. In some ways that seems quite a good local model to work from. You know, that issues come up from the local area initially; force you into looking at a much wider level to solve those issues. And then, as a local agency, really setting up some sort of city-wide (or whatever) project that can reasonably deal with that, at that level.

A Unitary approach can open up such possibilities, but — and this is a vital point — *it does not say how choices should be made, and by whom.* However, a lack of answers to these questions is not an oversight. The reason the theory does not specify answers, is because it includes an implicit assumption about the nature and causes of social problems. They are assumed to be due to *malfunctioning* of the social system. Therefore, the goal of professional intervention is to discover when pieces are failing to function together — as it is assumed they ought to. Dismantling the whole into parts and sub-parts, the agency worker is supposed to find out where different "cog-wheels" and "gear-wheels" are not meshing properly.[6]

In Unitary theory, therefore, the choice of 'system' to work on and with, is a technical/managerial one. As a result, like its systems framework origin, it has little to say about the social and political relations involved in co-working, either with colleagues or users. In the end, it is system work, not social services work.

Beyond Unitary Theory

Dave Holder and Mike Wardle drew from Unitary theory to explain Bishop Auckland's approach. But by now, it will be clear that Unit practice actually went beyond a Unitary framework. This is why their book remains valuable, especially in its description of team building; the tensions involved in learning and working together; and some of the conflicts between a formal hierarchy and a collaborative work group. They also offered more than 'integrated methods' in their work with users — though this may not be immediately apparent. Holder and Wardle describe the process whereby families were stigmatised.

> The role of Graham Street as a negative reference point for the community at large has had implications for the residents of the street. Even on the street itself we can observe a social hierarchy as some of the residents attempt to distance themselves from the 'supposed' sources of stigma. Within the street community there is a general consensus that a small core of families are the source and cause of Graham Street's bad name.[18]

This image was not only reflected by the public agencies, it could be reinforced by them — including FSU itself. "A large part of the street will know or experience that FSU works with the 'worst' of the families."[19] When a girl from one of these families joined a Unit group, she was stigmatised by the other members. Her stigma matched the way her family were treated on the street and by many of the public agencies. Only when the Unit began to understand and confront the whole process, could it start changing it.

Similarly, Holder and Wardle describe how casework and community work were originally separated in what they called "collusive tension". Workers acted on an unacknowledged division into stigmatised casework users and 'respectable' community work ones.

To see why this goes beyond Unitary theory, (rather then offering examples of its useful application) consider aspects of Newcastle Unit's work. They too, had their 'Graham Streets'. Lilian White mentioned Mill Lane, in years gone by, she said, reputedly used by the Housing Department to 'punish' tenants. She also remembered how, as a local herself, she'd heard of the Unit's reputation for "dealing with the 'worst' type of families".

> *Lilian White*: Certainly the referrals we used to get from the social services was the family that nobody wanted to know.

Both Parveen Akhtar and Pam Carter mentioned Asian users who were reluctant to come to the Unit because other people had said, "it was for problem families". Elliot was told: "If you go there you must be very down; right at the bottom of the social structure".

The crux here is not this state of affairs, but the choice of responses to it, made by both Newcastle and Bishop Auckland. From a systems perspective, the question is whether such a set of relationships causes conflict or malfunction between different parts of the system. So the "collusive tension" described by Holder and Wardle isn't necessarily a problem — it may be a *solution*.

Let me make this plain. Bishop Auckland Unit were not actually asked to make life fairer or easier for the families of Graham Street. The fact that they suffered stigma was not why the Unit was invited to the area. FSU was funded to prevent, or at least reduce, the problems and headaches *of the public agencies* — problems of crime, vandalism, and truancy, which they had located in the street.

> When the Unit arrived and visited all the agencies we were told the cause of the problems. First the estate, second 'those people' in Graham Street, and third the Edwards family.

So, who chooses the action system? Who defines the problem? Who is to set the target system? Initially, Bishop Auckland Unit were supplied with one answer: the public agencies. The

Unit's response was to insist that it ought to be the team as a whole, taking as its central criterion, an understanding of the needs and interests of users. And that meant working with family members, neighbours, and local agencies to change *what might be a fairly stable system*. Such a decision needed the Bishop Auckland team to look behind problems as defined by the agencies. And this, in turn, required political judgements that Unitary theory does not make.

Conclusion

I began this chapter by asking whether the Newcastle team should have been more integrated in its working methods. If the question assumes a Unitary model, there is little in such a theory to lead us away from an individualistic work group. It's therefore essential to distinguish the interactive approach used in Newcastle from the model proposed by Unitary theory. Newcastle's view was in no sense one of the different parts of a system in mechanical interaction. Nor was it a social work version of such a theory where the professional worker or agency is always the change agent; a subject who acts on other people and agencies as targets and objects.

There's a superficial resemblance, in that an approach aiming at empowerment, at dialogue and debate, focusses on relationships *between* as well as within. But priorities, methods of work, and co-ordination between team members are not assumed to be neutral technical issues. Nor do they emerge from an examination of 'needs' or systems. There simply isn't a smooth straightforward means of fitting the pieces of work together, shorn of political and ideological choices.

Newcastle choices were that integration and co-ordination ought to be a matter of pushing back and forth between people who were themselves subjects. This meant that, among the different sorts of work, there could be no neat slotting together of parts. Instead, there were only temporary agreements; phases with a great deal of overlap and sharing, and other times when:

> *Pam Carter*: There's just, sort of, acceptance that each other exists and we respect each other's work.

But then things change once more. New people ask old questions; pressures from outside shift; the pattern of users' demands makes the old balance no longer possible. Perhaps Newcastle had its periods of "collusive tension" when they didn't look too hard into each other's areas of work. But the phase that followed, the opposite of collusive tension, was not honest harmony but honest tension.

Ten

Collected Works

Exploring different aspects of Newcastle's practice has meant setting the Unit within a number of frameworks. We've looked at it as part of a national charity; as one of many small social services agencies; and as a 'voluntary' agency in one city. The context of this chapter may seem more open to challenge than many: a comparison with collective teams elsewhere.

In chapter four, I mentioned socialist and radical writing on social services work which advocated greater collective working — meaning that groups of workers should organise together as a way of developing democratic services. Would such writers see Newcastle's self-management fitting this frame? They might, provided they agreed with my approach to working collectively as *something people do* — a cluster of *processes*. Not everyone would accept such a definition. People elsewhere who talk about "running as a collective" may seriously doubt whether a team like FSU was a 'real collective'. Making that judgement, they have in mind a particular *form* of organisation, defined by certain rules.[1]

The idea of a defined collective form comes from left-wing political traditions. Socialist and anarchist collectives have a long history,[2] but describing a public service agency as a collective usually refers to a fairly recent development. From the early and mid nineteen seventies, a large number of formally collective agencies were set up in Britain, (as in other Western countries) from law centres to community projects, and advice centres to nurseries.[3] Some have disappeared, but many have thrived.

There was parallel growth in their sister organisations, the co-operatives. In the 1970's a new wave of worker and housing co-ops renewed the movement's commitment to egalitarian and democratic principles.[4]

The Ground Rules

Thinking of a collective as an organisational form was the standpoint of Newcastle's West End Resource Centre, (itself a collective) when questioning Elliot Yabantu. And it was Ian Bynoe's former job in a law centre which prompted him to ask how collective the Unit could be with the secretaries 'below' the staff team.

What are the characteristic features of collectives in this sense? Jane Mansbridge, researching United States 'New Left' collectives in the 1970s, described: "face-to-face, egalitarian, consensual democracy", expressed and governed by "ground rules". As groups adopted formal structures, such rules laid down internal equality among members, with one-person-one-vote, and major decisions taken by the whole group.[3]

The 'New Co-ops' have very similar ground rules, and, of course, a co-operative not only aims at common control, but achieves common ownership. By limiting shareholding to members, outsiders are prevented from gaining legal control. Members' own share-holding is also restricted, to avoid unequal power and an unequal share of profits.

In both co-ops and collectives there will be other ground rules for equalising what we might call the *extrinsic* rewards of the job. For instance, pooling salaries allows equal pay,[5] or at least a reduction in differentials. Sharing out the *intrinsic* costs and benefits of work is more complex. But often different types of work — 'manual and mental' — may be rotated or shared.

Not Really A Collective?

Newcastle didn't claim to be a *collective* in this formal sense. Nor had they set out to work collectively. Their proposal to self-manage only came at the end of a series of changes in the Unit's ways of working and thinking. So why make the comparison at all? Couldn't we drop the word, describing them simply as a self-managing or collaborative team?

I have several reasons for sticking to the term 'collective'. One argument — put forward in earlier chapters — is that examining *process* is far more fruitful than just focussing on sets of rules and structures. In this respect, collectives are no different to any other work group. Compiling a list of ground rules suffers from the same shortcomings as other attempts to reduce teamworking to a description of structures. It doesn't describe and can't explain the kinds of changes in working relations essential to any group setting out to share and pool.

Let me give an extreme (though, sadly, far from rare) example. There are work groups calling themselves 'collectives' who fulfill each one of the formal organisational rules. Yet their members work separately, rarely learning together. They may not even talk to, or like each other very much.

On the other hand, the fact that very many collectives *do* run successfully is a good reason for not fencing them off from teams like FSU. Why sort and pigeon-hole, when knowledge should and could be shared? The potential for pooling isn't limited by which groups are, and which aren't labelled collectives. All collaborative teams can learn from one another, and their experience will benefit others wanting to move towards self-management.

Taking this wider view means looking at how people succeed or fail in working together, rather than comparing their structures and rules. So, at Newcastle, sharp questions from outsiders about the Unit's secretaries were accepted as fair comment by workers who wanted everyone included in self-management. But, it's one thing to raise the tensions and problems of separate working, and quite another to invoke the 'ground rules'; cutting short any exchange by saying, 'You're not really a collective, so there's nothing to debate, is there?'

The Politics of Work

Members of many collective teams see the 'ground rules' as essential to their whole way of running. It may seem as though I'm asking them to forget their history and abandon their principles. So, let me stress that I am not insisting the ground rules be put aside or ignored. Rather that we take them as a key to open up discussion rather than shutting it tight down with the statement: 'We are a collective'.

Suppose we think of the rules as the 'what' and 'how' of collective working. Take, for example, one-person-one-vote. Collectives and co-ops tend to see this as one of their *principles*. But isn't it actually a tool, a *means* of ensuring democracy and equality? In other words, underlying the ground rules, there is a further set of questions asking 'why'. Collective and co-operative forms should be thought of as organisational an-swers to vital political questions about the nature and pur-pose of work.

What are those questions? I mentioned that collectives have their roots within the practice and ideology of left-wing movements, though not any single political tradition. There have been socialist, anarchist and feminist collectives, bor-rowing from and influencing each other.[2] Their common link is the challenge to traditional forms of organising work where *somebody else owns and controls the workplace and its product.*

The classic critique here was Karl Marx's discussion of work and alienation. He described how the factory system with its detailed division of labour led to workers who were alienated: from themselves as individual people; from fellow workers; from the day to day work itself; and from the prod-ucts of their work. Many other critics — often non-Marxists —have followed his broad scheme.

Both socialists and anarchists have advocated workers' control. Both traditions distinguish useful work producing what people need, from production for profit. A further chal-lenge concerns the quality of working time. Why should some people have pleasant and personally satisfying jobs, while others spend their lives on tasks which are dirty, repetitive and boring? More recently, feminist critics have enlarged this debate to include women's work and its status.

Behind collective 'ground rules', then, are some long and profound political debates. Not that collectives and co-opera-tives are *the* answer. But their aims of common work, com-mon ownership, common wealth, and common control each deal with aspects of an alternative way of working. The ques-tions have not been simply about building democratic, self-managed workplaces, but also about making work useful and satisfying; human-scale, and respecting people's dignity.

A further question is how far our society actually permits workplaces which avoid alienation. Can people build these new social relations among themselves as workers and be-tween workers and service users? Let me make it plain, I'm not proposing some impossibly tall order: anarcha-feminist-socialist work relations in one Family Service Unit! My sug-gestion is a lot more modest. It's that we need to understand such aims if we're to get beyond sterile debates about whether a group exactly practices collective rules. Rather than consider-er Newcastle FSU from the viewpoint of collective ground rules, all collective teams need reconsidering by a politics of work which has not fossilised into a single fixed structure.

Politics into Practice

In the early years of many 1970's collectives, their politics of work was quite explicit. Their founding mothers and fathers were often young, and frequently, had been influenced by the libertarian ideas of the 1960's, especially of May '68 and the 'counter-culture'. Lawyers, teachers, social workers, and community activists took their first steps in a 'long march through the institutions', trying to put their politics into practice in collectively run workplaces.

Anthony Sager mentions the weekly study sessions in a Boston legal collective, where reading included Marx and Mao.[6] In Britain, Sheila Rowbotham linked the practice of a London community nursery to the experience of storefront daycare centres in West Berlin.[7] Sometimes the ideas and values can be traced through the years. David Moberg tells how the Highlander Centre in Tennessee, set up in 1932 with inspiration from both socialists and the Danish Folk Schools, spread its ideas to North American Universities in the 1960's.[8]

Yet, it's also true that not every collective was aware of inheriting or borrowing the forms of direct democracy. Jane Mansbridge makes this point, again writing mainly about collective groups in the United States.

> By far the most astonishing feature of this phenomenon was its spontaneity. The New Left's affinity for the ground rules of Unitary democracy was certainly not inherited from the Old Left. There were stronger precedents in anarchist history, but few in the New Left knew that history.[3]

This applies to members of some British collectives who had only the haziest ideas of the politics involved — though often a very clear view of the collective structure they wanted to work in.

It's fucking left-wing isn't it. Basically left-wing, socialist... If they've been used to giving out orders I'm sure
they'd find it frustrating. I don't think it would work.
Everybody would tell them where to put their orders.
I'd tell them to bring it up at the Monday meetings.
'Don't tell me. Tell everybody else! What they say, I'll
do'.[9]

Perhaps a more important point is that now, ten to fifteen
years later, fewer and fewer members of collective teams have
this political pedigree. So whether or not a particular group
had counter-cultural beginnings, the question becomes: what
about new staff? Some people join such teams because they
are socialists or feminists, and others because they want a job.
Newcomers can find it pleasant to share work and have equal
pay, or they might want to change the work arrangements
they find. Whatever their views, the structure and rules are
given; the collective is the status quo. (Staff joining Newcastle
FSU were in this position after joint management was agreed.
Newcomers had to adapt to rules which existed already, and
which others had chosen and shaped.)

   These kinds of changes within collectives can easily be
seen as confirming a need to strengthen the 'ground rules' in
order to carry the weight of collective principle. This could
appear more vital when a team sets out to widen recruitment
by hiring people who are not necessarily feminists or socialists, and who may lack a background in participatory politics.
In many British collectives, the recruitment of new staff who
don't share the values and attitudes of former members has
often brought conflict, and sometimes crisis.

   Arguing for a politics of work as the 'why' behind collective rules, I am not saying that successful collective working
requires members who are socialists or feminists, or who
"have to share the same basic assumptions as far as politics
goes".[6] Clearly, people's politics are important in giving life
and direction to the agencies they set up or run. But even socialists and feminists can lose sight of the questions about the
nature of work relations that collective teams try to answer.
Besides, stipulating that all new members must fetch their
politics with them on arrival is unrealistic for most agencies
and, crucially, denies the values of democracy and equality
underlying collective working.

In any case, you don't need to read Marx to feel alienated, nor to find a collective workplace less alienating. Throughout this book I've argued that how work is organised and structured is inevitably a matter of ideology and politics. The opposite belief — that it can be neutral and technical — is itself an ideological stance.

One aim of a critical politics of work is to make such assumptions explicit. Just as hierarchy is neither fixed nor inevitable, the rules developed by collectives also depend on choices people have made. But knowing the rules is not the same as understanding the politics behind them. In fact, the 'answers' may no longer make sense if people stop putting the questions. The solution can't be to reinforce the rules and structures. That's like repeating things louder to someone who speaks another language.

Rules as a Template

There's another argument in favour of the primacy of formal collective rules. It would accept the need for a politics of work, but *in addition* insist on strict adherence to the 'ground rules'. This argument sees the rules and structures as a template by which collective practice is measured. Specifically, it allows us to gauge how far a group has moved away from self-management and egalitarian structures. For example, they appoint a co-ordinator who is, in practice, the boss; or they give different status and rewards for different work, perhaps contracting out the least popular work, or introducing pay differentials.[10]

This argument accepts the importance of process, both for internal democracy and in social relations. Collectives should aim for a qualitative change in how people treat each other as fellow workers. Nevertheless, this must take place within a framework of rules distinguishing what is and isn't a collective.

Some of the North American research on collectives interpreted change in this way. Groups were seen as compromising their principles by failing to stick to their original formal structures. For example, totally participatory teams developed specialisms, and gaps grew between the full time workers, and the part-timers and volunteers.[11]

This seems a powerful argument. It suggests, for example, that when a group reintroduces hierarchy, we refer to the ground rules, rather than its internal running, to decide that a shift away from democracy has taken place. However, as I'll argue in later chapters, power relations are usually more complex than this. Even groups with equal formal power can suffer from the 'heavy votes' of a few members.

Division of Labour

What if we apply the 'template' to the issue of division of labour in a work group? Is it a falling away from collective working when a team becomes more specialised or, like FSU, retains specialism? Here's a clear example of rules on job rotation, from a Canadian women's collective.[12]

> The collective decides together what jobs there are to do and how to do them. Collective members may then volunteer for different jobs. If there are some jobs remaining one member might ask another if they are willing to undertake it. Jobs may also be divided evenly and rotated weekly, monthly etc. Each member receives equally desirable and undesirable tasks. Some collectives share tasks with more than one member. This means that a specific task is undertaken by two or more members. Sharing tasks helps to reduce: isolation; initiate learning from each other.
>
> Some collectives encourage members to learn new jobs through job sharing. One method of job sharing is to have one member with the specific job experience and the other not. This allows the member without experience to learn new skills and to be able to assume more responsibility for that task at a later time. Undertaking new jobs helps to: diffuse power; share knowledge; initiate learning of new skills. All work positions in a collective are treated equally. There is no hierarchy of positions.

How far have collective teams in Britain followed such practice? An early feature of many groups was an almost arithmetical sharing out of work. The law centre where Ian Bynoe once worked, practiced 'self-servicing' — everyone doing a large part of their own typing. In addition:

> *Ian Bynoe*: They brought the provision of services into every job: meaning casework, advice work. Everyone was expected to do their round of this-that-and-the-other. I saw that as producing enormous versatility, so that any person answering the phone would be able to diagnose a lot, and provide an answer to a lot.

On the other hand, comparing Newcastle with how collectives run, it's important to say that over the past decade many British groups have developed increasing specialisms among their members. In social services, housing agencies, women's organisations, or in legal and advice centres, it's now rare to find an established collective which rotates or shares out all its work or even a major part of it. There is specialisation of all kinds. For example, advice workers may concentrate on welfare rights, housing, or immigration problems. Other agencies have hired specialist fundraisers, cleaners, administrators, typists, and ethnic minority workers.

Newcastle's own scheme wasn't based on an investigation of other collective teams. Ernie Dobson and Chris Johnson had worked in small collaborative teams elsewhere, and Chris took a special interest in co-ops and co-op training. They had links with other collectives in the city. Beyond this, the team as a whole didn't properly tap the available experience — like Ian Bynoe's knowledge. Even so, without deliberate borrowing, the model they developed was much closer to many other British collective teams than, for instance, the description written by the Vancouver women's group.

What we make of this convergence depends on how these changes are interpreted. If the ground rules are a template — then it's hardly persuasive to compare one team with a number of others that had themselves 'fallen' away from how they were supposed to run.

Did They Fall or Were They Pushed?

Does this departure from the rules amount to failure? Let's look more closely at the reasons certain aspects of 1970's collectives turned out to be temporary. One feature of groups with extensive job rotation, was that staff were often young people in their early twenties. It was frequently their first job in 'human services' and many groups were breaking new ground — developing services that had not existed in that form in Britain. It meant that workers might be learning the job as they went along.

> We were, much more than people now, real amateurs. We were the weirdest collection of people, none of whom really had any experience of that kind of work. Partly because there wasn't any way you could get experience; no one had ever done it before. So you sort of bumbled along.[13]

Many collective community projects started on a shoestring and ran with the help of volunteers. Even when they got public funding, pay often remained low, numbers of staff small, with people expected to work long hours.

As time went on, an expansion of grant aid from either central or local government brought these agencies closer to the scales paid by the 'statutory' sector. Undoubtedly, the reason why some collective teams modified job rotation was influence from outside. In many cases, management committees or funders exerted pressure against the 'inefficiency' of 'over-paying' secretaries and cleaners.[14] And aside from being pushed in this way, teams have fallen. The spurious objectivity of job evaluation has tempted many professionals back into pay differentials.[15]

Other, internal changes brought their own pressures. Originally, everyone answering the phone and cleaning the toilet may have been seen as socialist virtue; it was frequently a necessity as well. But as staff got older and had families, they weren't prepared to work the long hours when somehow everything got fitted into the working day — including clearing the rubbish and washing the tea towels.

A further change was in the growth of workers' skills and experience. Few people 'bumbled along' any more. Salaries comparable with outside agencies meant collective teams could attract more experienced and qualified staff. The result was that many teams faced a tension between the notion of workers as generalists, and the provision of different expert services to users.[16]

Nobody Enjoyed the Scutwork

How should these developments be judged? I've suggested that we need to look behind the ground rules and ask critical questions about work. Take, for example, typing and cleaning. As Ian Bynoe explained: "FSU isn't into those sorts of shibboleths which you get in the law centres, about how self-servicing is the be-all and end-all". In the early days of many collectives, rotating 'dirty' work was seen as a matter of principle. Here's a description of a law collective in Cambridge Massachusetts.[6]

> All the members of every group — lawyers, law students, paralegals — were equal in status and responsibility... To realise this equality, the group had no secretaries or receptionists: each attorney or legal worker was to do his or her own typing, copying and filing. Telephone answering and reception duties were rotated; so were the jobs of cleaning and buying supplies. Nobody enjoyed the scutwork, [servant's work] or thought it was efficient to do it that way. But all believed that hiring someone to do the firm's dirty work would be unethical — and probably also that it was a 'culturally revolutionary' act for lawyers to do the non-professional work.

FSU took a different view.

> *Ernie Dobson*: I used to think, yes, self-servicing was the way it ought to work, really. But another way of looking at that is to see [typing] as a skill which they're very good at, and which is a useful skill in the Unit. And to recognise that, rather than trying to do it.

Ernie wasn't ducking the cultural revolution, but simply asking why it required abolishing the jobs of people like Carole Tate and the secretaries, who took pride in their work and were concerned that it was well done. If we start from a *politics* of work, it becomes ironic when self-servicing and job rotation seem to imply that secretaries' and cleaners' skills are the least valuable. Why else call them *scutwork*, or *shitwork*, another term frequently used to include clerical, cleaning, or maintenance work?[17]

Owning the Collective

We ought to ask — not simply assume — whether people are
alienated from their work, their colleagues, and the agency as
a whole. For example, would someone doing filing and typing
be happier, more fulfilled, and have more dignity by taking a
share in all the other work going on? We shouldn't answer for
them. Though perhaps we might guess their view of self-servicing if it meant they were out of a job, while professionals
conscientiously rotated the 'dirty work'.[18]

What of other specialisms? Are you more estranged from
what you do every day and what your work produces, because
you do it with increasing skill? Or is it more satisfying to feel
part of a whole team,[19] and to take a share in each task as the
group requires? There isn't one simple answer, and I'm not
putting forward the modified practice of many collectives as a
new blueprint for avoiding alienation and deskilling.

But when collective teams debate their practice with each
other, and with outsiders, it's not enough to justify rotating
work by repeating, solemnly, "It's because we're a collective".
The Vancouver collective I quoted earlier, asked, 'Why operate collectively?' Their answer was:

> Because we are looking for respectful and kind ways of
> working together... Collectivity offers us more control
> over our lives, helps us to respect others' ideas and con-
> tributions and allows us to share tasks, rewards and mis-
> takes.

The challenge to collective rules and structures must always
be whether they are a means to achieve this end. For teams
change, and the world outside them changes too. In order to
face these changes, members of collective teams should be
ready to reach their own understanding of the forms they've
inherited. I don't mean they should interminably rethink the
basics. But if new members are to feel they 'own' the collective, they must be able to discuss knocking down walls and re-
building. Otherwise, once the process of adaptation ceases,
they will find themselves caretaking a monument.

In my view, collective working *can* accommodate a
diversity of complementary skills — different people making
different contributions. If I'm wrong, and it means job

rotation, self-servicing, and work groups made up of generalists who do similar jobs, it can only remain something unusual and marginal. But if I am right, then it has far wider application. It offers a possible model for all sorts of teams where the 'helping professions' are brought together in the hope that specialist skills will be blended to give a better service.

PART III

COMMON JUDGEMENT

"An incessant number of meetings about meetings". That complaint came up in Newcastle, just as it often does about collective teams elsewhere. A second linked criticism is that teams are inefficient at reaching decisions. Of course, these arguments don't stop at collectives as such. They may be used to attack any scheme for increasing worker participation as inevitably more costly in time and money — 'the cost of democracy'.

The next two chapters examine these criticisms. Do self-managing teams meet again and again? Chapter eleven queries the 'arithmetic' used to measure meeting time, and suggests we ought to look closely at who does the counting. Also, that we pay more attention to the *quality* of what goes on in meetings.

Chapter twelve then looks at 'outcomes' — whether the effort and time put in justifies the results produced. The usual question here is whether collective discussion produces better or worse decisions. But how far does the notion of *decision-making* itself assume hierarchy? I argue that a more fruitful approach is to ask about *judgement building* within a team or work group.

Eleven

Meeting

"The Core of Our System"

Looking at Newcastle's planning and managing, we find broad similarities with Family Service Units elsewhere.[1] There were weekly team meetings and — as in some Units — group supervision and discussions. Newcastle's 1984 annual report described joint management and began to suggest the difference. Team meetings were shown both as a way of fitting together the various parts of their work, and in a real sense, as the collective-in-assembly.

> The core of our system is a weekly meeting of the Unit's fieldworkers, which makes all the major management decisions, eg. what grant aid to apply for, which areas of work to develop, what sort of staff to recruit. It also makes more day to day decisions, such as drawing up rules for the use of our minibus or duplicator, making arrangements for visitors.
>
> Fieldworkers are delegated to take on responsibility for particular areas of work, such as liaison with the management committee, recruiting staff, and they report back to the group. This also means that if someone is absent or leaves, there are usually other workers who can take over without too much trouble. Workers also meet in twos and threes to plan for our work with people, how to respond to a particular family or group, how to contribute to a campaign, which work to ask a student to do etc.

I want to try and get behind the formal pattern of meetings, saying something about how FSU workers ran and thought about them. Let me explain why I'm taking this approach.

Boxes and Lines

One of the many small mysteries in writing about social services, is a lack of description of meetings — despite wide agreement on their importance. Given the conventional stress on liaison and co-ordination, this is rather curious. Of course, not all staff meet regularly. But within social services agencies generally, there is no shortage of committees, working parties, and so on.

Sometimes, the structure of these groupings is presented; one method is a chart with lines and boxes showing formal links between groups and sub-groups in a department. I haven't drawn a chart like this, because it's rarely helpful for our purpose here. To see what I mean, suppose that staff in an organisation are asked to meet together and share their knowledge and skills about an issue or set of problems.

It would be important to know some 'formal' aspects of such a group: who belonged to it; how often it met, and whether members represented interests outside. The results the group produced might be more understandable if we knew about certain 'informal' links. Were some members allies, and others not? Who caucussed beforehand?

But now switch focus to teamworking. All these pieces of information — apparently the 'hard facts' about something called a group or working party — don't actually tell us much about the central questions we want to ask. Was there much collaborative work? Were the skills and experience available within the group and outside it, pooled and used to the maximum? How could teamworking be encouraged and built upon in this setting?

Just as with the label 'team', calling a work group a committee or working party may mean nothing other than the same people coming together from time to time in the same room (and sometimes not even that). So what appears as organisational analysis — classifying a work group as a unit, or drawing a line on a chart to indicate it as one — turns out in crucial respects, to be illusory. Again, we meet the pitfalls of a technical/managerial approach to organisations.

Unfortunately, such linear ideas aren't confined to management theory. They affect people's everyday thinking about their workplace — quite often including people who work collectively. And because the model is not a set of neutral tools, but actually a system of precepts about organisations, it shifts almost without our noticing, from trying to describe what happens to *prescribing* what ought to happen.[2]

The prescription is this: if our conception of an agency and the map we've drawn don't fit the reality we see, then the *organisation,* rather than the map, is at fault. For an agency to function 'as it should', it must become more like the map. If lines of communication seem slack, they should be tightened. The pyramid of power and authority lacks clarity? Then it must be sharpened.

Applying such habits of thought, the collective team is judged and found wanting. Decision-making shared between so many people is seen as an inherent problem — it constitutes *noise* and *static* to be filtered out.[3] There can be no ambiguity over who has which tasks. The very idea of a group of *bosses* self-managing in a team meeting is anathema.

The Quality of Collective Meetings

Of course, you needn't go all the way with this model to dislike work meetings and to groan when you find your name down for yet another. This was certainly my own prejudice before beginning research with collective teams. Till then, working mostly in large hierarchies, I was cynical about meetings where people didn't meet, and committees with no commitment. With experience of a variety of self-managed teams, I am far more positive about co-operation and its potential — a personal confirmation of the findings of research on collaborative groups.[4] I've also noticed some less obvious points.

For one thing, it's not easy to convey the *quality* of relations among a group of workers meeting together. It's much harder than listing structures and membership of committees perceived as separate entities — things with a factual existence of their own. But I'd ask readers to consider how often this 'hard data' turns out to be the empty shell which 'soft' work groups leave behind as they change and grow.

Then, paying attention to the quality of people's sharing and engagement in collective teams, I've learned to think again about 'noise' and uncertainty, and the criteria for judging what makes a good meeting. In a place like FSU, 'successful' meeting is more than just making efficient decisions, or the stringency with which topics are discussed and action agreed.

Thinking Out Loud and Plain Speech

Lilian White: I still feel as though I want specific recommendations to go away and implement, you know, as from tomorrow. And I don't feel like we're getting hold of very many.

Shirley Forster: Can't we just have a brainstorm and get some ideas out instead of just having a discussion?

Lilian: We keep trying to!

Shirley: Smack anybody who interrupts.

Anne Davies: There's a bit of reluctance to say, 'We will do this', when there are much wider issues around us.

Elliot Yabantu: Do we do that, even before we've decided policy?

This rather muddly bit of conversation was recorded during a study day in 1985. It was a sample of several hours which was neither an orderly planning exercise nor an incisive debate. How does it fit the team's aim of plain speaking; the high value they placed on individuals owning and asserting their views and judgements? Well, it's important to appreciate that a requirement for this to happen is people's willingness to *think out loud*. Though sometimes when they do, it can seem muddled and messy.[5] Here's Shirley Forster's comment on the exchange above.

Shirley: I think the quote demonstrates confusion between two people who are old hands at a particular sort of problem solving they've evolved; brainstorming as equivalent to lateral thinking, to be followed by sifting and evaluation of ideas, both theoretical and practical — Lil and I: and two people who aren't working this way, and are trying their own problem solving methods — Anne and Elliot.

I think it also shows the importance of space for speculation. What you think out loud can then be unfinished and open-textured, even playful. Shirley's mention of brainstorming gives the flavour. The general idea is to encourage lateral thinking around a topic. People take risks; come out with disconnected, wild, wrong, but possibly creative ideas and suggestions. In chapter three, I quoted another meeting, when Ernie Dobson asks, "Somebody help me out", and Lilian White replies, "Yes, I'm getting into it now".

In hierarchies, brainstorming is usually presented as a *technique,* with care taken to separate it from the normal way of doing things. Permission is needed, otherwise staff won't risk losing face or looking foolish. Ernie linked this with status — especially that of male managers in hierarchical agencies.

> *Ernie*: 'Cause it involves a lot of openness and trust. And a lot of being able to say to somebody — either individually or bringing it up in a meeting — 'Look, this happened to me yesterday and I really haven't got a clue [laughing] about what I'm supposed to do'. I think it's more difficult if you're a sort of *qualified* man who's got this kind of status and image to look up to; to be seen as somebody who knows what he's doing, and an expert.
>
> My experience of working in [local authority] area team is that on the whole most men behave like that. Wouldn't dream of going to a colleague or coming to a meeting: 'I don't know what to do'. People go, 'Ah. Hmm. He doesn't know what he's doing. He won't get to be a senior, you know'. If you are a senior — and that's one thing about hierarchies — if you're in the hierarchy you've got to pretend that you know what you're talking about all the time.[6]

Writers on management[7] and politics[8] have explored the problems involved in 'speaking truth to power' — especially passing bad news upwards. Who wants to tell the President what he'd rather not hear? Ernie's example is the other side of that coin — the need for someone in authority to appear fallible and show weakness to subordinates. The implication is that a group of peers can avoid this sort of inhibition. At the simplest level, it meant that discussions at FSU could be interrupted by requests for basic information that other staff had assumed was common knowledge.[9]

I'm not saying we ought to value meetings solely for rough, half-baked ideas, or participants' confessions of confusion or ignorance. As Lilian said, there has to be action; a conclusion. People's learning, talking-out the issues, reflection and disagreement must eventually become focussed, shaped and definite. But this is not the same as getting smoothly through the 'business'.

Lilian illustrated how a smooth running meeting may show the very opposite of plain speaking. In 1984 and '85, she represented Newcastle at the quarterly meetings of the Unit Organisers. That group faced the problem of many UOs not attending. Others left before the end, while important decisions remained to be made.

> *Lilian White*: The way I explained it was that my attendance was there as a commitment by both staff and management committee to the national organisation. That, in fact, the choices had been taken away from me. I couldn't choose to stay [in Newcastle] and work on something else. I'd been allocated the task of going to the UO's conference.

The UOs opted to pass the problem 'upwards' to National Council. At the same time, observed Lilian, "they didn't actually challenge the UOs that were leaving early". They chose, in effect, to export disagreement and conflict somewhere else.[10] This isn't to say that UOs meetings were otherwise plain sailing and that conflict was never brought to the surface.

How far was conflict avoided in Unit meetings? There was little open dispute in those I attended. Although this wasn't how people remembered past meetings, for instance, about Lin Harwood's work. Staff stressed that there *were* disagreements, though few emotional outbursts. Ali Rhind felt there wasn't always plain speaking. At a study day in 1983, she'd brought up her worries about work.

> *Ali*: I was feeling pretty desperate. And I would have actually liked to leave. I eventually screwed up all my courage (with support from Sally and Pam) to say to everybody else how I felt. I felt very unconfident; I

didn't feel I was doing a very good job. I think I was
quite clear about it. It felt a very daring thing to do.
     And everybody said, 'Oh, we all feel like that too!'
And I felt completely deflated, put down, unrecognised.

The point here is not who was right or wrong,[11] but whether a
particular forum enables disputes and crises to be raised and
discussed. Though the issues in each example were much
wider than meetings as such, this is where they should become
visible.

Better Meetings?

Newcastle workers sometimes complained about meetings.
Broadly, though, they took them as a serious part of the work,
not an extra chore or a diversion. Only the secretaries (who
didn't go) made comments implying that meetings were a
waste of time.
     When Unit staff met, my impression was of people engag-
ing with each other in an open and creative way; listening and
sharing. Workers wondered how I'd transcribe tapes of some
of their discussions, with people interrupting and talking over
each other. But there was virtually no problem. Interruptions
were rare; there were often silences between contributions,
and an evident willingness to let people finish their say. I don't
overestimate the significance of this; people recalled earlier
years.

> *Ernie Dobson*: A really powerful group of experienced
> people who'd been here some time — we kind of com-
> peted with each other at meetings. To get your word in,
> basically. And that's changed.

At different times, reviews of the meeting process had been
put on the agenda, but this was apt to be dropped. The format
of meetings was changed too.

> *Shirley Forster*: It was done to focus discussion on the
> meat, and avoid the trivia of minutes and
> correspondence into which we were all willing to be
> sidetracked.

Ernie thought there was an inevitable compromise between getting through the business, and making space. "We do have a form of meeting where you don't actually have to agenda everything". He remembered when it had been: "much more formal. And there was a much higher level of dissatisfaction than we've got at the moment". [July 1985]

The person chairing changed every six months. Being chair and taking minutes were both regarded as important and learnable skills, (and were included in the programme for students). Some of the techniques for meetings adopted by groups elsewhere have been aimed at making sure people who are less confident and assertive get a chance to speak. [12] Newcastle workers were generally aware how their more confident members often said the most, and on occasions some of the longstayers held back.

> *Pam Carter*: Several times today I've been really wanting to say something, and thought, 'God, I've said an awful lot. I'm leaving and I've said far more than lots of other people'.

It seemed to me there was one clear weakness. The Unit had barely begun to explore the wide range of published material about the nuts and bolts of setting up and running collaborative meetings — some of the best directly from the experiences of collectives. [13] As a result, they sometimes made simple mistakes. For example, they might plan a succession of different meetings, with no change in rhythm programmed in. I asked why they didn't use the Elswick swimming pool right next door (for which the Unit had helped campaign) as a break between meetings.

> *Anne Davies*: I actually do that sometimes. I just find it impossible to go from one meeting to another, because I'm not concentrating. But it often happens here that we happen to have meetings on the same days.

> *Ernie Dobson:* I seem to do that quite often with students. Not going for a dip in the pool but, if it's not something that we're tied to the Unit for, we'll go into the pub. Break up the routine.

Anne: You do that ever so well with your race awareness training. 'Cause you change the method of working
regularly throughout the day. You don't do any one
thing for long.

★

After they'd left the Unit, both Pam Carter and Shirley
Forster wrote querying the comments above.

Pam: You say we didn't try making the meeting
process an explicit part of business. This is interesting
because I've been carrying round in my head the idea
that *we did*. So I've been thinking about how this
difference in perception has arisen. One point is that
we thought more about 'process' in Family Discussion
Group than in Unit meetings.

We did try to do things like have a 'meeting
review' slot in Unit meeting — discussing how it had
gone. But somehow it didn't work very well. I feel there
may have been some reluctance to talk about 'process'
any more than we did because it sounded a bit 'social
worky' and was vaguely associated with T-groups and
things like that. So process was talked about in terms
of changing structures/agendas etc.

At times when we had 'big' difficult discussions we
asked someone to plan a structure so that everyone
had their say. Perhaps we discussed process 'just
enough' — that is, sometimes from our experience,
such discussions arise because things are going badly.
otherwise they seem empty.

Shirley: We did spend more time evaluating how to
meet — good structures, how to become skilled at
using meetings — than you imply here... Agenda-ing
reviews of the meeting process at different times
worked for a period. Then didn't — got dropped —
came up later on.

Didn't you say something about collectives always
need to reinvent the wheel? Well, they do — 'cos the
process of arriving at collective working is important.

You can't just follow a recipe — or put it on like a new dress.

When Group Process is Closed

Pam and Shirley were debating 'How' and 'How often' the team reviewed its process. For many readers these questions will be beside the point. At FSU, at least they accepted the need. When staff were disgruntled with meetings they could go over what was happening; revamp the rules, experiment, and try again. But what about a workplace where that isn't true? What if the very idea of such an overview meets incomprehension or opposition?

This situation has been described in writing on all kinds of groups, but particularly in commercial companies. Staff are caught in a double bind. They'd like to break out from what they rightly see as inhibiting working relations which stifle open discussion. But how can they initiate such change when the climate itself prevents criticism being put on the agenda and openly debated?[14] In many public services as well, the openness required for team building will be undermined by closed unselfcritical meetings. It's a chicken and egg problem: to change poor meetings, you first need a 'good' meeting to discuss what's wrong and should be changed.[15]

I hinted at the outcome before. 'Business' moves along briskly and smoothly. Most people take no risks, say little, and regularly come away frustrated. They know how anyone complaining can easily find themselves cast as the cause of the problem. Naturally, the smoother the surface, the harder for somebody to raise anything which causes ripples, let alone that makes waves.

A sign of what's happening in the depths is when a minor item on the tail end of an agenda turns into a major argument. Who isn't taking their turn washing the cups? Energy and anger erupt at this point because it's so much safer.[16] One irony is that such mock battles confirm everyone's prejudices. Staff cynical about meetings get irritated listening to storms over tea cups.[17] Bosses who don't expect staff to offer anything helpful on major issues, repeatedly see time and effort taken up with trivia. And the people who really wanted to talk about the washing-up? They aren't happy, because they sense their small item has been hijacked.

Breaking the Circle?

Recognising this closed process can be a first step away from
reinforcing it. A possible second step is to begin questioning
many of the rules about meetings which are thought of as giv-
en and neutral. These traditional 'rules of order' — committee
procedure, rules of debate — are heavily criticised in practical
writing about collectives. They are viewed as ineffective and
alienating, with alternative collective rules put forward. The
argument is an important one and worth taking a little further.

> Some people thought I was joking when I mentioned
> committee procedure as part of our cultural heritage, but
> the joke is on them, if they are serious about democracy,
> for these are the means of its working.[18]

This quotation, from Raymond Williams, illustrates how we
are used to thinking of committee procedure and the rules of
debate as a means of ensuring fairness. Giving people turns to
speak, having them speak 'through the chair', and so on, is
supposed to control abuse of power. But this ignores the use
of traditional committee procedures as a way of *disabling* participation.

> *Ernie Dobson*: At the Union meeting, the national
> working party, what happens is that you come to this
> item on the agenda. You've waited for two hours of this
> boring stuff. And then people are allowed some time to
> state their position. Then you take a vote. You don't
> discuss anything. There's a series of people stating
> their positions. To be 'fair' of course, people can only
> talk once.
>   And nobody's happy with it. There's nothing
> positive about it at all.

I'm not arguing that groups should simply abandon traditional
rules and adopt new ones. The choice is not between 'our cultural heritage' and a new blueprint. But, using the framework
suggested earlier, we ought to ask whether particular procedures are rules of *deference or reference*. For traditional rules
aren't always a neutral framework for ensuring fair play. All
too often they turn out to be rules of deference, serving to en-

dorse and strengthen existing (unequal) power relations.[19]Anyone really serious about democracy will make the whole issue of rules and procedures at meetings open to question and experiment.

Informal Rules and Informal Meetings

Some of Newcastle's rules of reference weren't written down, or even told expressly to new staff. They were part of the normal way the group did things — conventions that established staff took for granted. One convention was that Unit workers expected to 'grab' each other for time to discuss something. Someone would say, 'Can I book some time with you?'

So, first thing in the morning, Lilian would be talking to a student about work with a particular family. A little later Elliot and Parveen could be found discussing the latest developments in the City's plans for ethnic minority posts. Over the day people's time interweaved, as they consulted, questioned, planned and checked-out parts of the work. Because this was an unwritten rule it could cause problems.

> *Parveen Akhtar*: There was a period when I wasn't
> approaching people. And yes, it partly had something
> to do with collective working as well. I just didn't see
> one person I could turn to. It always meant exploring
> avenues; who do you go to? And getting people
> together. Sometimes it's a lot easier if you have
> concerns — I do think, before bringing it to a big group
> discussion — to have, sort of, reassurances or be able'
> to talk about things to a person. Pam used to sit next
> to me and I've often spoken to her about things before
> taking them either to the Unit meeting or elsewhere.

On the other hand, 'grabbing' someone didn't mean a free for all. So, at one stage outsiders were told that someone 'was in a meeting' as a way of filtering calls.

> *Pam Flynn*: Now that has stopped, because I
> complained quite vehemently. And it was simply a
> matter of parlance, apparently. If people were talking
> like you and I are, it was deemed to be a 'meeting' and
> it wasn't to be interrupted by a phonecall.

But Pam was right in thinking workers were reluctant to be interrupted. The obligation to attend a meeting as an active listener and contributor had, as its complement, the expectation that people would not double book, nor come with their minds elsewhere, or followed in by a stream of phone calls. To put this more exactly, an agreement to meet implies agreement *not to do other things*. This was how Lilian White saw the obligation of any Unit to make space for a worker — herself included — expected to attend UOs' meetings.

> *Lilian*: If any other Unit couldn't carry out that responsibility it should've been referred back locally to the management committee to try to help them [UO] make space to go to the meetings.

Conversely, clearer boundaries need setting, between meeting and not-meeting. (Despite Pam Flynn's comment!) 'Can we arrange to talk?' implies *not* raising a topic piecemeal, but putting aside time for a full discussion. So short informal chats ended with, 'Well, maybe that ought to come up at Groupwork Discussion Group'.

The idea then, is that time for supervision, meeting, and so on, were agreements to *hold over and postpone* talk and discussion. As we'll see, this feature — setting aside a time to meet — is especially important as we come to the question of whether collective teams have too many meetings.

We'll Meet Again and Again?

> *Margaret Chiles*: There seem to be an incessant number of meetings about meetings. And it's quite difficult to actually — you phone up and, 'They are in a meeting'. That was the feeling quite a few people have got. They seem to have so many meetings about whether they're gonna have meetings. I mean, that might have changed, because that was months ago, you know.

It isn't just Newcastle. Conventional wisdom is that collective working entails many more meetings. Members of collective teams themselves get defensive about the time taken by self-management. And it's often one of the first things outsiders raise, sometimes with the caricature of a group where every-thing must be discussed with everybody.

This view is repeated by writers on collectives.[20] Here's a comment from Joyce Rothschild, author of detailed case-study and theoretical research on collectives in California, and someone broadly sympathetic to them.[21]

> Democracy takes time. This is one of its major social costs. Two-way communication structures may produce higher morale, the consideration of more innovative ide-as, and more adaptive solutions to complex problems, but they are undeniably slow. Quite simply a boss can hand down a bureaucratic order in a fraction of the time it would take a group to decide the issue democratically.

As a research finding, this seems pretty clear. But is it a find-ing? If we look closely at Joyce Rothschild's argument, a num-ber of questions emerge.

To begin with, it's hard to see why she chose to compare a collective discussion with an instruction handed down by one boss. Three of the five agencies she researched were in the 'human services' — a medical clinic, a free school, and a legal collective. Each of them, in its corresponding non-collective form, is usually a complicated hierarchy rather than a single boss. Partners in a law firm, and staff in clinics and schools have complex problems of co-ordination and liaison. Nor was her choice of agency unusual. Other research in the Unit-ed States suggests that education, law, social welfare and med-icine were very strongly represented among alternative organisations adopting collective working.[22]

Of course, some organisations do adopt or attempt man-agement by instruction. "I'm the head, and you don't make any decision without you come and check it out with me", was how Joan Smith characterised this kind of management. But it rarely works out as planned. It's true that the classical theo-rists of bureaucracy suggested this was how it *ought* to func-tion.[23] However, writing about the psychology, sociology and organisation of work has been centrally concerned with why subordinates don't always follow instructions. Some writers even argue that this is the reason why schools of management and industrial psychology receive a large slice of their funds — to aid industry and government overcome the problem.[24]

So, Joyce Rothschild is comparing collective working with an *idealised* stereotype of how hierarchies are supposed to function. And when you take as your baseline, a boss who knows the answers and issues instructions, it's quite easy to think of collective teams as longwinded and uncertain. Here's one of the students on placement at Newcastle FSU.

> The type of democratic management system they're implementing in this Unit, I found it difficult to come to terms with it. I mean, I like the idea of it. It sounds very good. But putting it into practice is an entirely different matter. Because at times I have looked for a line manager — someone who would be there in a supervisory position; where I could go to them. It would be their job to sort out this problem, thank you.

Other students challenged her. They'd been in social service teams on Friday afternoons, when the senior and district officer were never around. She replied by offering a conventional hierarchical model.

> But then you could go one up again, couldn't you? You know, in a hierarchical system you can always go one up.

Sometimes this tendency to idealise hierarchical decision-making is shared by members of collective teams — usually people who've never worked in a hierarchy. A feature of the Newcastle staff was that everyone had previous experience of the messy realities of social services, other public agencies, or large commercial companies. "In social services," said Shirley Forster, "my boss was on the phone half the supervision session". Elliot Yabantu mentioned a job in South Africa. "The people who really do the work are — for example in administration — the clerks and people like that who write letters and interview Township residents. And really the white official is simply there to sign. Because your black signature doesn't count."

Returning to Joyce Rothschild's comparison, we find a further oddity. Her example of collective decision-making implies a second stereotype — that everyone does everything, and spends forever discussing it. But this had actually ceased to be a feature of the groups she researched. During their very early stages, some *had* spent an inordinate amount of time in meetings. An alternative newspaper, for example, took three days a week! But, as Rothschild herself pointed out:

> Very little time remained to do the tasks of the organisation. Members quickly learn that this is unworkable. Meetings are streamlined. Tasks are given a higher priority.

The newspaper reduced meeting time to around four hours a week. Staff in a free clinic met weekly for an average of seventy-five minutes, with decisions delegated to individuals outside the meeting. Such streamlining is characteristic of very many collective teams.

I've already suggested that most of the British groups formed during the 1970's passed through a stage of working very long hours with correspondingly long meetings. It's part of a three stage pattern which we'll recognise. Following the removal of hierarchy, (or perhaps the rejection of one or two "sometimes charismatic figures"[25]) there's a second phase of direct democracy. This usually takes the form of discussion and decisions made in full assembly. In the third stage, power is delegated, perhaps with some form of representation.[26]

Newcastle's experience confirms the expectation that time spent on meetings increases when collective working is launched, and then falls noticeably. This is what the most critical members of the management committee had experienced, and it matched the workers' own perceptions. Lin Harwood, who left around the time joint staff management was underway, was scathing about the time taken.

> *Lin*: Oh my God, it was terrible. That was one of the things. You literally were in meetings half the week. It got so that if you didn't do it in a group, it wasn't legitimate. It wasn't legitimate unless it was done by everyone. And we were all trapped in that.

Two years later, the weekly staff meeting was down to ninety minutes (well... stretching sometimes to two hours), with other meetings shorter. For any team, whether there are more or fewer meetings also depends on events outside. During my contact with Newcastle, crises about funding and on casework required extra staff meetings and urgent talks with management committee members. The numbers and kinds of meetings are also affected by those other phases people mentioned — the cycle when there's a period of introspection and discussion, followed by a time when fresh energy is redirected outside.

Visible and Invisible Meetings

So far, I've suggested two broad points about a comparison of meetings. First, we should avoid stereotyping collective and hierarchical workgroups and compare, instead, what actually happens in them. (This, incidentally, seems an exercise that has never been done.) Second, we should pay careful attention to each group's stage of development. However, our problems would still not be over. There's more to it than, for instance, taking a group like the free clinic or the alternative newspaper, and arguing that seventy-five minutes or four hours a week isn't so bad.

For members of collective teams are managers, as well as workers. So, comparing Newcastle with a hierarchical team offering direct public service, we'd need to 'add up' meeting time, not just for people on the same grades, but for all staff who do some of the management work. (The 'costs of democracy' might be calculated, as well, with comparative hourly wage rates in mind.)

This leads on to what might be called the 'visibility' of meetings. In a hierarchical agency, it's hardly remarkable when managers attend meetings; they are doing part of their ordinary jobs. But when direct service workers meet, remarks are likely, since services to users are interrupted.

Not all meetings are this visible. Any workplace may have a range of informal contacts. Research confirms the commonsense view of the value and importance of such "informal interpersonal relations between peers".[27] As Bishop Auckland FSU found:

> There is an equally important use of time in informal situations during coffee breaks, lunchtimes and generally around the office, where ideas can get their first airing;

interest can be shown in what other people are doing and information can be shared.[28]

Earlier, I described Newcastle workers agreeing *not* to discuss something informally. Obviously workers in collective teams do chat with each other. It wouldn't make sense for people involved together in a piece of work to bring all the detail to, say, the team meeting. But, Newcastle's convention was for staff to postpone and reserve discussion for meetings that were formally programmed. This might mean paired supervision, or one of the Unit meetings. In Pam Carter's words, "It had all been, paradoxically, much more formalised in the Unit".

Now, let's go back to Lin's point about 'legitimacy'. The question she implied was actually: when is a meeting not a meeting? In a hierarchical team a meeting is legitimate because it's authorised by staff of a particular status. It probably begins when they turn up and ends when they leave. As a result, the caucus beforehand, or the 'quiet word' afterwards, is easily overlooked; all the more so when a major reason for getting together outside the *official* time, is so that people can talk privately.

Now clearly, this has implications if we're asking whether a collective team has *more* meetings. Leaving discussion to the scheduled hour may not decrease time spent, but it sure makes it more obvious — and recordable. In another group, time may be largely hidden, or at least not considered part of legitimate meetings.

The problem is not simply technical, since it involves issues of power. Hierarchical managements may be unwilling to recognise informal meetings as a legitimate part of the job, because it cuts down their control. Workers may feel the same way — preferring to keep to themselves the time they "liberate" from the employer for their own or the Union's business.[29] One reason why research into social services teams has rarely explored informal meetings, may be a reluctance by staff at all levels to be candid about how much coffee drinking and chatting is actually 'work'.

Conclusion

Where does this bring us? Does self-management take up
more time? No serious examination of co-operative or collective working would suggest that a commitment to participation of all members in an agency is going to be short and simple — especially if workers' previous experience is of traditional decision-making.

Beyond that, I can offer a speculation; a guess based on
the groups I've researched with. What is presented as a truism
— that participation takes a lot longer — may hold true only
in the short run, while the habit of democracy is being established. Once established, and purely on a quantitive basis,
collective teams are probably no quicker and no slower.
There may well be a 'Law of Conservation of Meetings'.

Certainly, we should not observe sagely that, "the demands of democracy can conflict with getting the work
done", [30] as if the demands of hierarchy never did. Or as if it
was always obvious when work stops and talk begins.

Twelve

Building Judgement

People may judge collective working as slow, yet balance their assessment with a further argument. Speed, they say, isn't everything. In fact, there are some circumstances where careful, thoughtful discussion is a positive advantage. So, in the last chapter, we had Joyce Rothschild's suggestion that a collective team may produce "consideration of more innovative ideas, and more adaptive solutions to complex problems".[1]

At FSU, Lin Harwood's comments matched this interpretation. Lin was not impressed by the daily business of collective management — "You couldn't buy a toilet roll without having a meeting". But at the same time, she was very positive about casework discussions.

> *Lin*: I think the families and the people we were working with — the kids or whatever — got a really good deal out of that. Because we would all sit down, and someone would say, 'I feel particularly stuck with Mrs So-and-So. There's this, this and this'. Within about ten minutes people would have had fifteen ideas about how to tackle it. I thought that was brilliant.

The underlying idea is that different types of decision-making suit different kinds of problems - a sort of, 'horses for courses'. Collective teams show their strength when faced with complex, longer-term problems which require time for discussion and reflection. Conversely, we can expect hierarchies to have the edge when it comes to sorting out this afternoon's problem with an authoritative rapid decision.

The Long and the Short and the Simple

However, this apparently straightforward comparison begins to go awry as soon as we look closely at particular examples.

Take Lin Harwood's comments about casework. Supposing another agency refers a family. Won't that agency (and the family themselves) already have its own ideas of what needs doing? Recall too, the student who expected supervisors to: "sort out this problem, thank you." In either case, fifteen new ideas from next week's meeting may not seem quite so brilliant. In particular, time taken with users and colleagues to *redefine* a problem can be seen as simply inefficient.

A further difficulty arises in evaluating the action taken. Who defines success? Workers? Funders? Or even users? In its services for Asian users, FSU aimed to "make a molehill out of a mountain". Perhaps some outsiders would have seen things the other way round.

Another question is deciding which are short-term and which long-term goals. Again, taking family work as an example, one reason for planning and review is precisely to avoid a series of temporary 'solutions'. The same applies to apparently commonsense short-term tasks. So yes, it would be daft (and uncomfortable) if FSU had no toilet paper one morning, because nobody was authorised to pop up to the corner shop in advance of the team meeting. But it would also be absurd if there was never time on the agenda to agree bulk buying supplies.

Delegating Responsibility

I realise all this could read like an excuse for unnecessary delay in a team's work, with meetings clogged up by petty decisions. This isn't my intention. In any case, how true is such a picture? In the last chapter, I criticised some of the writing about collectives for basing its conclusions on quite early stages in groups' development. This has contributed to a stereotype of collective working, not just as a roundabout of endless discussion, but with nobody willing to get off and accept responsibility for a decision.

However, collective teams aren't static. Newcastle, in common with many other agencies, had developed extensive delegation to individual workers and sub-groups. Day to day, and week-by-week, staff had discretion in their jobs. There had been delegation while Joan Smith was still the Unit Organiser, though it's worth remembering how differently workers had felt while "the buck doesn't stop with you".

When authority comes from the staff group, people are expected to take a good deal of personal responsibility — and to report back.

> *Lilian*: I speak at the [UO's] meetings. Well, most of them. If I've got anything to say or contribute, or if there's anything the staff group want brought forward. I'm very careful about views that I'm expressing that are mine, and I keep them separate from a staff group response.

Given that people at FSU could act on their own to a wide extent, did they? Or was there a tendency to push things back; unloading responsibility onto the group? The only pointers in this direction related to money. Ian Bynoe saw one of his functions on the management committee as ensuring that resources, "are not handed over to a bunch of dishonest cowboys".

> *Ian*: I'm on the Finance Sub-Committee, and I'm often surprised at the small amount of the expenditure we're expected to approve. Which in many voluntary organisations, I wouldn't have thought management committees are involved in approving. It's a bind, but it shows a good philosophy. Nobody's on the make in that place at all.

Ian's comment implies a wider point: what one person sees as dithering indecisiveness, someone else regards as a proper safeguard. Putting it another way, action taken invariably has a political and professional dimension as well as an organisational one. Spending actual cash (especially 'public money') is always a good example of this. As Ernie Dobson pointed out, an agency's misuse of money could make the local paper, but:

> *Ernie*: I don't see a headline in the Chronicle saying: FSU MISUSES COMMUNITY WORKER'S TIME!

Where does this take us? I've tried to examine the questions and criteria which are used when collective and hierarchical decision-making is compared. The fact that they aren't much help, doesn't avoid a a judgement being made. On the contrary, it suggests that we probably need different questions and a different framework for asking them. One more example will show what I mean, and suggest a possible way forward.

Ambiguity, Uncertainty and Imperfection

One theme running through this discussion is the notion of *decisiveness*. There's the criticism, implied or explicit, that collective working suffers from indecision; with people shelving responsibility and avoiding tough choices. This is set against a contrasting image: the decisive, or even *incisive*, hierarchical manager, who cuts acutely through the tangle of information and discussion, to issue necessary decisions.

Given that not every boss succeeds in handing down rapid bureaucratic orders, even so, isn't this how hierarchy is supposed to work; something built into it?[2] That picture is confirmed in countless books about the qualities needed for successful managers; with descriptions of decisiveness, creativity, and personal charisma.

However, I want to mention one, perhaps surprising study. It doesn't so much contradict this literature, as ask whether it may be specific to our particular culture and its ways of thinking and behaving.

In the 1970s a number of writers on business were intrigued by the commercial success of Japan and the increasing involvement of Japanese companies in the West. They examined what seemed the very different basis of Japanese management practice.

Richard Pascale and Anthony Athos compared businesses in Japan and the United States.[3] They suggested that the latter often had "an energetic kinetic image",[4] with a belief that good managers move from facts to options to decisions — "bam, bam, bam". Japanese companies had a quite different ethos. Their managers rarely made rapid decisions, thereby closing off other options. Instead, the companies preferred people who were able to welcome ambiguity, uncertainty and imperfection. In a Japanese company, day by day decision-making was less about finality and control than, "accommodation to a continuously unfolding set of events".[5]

What happens, then, if there is a need for major changes and shifts in policy? Here, Pascale and Athos stress several aspects which find echoes in collective teams. Japanese managers are encouraged to be far more reflective. When decisions are to be taken, the company will invest considerable time in sounding out workers at every level, exploring the various options, and building support for the changes finally agreed.[6]

Let me stress that Pascale and Athos aren't proposing a 'better' Japanese model, waiting to be taken off-the-peg. On the contrary, the heart of their book is not about applying Japanese methods, but what we can learn about our own.[7] When they compared Japanese ways of thinking with the *practice* of firms in the United States, they frequently found it much closer to the Japanese model. Despite the bam-bam-bam rhetoric, many American managers were valued for juggling decisions, rather than just making them.

> Juggling captures the dilemma nicely; any effort to grasp two pins results in the remaining pins falling to the floor. Many managers, schooled in the supposed virtues of being firm, explicit and decisive, spend their entire careers clutching for some pins.[8]

It becomes crystal clear that our ideas about organisations and ways of behaving in them, are neither commonsense and obvious, nor neutral and scientific. They are the customs of our culture.

A Letter to Shirley Forster

After Shirley left FSU she continued to see chunks of draft, and sent me long critical letters. What follows is a shortened version of one of my replies. Earlier, I mentioned her views on the study day. I wrote trying to explain what I was getting at; how there are different ways of thinking about decision-making.

Dear Shirley,

I was really pleased to get your letter. Your comments will be taken to heart. (ie. incorporated!) I want to try something out on you.

Bear with me for a bit if this seems to wander off the point.

When I'm writing about the Unit, I'm thinking about how it might contribute to a wider sort of discussion — among students, and staff in different agencies, as well as in FSU. Now there are conventions about how you're supposed to write something as a book. Usually it's meant to be polished, finished, close-textured. People don't expect to be able, or be invited, to respond to a 'text' book.

But, say I wrote something rougher and unfinished (not really a 'proper' book). Would readers feel they'd been cheated? Wasted their money? Or that I don't really know my business?

The point is that some things I have to say are tentative. And even when they are much more worked out and complete, I don't want to bang people over the head with FSU or my ideas on it. I want to put things in a way that respects readers' own views and experience. But I want to get across the idea that there just might be an alternative view or explanation around. Or even provide a guess about what happens that might go against their expectations.

So, I'm trying to imagine a sort of discussion with a reader which could be like your description of the discussion at the study day. You talked about lateral thinking and brainstorming between you and Lilian. To me, that didn't catch the complexity of what was going on. I thought of it as judgement building. Because, what seems to happen in Unit meetings is that the group building its judgement is just as important as decision-making.

Trying to understand this, I've begun to see there's an ideology of decision-making. What kind of ideology? Try this description against your own experience.

The term 'decision-making' is used in two main ways. Either it's used to mean one separate stage — like somebody saying, 'We must stop talking about this, and move to a decision'. Or it describes the whole process of discussion and action to get things done. The second usage would be a question about 'the Unit's decision-making', covering everything from why something got discussed, to how it was agreed and implemented.

Either way, what's usually implied is hierarchy. Higher and lower status people are assumed to take different parts in the process. For example, we could think of change needing a whole sequence of stages — initiation, search for solutions, discussion, and decision. Then decision-time becomes the big one; the important bit which actually matters, when someone has to say 'yes' or 'no'.

And that someone, of course, is the big person. Do important people make big decisions? No, important decisions make big people.

Calling the whole process decision-making isn't much better. All prior stages are now steps leading up to the decision, which is still the peak or culmination of the process. Steps afterwards are seen as leading down and away from it — something left to the underlings who implement what has been decided up above.

So we all 'know' that 97 people can't make a decision. Only what this means is that 97 important people can't intervene at the one most important point in the decision-making process. The whole thing then gets muddled up with status and power: who has the power to decide; who's getting paid for taking all that responsibility; and who's going to carry the can?

When hierarchical groups use brainstorming, this is one way they try to escape the effect of everything revolving round decision-making. But what the Unit seems to have is something more than that. There's a lot of listening, a willingness to pull each other along. People think it's as important to get other people to understand the issues, as to get the meeting to decide on a concrete plan, product, or result.

There must be results and concrete plans, of course. But in a funny way these are the implementations of people's judgements. Do you see what I mean? It's as if the goal is to arrive at a group judgement on something. Once that happens, decisions to take certain action, or not to do something, are almost the formal part of the business that needs sorting out at the end.

I'm not saying your meetings and discussions have decisions that, sort of, emerge from them as an afterthought. But there is an atmosphere where people can be half-baked, tentative, a bit rough, unsure. And what this does is foster and build and consolidate the judgements that people are making and gaining.

Judgement Building

I mentioned my own change of mind about what happens at meetings in a collective team like FSU. Listening and watching, what I saw and heard failed to fit the ideas I'd brought with me. The writing about meetings and decision-making seemed hardly more helpful.

One reason the wrong questions get asked is because, invariably, the starting point is: decisions. How do they arrive at them, and how effective are they at making them? These ques-

tions contain a way of seeing group process as a journey towards something. The route might be interesting, but the ter-
minus is decision-making. Implementation is what we do after we get there. I've fallen into the same trap myself — as
have people with greater experience of collective work.[9]

Despite using the wrong questions, I often got answers to
many of the right ones. Asking Lilian White about decisions
at Unit meetings, her reply went beyond that, to whether they
were a forum which enabled her to understand and absorb
the issues, and to contribute.

> *Lilian*: 'Cause when I first started at the Unit I was
> very underconfident, very unsure of myself. And I
> spent a lot of time always with quite a few things going
> over me head. If I'd had a very strong objection to
> something, I would have said. But otherwise I didn't. I
> held back quite a lot.
>   I'm much more actively involved in discussion
> now. Whereas I tended to be, sort of, quiet, passive I
> think, before. It's hard to describe. I think what I feel
> now is people are much more responsive because I'm
> giving a lot more.

One problem mentioned earlier is the difficulty in describing
the quality of people's meeting. Somehow the right words
don't seem to be there, and the words we use carry the weight
of the old cultural values; they can easily sound muddly and
indecisive. I'm suggesting a tension here; that collective discussion and debate needs to break free of the gravitational
field of 'decisions'.

I've tended to speak of *dialogue*, and *forum*. The latter fits
well, as it still carries some of its original meaning of a place
for public discussion, where people meet face-to-face, to listen, discuss, and appraise issues. Newcastle workers used other words quite often — *sharing* and *reflecting*, for instance.

> *Elliot Yabantu*: We have as a staff group decided that
> there's going to be time for reflection on individual
> workers' work. Though in a sense there is that already
> going on, like at Family Discussion Group. That is,
> apart from the general reflection on the direction
> which the work is taking.

I hope that quotations taken from interviews and meetings, give some flavour and feel of a team whose members expected ideas and information to be sifted, and views to change. It n.ay be that the Unit was in a particularly calm and even period. Though workers were sometimes passionate and often committed to the principles underlying a discussion, their exchanges remained open, and were frequently tentative.

Building On

The framework I've sketched links with wider issues discussed later. There's the question of how people *learn* in groups, since another way of talking about judgement building would be to ask what it is that a group knows and how it puts together this knowledge. So too, the ideas here can throw light on issues of *power* and *equality*. Commitment to a democratic work group as a forum, with informed and participating members, has sometimes been seen as one of the more 'utopian' (in the sense of unrealistic) of the co-operative ideals.[10]

To sum up, there is a need for an understanding that breaks loose from traditional ideas about structures of meetings, and rules of procedure; and from a hierarchical view of group process which places the decision at its apex. An alternative viewpoint is essential for collective and co-operative teams, as well as collaborative teams within a wide range of hierarchical agencies. And it doesn't stop there. Without an alternative framework it is extremely easy to misunderstand or even undermine many self-help, neighbourhood or 'community' groups.[11]

> *Ernie*: It's interesting, the parallel with [Elswick] Festival meetings and the Festival itself. I always find it quite amusing how frustrating and difficult some of the full-time youth and community workers (people who work in centres and things) find it to cope with the Festival. They come along to meetings and they just cannot cope with them. And they walk in and say, 'Well, you can understand why I never come to these meetings'. When it comes to the Festival, at the end it's always a bit of panic, and some things go wrong. And there's always [professional workers around, wanting

to organise it and get it tighter and planned; deciding in November what we're gonna do in July. That's the way they operate.

And they find it really difficult to relate to a group of people who turn up, and do actually get through what they want to talk about. And who will discuss it again maybe two or three times. But they get to where they want to be. By and large they do without an agenda. But they do it and it works.

PART IV

COMMON WEALTH

The two chapters in Part IV are about very different topics. Let me explain why they are paired.

Chapter thirteen follows on from the discussion of judgment building to look at co-learning and knowledge. What's different about learning together in a collective team? Chapter fourteen then explores how such teams tackle the organisation and use of their own workspace. One feature of Newcastle FSU's development was the reorganisation of the Unit's building to enable this 'resource' to be differently shared among staff and users.

The link made here is between two kinds of 'assets', usually treated as belonging to the agency. In other words, the normal way of thinking about these issues would be to see FSU as the *owner*, hiring the experience and skills of 'its' staff, and renting or owning the actual physical facilities offered to workers and users.

The idea that 'wealth' is what buys labour and plant, is deeply ingrained in our culture. The reverse - that *labour* should hire *capital* — is a fundamental co-operative principle. But what does that mean in the context of a team like FSU? How can we talk about the agency's building as common wealth? It can't mean that workers owned the Unit in a literal sense — in the way that a co-operative legally belongs to its members.[1]

And what of common learning? People's individual skills and qualifications may count as their 'wealth', but why extend this to talk about what a team learns together? How can workers actually 'own' anything more than they can take away with them and sell elsewhere? My suggestion in these two chapters is that, even without a formal legal co-operative framework, there is still the possibility of *our* knowledge and space — and not simply the opposition of *theirs* and *mine*.

Thirteen

Learning and Knowing

When the 'business' of meetings is seen as decision-making, then time and effort for increased participation are treated as 'costs of democracy'. One implication is that an informed work group is a *liability*. Not surprisingly, this is how wages and salaries are viewed by the business convention which counts people as 'labour costs', to be kept as low as possible.[2]

I've argued an alternative view: that meetings are part of *judgement building* among members of a group. It follows that in any team, the process of learning and evaluating is both part of the work, and something which can add to the group's resources (its assets). Skills and experience of staff become collective wealth. A democratic team, with an informed and interested group of colleagues, corresponds to an informed group of citizens who learn about and involve themselves in a public issue. Collective learning, then, is an essential exercise and expression of collective working.

Understanding this link doesn't solve the problems of learning within a team. For one thing, it's not organisations which learn, but individual staff who work there. So a key question highlighted by an egalitarian team is precisely about *inequalities* in knowledge: who knows and how much do they know? There are inevitable differences between experienced staff and newcomers; paid staff, volunteers and users; and among a workers' group where people have specialisms.

Writers describing the early stages of collective teams have suggested that these tensions were ignored or even denied. Members imagined they:

> could solve all the problems of inequalities caused by the division of labour and inequality of skills by simply declaring the problem null and void. Rotate all skills. Keep everyone moving so that power never aggregates.[3]

Recognising this *oppositional* stage of collective working, we'll also see some of the conflicts that teams must tackle if they are to develop further. So this chapter examines some FSU examples of the tension between individual and collective learning; what room is there for 'my development' when the stress is on learning together? I'll go on to ask whether the formal hierarchy of position is replaced by a *hierarchy of knowledge*. In particular, what did *learning with* mean, when it came to students and users? In the last section, we'll explore the issue of users' knowledge and learning. Can collective learning build a new relationship between professional and client?

Underlying these issues is a further question which applies to problems of learning in all kinds of teams and agencies. How do people learn to learn? When knowledge isn't pooled, frequently it's because teams are failing to do this. As the management writers Chris Argyris and Donald Schon observe:

> There are too many cases in which organisations know *less* than their members. There are even cases in which the organisation cannot seem to learn what every member knows.[4]

Does collective *co-learning* provide ways out of this? As usual, a collective framework doesn't offer tidy answers. But it does suggest fruitful questions, worth exploring by any team.

A Place of Learning

A conventional workplace has its learning and teaching. People may not think of their agency as a place of learning, but the most rigid hierarchies train employees; and supervision includes some instruction as well as control. Staff absorb new policies; learn revised procedures. Information flows around the organisation — upwards as well as down — as data are collected and reports written. At informal discussions, workers gather their own knowledge. Becoming a new staff member means learning the ropes — with or without formal induction. You need to know the official rules you're supposed to keep to, and the unofficial ones that make them workable.[5]

How is this different in a collective team? In particular, what marks out Newcastle's practice from that of many other small teams in human service agencies? That includes FSU itself, as a national organisation which emphasises training and regular supervision.[6]

What I've described at Newcastle very often related directly to teaching and learning. Much of their their work with users was explicitly educational rather than, say, therapeutic. We saw how family casework changed when workers came to oppose a paternalism which created or reinforced users' dependence. Instead of families being passive recipients of the Unit's work, (consuming expertise or second-hand clothes), staff wanted users to learn with them, and to achieve confidence to do things for themselves. This critical view of social services work with families is at the heart of Joan Smith's book.[7]

It's no coincidence that many of the Unit's projects had an educational theme. The Women's Workshops' stated objective was to enable women to learn practical and social skills. Described as 'self-help' groups, in this context self-help meant independence and self-determination. Admittedly, research on the workshops by Fran Martin questioned how far members actually felt they 'owned' them.[8] Even so, most workshops eventually became part of West End Leisure and Learning, a self-managed community education project.

Similar thinking lay behind the Unit's development of services generally. The question, 'How can we learn about?', had been edged over by, 'How can we learn with?'. This needed an altered approach to knowledge. It was no longer a question of gathering data on people's private troubles, to be measured and charted by the professionals and made into *their* understanding of public issues.

Even when the Unit came close to conventional teaching, they stressed an interactive view.

Shirley Forster: It's questionable how much benefit you get from race awareness training if you're sent, and if you don't go of your own volition. The process of me doing a race awareness course consisted of Ernie gradually getting me interested over a period of something like two years. And saying little bits here and little bits there, until I was eventually interested enough to take a risk and do the thing.

But the link went beyond a list of different work. For we've come back, by another route, to the Unit's aim for a consistency between how they tried to work with users, and their wish to self-manage. The link is not simply learning, but a particular approach and philosophy of *co-learning*. In one way or another, ideas about co-learning and co-teaching emerged again and again. They were used to explain Joint Staff Management in the annual report as the process of workers, "drawing from each other's knowledge" and pooling, "imagination, ideas and enthusiasms". It was, said Lilian White, part of the basic assumption underlying their way of working: "The philosophy we use throughout the Unit".

> *Lilian*: It's something to do with the whole range of skills that staff group has, and how we lend to each other. There's always things you can pool.

Let me clarify this by returning very briefly to the work of the Educator, Paulo Freire. In chapter one, I mentioned his influence on former FSU staff, suggesting that Freire's ideas illuminate later developments at the Unit. (Though they didn't explicitly use his work). Every educational practice, says Freire, implies a view of people and of the world. To see knowledge simply as instruction is to view people as empty vessels waiting to be filled by experts.

> The 'banking' concept of education in which the scope of action allowed to the students extends only as far as receiving, filing and storing the deposits.[9]

Freire denies that an educational programme can be simply what "the *educator* thinks best for *his* students".[10] Instead, he insists on the necessity for people to engage in *dialogue* as co-learners and co-teachers, in a "restless, impatient, continuing, hopeful inquiry".

Informal and Commonsense

Some readers may feel we've gone too quickly from learning among a staff team to learning with users. So let's retrace our steps more slowly, beginning with the team itself. A first question might be whether we really need terms like *dialogue* and *co-learning*. Don't all sorts of teams borrow and share skills with one another, in an informal and commonsense way? I'm not claiming that groups working collectively have a monopoly of shared learning, and FSU certainly weren't a model learning community.

Let's accept then, that collaborative learning and pooling goes on in many teams. Staff see the good sense of skill-sharing and swopping experience. Won't such 'natural' co-learning be welcomed by their organisation?

The answer isn't straightforward. For one thing, there's a likelihood of conflicting expectations about what people need to learn, and how this is taught. What happens, for instance, when a group's informal skill-sharing doesn't accord with their agency's training policy? Another question asked before, is how far the more casual "sloppy" and exploratory kinds of creative learning are allowed 'in the firm's time'. Does leaning on each other's skills extend to lounging over cups of coffee?

Add to these problems the many instances where colleagues do learn from one another, but don't necessarily recognise and value it as such. I'm thinking here of the help FSU's secretaries gave to students, and how Shirley Forster wanted this made visible and appreciated. Knowledge and skills are often hidden or overlooked in this way. Unrecorded, they end up being noticed only when lost. It's not just that colleagues can take each other for granted. You yourself may not appreciate the value of what you know, unless other people recognise how it contributes something useful and worthwhile. Donna Akhtar's knowledge of languages was another Newcastle example.

A commonsense 'we-are-doing-it-already' approach faces another problem (literally a final one in some cases). Quite often, the issue is not encouraging team learning, but *defending* it. For at least two thousand years people have recorded the phenomenon that just when a work group starts becoming a team, the powers-that-be reorganise it out of existence.[11] I'm not saying work groups should never be split, nor staff transferred. But when teams do create common wealth by learning together and building judgements, there is a hidden cost if they are dispersed. So 'defend' here, simply means recognising and stating the case for keeping an effective co-learning team intact.[12]

But being able to say explicitly what you want acknowledged and encouraged, requires understanding what you have, and describing it. If the reality of team-*working* is hard enough to describe without cliche, how much harder it is to convey more than agency rhetoric about team problem-solving and sharing knowledge. After all, no job applicant would ever hear: 'There are no opportunities for training. You will find your colleagues unstimulating, unwilling to share skills, and interested in the development of your knowledge only as it impinges on them'.

However, suppose that description was largely true. Just as the label 'team' is no guarantee of shared work, equally, there are work groups who don't often share skills or learn together. It's vital to see that this is not just bad luck, or a matter of personalities. Training in a hierarchy mostly assumes that knowledge comes down from the institution to the individual. There's the hint too, that newcomers have little or nothing to teach old hands.

In addition, it's frequently assumed that a team leader or manager simply assigns work to different specialists. The notion is that staff with the necessary experience and qualification can be hired and then simply 'added' to a work group. Specialists are tagged onto a team — with the proper lines and boxes drawn on the chart, but without providing for colleagues to learn from them. To adapt Freire's terms, a work group is treated as a bankable selection of complementary resources; a varied portfolio adjusted to keep its value in a changing market, with deposits of knowledge drawn out as needed.

Consistency of Practice?

So far, I've argued there will be serious problems without clear and deliberate co-learning among colleagues. But what of the further links Newcastle FSU made — their aim to apply co-learning to managing the Unit, and in relationships with users as well? In other workplaces these links are not necessarily made.

Take the well known example of large commercial corporations which set up staff learning groups with a no-holds-barred peer dialogue. These companies realise how a hierarchical pyramid, with its pattern of competition and deference, inhibits learning and problem solving. In particular, internal communication becomes choked; ideas and thoughts camouflaged and guarded.[13] Staff in this situation defensively control and censor information to the point when it becomes bureaucratic propaganda — to which other people stop listening.[14]

Solutions are tried out according to fashion. Two examples are *quality circles*, where employees from different levels of a company are brought together with a problem solving brief; and management variations on *'T'-groups* (therapeutic group techniques). These have in common the creation of a separated space where people are allowed or encouraged to be far more 'equal' and open with each other, despite status differences. There is always the proviso that things must be kept within strictly defined institutional limits. What staff learn together and try to come up with, are answers, or at least suggestions for problems set by the company. The firm is paying.

To imitate collective teams like this, pays them an implied compliment. But it also challenges the consistency of aims described at FSU. Apparently, there are a set of choices. We can have segregated, staff-only, learning and problem solving groups. Or we might set up a small circle where one or two staff learn together with users. Alternatively, users can be encouraged to come together. But why should these various options be linked? And why should any of it imply a corresponding change in the management structure of a team, and *its* group learning or supervision?

'The philosophy' at Newcastle led them to reject such separation on two counts. First, it was a question of ends. Co-learning, with the aim of an honest and open dialogue, was valued as an end in itself. Which meant that it was a goal for all aspects of the team's work; what was 'right' in one place was also right elsewhere. The aim was to enable everyone to become co-learners rather than some people remain passive recipients of other's expert knowledge.

So the fact that a segregated learning group may be feasible, didn't make it desirable. They believed (as do many other social services workers) that open honest communication is essential for a family's learning and problem solving. How could they justify something different between workers and family members? Or within the group of workers?

Second, the argument is that such ends can't be detached from the means chosen to achieve them. Separation is possible in a quality circle because the end is different. Sure, collaborative learning is encouraged. But only in a setting where members have a restricted time and place to meet, with management choosing the problems they tackle and the particular methods they use. It's also likely to be quite removed from work members normally do. True, staff taking part in quality circles often find them challenging and even enjoyable, and this is a welcome spin-off.[15] But there's no doubting why hierarchies favour them. Their primary purpose is producing something useful *to the company*.

In contrast, for collective working, the end isn't just efficiency, or even personal growth. It includes empowerment and self-determination. Why, then, would a segregated learning group pose a problem for a collective or collaborative team? The answer is shown in the following example.

Learning Networks

How does someone learn to become a member of a social services team? For 'professional' staff, the conventional answer is that before coming to an agency, they have to attend a formal training course. Courses certify that students are competent practitioners with the necessary skills.

Now, there's a recurrent question of the 'fit' between what and how people learn, and their jobs afterwards. Suppose we ask, not about individual competence, but whether students have learned to contribute to a team? Here, the problem becomes acute. Professor Phyllida Parsloe — whose department runs a professional training course — considers that social workers are often unprepared to work collaboratively. She thinks this is partly due to courses where, "the practice, theory and teaching methods emphasise individual behaviour and individual learning".[16]

Parsloe proposes a change: that students should learn *within* as well as *about* groups. Both aspects, she says, are needed in equipping them to become full contributing members to other collaborative groups they join. The course curriculum would include both material about collective teamwork, and methods of learning which provide experience of collaboration. It should:

> Ensure that students analyse their experiences and think how they can use them in the work group of which they will be future members.

How does this relate to co-learning inside an agency? Well, it's important to understand that the problem Parsloe raises is not confined to training courses. The challenge of teaching the right content and best methods isn't faced, unless we realise how wide is the 'syllabus' and extensive the 'school'. Let me be clear, I'm not saying a team is or should be *like* a training course. The point is that every part of the work within an agency, in one respect, *is* a training course. With or without it being designed as such, people watch, hear, feel, ask, absorb, try out, talk over, practice, argue... and are thereby learning.

But the idea of co-learning goes further still. Just as learning is not restricted to courses people attend, it extends beyond what are usually taken as an organisation's boundaries. At Newcastle, users were included; so were groups within the city and in other parts of FSU that Unit staff belonged to.

In other words, there was a *learning network*. Training courses were one part of it. But, just as important, people were doing their learning, and building their judgements, in a series of forums. Workers belonged to the staff group; they were members of more than one subgroup — which were sometimes separate and sometimes overlapping. They learned in paired and group supervision; in support groups; and wherever they worked, including with families and community groups.

All organisations have more or less developed sets of learning networks.[17] Some of the issues discussed before are about links *between* different groups, while others are concerned with how intentional learning can take place *within* a group. A quality circle illustrates this, since it isn't just bringing together different staff with varied knowledge. Its starting point is that knowledge built by distinct work groups has not been linked. Perhaps staff don't realise what they know. Maybe knowledge is hidden; or groups are in conflict.

The hierarchical solution is a new segregated subgroup with overlapping membership. Very plainly, the collective answer would not be to constitute a new group, or at least not without asking how and why the learning network isn't working and doing something about that. Intentional collective working includes the aim of having clear, open, linked learning networks.

The Hidden Curriculum

There's a further, less straightforward dimension to this problem. Because institutions teach more than what's on their 'syllabus'. Take Parsloe's proposals. How far could they be effective — or even permitted — if they ran against the underlying assumptions of the institution? This 'hidden curriculum' is unlikely to favour co-operation and collaborative teamworking. Depressingly often, the British higher education system teaches individualistic competition, hierarchy, and that success is always at the expense of others.[18]

Educational institutions and social services agencies are both complicated bureaucracies. What people learn or teach there depends on the interplay of the same complex aspects — of power, people, and values. Which means that staff who deliberately set out to make changes need to reckon with the overall pattern of social relations within their agency.

This may seem too gloomy. Readers could protest that they've been on courses offering open dialogue, intense learning, and the exhilarating experience of sharing their ideas and building judgements with other participants. But, crucially, were they able to build-on from this? Suppose you return to a work group where there is no open learning. Your work colleagues can be defensive about what you bring back *and* about the process within which your new learning was built.[19]

We can now see the practical reasons for trying to achieve co-learning in every part of an agency's work. Without such consistency, what is learned in one place can be undermined or unlearned in another. Like colleges, social services agencies contain their own complex learning networks, which are as likely to collide and compete with a shift towards collective learning as to enable and encourage it. If we want people to learn interdependence, and to enable others to collaborate, we require a means of learning that is itself collaborative.

Without consistency there's the danger that building confidence and judgement will be undermined elsewhere within the learning network, or contradicted by the hidden curriculum of the agency. Closed segregated learning fits closed segregated working. Relations of deference and dependency match forms of learning that reinforce powerlessness and incorporation. In contrast, open collaborative learning — the dialogue of co-subjects — is an essential means of empowerment.

Individual Knowledge and Expertise

Members of any work group are inevitably at different points in their personal learning. They have varying interests, talents and, in developed collective teams, differing day to day work. So learning collectively doesn't imply a fixed 'syllabus' — with everyone in a team somehow following the same topics at the same rate. They are always learning parallel to each other, even if they work together. The vital question, though, is whether people keep their skills and knowledge to themselves, or co-learn, co-teach, and make their questioning and inquiry joint activities.

At FSU, workers with more skill or experience found themselves alongside colleagues who knew much less. Students came to the Unit to learn; and among the staff group it wasn't that newcomers had nothing to teach, but that experienced workers had more.

This issue of expertise is crucial, as it's often used to justify hierarchy and professionalism. It's argued that you can't realistically expect staff to go on contributing unequally. Why should someone take part in a team where — because of an imbalance of skills — they are constantly doing more of the 'teaching'? The implication is that collaborative co-learning may work when staff are more or less equally skilled (or equally unskilled), but this is bound to be rare and temporary. Even in a team of equals where nobody leaves, some workers learn better and faster. So, how far does co-learning depend on equality of skills?

The question seems even harder to answer when we talk of co-learning with people outside a team — in particular with users. Aren't staff paid for expertise users don't have — and more than that, may have neither the opportunity nor wish to acquire? For example, if I don't understand welfare rights, perhaps I only want access to someone who does, not a welfare rights course.

In chapter nine we had Howard Goldstein's picture of the social worker's office with, "The trappings of professional insignia". They are no invitation to co-learning, but signal deference to the professional's certificated expertise — a mastery of what's called 'the body of knowledge' (a pedagogy of the impressed). The body is a corpse, of course, unless living people understand and use what they know for living purposes. Yet the practice of co-learning can't deny that differences exist between people. How should these be tackled?

We can begin by saying that an interactive process of 'learning with' does not mean rediscovering and reinventing everything.[20] It also entails a challenge to such notions as objective neutral knowledge 'out there'. A further point is that speaking of people learning together and in networks, in no way denies the plans and hopes they have for their own futures. Differences between staff will surface when individual workers think about their own careers — which won't be tied to one agency.

Staff Development — Whose Responsibility?

Let's look at these issues taking some practical instances at FSU. Here are my notes from a staff meeting, followed by an extract from the management committee minutes.

Ernie's Course: Ernie Dobson tells the team that he wants to do a part-time MSc on Race Relations at Bradford University. He can pay his own fees. Can he have time off to attend?

People acknowledge he would get a lot from the course, and support his going. Then they begin asking how academic or how practical it'll be, specially for the Unit's everyday work, and generally with the black community. Members pointedly ask Ernie how he plans to pass on his new knowledge. At one point he jokes [?] "I'm beginning to wish I'd never raised it at all".

Other issues brought up. The course means time (a day a week). Which bits of Ernie's work are going to get left, and which passed over to someone else?

From the minutes of the Finance Sub-committee of Newcastle FSU Management Committee. Item 2: Ernie's Course.
Ernie's request for help to defray his course expenses was granted as follows:
1) £75 for books was agreed.
2) £45 out of the Punjabi course allocation was agreed.
3) Concerning the costs of the course, the meeting resolved thus: The committee recognises the interest of FSU in Ernie's course and as such the committee is prepared to defray Ernie's costs with regard to fees.

Two snapshots then, showing a common enough event in an agency like FSU. The only complication was that Bradford was eighty miles away, offering an academic qualification that sooner or later, might get Ernie another job.

What difference did self-management make? Well formally the decision belonged to the management committee. But, all the same, it was Ernie's colleagues asking what use the course would be for the Unit's services. They expected to set criteria and make their own judgements. To some extent they began to make conditions — asking Ernie to be a resource person for the team (not just for users) and to report back on his learning.

Formal practice in a hierarchy is for these decisions to be made from above. FSU Unit Organisers made a strong claim for this function, when a UO's Working Party described their responsibility for: "individual staff development... by ensuring supervision, assessment and training."

We find a similar attitude reflected in the writing about training and supervision in social service teams. From what I said earlier about how teams are often seen, this is not surprising, and it holds true even when people are broadly sympathetic to collaborative team models.

One example is in Allan Brown's book on consultation, intended to be a practitioner's handbook.[21] Brown warns that a team won't be able to meet all its learning needs internally. He makes the useful suggestion that each worker negotiate, "a programme of supervision, consultancy and training" with both their formal supervisor and their colleagues. But instead of developing this idea, Brown goes on to focus on the role of the team leader as facilitator of learning — the "key figure" who must "negotiate across team and agency boundaries".

At Newcastle, Joan Smith was increasingly unable to meet staff's training needs, especially as the range of work widened, and with it, the experience and skills of team members. But this problem isn't solved by Brown's idea of the team leader as a sort of one-way gate to outside learning. For how are people to discover when they don't know something? "Recognising the need to ask"[22] is as important for the teacher as the learner. Again the collective answer is to build open learning networks.

In practice, members of teams have access to a far richer and wider range of learning "resources", both across the team's apparent boundaries and within them. Even with something as formal as an outside course, the rules which are meant to govern who goes and who says so, are unlikely to be the whole story. Like Ernie Dobson, staff in many agencies do a bit of negotiation and boundary-crossing themselves. In both collective and hierarchical teams, people's plans and choices play a part in what gets learned. Individuals may be as much (if not more) concerned about updating and improving their skills and expertise, as the organisation will be in training 'its' employees. Nor does this mean just the 'professionals'. During my contact with FSU, though the secretaries were generally resistant to suggestions about going on courses, they were interested in gaining new practical skills.

It's worth noting that other workers weren't antagonistic to Ernie's course. It was accepted that people had personal goals, which might involve going outside. Learning together wasn't the only legitimate learning. Though, it's fair to say that the team's decision was neither difficult nor controversial. A longstanding member had asked to go and learn about an area the Unit wanted to promote and improve. For several months, no one pushed Ernie into keeping his promise to run some sessions on the Bradford material.

By contrast, six months later, when the Unit agreed some financial support to Elliot Yabantu to go on a social work course, people told me that the discussion was much sharper. Some workers felt — and said — quite strongly that Parveen Akhtar had a prior claim. They also quietly encouraged Lilian White to apply for a social work course, (begun in Autumn 1985). Her sister Brenda (Pool Girls' Club worker) was nagged until she took the plunge and got a place on a youth and community work course a year later.

Hopes and Fears

The issue of individual learning needs to be aired if a work group is discussing any move towards co-operative or collective working. Learning collectively may be felt as potentially exciting, or threatening (or both at once!). There's the notion of putting together people's different knowledge. It, "liberates resources and raises all sorts of thresholds", said Ian Bynoe. At the same time, there's an implied promise of more space for *individual* growth.

> *Chris Johnson*: It gives people time to grow and learn new skills, and take on new areas of responsibility.

But this has another side too. Sometimes, when people become members of collective teams, they mention a feeling of being 'deskilled'. Perhaps their previous training and experience has equipped them for a particular job within well defined limits — teacher, caseworker, lawyer. Suddenly their colleagues are asking them to take on new work; tasks which they may have seen as 'admin' or 'unskilled'. At the same time, their existing skills are questioned, and they're expected to learn in new ways.

Unlearning and new learning may be hard and painful, especially when you're really good at something. Ali Rhind could only partly use her community arts skills in the Women's Workshops.

Ali: I feel as though a lot of my skills, there isn't any-where else in the Unit that it can be used. I feel that they're not valued or used.

For someone thinking of their career, it can easily seem as though joining a collective team implies submission to the group, not just of their present skills, but their future learning as well. Later I'll be talking about the judgement of our peers, and how this isn't comfortable. The acceptance of 'us' as a team implies a responsibility to fit what you know and learn and teach, within the pattern of services the group and its us-ers are developing.

So tensions between knowledge and experience as the *as-sets of an individual*, and those *of a group*, don't disappear with collective working. Common wealth isn't a formula for ban-ishing personal hopes and fears. But, looking at it another way, neither does building skills and learning as part of the common wealth, prevent individual accumulation. It's as though people realise their share in the equity when they leave. In fact, one of the ironies of collective working is how workers gain a range of marketable experiences in areas denied to subordinate staff elsewhere. Supervision, and man-agement generally, are obvious Newcastle examples. So is money.

Shirley Forster: I wouldn't have touched that stuff with a barge-pole two years ago. I'd have died. I mean, when we came into being a collective I said, 'I'm only willing to join this if I have nothing to do with the money'. And now I've actually been to talk to the Councillors about our grant and, I hope, talked reasonably intelligently about it.

What about individual 'professional development', as the phrase goes? Pam Carter's experience at FSU, added to her previous work, took her to a senior lecturer's job. Chris John-son was able to follow up the co-op development and wom-en's employment work she'd started doing at the Unit. Angela Sewell became a Social Services team leader.[23]

Shirley Forster, despite being positive about widening her own skills, still had mixed feelings. For one thing, as the most experienced field social worker, she missed Joan Smith.

> *Shirley*: What I find quite hard — what I miss Joan a lot for — is having somebody around who's got a lot more experience than I have.

On the other hand, she was enthusiastic about pooling ideas — for instance, material Pam Carter brought back from a course.

> *Shirley*: We've really worked very hard using those ideas and sharing them. I feel like we've understood — Pam's gone on the course and picked up material — but then I feel like the rest of us have understood it very quickly.

Newcastle can be criticised for failing to develop an overall programme of learning, of the sort suggested by Allan Brown. But they did have a clear understanding of the mutuality involved in this process — the quite generous giving and receiving that has to happen within a team and outside it. They were also realistic, not just about the creation of common wealth, but of limitations in distributing it — arranging the time and effort needed in co-learning and co-teaching, and simply in covering for other people when they're away. (And straightforward spending, since course fees come from a limited budget).

The very notion of co-learning includes the responsibility that people carry for their fellow workers. In a hierarchy it's all too easy to avoid owning your share. Instead of taking responsibility, the whole blame is fixed on a manager, supervisor or training department for not offering enough.

What, I hope comes emphatically from this discussion, is how thinking of *our* knowledge and learning offers a way out of one of the worst dead ends in thinking and writing about teams. When *our* includes users as well as workers, other practitioners and local people as well as management committee members, the world can no longer be divided between the individual professional — pushing for autonomy — and the bureaucracy insisting on hierarchical accountability.[24] *My* professional development versus the agency's training policy are not the only two options.

Co-Learners or Practice Teachers?

The presence of students at FSU may seem one aspect of their set-up which challenged the notion of co-learning. Students on practical placement came with their own individual learning very much in mind. Unit staff recognised this, and each student was asked, as one of their first tasks, to draft an agreement between them and the Unit, setting out what what they expected FSU to offer — but also *what they brought*.

All the students I met were on qualifying courses, either in Social Work, or Youth and Community Work. Except for a community work student supervised by Ernie, all were part of the Student Unit, with either Pam Carter or (later) Angela Sewell as their formal supervisor. Though most students worked closely with other staff, especially when involved in groups.

In a paper on training, Shirley Forster and Pam Carter raised some interesting questions about students learning groupwork.[25] One of their starting points was to ask what they were actually teaching. Women students in particular were offered the chance of a wide range of group experience, including the Pool Girls' Club, Women's Workshops, and the various Unit meetings. As people learn about groups from being in them, one way to teach students is direct them, pushing them in at the deep end. Once they're involved, a supervisor can sort out how they do it, as the group goes along.

> *Shirley Forster*: Because you've got more experience you can see things that they can't see. And for the sake of speed and getting things done you just wanna tell them [laughs] rather than have them work it out.

But FSU preferred students to work things out jointly with staff.

> We encourage students to consider the assumptions and beliefs which guide their own work and which are not very conscious. We also encourage them to contribute to the development of our ideas. They have the opportunity of applying their ideas in their work within the Unit, as

they contribute to the development of aims and directives in the planning stages and their actual practice. This is especially apparent in groupwork as each new piece of work is planned from the start — even more consciously than casework.

This meant helping students think critically about what they were doing and learning. It was also important for them to be able to fit previous experiences into their groupwork. Both of these implied that staff should appreciate and value what students had to offer. But placing students' contributions alongside those of experienced staff, again raises the issue of unequal knowledge and expertise. As Shirley and Pam observed:

> We've become more aware of the amount of support students need to feel able to contribute their skills and ideas, and of the way we can use our greater experience to help them rather than intimidate them.

Shirley and Pam were especially interesting when they described changing their minds about what they ought to be doing. There was an early stage, they said, marked by deep distrust of groupwork theory.

> *Shirley*: We spent quite a lot of time thinking about theory and whether we wanted to teach students any theory or not. And moved through the whole thing of saying, 'We don't want to have any theory', because the theory you read in books isn't related very much to practice. And what we want to do is just to build up a theory from their actual practice.

A reaction to 'theory in books' led them to downplay the very real differences in levels of knowledge and experience.

> *Shirley*: We did all sorts of things like saying, 'If you run a group the students know as much about groupwork as you do, really. So you all muck in together'. And in practice that's not true. You actually know much more than students do.

Pam: We realised how much we were, sort of, saying, 'Oh, anybody can do this. It's just about making people cups of tea and being nice to them'. And realising students were incredibly intimidated by this — very much in awe of what we were saying. Either that or dismissed it completely because we weren't really recognising or giving them some kind of awareness of what it was we were really doing and saying. Yes, I think we've begun to clarify all of that.

Their paper makes this clearer.

Like many social workers and community workers our relationship to 'theory' has been an ambivalent one. We've held it in awe — 'someone else's language, not our own' — 'jargon', etc. But of course we've absorbed it, used it consciously and unconsciously and do recognise that it helps us get beyond the individual, and the immediate and to learn from our own and other people's experience. The experience of this project has aided some of our staff group to feel more comfortable with 'it', understanding their own role as co-workers and sometimes as practice teachers.

Here's an example where Unit members explicitly faced the issues raised by co-learning with people who had different levels of expertise. So what does it really mean to respect people's skills and ideas, when they are newcomers, and when there's a gap of five to fifteen years between them and workers in the job?

A Hierarchy of Knowledge?

Students saw a similar contradiction inside the staff group itself. They came to a team which, they were told, tried to work collectively; "making the best use of workers' potential, respecting each other as equals". Yet, plainly, workers' skills were not even roughly equivalent. In fact, students identified an informal ordering — a weighting of people in the staff team which reflected length of experience and relative expertise. Shirley and Pam themselves were viewed by students as among the more influential members. So was Ernie.

Ernie Dobson: [speaking at a team meeting] I know I'm
a person who does a lot of talking. Who's been here a
long time. [pause] And I've stopped talking and, like,
there's silence. Or I know who's gonna talk.

In practice, the link between experience in the job and influence in the team was not so exact. At any one time, there were
subtle variations in who initiated, led, or pushed things. For
instance, it was Ernie doing "a lot of talking" who had his
course plans dissected by his colleagues. Nevertheless, such
variations in competence and knowledge are likely in most
teams. And differences will be quite sharp when students or
inexperienced workers come to an agency.

So is the result a *hierarchy of knowledge* just as real and
powerful as any formal hierarchy of position? In which case,
what becomes of the determination to build forums where co-
subjects learn together? Have we simply returned, by the back
door of professionalism, to expert knowledge communicated
to colleagues and users?

It's possible to interpret Pam and Shirley's argument like
this. Here were workers starting with a commitment to value
the contribution of students in the way the Unit tried to do
with users and other local people. "You have as much to give
to this work as I have", they said. But it turns out to be something "which wasn't true in practice", leading to their honest
admission of "our greater experience".

However, when Pam and Shirley gave their own meaning
to this sequence, they certainly didn't see it as arriving at professional realism. True, they drew the conclusion that Unit
workers, as practitioners, had a range of learnable skills —
craft skills, if you like. But their claim was not to professional
status, but a *practitioner's knowledge*.

This vital distinction goes to the heart of a confusion
about expertise, hierarchy, and status; a confusion found
among workers in many teams. It's important to say that Pam
and Shirley, (themselves professionally qualified) weren't trying to have their cake and eating it — with a dollop of radical
rhetoric on top. How then, was it possible for them to own
their expertise while denying the status and power which apparently went with it? Let me explain the distinction.

The Body of Knowledge

The explanation returns to a point made earlier: co-learning includes a particular approach to knowledge — one which challenges the idea of knowledge 'out there'. Perhaps some readers will consider such questions rather abstract (as did one or two people at FSU). However, while the argument is usually presented as about something detached and objective — 'the body of knowledge' — the issues at stake are power and politics.

This is made crystal clear by Adrian Webb and Martin Hobdell, writing about teams in health and the personal social services.[26] Inside hierarchical institutions, they say, there is a "struggle between professional and bureaucratic ideologies" for status and power. So when professionals insist on their independent professional knowledge, they are laying claim to a degree of power and autonomy *over against* the bureaucratic hierarchy. Webb and Hobdell label this the distinction between professional's "authority of knowledge", and the official's "authority of position".

What's involved here is a power strategy. To conduct the struggle in these terms, it becomes essential for professionals to present 'the body of knowledge' as something detached, rational and objective. This separates it from the positional authority exercised by virtue of someone's job. Increasingly, say Webb and Hobdell, professionals rely on the academic status of their knowledge, plus the length of their training. Whether or not people believe in 'the body' of knowledge, they recognise that for *them* to be taken seriously, there must be at least, a grand mausoleum.

However, on reflection, it's evident that the struggle is not actually between knowledge and hierarchy, but between *two* hierarchies. Compare a training course, say, with a large bureaucracy (like a company or a social services agency). In both, people with positional power endow certain kinds of knowledge and learning with their approval. Specified information is chosen and a particular 'official' interpretation offered. In each case positional authority is used to shape and select what is and isn't legitimate knowing. When people speak with this kind of authority, they silence others; knowledge itself is validated or ruled invalid.

In other words, whether at an academic or professional level, the issues are as much about hierarchical authority as in any bureaucracy. It may seem odd talking about professionalism in this way, as its rhetoric often has an egalitarian flavour (all professionally qualified teachers, or social workers as peers). But in practice a hierarchy is created and carefully guarded, with boundaries between 'lay' and qualified, and between different professions.

I'm arguing that professionalism is simply one variation on the general strategy which tries to weld competence and knowledge to grades and classes as a source of authority. The fine gradings of a hierarchy are also supposed to correspond to differences in ability and experience.

What Clients Know

Webb and Hobdell realise that, given this set-up, there isn't much "consumer sovereignty" Indeed, there's "a tendency to treat the patient or client as a passive recipient of the service" and, "in isolation from their immediate social world". But, they say, users know things too. They have their "own definition of their needs". They know "the resources which they can muster", and whether or not they are satisfied with their treatment by the agency.

Webb and Hobdell propose tipping the balance towards users, and their suggestion for doing it is a revealing one. There is, they say, a third sort of authority: an *authority of relevance*. This means information and knowledge, "relevant to the client's own feelings of well-being", and which has been excluded from decisions made about them. Are clients, then, to be regarded as 'authorities' on their own views and feelings? Not in the proposal put forward by Webb and Hobdell. Instead, they ascribe authority of relevance to *para-professionals*; urging senior professionals and administrators to listen more to people like care assistants, social workers and home helps. The client may have told the home help of his worries about his cat. A social worker may be aware of the client's fear of death. (Note how users recognise professional hierarchy in their choice of confidant!)

This vividly illustrates how professionalism — wedded to the body of knowledge theory — obstructs even modest proposals for improving services. To be fair, it seems that Webb and Hobdell are actually after, not relevance, but increased *reference*. They'd like to see senior professionals put aside who's who, and ask, 'who knows?'. But they are well aware that services operate within a framework dominated by deference, and their discussion plainly acknowledges the existence of professional hierarchies. Higher status is accorded to senior professionals, with even more rarefied levels for those associated with academic theory.

It's worth noting this pecking order. It descends from the high peaks of 'pure' knowledge, through 'applied' research, and applied knowledge on training courses, sinking down to the day to day skills learned by professionals. Further below comes what receptionists, secretaries and even clients know. It is no wonder that academics' most recent approaches to users' views and experience have been labelled 'client studies'. But we must ask how often this means studying users as objects and re-presenting them to practitioners as legitimate knowledge.[27]

Practitioners' Knowledge

Let's now come back to the questions asked earlier about co-learning. Newcastle staff, I suggested, acknowledged their skills, but not professional status.

> *Ernie Dobson*: I feel we haven't got any unqualified workers here. I feel all workers here are qualified. We considered that when we were picking.

He didn't say that staff need not be qualified. The point was that the expertise of so-called unqualified people was legitimate and valid in its own right. But how feasible was this? Is there a practitioner's knowledge which can escape being locked into the hierarchy of professionalism? It would need to avoid treating users' knowledge as some sort of supplementary knowing: clients' data channelled as home helps' information. How could this be done?

Some preliminary points. Though I've drawn on Newcastle's experience, as usual there wasn't a Unit 'line'. Staff had mixed feelings about professionalism and, just as Pam and Shirley described with groupwork theory, there was distrust, awe, and the recognition that ideas and institutions were 'out there' anyhow.

In any case, I'm not talking about something unique to FSU, nor to collective working. Many sensitive and skilled practitioners do engage in co-inquiry with users. And there are very many workers in human service agencies who are profoundly sceptical about professionalism, or are anti-professional in the sense that they deliberately oppose "professional insignia" and the deference that goes with it. However, as we saw with Pam and Shirley, recognising practitioner skills goes beyond this.

The Reflective Practitioner

Perhaps I've centred on what practitioners' knowledge isn't, rather than on what it might be. If so, one extremely helpful examination of the knowledge that practitioners actually use is made by the writer Donald Schon, some of whose ideas I've already referred to.[28] Schon takes his material from widely separated fields. Psychiatry, architecture, management, and a Third World aid project are just some examples.

Put briefly, Schon argues that "the reflective practitioner" in many fields will "exhibit a kind of knowing-in-practice", which is part expertise and part artistry. This art of the practitioner, "may mean intuitive judgement and skill, the feeling for phenomena and for action". It will also include, "reflection in a context of action" as the practitioner tests, criticises and restructures their own understanding of what they experience.[29]

Not every practitioner automatically behaves in this way; Schon is describing competence, and sometimes excellence. It includes a grasp and understanding of broader ideas and theories, but using them in particular ways to frame and test each problem. This is how Shirley Forster answered my question about the use of theory in Family Discussion Group.

> *Shirley*: I think we haven't used theory in a very
> specific way. We haven't done things like discuss it
> and say, 'Let's deal with this family using a task cen-
> tred approach, and then let's try it using behaviour
> modification, and then let's use something else and see
> which is the best. We very rarely do that. We tend to,

sort of, work from those ideas. I think they're in the
back of our heads. But what comes out doesn't sound
very much like the original theory.

Donald Schon is fascinated by how practitioners learn by doing. One explanation he gives is that they "build up a *repertoire* of examples, images, understandings and actions".[30]
Practice is always a kind of research, and inquiry should always be "a reflective conversation with the situation".

Though he uses phrases like "the art of practice", this
isn't something mysterious and unteachable. The main examples he gives are especially apt in this chapter, since they're of
practitioners as teachers: an architect with a student; a psy-
chotherapist supervising a trainee. Schon asks how people
come to learn from and with others, who they regard as
skilled and competent: a therapist, for instance, but also a
musician or a sports coach. He tells the story of a systems engineer involving local people in investigating and designing
ways to reduce malnutrition in Colombia.

Schon's notion of a reflective practice becomes clearer
when he describes how practitioners could work with clients.
He rejects the traditional approach — the autonomous professional who offers a service, says 'trust me', and expects deference. We'll recognise Schon's alternative.

The new relationship includes the practitioner recognising
her own experience and skills. But Schon insists that, in using
her expertise, she has the obligation to lay out her meanings,
understandings and uncertainties, openly to the client — to
"make herself readily confrontable". At the same time, she
must assume that the client too can mean, know, and plan.
The aim is — quite literally — a conversation where they *both*
reflect on the work they're doing; asking, listening, telling,
clarifying to and with each other their thoughts and feelings.

This means the client is not offered the comfort of "being
in good hands", but invited to a joint inquiry which tries to
"make sense of his case".[31] Both client and practitioner require each other's knowledge, and both are entitled and invited to say what either doesn't understand or agree with. The
interdependence of the relationship extends to a joint discussion of what is and isn't effective.

I don't want to stretch Schon's framework too far. The reflective conversation he describes is not identical to the notion of dialogue I've used to talk about FSU. Yet his ideas do make sense of the Unit's attempt to disentangle practitioner skills from positional authority; and to offer those skills — whether to colleagues, students, or users — in a way which respects their knowledge and experience, without denying the practitioner's own. Having theories "in the back of our heads", isn't the same as becoming keepers of all knowledge. The switch from "you all muck in together", to "you actually know much more" was not a return to professionalism.

What happens is that beyond anti- or counter-professionalism, there is a stage where practitioners attempt to find a synthesis. The practitioner becomes a learner as well as a teacher, and invites colleagues, students and users to become the same.

There were similar patterns in many of the collective groups founded in the 1960's and '70's to provide services. Understanding how traditional professions were servants of the powerful,[32] many groups reacted by taking an explicitly anti-professional stance. They stressed the mystification of professionalism. 'How you can do it yourself' and 'none of us are professionals' expressed both a critique and a programme for the alternative agencies.[33]

As workers in those agencies themselves became skilled and experienced, emphasis shifted to a need for counter-professionals — 'people's experts' who would make technical expertise available to disadvantaged groups.[34] Schon is well aware of the important gains made by the American counter-professionals. But he is right to point out that:

> there is something inconsistent about a demystification of professional expertise which leads to the establishment of a breed of counter-professional experts.[35]

One implication is that, after anti-professionals have thrown hierarchical knowledge out the window, the counter-professionals smuggle it in up the backstairs. And this is bound to happen, continues the argument, unless there is a different relationship built between workers and users and among fellow workers. As Pam and Shirley found out, it will also be doubly mystifying if, instead of making themselves readily confrontable, they were employing and denying their expertise at the same time. That is trying to have it both ways.[36]

Pam and Shirley didn't talk about demystifying knowledge, but two words they used a lot were 'awe' and 'intimidate'. So, staff were sometimes in awe of theory; students intimidated and in awe of workers' expertise. It was this reverence and fear they wanted to dispense with. It's not that easy, of course. The tensions involved in trying to work out ways of owning and opening up knowledge are all the more difficult for being a departure into a new and relatively uncharted area. In this I think the Unit were actually more ambitious than Schon, and therefore preparing to take more risks.

Although Schon offers a helpful model, FSU went further in their understanding of the 'hidden curriculum' involved simply in having a hierarchical agency and professional structure. Unlike Newcastle, Schon's argument takes the existence of the context of the client/practitioner relationship as something given. FSU asked whether the very existence of professions and a hierarchy of formal positions might be a means of teaching and learning in itself. The ways of relating proposed by Schon will then be undermined, however open and committed the individual practitioner may be.

For it seems that Schon failed to consider (for practitioners' students as well as their users) the danger that a major *lesson* people often learn is their 'need' for instruction from an agency. The committed counter-professional (as much as the traditional professions) can reinforce people's fears that their own knowledge about their world is less important and legitimate than what they learn from a 'supervisor' about the world.

A Comment From Shirley Forster

Shirley: You, the worker, know more of the resources, methods, and ways of responding. But the user knows more about their concerns and which bit of your repertoire might be most useful. It takes a lot of confidence on the part of the worker to let the 'client' choose. So often, your status, and self esteem is derived from knowing best, deciding 'about'. And your training builds you up for this. So that when the poor 'client' expresses their views they can be interpreted by the professional as aggressive, manipulative, non-co-operating, and all the other labels used to disqualify them and say, 'we know best'.

Fourteen

Making Space

This chapter starts from the notion of an agency's building as *common wealth*. It's hardly the first thought that comes into people's heads. Whether it's social services, or libraries, or parks, calling something *public* can mean only that the government or local council owns it; not that it feels like *ours*.

Agency workers often share similar attitudes to their workplace. The physical building, of all 'structures', seems fixed and given; the result of someone else's plans. Where adaptations are made, staff may find they are now the 'clients', as architects and builders take over the design of their workspace.

On another level, the use of a building can seem as fixed in place as walls and corridors. Within a team or a department, who has which space and how much they have, can often be guessed from the shape of the organisational pyramid. After accommodating managers and money (the safe, computers, ledgers etc), there won't be a lot left to argue over.

Collective teams face each of these issues, but can open them up in a helpful way. Take the problem of the 'fixed' building. One task for any team is to avoid simply becoming consumers of other people's products.[1] The discussion of co-learning in the previous chapter suggests an alternative. Agency staff know things too, and their knowledge of how a building is used should be part of a critical dialogue with practitioners like architects.[2]

Questioning the existing use of a building is likely to be harder when it involves challenging the prerogatives of hierarchy. The boss's large quiet office may be justified on functional grounds, but you won't often get the chance to ask him. Common wealth doesn't necessarily mean equality, but it describes a situation where a team's space and how it's divided up and used, is something for the team as a whole to discuss and agree.

The remaining area — for who else is the building a resource? — is even more complex. All too often, schemes to increase access and openness to users fail to look carefully at the concrete detail of how offices run. Plans are shaped and coloured by an almost symbolic concern for dissolving boundaries and 'bringing people in'.

Newcastle FSU re-organised their offices on two separate occasions, not just to suit themselves, but with a clear idea of how they wanted users and staff to share the building. They tried to provide open and welcoming space, in a way they hoped would encourage certain kinds of social relations. As I'll show, this was not a peculiar feature, but follows the pattern in many other collective teams.

Exploring these similarities, we can begin to suggest how other teams might use this experience. A collective team redrawing the boundary between workers' space and public space faces the same physical options and constraints as any other. No collective magic exists for avoiding noise, dirt, problems of confidentiality or theft, or the general need to get a quart of workers and users into a pint pot of a building. Even so, it's a big advantage to begin with the question rarely put in other settings: how should space be used as part of the common wealth of a team and its users?

Tracing and Trailing

The work routes of a team extend outside agency walls, but its building is likely to be the central workspace, as well as an expensive, scarce resource. Suppose readers had been able to trace comings and goings at FSU, looking for broad continuing patterns. We'd recognise many of these trails of movement in and around the building. Tracks would form temporary 'knots' showing meetings; with small whirls around central points like the secretaries' room. There would be major crisscrossings, most marked at the kettle. We'd notice how some people worked closely with colleagues, while others more often worked parallel; as individuals or in separated groups, like Sally Walker and Shirley Devlin in the Women's Workshops, or Brenda White in the Pool Girls' Club room.

Add sound to vision, and there'd be times of quiet and then pockets of noise and hubbub. We'd hear a lot of talking, in English as well as Bengali and Urdu; arguments; crying; laughter too. We'd find out who was quiet and who talkative; which workers circulated, and who spent more time in the building. The overall picture would let us make some fair guesses about the different frameworks we've looked at already — for co-working, co-learning and judgement building.

A spatial portrait can be a useful way of approaching any workplace. Concrete physical aspects can be overlooked — sometimes until we literally trip over them. I'm not saying links between the physical environment and social relations are straightforward — that one determines the other. But certain kinds of interactions are made easier by particular physical layouts, while others are hindered. Staff who move offices will frequently experience this.

Space for Teamworking

If we want to encourage teamwork, we can't ignore the issue of shared and separated space. An office divided into individual cubicles and with nowhere to meet, is going to cause problems. On the other hand, an 'open-plan' won't guarantee open relationships. People are apt to use their ingenuity to find private space; 'building' it with screens, pot-plants, or working away from the office.[3]

Quite often, it's possible to 'read' a workplace in spatial terms and see which workgroups are teams and the ones which aren't.[4] One example is in a study of a gypsum plant by Alvin Gouldner.[5] He found a strong contrast between two categories of staff — miners who mined gypsum, and surface workers who made plasterboard from it. The miners worked in small teams which were closeknit and physically interdependent. Their workspace was separated, not just from the rest of the plant, but to a large extent from management oversight. By contrast, surface workers, who didn't form teams, normally had to remain at fixed points in the manufacturing process, with far less chance of social contact with each other.[6]

If this seems a long way from a social services agency, then consider how at FSU there were also two groups of workers — one wanting to self-manage, and a smaller group who asked to be left out. The majority, the fieldworkers, enjoyed much greater flexibility in organising their time and in moving around. The tasks of other staff — particularly the secretaries — meant they had fixed hours and stayed put.[7] The same applied in the Women's Workshops, where Sally Walker and Shirley Devlin worked separately from each other and from other Unit staff. It's likely that this difference contributed as much to who felt part of the team, as who was full-time or part-time. Spatial divisions were certainly reflected in how Sally and Ali saw their disagreements. Sally called it "the sort of upstairs/downstairs relationship".

> *Ali Rhind:* It might have been better if I'd been based here [in the Workshops]. It might have been easier. Because I think Sally sometimes felt that — you know what I mean — that I was involved in all the stuff up there and not enough at the workshops.

Other staff commented on the difference made by who worked where. Parveen Akhtar could chat informally with Pam Carter when they sat next to each other. Pam observed how, without such close contact, it became harder to raise a personal matter with someone.

Boundaries

Earlier, discussing meetings, I focussed on *time*. But space is just as pressing. Or, to be more exact, the need is for boundaries *between* spaces. If people are to meet and not be interrupted, they must arrange with other staff that boundaries are respected and maintained. FSU had a system for booking rooms, which prevented case conferences or meetings clashing. It was also so Carole Tate could plan her cleaning to avoid meeting times, or vacuum cleaning next door.

In general, meetings needed the secretaries outside them, intercepting and filtering callers. This is such an obvious feature of office life, that we easily forget how some workers' quiet concentration is 'paid for' by their colleagues.

> *Evelyn Rae:* When you're on your own you can't concentrate on, say, a Court report or anything. Be-

cause you have to answer the door and you have to answer the phone. And the phone's always ringing, you know. I think, again, sometimes the workers don't realise that, and they put work in expecting it [typed]. And you just can't do it. You haven't got the time — well, you can't split yourself up. And then people come in and want to talk to you. You can't really say, 'Go away, I'm too busy'. You have to be polite to them at least [laughing].

The problem here is more than providing insulated space — although Unit staff were very slow to do that for the secretaries. People whose work ties them to an especially busy room can't just move to a quiet area.

Shirley Forster: I go in and I interrupt them. If, say, Evelyn's typing something of mine that I really want typed and I wannit, like, quick, and somebody else is gossiping to her, I think, 'Argh!'. But I go and do exactly the same thing when she's typing somebody else's. They haven't got anywhere quiet where they can go and work.

There can be discrimination which confirms the separation of admin work, and of staff who do it. It's not uncommon, for instance, to have a training policy which maintains existing patterns of work by sending admin workers on admin courses, while other staff get 'professional development'. Allocating space according to what people do at one particular time, tends to have the same effect. Staff who already have access to quiet, comfortable, insulated space, are encouraged to produce thoughtful concentrated work. This further justifies the original discrimination.[8]

To give occasional access to such facilities is not the answer. In chapter twelve, we saw how people need time for trying things out and building up confidence. Like anything else, it takes a bit of practice.

Shirley Devlin: I come on Tuesdays and Wednesdays to look after the kids. I feel in control; I can handle it all. But when I come to woodwork, occasionally I feel very insecure, panicky. It's hard to explain. I think, 'Oh,

what a fool you are, Shirley. You cannot do this'. It's
because it's all new. And I think, 'Ee, I really shouldn't
keep asking'. I see all the skills some of the women *can*
do. And I cannot. And I think, 'Oh God, it's hard'. I've
only been to five sessions, but, like I say, I would come
more often if only I could walk in the door. It's hard
for us.

Coming In

Let's turn to the question of the Unit's openness to 'outside' —
users especially. The issues are complex, not least because
when we talk about spatial relationships, our words often
have extra levels of meaning. Phrases like 'opening up', and
'letting someone in', are also metaphors for personal and social relations. So what were users' feelings about coming in?
Some people said they felt quite at home in FSU. George
Cross had known staff for years, and had a regular 'route'
which began in the secretaries' room. Jean Tams also felt
comfortable.

> *Jean Tams*: I'm just cheeky. I just walk around.

These were two old hands; what of new and potential users?
For a long time, some workers had felt that the place could
and should be a lot more accessible. Elliot Yabantu, for example, was critical almost from his arrival.

> *Elliot*: When I came for the interview I couldn't find
> the place. I went up and down.

Pam Carter agreed.

> *Pam*: Because we haven't got an open door to local
> people. Nor have we got an open door to other
> agencies.

A chance to rethink their use of the building came at the end
of 1984, when funding ran out for the Women's Workshops.
Many of the workshops moved to West End Leisure and
Learning, leaving space on FSU's ground floor. They
reorganised, making a ground floor room into the lounge/re-
ception. The secretaries moved to the adjoining room, next to

the front door, which now remained unlocked. Other workers had more space upstairs. Reasons for the change were listed in the annual report.

(1) Messages from the community that our offices and premises are not very welcoming and the locked door puts people off coming in.
(2) Some of the workers' feelings about their rooms not being private enough.
(3) The staff's feelings about having the front door locked being a bad idea.

It wasn't a fixed solution; nobody claimed they'd 'got it right this time'. Even so, it's worth comparing the 1985 re-arrangement with the earlier one. In 1977/78 the team were also in search of a welcoming and open layout, and their alterations were very much in line with other developments underway. The large reception room (then opened up on the first floor) was planned as a common room for staff and visitors — including users and workers from other agencies. An important difference was that, where the 1985 changes increased workers' personal space, the earlier arrangement carved out the semi-public reception area by decreasing staff space — to the extent that fieldworkers stopped having their own desks for a time.

> *Alison Harker:* We then moved all the desks into the next door room. But people actually spent fairly little time in there. People spent time in the kind of communal bit.
> I did have a desk initially. And then it just seemed daft having desks... We had filing cabinets, and we all had trays. If you wanted a quiet space you just found a space. You could go upstairs; that was the quiet area.

I don't want to over-stress this. Not having private desks seems to have been something felt, rather than thought through. Even so, it was important as a signal of how things were then moving. The fact that it can feel "daft" to have private space, links directly to the team's developing notions of how openly an agency ought to be working.

So how should we understand the later plan? One interpretation is to see it simply as a swing of the pendulum —
back to a more open building, but this time not going so far.[9] I
want to give an alternative view, but before explaining it, we
need to set FSU within a wider context.

Open Doors

With space, there's a striking similarity between FSU and other teams working collectively. Opening up to users is frequently signalled by removing boundaries. Here are two comments, first from a description of the Harlesden Community
Project, the second by a worker in a London collective working with elderly people.

> People were encouraged to drop in whenever they felt
> like it and were offered cups of coffee.[10]

> I don't think of the pensioners as being part of the
> outside world. I see them in here with us, really.[11]

In a third team, Essex Road social services, the pattern was
even plainer. For several years this local authority neighbourhood office had one person one vote; group supervision; and
a substantial measure of task sharing, cutting across the formal hierarchy. Two other distinctive features were: an open
door policy, making users welcome throughout most of the
building; and a fieldworkers' workroom where desks were collected together as if for a conference, and used communally.
From their team leader's description, it would be hard to
imagine a more explicit rejection of private working.

> We were determined not to reproduce the bureaucratic
> organisation we had left behind, and the rooms we had
> acquired were equipped with a minimum of formality.
> No social worker had an individual desk, instead the
> main room was furnished as a sitting room. There was a
> small kitchen, a group room, administrative office and
> an interviewing room. We set out to explain to local peo-
> ple why we were there and to invite them to use the
> building.[12]

Developments like this have been claimed as part of 'community social work', with decentralisation and local 'patch'
teams seen as essential steps towards agencies becoming
more responsive and accessible to users. However, this really
misses the essential point about teams like Essex Road or
Newcastle FSU, which is that a number of apparently separate features are *linked*. Whether explicit or not, there is an
underlying unity. So the changes at Newcastle weren't 'just'
collective working, any more than Essex Road was 'about' going local.

Here's another example, from The Limes Grove — a
NHS General Practice in South London, where doctors, other
health workers, and reception staff shared in the running.
They made decisions by consensus, and there was equal pay.
They aimed at accountability to patients, who were involved
in major decisions. Here's Anne Karpf, a visiting journalist.[13]

> Perhaps the single most demystifying aspect of the prac-
> tice is that the patients are offered (and many take) the
> choice of having their consultations in the reception
> room rather than necessarily closeted in the doctor's
> consulting-room where health issues become
> individualised again. (This doesn't mean that patients
> are forced to bare either their bodies or their souls. They
> seem to find it easy to say,'may I see you in private?' and
> the workers seem sensitive to people's need for privacy.)
> Public consultations are one way of lessening medical
> power, since doctors are to some extent subjected to the
> scrutiny of patients as a group — at least that's the theo-
> ry.

First Come First Served?

As we've seen, an 'open door' had been adopted at Newcastle,
but then dropped a few years later. It suffered from a major
drawback. A small number of users stayed in the building for
long periods, and took up substantial staff time. The open
door turned into first come, often served.

> *Blanche Callan*: X and her sister used to come in as
> well; with the kids. And spend all day, every day here.

Yvonne Waters: They sent out letters to various people saying that they were welcome to come into the Unit, but times would be between such-and-such. And a lot of them took umbrage. They thought, "We're not welcome to come in'.

Had FSU failed to stick to its principles? In other words, should we measure successful collective working by the openness of a building to users? In that case, the Unit's 1985 reorganisation looks like a half-hearted attempt to do what it and other teams had done before in a more full-blooded way. However, I suggest the issue is not so straightforward. To explain why, let's return to the discussion about dividing space between workers.

Why Barriers Come Down

For some outsiders, notions like not having private desks, or inviting users "to drop in whenever they felt like it", will simply confirm their picture of collective working. They imagine everyone continually sharing everything; endless meetings; vaguely demarcated work and workspace — features which appear to proclaim confusion and weakness.[14]

The opposite view is taken by many members of collective teams, for whom common open space represents a strength. In particular it challenges those barriers (internal or external) defending closed *private* space. We can see how this comes about.

Particularly in the early stages of co-operating as a team, energy will go into developing co-work and co-learning. Staff try out pairing and group projects. They take time to show one another what they do, or tell each other about their work. The accent is on physical proximity and a great deal of mutual access. Becoming a team, one of the first things that demands questioning and change is the existing pattern of privatised space. Once people have positive experience of sharing space they want this extended. Beginning to build common judgements leads to experimenting with ways to dismantle barriers which have isolated staff and individualised work, both within and outside the building.

Aside from being a reaction to individual, privatised work, this kind of development is also counter to hierarchy. It isn't hard to see why work groups within a hierarchy rarely sit down and discuss space as an overall resource.[15] Existing rules of deference tend to divide up workspace largely in line with people's power and status. As well as the boss getting the quietest, most comfortable room, his boundaries will be better protected.[16] The extent to which someone can intrude into a colleague's space (e.g. interrupt them when in a meeting) is itself a measure of the 'intruder's' superior position in the hierarchy.[17]

Given this experience of organisations-at-large, it's not surprising that teams who begin to control their own building are suspicious of private space as such, and the way it complements hierarchy. So people may be wary of claiming *personal* space for fear that colleagues are going to see it as private.

Since I'm talking here about the earlier stages of collective working, members of many small teams could rightly protest that their agency had no alternative to everyone working in the same space. Cramped accommodation and funding-on-a-shoestring were often facts of life, not ideological choices. However, a feature of some small teams is that staff stay huddled together after funding improves and there *is* more space. The following comment comes from a London welfare rights collective.[18]

> At various times there are five people working in the one room; with two desks, two phones, and one of the desks covered with a big typewriter. So now there are two rooms. But we're finding it difficult to get out of this one.

Let me summarise the argument so far. When teams begin to work collectively, they often follow similar patterns in organising and using their physical workspace. What links them can largely be understood as *opposition* to the ways most bureaucratic and hierarchical organisations pattern their workspace. Such patterns individualise staff and strengthen chains of command; generally inhibiting day to day co-operation. They also contribute to setting up barricades against users.

The likely response of collective teams in their earlier stages is to focus on removing boundaries and barriers, and trying to avoid new ones being set up.[19]

Dividing Up 'Our' Space

But now think back to what I said about meetings at Newcastle. Because there is the apparent paradox that open effective meetings meant agreements on *closure*. They required ground rules about *not* discussing things at other times; not bringing in extraneous items. You make space by setting boundaries; respecting and maintaining new barriers.

This was one of the ideas behind the Women's Workshops (and 'women only' space in many other settings). Workshop users were encouraged to see the ground floor as 'their' space, with upstairs separate. Ali Rhind added a further reason; to distinguish the workshops from the rest of the Unit as a *social work* agency.

> *Ali*: Because for some people there is in fact quite a lot of stigma attached to a social work agency. And we're not offering that. We're not social workers. So for people to be able to see the separateness — for the users to be able to see that we are something different — that is *there*. They can have access to that.

In a sense, I'm saying that a network can be viewed either as an arrangement of spaces, or the lines separating them. But then, if closure and boundaries are as important as access, where does this leave the original aim of openness to users?

We've looked before at the dismantling of barriers, but from a different angle, when I talked about the *conventions* affecting how people from outside relate to a collective team. Janet Williams described Newcastle going through a sequence of changes. Initially there was an etiquette based on line management through the Unit Organiser. This was followed by a phase when Janet, at least, felt that workers were actively opposing conventions as such. In her words, after they opened the door, she was "left to get on with it".

> *Janet*: They went through this phase of rather,'This is how we organise ourselves; the rest of the world's gonna have to fit round us'.

But later, came a third stage when, "they'd got themselves sorted out". "Having acknowledged other people's need for clarity about these things", they made sure she knew who was dealing with what.

We find the same underlying sequence in the division of space as with other issues. When collective teams try to avoid all barriers and divisions, it means they've moved from the first to the second stage — from *deferential* to *oppositional*. A third, *referential* stage is marked by the negotiation of new agreements about dividing up 'our' space, where that negotiation is open, collective, and confrontable.

Rationing

Such a framework is open to criticism. I'll admit straight off that what happens in practice is rarely as neat as my description. Readers may also wonder if it's too pat in a different way; an excuse, rather than an explanation for Newcastle's new barricades? I'll come back to that. First let's examine a broader question: whether the framework is actually necessary. After all, don't we already talk about 'choosing priorities and 'rationing resources?' Why isn't this enough?

Plainly, many aspects of space can be discussed in this way. Given that there are only so many rooms in a building and hours in a day, choices must be made between competing needs (e.g. new users versus the group that spend all day, every day in an office). But it's not just slicing up the pie. There are demands for an agency's resources which appear incompatible — like Women's Workshops and social work — or some users who disrupt others.

> *Brenda White*: The last couple of weeks [three girls] were really difficult to handle. They made a right mess of the toilets. Some of the younger kids had been painting, and they came along and they stuck them all over the wall and destroyed them.
> (Incident at the Pool Girls' Club)

We need to look beyond explicit rules of rationing to those often unstated and implicit choices people make — like staff working at home, or erecting filing cabinet barriers. For once

such a notion of *hidden rationing* is introduced, we realise how
there cannot be a truly open door. The outcome will always be
a pattern of use shaped by hidden and implicit divisions of
time and space. Certain users will be inhibited or edged out
by others.

The idea that it's enough for there to be a neutral com-
munal area for different sorts of people to rub shoulders,[20] ignores the fact that the world outside is not neutral. People
bring in all their divisions and antagonisms — of class, race,
gender and so on.[21]

> *Brenda*: I went, 'Oh, hello girls. Come on in'. And
> everybody's going, [whispering] 'But it's the gypsies,
> Brenda. It's the gypsies. We can't have them here.' I
> said, 'Don't be daft'.

A further point about this 'hidden rationing' is that a team's
building is itself never neutral. People are put off by more
than locked doors; the feel and smell of a place can close it
just as effectively to whole sections of potential users. Staff
need to realise that even what they wear, and the pictures on
the wall contribute to this. All agencies give these physical
'messages' which outsiders 'read' whether they are aware of it
or not.[22]

> *Pam Carter*: The odd thing is that when Health Visitors
> and people like that come, they always seem really
> quite confused by the apparent informality of the
> place. I mean, they never — they hardly ever accept
> cups of coffee. Seems really peculiar. And that's partly
> viewing the Unit as an odd place. We're always having
> to be very careful to be seen to be *professional* — not to
> seem like a bunch of hippies.[23]

Exploring the 'hidden dimension' of rationing confirms the
framework I put forward earlier. For a collective team, it
matches the distinction between an oppositional view and the
later referential stage. A group of workers can't be neutral
when responding to users. Not choosing, always means that
you or others make implicit or hidden choices. But what of
the distinction I made between reference and deference?
Can't we understand the allocation of resources like space

within a hierarchy by talking about rationing, rather than deference?

The separation and allocation of hierarchical space *is* a form of rationing, though rarely presented as such. When some staff get more space, the implication is that others get less — and probably that many people get to make do and share. But the result is more than a simple narrowing of choice. Taken for granted assumptions about how a building is used, effectively prevent the issue even occurring to many people. They end up planning plants and carpets in the reception area, in the belief they're reorganising the agency's space.

The problem is that so many of the criteria used are hidden and implicit in this way. Even if the allocation of office space is *formally* an open exercise of power, there's an overlay of convention linked to status. For example, a colleague is summoned with: 'Come up to *my* office'. Such unwritten rules operate in many different settings.[24]

Priority or Privilege?

To restate the argument: although the concept of rationing is useful, it's incomplete without the distinctions I've suggested. Take the example of priority access. What happens when people outside an agency want to jump the queue with an urgent need?

> *Pam Flynn*: But you want to communicate immediately when possible. If I've got, you know, a funding application to fill out and I want an answer now, then if I've got to wait a day it screws up my thinking.

Other Newcastle management committee members raised this issue. Tony Boyd and Peter Stone wondered whether an outsider would get the same kind of emergency response from a collective team as a hierarchy? In fact, the Unit gave priority for emergency access, especially if it was a phonecall about a child at risk.

But there's another side to this. Most hierarchies allocate a slice of their resources for responding to other hierarchies. For instance, agency filtering systems permit staff in one agency to speak to people of equal status in another. This *dual rationing* system is rather like senior officials in communist countries being allowed to use special shops. In Britain arrangements are made for social workers to by-pass the Social Security switchboard. (A privilege which becomes a liability when users find ordinary access increasingly blocked.)

The existence of a dual system is shown by the way hierarchies respond to collective teams. When teams adopt an open door policy, there's an implied rejection of privileged access. Everyone is asked to accept the same reception procedure. It's also one of the ways collective teams attempt to switch resources from servicing outside hierarchies to serving users. In general though, any such shift is apt to be interpreted as 'inefficiency' by people normally granted these privileges. (Though, of course, they wouldn't see themselves in this light.)

That's one reason why simply opposing privileged access isn't enough. The need for a third stage *is* a need for rationing, but a special kind of rationing. Clear open choices are necessary, but with the aim of a continuing critical discussion about them — a discussion which includes an agency's users, other practitioners, and those officials and politicians who will meet the new rules and policies.

All Too Pat?

Finally, let's return to the question of whether the model I've presented is just a rationalisation. After all, one criticism in research on social services teams is that, too often, they are closed and defensive. If the internal strength of collective teams enables them to be more open, am I offering them an excuse to rebuild walls?

But I've argued that there aren't only two options — closed or open. Nor am I suggesting an oversimple third stage solution, neatly synthesising the problems involved. If there *is* oversimplification, it's when there's talk about open doors and 'bringing the community in', while ignoring the implicit means that people find to re-establish boundaries and separation. For this reason, the ideas in this chapter apply to decentralised or 'patch' teams as well as those working collectively.

"Good fences make good neighbours" wrote the poet, Robert Frost,[25] and people draw lines and set markers in the most apparently 'open' spaces.[26]

Lin Harwood: We did have desks, but we didn't have *desks*; everybody always sat in the same place. It's like the sofas in your front room — we tend to sit in the same place. It was like that.

Alison Harker: Once we'd opened up the big |reception| room, I overlapped with Chris Johnson for a about a year — a bit longer perhaps. And she and I always seemed to end up on the same big cushion which was near the radiator.

The outcome can also be far more serious. Politicians provide staff with another kind of 'Brasilia'— new open plan offices — and wonder why they're building their own internal 'shacks' to protect themselves from the noise and bustle.

The lesson is not that openness is a sham, but that unresolved tensions remain. I've suggested that without policies to secure a fair use of an agency's resources, the likely result will be to reflect (and maybe strengthen) the divisions that exist outside. Patterns are set whereby an agency serves — or is thought to serve — particular families, certain racial groups, or one kind of child. Potential users are discouraged from even coming on the premises.

As readers will see, we've taken a back door into the politics of equal opportunity — something very much in the minds of FSU workers, when they asked how many local Asian people used the building and felt comfortable there. The issue was not only the fair allocation of a local resource, but about separation. A building can't determine social relations among users and between users and Unit staff. But it can let or hinder new relationships. So we actually need to pursue not just openness, but equity. And equity means discussing 'why' and 'why not'; acknowledging the existence of continuing tensions. It's these that need bringing into the open.

PART V

SHARING POWER

This final section explores different aspects of power. Power sharing is a core issue for collective working, and perhaps its acid test.Chapter fifteen begins with an issue raised by many critics, and some supporters of collective working. Since this way of working is apparently designed for *consensus*, order becomes a matter of mutual agreement. So what happens when things go wrong — sometimes badly wrong?

> *Shirley Forster*: Because management's a shitty job. It was great, you know, when you're in social services you know how crap the management is. And it gives you an excuse for all sorts. When you're actually sat there with a budget of so much, and so much to do with it, it's dead hard. We learnt that it was dead hard. We stopped doing all the snidey comments behind the UO's back that we used to get up to. Because we had to do it; we had to be responsible ourselves. And that responsibility for your work gives quite a different feeling to having somebody else do it for you.

Chapter sixteen briefly discusses some of the links between collective working and gender. Not only was Newcastle FSU mainly a team of women, they had been strongly influenced by feminism, with its own special contribution to equality.

Lastly, chapter seventeen looks at the possibility of extending the experience of collective working beyond a workgroup and into the wider community. How far are there lessons here, not just in the involvement of agency users, but for all kinds of groups where people are asked to participate as citizens?

Fifteen

Power and Control

Shirley Forster: In some ways I think we were more ruthless. That partly reflects that people actually felt more responsible. Because they couldn't say, 'Ah, UO's job', or 'Management committee's job', whatever. You felt responsible for sorting this out, so you got on and did it. Which isn't to say that conflicts don't happen, because they still will.

Shirley, Lilian White, and I led a small group discussion during FSU's 1985 Annual Conference. We described the development of Newcastle's self-management, and the link between this and *empowering* users — both, in the Unit's view, about people working together in ways which enabled them to have more control over their lives.

There's a question outsiders often ask about power inside a collective team. Here it came up simple and sharp: "What would happen if somebody needed to be disciplined?" Shirley and Lilian gave a blunt answer. Yes, they did sometimes need to exercise such power. Collective working meant members having to do as the staff group wished — which might entail directing and controlling them. "It has happened" Shirley said, thinking of two occasions when they'd warned someone about poor work. She went on to spell out how people took responsibility because of joint management, not in spite of it.

I don't mean they were happy about using sanctions. In fact, staff were reluctant to let things go that far. First they would try and help the person work better.

Lilian: I think, within the management team, there's much more opportunity to get in there early to sort things out before they get to an official procedure.

Shirley: There is a certain space for people's feelings. But you can waste an awful lot of time being sorry for people when what you need is to sort out the work that needs doing, or to provide whatever help needs providing so that the person can do the work.

Their views were endorsed by other Unit staff.

> *Ernie Dobson*: Our first response to anybody would be to try and be helpful and supportive; to see if there was any way that they could feel happier and the team could feel happier with the kind of work that we wanted the person to do. Or whether there were some changes that could be made which would be appropriate and valid. But if that broke down and didn't work, I would hope we would have clearer mechanisms for dealing with it.
>
> Given the system of assessments we have, if you don't perform in this way, then we as a group say you're going to have to improve. If you're not working in the way we expect, then you'll reckon to get the boot. Now we have that power and I've no doubts that we could use it.[1]

Making Someone Do Something

"The purpose of locating power is to fix responsibility for consequences", argues the political philosopher Steven Lukes.[2] Here were Newcastle workers making very plain statements about using power and owning their responsibility. Elsewhere, thought Ernie, this was something "people are vague about — they try to skirt round it". FSU weren't skirting; power and control should be exercised openly and clearly. Roughly summarised: 'we can, we should, and we do'.

Writing on collective teams has frequently cast doubt on this view. Critics have asserted that such teams find exercising control a serious problem. The arguments range from: 'They can't, and they don't' to, 'They ought not to anyhow!'. For many outsiders, the biggest problem is the absence of hierarchical control. Haven't collective teams abandoned the most effective mechanism for *making someone do something*? Here's Tony Boyd, from the management committee.

> *Tony*: Supposing somebody takes the afternoon to go
> to the hairdressers or something? Who's going to say?
> And who's going to know? Whose responsibility is it?

A complementary argument is that in a collective team, everything is far too *personal*. Suppose somebody does know, and does say. Don't the rules and procedures of hierarchy at least allow someone to defend themselves against unfair criticism? So what's to ensure that collective judgements are *fair*? Tom Hammill, also on the management committee, made this point. Though he wasn't denying there was personal influence at Newcastle University, where he taught.

> *Tom Hammill*: Yes, but we do have a formal chain of
> responsibility/accountability. I think it puts some *limits*
> on influence — informal influence. It gives you,
> perhaps, more opportunity to correct things.

The Unit Organiser's group had expressed similar worries about joint management. Might it cover up and collude with poor work — especially when a worker was liked and trusted? Such doubts have been raised about teams elsewhere. In trying to be 'supportive', will they be too soft? Are members ready to confront poor work when they have to keep working next to the colleague criticised? Curiously, the opposite point is also made: that teams can be unfairly hard — perhaps scapegoating certain members.

> *Tony Boyd*: There might be the sort of ganging-up
> thing that goes on.

All these supposed weaknesses are brought together in the charge that collective teams operate what's called, 'community justice'; informal, interpersonal ways of resolving disputes. Which leads to the argument that they are actually worse off than with clear hierarchical rules. The 'ganging-up thing' is sometimes called the "Tyranny of Structurelessness", meaning that hidden behind a curtain of formal equality, the reality is a controlling caucus or group, tightly pulling the strings.[3]

> *Tom Hammill*: Whether de facto, one or two people
> have power without the formal responsibility and
> accountability.

I mentioned one further criticism — that colleagues should not be disciplining each other. This is based on a different set of principles, and challenges the whole idea of a collective team using power against its members.[4] For example, it would reject Shirley's comment about workers being "more ruthless" with each other. If there's such enforcement, how could a workgroup be *co-operating*? Joan Smith hinted at this argument when explaining why supervision and support weren't delegated during her sabbatical.

> *Joan*: If it isn't shared and mutual, does it have any meaning?

Doubts like these match feelings among many members of collective teams elsewhere. Having to sanction or discipline members is felt as a *failure* of collective working, rather than an integral part of it. After all, aren't they aiming at "kinder and more respectful ways of working", and with making the workplace less alienated? So how can this square with accepting that some of those same colleagues can "reckon to get the boot"?

There's the linked idea that working hard and well is a matter of *self-motivation*. If you believe in and want to do the work, you will need neither carrot nor stick.[5] Sometimes there's even the notion that a collective ought to allow virtual autonomy for each staff member; that other workers may persuade, but not direct. Here's a worker in a collective advice centre.[6]

> Working collectively means for us that we are free of interference from each other. We do not accept that collectivisation involves or requires any degree of regimentation or strict control by the group.

Power Between

Let's take the above points in turn, beginning with the argument that exercising control is intrinsically difficult without a formal hierarchical pyramid.

Readers will have no trouble spotting the underlying assumption here. It's the notion that power itself is hierarchical. Formal accountability is always 'upwards', while control means checking and restricting those 'below'. The classical description of power in a bureaucracy is of something a superior delegates to a subordinate. The problem is balancing the need to give discretion, with the wish to control what subordinates do.

Such taken for granted top-down thinking permeates conventional views of management. So people talk about 'leaderless groups', and questions to collaborative teams imply the unspoken phrase, 'Now that you don't have a boss'. With just two apparent options — over or under — workers are often wary about notions like empowerment of users. If there is only directing or being directed, increasing client control looks suspiciously like swapping one boss for another. It's therefore crucial to state that *there is no logical reason why power has be synonymous with hierarchy*. Nor must the use of power inevitably create it or be tied to it.

Muddling the two is the cause of a number of misconceptions about collective working (including among some people working in collectives). For example, it leads to confusion about delegation. A group delegating power does not thereby set up a hierarchy. There can be a different kind of power relationship — power between — which is just as much about accountability and control.

Take Lilian White's membership of the Unit Organisers' group. Although Lilian had authority from Newcastle, she was its delegate and accountable to the Unit for her actions. She felt some of the UOs misunderstood this.

> *Lilian*: I would discuss the agenda for the UO's meeting before going, and at times have been mandated to vote on certain things. I might appear to be quite rigid. There's not always that constraint. There's quite often a lot of room for negotiation.

Asking: 'How do you make someone do what they don't want to?' is a fair question. But it is *not* the same as, 'Who comes down and sorts you out?' The Newcastle staff team required Lilian to give an account of her actions, and they needed ways of ensuring she voted as mandated. But the vital point is that without hierarchy, the tasks of review and control don't vanish. They are, in Chris Johnson's words:

The biggest challenge to collective working generally — once you've no longer got the bad guy to do the management.

We can put this more positively. A work group beginning to pool its effort and skills has an *opportunity* to explore the use of power without tying itself up in vertical chains of command. How far is a team member mandated and how much room have they for manoeuvre? Questions of motivation, sanctions and rules can each be discussed far more clearly by untangling them from the automatic assumption of hierarchy.

Clearly, it would be helpful to use an analysis of power which puts such questions into a neutral form. Instead of assuming hierarchy, we need to be able to understand power and conflict so as to include 'horizontal' relationships among and between, as well as above and below.

A neutral model is proposed by Steven Lukes.[2] For Lukes, power involves conflict of interest. Though conflict can also be pursued by persuasion and influence — falling short of the exercise of power. He assumes at least two parties in conflict, and that power is exercised when one of them (call them A) gets the other (B) to act in a way which is against B's interests — as perceived by B. The two parties needn't be individuals. Groups and institutions exercise power between each other.

If this seems an over-abstract way of approaching a small team, consider how it fits each of the changes which took place at the Unit, not just internally, but in relation to national FSU, the City Council, and so on. Whether in a team or a large organisation, we can never properly understand conflict and its outcome if we focus on the up and down of formal line management.

Rules — An Opportunity To Correct Things?

What then of the up and down of formal rules, and the claim that at least bureaucratic hierarchies offer staff the protection of orderly procedures giving "an opportunity to correct things", as Tom Hammill put it? The implication is that collective teams are *disorderly* and *unruly*. Newcastle's experience can be cited both for and against such a view.

Formal rules there certainly were. For instance, one condition laid down for national agreement to joint staff management, was that the Unit amend formal Discipline and Grievance procedures — national FSU's standard rules for all Units. Broadly, Newcastle's new procedures meant that its local management committee and assistant director had to agree to steps such as formal written warnings, and dismissal. There was provision for trade union representation, and for the involvement of the national director.

During discussion about the new procedures, Pam Flynn suggested a more radical change. She proposed a right of advocacy for committee members belonging to a worker's support group, and with a special interest in that area of work. Advocates would have been able to make representations on behalf of workers; a right in addition to having a union representative.

> *Pam Flynn*: I've been involved over the years in being in one or two different management set-ups where people have not worked well. Or have actually needed to have procedure brought against them. Or to bring procedure.
>
> I'm a very active trade unionist and so I'm very clear on structures. I believe that people — just in their day to day work — it is useful, if you have a management committee, to have a particular member of the committee who is on your side; who knows your work well; who knows the issues involved in it; who supports you through it. And if it comes to grievance or discipline, can act as your advocate.

Though Pam's scheme wasn't adopted, it's significant as an attempt at a genuinely non-hierarchical procedure — where people could be judged by and with their peers. Pam assumed that formal procedures can be productive and sensitive, as well as fair and open.

This was Ernie Dobson's view as well. As Union shop steward, he supported workable "clearer mechanisms", especially as the old procedures had turned out to be inadequate when Lin Harwood invoked them. Ernie felt that the defects then, were due to the Unit having been "in transition" to col-

lective working. So while the team had been involved informally, Joan Smith's position as UO had given her the short
straw.

> *Ernie*: Obviously, given the grievance procedure we
> had, the UO had a particular role to play in relation to
> that. When that happened we didn't say, 'Oh well,
> Joan. You have to do that now'. Obviously when Lin
> and Joan were in together, perhaps that was what it
> had to be. In terms of the preparation of what we were
> going to say, and looking at things we were gonna put,
> Joan didn't do that on her own. She always did it with
> other people. We prepared our answer collective; we
> prepared together. In fact we didn't do it in a big team.
> I mean, we asked around, but I think two or three of
> us together.

Ernie's confidence in formal procedures wasn't felt by everyone. Shirley Forster's views were also coloured by the dispute
with Lin. But she drew the opposite conclusion.

> *Shirley*: We've got a grievance procedure that was
> drawn up at the cost of sweat and tears. Probably is no
> more help than the old one that we had when there
> was a hierarchy.

Undoubtedly, such pessimism is shared by members of collective teams elsewhere. Why should this be so? Lin Harwood
suggested an interesting answer. It wasn't that she had been
dissatisfied with the procedure as such. On the contrary.

> *Lin*: The Union bloke just about burst a blood vessel.
> And talked lots of Unionese at her [Joan Smith]. I love
> the way Union people talk. It was a wonderful
> experience; I felt so supported; it was fantastic. All I
> had to do was sit there, and this guy just chundered on
> about this and that. And he said the Union would be
> very happy to take it further.

But Lin felt — was emphatic about it — that by the time
things had reached an adversary stage, formal procedures
didn't help. It was too late.

> *Lin*: By that time I knew — I must have known — I
> would have to leave when I'd done that. But I thought,
> 'I've had enough of this crap'.

The 'crap' had been meetings, rows, and long drawn out attempts — from Lin's point of view — to get the support of her colleagues. Once this had happened, she knew, as did the others, that subsequent formal steps were more like an official announcement of the breakdown than the start of a process to solve the problems. The game had already been played out. To take an analogy, something like Pam Flynn's proposal for grievance and discipline would have offered marriage guidance when what's wanted is a quick divorce.

Easing and Squeezing

The suspicion then — and sometimes people's experience — is that formal procedures are none too helpful. The explanation seems to be that all the substantive questions have already been decided. The real 'hearings' have been in private. In fact, didn't FSU carry on meeting privately ("We prepared our answer collective") *during* the formal proceedings with Lin?

   One inference is that social control in small face-to-face groups is essentially personal and informal; a kind of 'private' or 'community' justice. As a result, formal procedures, including the general law, become far less important, perhaps even having more of a ceremonial function. In such a setting, formal steps seem akin to a rite of passage; a ritual which changes the status of the person concerned. This certainly fits the experience of some teams where it feels as though an invisible wall now exists, beyond which someone has ceased being a colleague (and perhaps a friend).[7]

> *Lin Harwood*: All right, it was shitty. But I still liked all
> those people, and it really hurt me when I left and no-
> body said goodbye. There was not even: 'We're fucking
> glad we're getting rid of you'. There was nothing. It
> was like I'd never been.

Studies of small teams often reach similar conclusions. Joyce Rothschild, for example, found that collective teams do not accept "standardised rules to achieve social control", but rely instead on personal and moral appeals.[8] Some writers on management see agencies like FSU as having a predominantly "personal" organisational culture, compared with others which have strong centralised power, or a culture centred on the detailed application of rules.[9]

Such analyses lean on Max Weber's writing, early this century. Weber described bureaucracy as a technically superior mode of organisation — a judgement which has continued to influence thinking about organisations ever since.[10] He suggested that large bureaucracies with their complex systems of rules represent an advance over more 'primitive' and personal means of control. By comparison, small scale face-to-face groups are more like a 'community', with organic solidarity, and a process for easing or squeezing out people whose difference is not tolerated. The application of such a theory to squeezing out a member of a collective team hardly needs spelling out.[11]

The Tyranny of Structurelessness

The 'community justice' critique is sometimes pushed further still. It's said that informal and personal power can lead to the antithesis of formal equality. In chapter two, we saw Lin Harwood posing just this challenge to Chris Johnson; that Chris informally wore the mantle of Unit Organiser during Joan Smith's sabbatical.

> *Lin Harwood*: I told her. I said, 'In your own way
> you're being the bloody Unit boss here. You're telling
> us how this Unit's gonna be run'. I used to have a
> copy of that *Tyranny of Structurelessness* thing. It's like,
> if you've got a boss you can blame the boss, right?

Lin was referring to a well known feminist pamphlet by Jo Freeman, discussing the danger of a hidden, informal hierarchy emerging within a formally egalitarian group.[3] Chris, denying the charge, also mentioned the pamphlet.

> *Chris Johnson*: I think we were all very aware of those
> dangers. And as much as anybody could do, sought to
> combat that. We were aware of the individual power

> people could get. And I think we certainly weren't structureless. I mean, the whole thing of having to convince a management committee even before Joan left meant that there was actually a huge amount; more structure in it when she went than ever there had been before.

Jo Freeman originally wrote for the Women's Movement, at a time [1970] when its most common form of organisation was the small consciousness raising group. Freeman thought this had proved inadequate once women become involved in specific practical projects or wider politics. From time to time, people writing about collective teams take her pamphlet as a warning. 'Don't think you can just abolish hierarchy and run democratically', they imply. 'See here, someone from the Women's Movement *admits* it can't really work'. Invoking Freeman, critics have declared that "too much informality leads to undemocratic practices and the emergence of elites",[12] or asked why socialists and feminists have, "this addiction to such a self-defeating form of (non)organisation?"[13]

One edition retitled the pamphlet: 'Informal Elites'. A cartoon was added, with a woman pointing to the hidden "central committee" — a small clique gathered at the pub, who've ended up running things without acknowledging it.

This is the bit in the pamphlet which always gets quoted.

> If the movement continues to deliberately not select who shall exercise power, it does not thereby abolish power. All it does is abdicate the right to demand that those who do exercise power and influence be responsible for it.

Oddly, one part that's rarely referred to is Freeman's conclusion, where she makes the following proposals for *avoiding* a hidden hierarchy, and achieving accountability and responsibility.

1: "Delegation of specific authority to specific individuals for specific tasks by democratic procedures".
2: Requiring delegates to be responsible to the group, which has ultimate power.
3: "Distribution of authority among as many people as reasonably possible".

4: Rotation of tasks but so that the individual can "learn her job well and acquire the sense of satisfaction of doing a good job".
5: Allocation of tasks according to ability and interest; through apprenticeship.
6: "Diffusion of information to everyone".
7: Equal access to a group's resources, including members' skills and information.

For many people, this solution is likely to produce exactly the kind of structure they see as the problem. (Certainly the seven principles point nicely at what Newcastle came up with in joint management). But there's no paradox if we focus, not on structure, but on *power relations* — which is what Jo Freeman herself is centrally concerned with.

Freeman does not object to groups or individuals exercising power. Nor is she saying that informal elites are a type of "non-organisation". On the contrary, her crucial point is that the growth of informal elites within egalitarian groups can undermine *democratic* power relations. It replaces power between, with power over — but masked power; unaccountable and hidden behind a "smokescreen for the strong or lucky".

Her proposals are not to ensure formality as such; they're to prevent the abuse of informality by *hidden power*. Their aim is to fix responsibility by making power open, clear and confrontable.

Masked Power at FSU?

How far do these ideas help us understand events at FSU? When Lin Harwood mentioned Jo Freeman's pamphlet, she gave the example of Chris Johnson picking up unallocated bits of work during Joan's sabbatical. Chris herself explained.

> *Chris Johnson*: I certainly felt, because I was really committed to the whole thing working, very responsible for thesuccess of the operation. Which inevitably, perhaps, therefore means that you end up picking up some of the things.

Well, why not? Freeman argued that, even when a member is willing to take on a task, the group itself ought still to select; and the person concerned make a commitment. The point is not someone's bad faith or malice, but that: "individuals may exercise power, but it is the group that has the ultimate say over how it is exercised."

Sally Walker raised a different aspect of hidden power. In tensions between herself and Ali Rhind, she'd felt relatively powerless. Thinking back, Sally was puzzled why she hadn't pushed harder, or brought things to a head.

> *Sally*: I wasn't getting anything out of going to the Unit meetings, so I didn't go. Which meant that Ali was the one who'd go to Unit meetings, representing my views. All the way along the line Ali's made loads and loads of efforts to include my views and work as a team. But that was a problem because Ali was part of the Unit staff and identifying strongly as part of the Unit staff and getting their support.
>
> There was the other part-time workers, and I was, sort of, in limbo between. Because it was all meant to be equal, there wasn't any clear guidelines. So in terms of informal power, Ali had all the informal power.

Why didn't Sally tackle this? She had every right to. It was still a question she asked herself several months after leaving the Unit. It seems reasonable to say that Sally had faced a team with such greater power that she avoided making a demand on it. I don't mean that they ganged up on her. The significance of masked power is that it's exercised just as effectively by the processes and mechanisms by which things come up for discussion — or are left off. One person encountering what they see as a strong group, may simply avoid engaging that strength.

All Big and Qualified People

Here's another viewpoint, from someone who we haven't heard from a lot. When I met Brenda White she'd been Pool Girls' Club worker for two years; the job was 18 hours a week. Brenda wasn't an FSU staff member. Though the club started as a Unit project, it was independent. Even so, Shirley Forster was on the club management committee and supervised her.

Thirty to forty girls met in a room at Elswick pool. Brenda had a small office in a back room at FSU where she prepared evening sessions, and organised volunteer helpers. She supervised club activities, and then walked many of the girls home. A second session for older girls was just starting up.

> *Brenda White:* Really, in the last couple of weeks some of the girls have been coming in, and they're the height of me and maybe a bit taller. And I say, 'Ee, are thee growing or am I shrinking?'

Brenda preferred to be left largely alone to get on with the job. But felt she would get help from FSU staff when she needed it.

> I feel at ease to go and talk to any one of them. If they're sitting in the reception room, they've always got time to sit and talk with me. If I write something I always get it checked. I get the okay from Shirley and then I send it out. If it's just writing a brief note I get Blanche to check it with me.

She liked the idea of joint management with "everybody pulling together."

> I think it's best if you've got a group of people where you can sit and have a good natter about it; really have a good discussion and weigh up the pros and cons.

All the same, Brenda was very uncomfortable about power. She'd found it hard to direct a helper who wasn't working as she wanted.

> I'm not a person to do that. I can't do that. 'Cause the kids say to me, 'Are you the boss?' And I say, 'Oh, no I'm not. We all work together; everybody tries and helps here. It just so happens that I'm wrote down on the piece of paper'.

She described being on the receiving end of FSU's power. On one occasion, they'd asked her to store stuff in a toilet — something which rankled.

I went in each time. The toilet was staring us in the face and I had to pile all this stuff around. I thought, 'I shouldn't be doing this'. And I just refused it. I didn't, like, say, 'No, I'm not doing it'. I just stopped putting the club stuff in.

Well, eventually they said, "What's wrong with using the toilet?" And I went, "Oh, I don't think I should be".

Then Shirley says, "Do you want to come to the next Unit meeting and tell them about it?"

I said, "No, I don't. Just tell them from me." I'm stubborn like that, and I thought, 'If they can be good enough to make decisions without me there, well, why should I be there to make decisions about my stuff? Do I need their blessing about it?' Alan, I was really annoyed and I think I might have really blown me top, getting very upset. I had very little confidence in myself to start with. And I saw these as all being big and qualified people.

Brenda stressed that this didn't stop her liking the staff — "I couldn't think of a nicer team to work with." But they were, "a bit nigh-sighted at times". [ie. near, or short-sighted]

I don't know if it's fine saying that it's supposed to be a collective now, isn't it? Everybody's supposed to be in charge and responsible for one another and all this. Well, sometimes I have mixed feelings about FSU getting credit because of the Girls' Club. They have their meetings and they make decisions about doing this, doing that. But I never get to hear about them, and I get it as second-hand news from somebody else.

Like the times I've said to Shirley, "Hey, Shirl. This has been decided and I think I should know."

And she went, "Ee, yes. I'm sorry. I should have told you, but I'm that busy".

So I think if it's a collective and they're good enough to use the Girls' Club name, well I think it's only good manners to tell us what's going on. Although that might sound a bit nasty, I don't want to sound nasty. 'Cause I really like everybody here. Just sometimes I do feel more hurt.

Well, whose power and whose responsibility? Individuals who don't enter the fray and fight their corner? Or a team which doesn't do enough to acknowledge and counter the barriers which prevent them coming in? Brenda's view stressed her own lack of confidence and sheer dislike of potential conflict.

Brenda White and Sally Walker aren't the only ones whose experience could be explained by hidden power.[14] And, as I've said, examples from other collective teams have been used to suggest a weakness in democratic management. In a bureaucratic hierarchy, so the argument goes, formal power is located with the boss: therefore you know who to blame and who to oppose. A collective or co-operative group is seen as replacing this *overt power and overt opposition,* with *covert power* which is far harder to oppose because it's not supposed to exist. As Lin Harwood put it:

> *Lin*: If you work in a collective your right to be alienated disappears.

Questioning The Comparison With Hierarchy

Shirley Forster: We were asked questions that people never ask of the status quo. That was really the hardest thing: to be able to *prove* that what you had was better than people's idealised version of what 'ought' to be in a 'normal' working situation. Which in practice everybody knew wasn't true. But they wanted to know how we'd never managed to have any rows with each other; how we'd never missed doing a social work visit; never had a child beaten on our caseload. And of course, we were not allowed to say, 'Well, in your Unit with a UO, have you ever had a child hit on your caseload? Do you never fall out with each other?'

It's suggested that without hierarchical control mechanisms, the potential strength of a collective team remains unchecked; that its own rules and procedures will be ineffective and too often swayed by personal considerations. The charge (and it is a charge) is that Newcastle and similar teams operate a 'primitive' form of 'community justice', handling conflict substantially through social pressure, social approval or disapproval, or by an appeal to shared principle. The result predicted is an unfair and inconsistent use of power — perhaps even a hidden hierarchy.

In the second part of the chapter I'll look closely at this comparison, in particular, introducing studies which cast doubt on the argument that 'community justice' and 'hidden elites' are a special feature of collective teams. As Shirley Forster observed, attributing such problems to collective working is part of the process whereby hierarchy is judged by its official portrait, and self-management by its warts.

Certainly, it's true that this book includes views and experience from collective teams which could easily signal 'community', rather than a large organisation. Also, to be fair to outsiders, there are times when collective teams seem bent on showing themselves at their worst. More exactly, what sometimes happens is that they strive to present an image of harmony. Tensions are hidden or ignored — till there's an explosion. The upshot is a revelation of 'real' life in the murky depths of group process — dwelling on conflict and catastrophe. Even attempts to open up debate on the realities of self-management can be infected by this, and read like self-laceration.[13]

The Newcastle team weren't claiming an unreal unity. But they challenged the assumption that personal conflict and group power were distinctive features of collective working. What about the realities of hierarchical power?

Hidden Dimensions of Hierarchy

Returning to Steven Lukes, a central part of his analysis is of the hidden dimensions of power. He observes that whereas overt power can be recognised, and possibly regulated, the key feature of hidden power is the difficulty people have in locating and confronting it. Lukes' model is consistent with Jo Freeman's, but not confined to egalitarian groups.

Hidden power is exercised, says Lukes, when conflict of interest has been excluded from public debate and decision-making. It includes the power to set an agenda, or otherwise exclude from certain forums, issues some people would prefer not to discuss. (One of them being who sets the agenda.) As a result, though others appear to acquiesce in what happens, in reality their viewpoint has been prevented from being raised. [15] The absence of overt conflict means only that they have been "denied entry into the political process".[16]

The cartoon I mentioned before, is bitter rather than funny, because it implies a deliberate flouting of a group's openness and trust. But it would be wrong to think of hidden power always needing secret intrigue; the notion isn't limited to this. 'Covert' doesn't depend on conspiracy. In fact, the 'central committee' will often quite fairly protest that it did not set out to exclude anyone, and anyhow, 'If *we* didn't do the work, nobody else would'.

Lukes goes on to propose a third dimension of power. "The complex and subtle ways in which the *inactivity of leaders* and the sheer weight of institutions — political industrial and educational", serves to keep people out of the process and "from even trying to get into it". [17] He finds this even more insidious, since people are prevented from having grievances:

> by shaping their perceptions, cognitions and preferences in such a way that they accept their role in the existing order of things, either because they can see or imagine no alternative to it, or because they value it as divinely ordained and beneficial.

It's precisely when there are large and obvious inequalities that those with greater power have both the means and motive to exclude those with less, from the political processes. Absence of overt conflict can then be interpreted as *consent*. [18] John Gaventa used Lukes' model to explain why poor farmers in Appalachia appeared to accept domination and oppression by large corporations. The formal rights and channels open to them remained unused. Gaventa insists that, focussing on people's apparent choices, we ignore that possible use of power to stifle and exclude conflict. That only "blames the victim for his non-participation". [19]

For the present argument, the implications of Lukes' model are far reaching. Most plainly, it establishes that covert or hidden power in no way belongs to collective teams. On the contrary, the hidden dimensions may operate in *any* situation — among either individuals or groups, and whether or not they are in some formal hierarchical relationship. Don't organisations frequently have 'formal channels' which staff rarely use? How many bosses proclaim 'my door is always open', though nobody need look very far to find less tangible barriers?

When comparing workplaces then, we must make one very important and useful assumption. We're looking for the effects of both overt *and* covert power. Instead of hidden power in collective teams versus open power in hierarchies, the likelihood will be *both* kinds in *both* settings.

Tightening Up The Game

The importance of this will become plainer if we look again at the argument that covert informal power within hierarchies is at least checked and balanced by formal rules and procedures. Let's return briefly to Alvin Gouldner's research in a gypsum plant,[20] and then draw from a British study which specifically compared discipline in co-operative and hierarchial firms.

In chapter fourteen, I mentioned Gouldner's study as an example of the link between teamwork and space. However, his main focus was on bureaucratic rules and control, particularly during a change in management regime. In the plant a new manager was sent in to tighten up the workplace, and one thing he did was introduce and enforce tougher bureaucratic rules. Before then, management had been fairly lenient. There was, "an indulgency pattern", when workers were given considerable leeway and didn't feel they were being constantly checked, nor that management was always pushing.

> When workers lauded management for allowing the injured to work in the sample room, or permitting workers to take company material and tools for personal use, or giving those who violated managerial expectations a 'second chance', they were employing criteria legitimately applicable to the relations among *friends* and *neighbours,* rather than in a *business* and *industrial* context. [original italics] [21]

But ending this friend-and-neighbour regime did not produce a straightforward application of the rules. Gouldner analyses the complex interaction of new rules and the work practices they were designed to control. For example, a rule intended to specify the minimum performance of duties [do less than this and you'll be disciplined] turned into a maximum, since workers knew precisely how *little* they could get away with. Another consequence of tighter rules was to 'screen' the power of middle managers. Rather than own their exercise of power and responsibility, they'd say:

> *It's not my idea.* I've got to go along with the rules *like everyone else.* What *I* want has nothing to do with it.[22]

Ironically, the reverse was often true, too. Supervisors used their discretion to *ignore* a breach of the rules, in order to increase their power over workers. Neither at the leniency stage nor later on, did rules enable an 'impartial' process to redress the 'personal' aspects of work. On the contrary, rules were an integral part of power relations generally.

> Formal rules gave supervisors something with which they could 'bargain' in order to secure *informal* co-operation from workers. The rules were the 'chips' to which the company staked the supervisors and which they could use to play the game.[23]

Co-op versus Company Justice

Stuart Henry's research came to much the same conclusion. Henry compared disciplinary procedures in a sample of co-operative and hierarchical agencies. He began by assuming that co-operatives and collective teams would have a "form of peer group discipline", while large commercial companies would rely on formal rules and, beyond that, the general law. Both assumptions proved false.[24]

The co-ops researched (four housing and eight producer co-ops) did not keep to 'organic' or personal methods of controlling members, nor conform to a model of 'community justice'. It was true that they made allowances for members' personal problems, with more leeway for someone who was known and trusted. But still, a point would come when a group "would have to talk to the person concerned and say, 'If you are not able to do the job it may be the wrong one for you'. [25] Beyond that point, a large measure of control was based on social sanctions. Sometimes there was shaming and confrontation. "The rest of us are always criticising each other. This hurt their pride too much and they left".[26]

Peer group pressure was frequently formalised. Having a meeting about someone's work meant taking it seriously. As a co-op member explained: "Groups are sitting down and making judgement on a fellow member". And if that didn't work? When people persistently broke rules, co-ops used formal discipline, including some co-ops with an explicit policy of avoiding it. Several groups had highly formal review and appeals committees.

> The big stick — it's always there in the background.

> The atmosphere in the shop was so bad. In actual fact, we gave him a week's notice.

Henry compared this with a sample of private companies (including firms in transport, catering, metal manufacture and engineering). Some were authoritarian, with a 'management must manage' attitude. Others prefered consultative, or joint bodies involving the trade union. Despite the existence of formal procedures, a feature in every case was reliance on 'personal' or 'community' justice which was *used to make the formal system work*.

> Unofficially, normally one discusses what one's got in mind with the Union advocate before the case is heard. (manager)

Instead of the formal system providing an *alternative* — checking and balancing community justice — company managers were happy to use the latter to supplement their own power. It was an integral part of the discipline process, taken into account by both management and Union.

> If the others either side of him are hard working chaps they will jolly soon see that he comes into line in their own way. I don't know how they do it, but we suddenly find that that chap is suddenly working quite well. (personnel manager)

Shopfloor pressure against a dismissal was especially strong when someone's workmates felt that formal procedures ought to take long service or personal problems into account. On the other hand:

> It is interesting when, for example, we see that the view of the factory is very much in favour of dismissal, irrespective of what the Union representative might say. We know very well that the Union representative has a part to play or a role to play regardless of the offence, as a sort of advocate, but very often it is perceived that he is very happy to see the action taking effect. (manager)

Henry concluded that instead of two distinct types of workplace justice, a wide range of features were shared. Most significantly, though 'community justice' and formal rules are usually seen as separate, they actually form a single system with interdependent parts. It follows that understanding the operation of formal disciplinary rules and procedures requires a description of their *interaction* with all the other processes going on. Work groups, Trade Union, and managers, will each operate parallel *and* each have links with the others — shaping, influencing and changing them. This is borne out by Gouldner's research, and by many other workplace studies.

An important consequence is that in any workplace, making an intentional change is a lot more complex than simply altering the rules. Which is one good reason why a group won't sort out its problems of control by looking for the 'right' grievance and disciplinary procedures. A new set of rules will alter the existing pattern of relations, but will also be *absorbed into them*. Like any new 'legislation', how far it's enforced and how much it's a dead letter, depends on existing power and influence.

Again this corresponds to Gouldner's study. The gypsum miners, with greater solidarity and physical separation, were able to resist new bureaucratic rules more effectively than the surface workers. It also suggests a similar result at Newcastle FSU. Though the Unit had not yet tested their new procedure, it seemed likely that its operation would be modified by internal group processes in the same way as the old rules.

Let me stress that findings like these are not exceptional. At least since the 1930's, writing in Industrial Psychology suggests it would be unusual to find a work group which *didn't* develop some 'organic' norms and sanctions.[27] Teams — and not just collective teams — may combine mutual support and · solidarity, with keeping members in line through a range of processes from the pull of friendship to the push of shaming and silence.[28] It's true that research on co-operatives often contradicts this conclusion, stressing peer presure, virtually as one of their special characteristics. [29] However, it appears that such research often fails to take the wider studies into account.

Could things be otherwise? Some writers on organisations have suggested we need *more bureaucracy;* tighter, more impersonal rules. For them, what I've written could seem like an excuse for 'office politics' as usual; co-ops and collectives sharing the rough and tumble of organisational life with teams in hierarchies. Members of collective teams sometimes think along similar lines, wondering (or hoping) whether there might be some foolproof neutral procedure for discipline. Is there a method which doesn't mean stomach churning meetings and the unpleasantness of "sitting down and making judgement on a fellow member"?

But the examples in this chapter (and discussion of rules and structures throughout the book) point to the impossibility of neutral rules operating in neutral space. Least of all can this happen *where rules are intended to regulate the exercise of power.* Since power entails conflict of interest, setting up a neutral formal procedure will simply ensure that 'public' aspects of the process are no more than a staged performance. The important action will then take place off-stage.

An Adversarial Solution

There's another approach to this problem, one which seeks to detach group power from bureaucratic procedures in quite a different way. Lin Harwood raised it with her comment about a "right to be alienated".

> *Lin*: An official structure you can feel alienated from. You can moan about; you can get cross about. You can involve the Union.

For many staff, "the opportunity to correct things" is not found in official rules and procedures. Indeed, it is the employer's power (expressed through those rules) which poses the problem. In response, workers 'below' push back collectively, building an opposing power centre. Their fellow workers, judging them to have been treated unjustly, have the power to come to their aid.

At first sight, this is an attractive option: a counterpoint to bureaucratic rules; an adversarial check to the problem of control. Workers' solidarity through the Union offers 'our' structures and rules to balance the power of 'theirs'. It means the type of 'joint consultation' described by Stuart Henry would be dismissed as *incorporation* — the Union trading away its power to oppose.

Of course, workers have many good reasons for opposing the "official structure". But an oppositional solution still ignores the crucial question which Lin herself finally faced. What happens when members of a work group need to moan and get cross *with each other?* Like Chris Johnson or Yvonne Waters at FSU, we may dread "horrid meetings". With Brenda White, we can dislike even the idea of making someone do something. People ignore or suppress issues, rather than pay for conflict in their stomachs. But problems of conflict and control won't go away because we belong to a Union shop, any more than in a co-op or collective.

Against this, it's sometimes argued that the overriding conflict of interest between workers and management *always* outweighs differences within a group of colleagues. There are dangers though, of trying to export all conflict outside a group. For one thing, there's a need to locate an 'other' who 'we' can unite against. It means that "those who can and ought to fix things" are always somewhere other than in the peer group of colleagues.[30]

Because, of course, colleagues do get cross with one another. I said earlier that some people question whether a collective team has any business exercising power over members. Yet the existence of a hidden dimension makes it difficult to see how any group coming together to pool its talents and resources can avoid this. Take for example, the advice centre worker who talked about collective working being, "free of interference from each other". That worker went on to describe the team squeezing somebody out. It was a member they'd put up with and regarded as "an eccentric".

> We did of course talk to the guy but this did not
> achieve any lasting improvement.

Nevertheless, the 'eccentric' did leave, shortly after formal procedures were begun, ie. after his colleagues had finally made their evaluation plain.[6] In other words, an attempt to avoid 'interfering' is virtually a recipe for covert power — which, unless owned, can't be confronted and challenged.

To ignore this — imagining that 'we' never exercise power inside our group, and have no conflict of interest — can also have more destructive outcomes.[31] Resentment against masked power within the group is stoked up, until finally there's an explosion. Alternatively, groups padlock themselves into needing 'them' (boss, hierarchy, or outside enemy) more or less permanently.[32] In this instance, going beyond office politics means giving up that secure and comforting thing — the prestige of the victim.[33]

A Gang Through Our Fears

There's another point, more easily seen in a non-profit agency like an advice centre, or FSU. When workers resist criticising and controlling poor work by colleagues, they hurt their users, not a company's profits. But whether we work in a 'human' service agency or not, what does it say about our own principles and integrity if we ignore and work round a colleague? Whether they aren't pulling their weight, or need help because they're floundering, are we justified in waiting till the boss sorts it out?

Successful collective working entails not just the right, but the obligation to demand and evaluate quality from fellow workers — and to have that demand made of us. It asks us to overcome our fear of 'community control'.

It's vital to understand this fear. For it is shared by each of the criticisms we've seen; the negative responses to a group of peers exercising power. Each reflects a deep ambivalence about teamworking. And though the doubts raised seem to focus on potential *problems* in working together, they are as much about its *successes*. Let me explain.

The word 'team' carries strong, positive meanings. But there are other words too — words like *clique, caucus, ganging up*. Because teaming up is always double-edged. We hope for and welcome the strength of a team, while at the same time we fear the power of a group. 'We' in this sense might be members of a team, or one of its users. More than likely, it will be a boss; pleased when a work group is pooling skills and showing sparkle, but at the same time worried in case a turbulent team gets out of control.

With this wider perspective, we can see how disciplining an individual is only one of the ways people may begin to feel a group as restrictive — a pressure, rather than a supportive strength. Which is why it won't do to talk about empowerment in the abstract. When people begin to exercise more control over their lives, power relations change in specific situations. Power isn't a *thing* to be given, (or locked safely away). It always describes a relationship between people.

Take the users of a social services agency. Strictly speaking, they aren't powerless, so much as **overpowered** by others. Changing this requires more than enabling them to speak and giving them a hearing. There comes a point when discussion and persuasion give way to pushing and pressure. Workers in a social servies agency may have encouraged (even applauded) users insisting on their rights from agencies such as DHSS. But will they feel the same if power is exercised against their own agency — or will that be called 'manipulation'?[34]

People's mixed feelings about a strong team come from the same realisation. It's all very well if there's harmony and agreement on shared goals; when a staff group are learning from each other, building confidence, and putting the pieces together. But what's going to happen when there are conflicting interests? Suppose a team starts pushing and pressuring, either members or people outside?

The ambivalence here is a distrust of all groups, but the power of a self-managed team can seem a special problem because it appears to lack those checks and balances associated with other groups. Without hierarchical rules and a ruler, will it be unruly? And, since a gang is a group seen through our fears, will its members gang up?

These mixed feelings are something no collaborative or collective group should forget. Managers can (and do) choose to jettison the benefits of shared skills, co-learning and co-working, rather than risk a threat to their own authority. For a member — or potential member — of a team, the group's power may also be worrying. If, like Brenda White, we "couldn't think of a nicer team to work with", we won't want to think of falling out with them.[35] The judgement of our peers often hurts more and lasts longer than criticism from the boss. Eighteen months after she'd left FSU, Lin Harwood said:

> I feel as unfinished with it now as I did then — which is probably why I agreed to talk to you. Because there's no resolution with those people, and I really like them all.

Facing The Judgement of Our Peers

Joan Smith: In the Unit you're much more answerable to the rest of the team, to your peers, than you might have been in the usual one-to-one supervision thing. There are supervision structures — formal and informal. Which means that you actually discuss your work; seek help, advice; share your anxieties about it; and look to see why something worked, so you can learn from it and apply it elsewhere. People certainly weren't left to get on with things for themselves. The exact opposite happens when you have peer supervision, and times when you meet as a group to talk about work.

One of the things that happened for a lot of people who came to work at the Unit is feeling quite intimidated and even afraid of working so openly. It actually makes you much more thoughtful and careful and answerable to others [chuckle]. It isn't saying, 'Go away and do your thing, I've got every confidence in you'. It isn't just saying that at all.

I've described how mixed feelings about the power of a group lead to two sorts of response. The hierarchical 'answer' is to adopt rules which formally exclude peer power, while tacitly welcoming and using it. The oppositional stance is either to deny its existence ("We are free of interference from each other") or to idealise workers' solidarity as somehow transcending the need for control.

There's a third possibility. In the last part of this chapter, I'll sketch some aspects of a collective team approach which aims at exercising power openly, while bearing the responsibility that goes along with it. It also means recognising and accepting the sometimes messy reality of 'community control', and realising that support and criticism are not distinct functions, but two sides of the same coin — an integral whole.[36]

In chapter twelve, I used the phrase *building judgement* to describe the process whereby teams learn together, gaining and making their own understanding of issues. Well, teams build judgements of one another's work in just the way they make other assessments and evaluations. People are judged from the moment they apply to join. The subsequent process by which colleagues take the measure of each other is no less an evaluation.

As Joan Smith suggested, staff with a background in hierarchies can feel "quite intimidated and even afraid" of making judgements about peers and of being judged. But they might ask themselves how far they assume simply a more powerful version of their previous experience — of gossip, cliques, and unowned, whispered criticism. Judgements are inevitable. They can't be abolished. But we can aim to unmask them, making them owned and open.

Take, for example, the position of the secretaries at FSU. Like admin staff anywhere, they had their own views on what was going on; about work and about their colleagues. As we saw, they passed on some of *those* judgements to students, as "verbal profiles of the staff". When Shirley Forster became liaison person with the secretaries, she set up fortnightly meetings to discuss their work. Shirley realised that the first hurdle to get over was their reluctance to open up and state views openly.

> *Shirley*: Their only way of making complaint was to slam the filing cabinet drawer very loudly when you were on the phone.

They had very little experience of actually being asked their opinion on things. So they varied between absolute silence to, 'Do you expect us to comment on that?' Or to take the piss out of it. Loads and loads of that. Because it was their chance of having years' worth of revenge on fieldworkers. Oh, I sat through many a tale of the sins of myself and the people before. But then, at the end of that, what's happened is that, in a sense, they're much more responsible now for their work, and much less just have their work handed down to them.

Supervision and Consultation

Let me make it plain that, giving the secretaries as an example, I don't mean the Unit split the tasks of review and control. The joint management team weren't consulting together, while 'supervising' the other workers.

In many agencies, consultation and supervision are discussed and treated as if they were separable. In hierarchies, the two aspects are then attributed to different *structures*, with 'line management' contrasted with consultant or 'non-executive' staff. The idea is that some staff control and direct, while others only advise and persuade; in other words, that influence can be detached from the exercise of power.

We can see this idea in the ambivalence which lower level staff in social service agencies often bring to the issue of review and supervision. The ideal supervisor is seen as someone with a great deal of experience, who is able and willing to share their practice skills. However, they shouldn't be directive and controlling. So, workers value 'staff support', but are fearful if it should become 'the big stick'.

But the distinction is illusory. The exercise of power is not confined to those staff who 'officially' and legitimately instruct someone else to do something. Just as superiors influence as well as direct subordinates, so individuals and groups will be bringing powerful pressure to bear on their colleagues, some of whom will be peers and some superiors.

Supervision is a process involving co-learning, and judgement building *as well as the negotiation and use of power*. It's not a *thing* a team has. Neither is it a structure, though the process takes place within a network of overlapping forums. For instance, at FSU, the pattern of interlinking groups and sub-groups (staff team, paired supervision, support groups) were forums for control as well as learning, support and persuasion. The learning network described in chapter thirteen was also a control network.[37]

This is why Lilian White replied to a question about *discipline* by stressing face-to-face contact in the various working groups.

> *Lilian*: For people who are outside of that team there's much less contact. Much less opportunity to work together to actually see what each of us are doing. And much more difficult to pick up if a particular worker's struggling and not being able to produce the type of work that is to be produced.

Best Criticism and Due Process

In many teams, people's mixed feelings about power are shown when they discuss *criticism*. Saying 'constructive' or positive' criticism, wrongly suggests there might be a way of shutting out the negatives. There's usually a confusion with hierarchy as well, if staff have been used to the boss taking the critic's role.

> *Pam Carter*: You don't know whether you're doing a good job a bad job, or what. 'Cause the general atmosphere was very supportive.

What Pam wanted to see was more *open* criticism. She had no doubt that there was plenty hidden. Like the views of the secretaries, it could be feelings and thoughts people kept to themselves, or shared off-the-record. A few months later, she saw an improvement.

> *Pam*: The incident I was describing the other day, when we said to one of the workers, 'You'd better go and do it even though you don't like it'.

Many reasons have been mentioned why people veer away from criticising their colleagues, and I've said that criticism stings worse the more you respect your critic's judgement. Yet this has another side. For one thing, the experience of teams like FSU suggests that anticipation of conflict is frequently worse than the event. People are rarely as fragile as we fear, and often, to travel fearfully is worse than arriving at open disagreement.

Second, avoiding appraisal of a colleague and accepting poor work from them can actually signify low expectations. The implication is: 'I wouldn't have expected you to produce anything better'. Whereas giving someone our *best criticism* is a demand for their best work, and is, in its own way, a compliment to their abilities.

Shirley Forster's wider aim in her meetings with the secretaries was enabling them to make their judgements plain and open; to invite their best criticism. This was long overdue, she thought. But it wasn't just a case of what *they* were due. The staff team also hoped to draw the secretaries into the collective discussions. Doing this would give other workers the chance to question and perhaps challenge their views. *Due process*, then, takes on a different meaning when, instead of inquiring whether the right set of rules and procedures are followed, we ask *what are people due?*

As usual, I'm not saying FSU got it right, or always managed to "get in there early to sort things out". Staff were frequently critical about their own failure to use power when appropriate — when it had been someone's due. For instance, Pam Carter mentioned how the team had avoided facing and settling problems between Ali and Sally in the Women's Workshops.

It would be easy to see all this as yet more evidence of "wimping about in great angst-ridden meetings" (in Pam Flynn's phrase), this time concerned with judging colleagues. So perhaps it's worth recalling that the phrase for a work group jumping to a rapid conclusion about a member is 'kangeroo court'. Aiming at a "careful and thoughtful" appraisal of someone's work, the result can seem as messy as any other judgement building. But we should judge a team by its reach as well as its grasp.

Team History

It's essential to notice that we're talking about judgements made over *time*. We learn about and assess our colleagues over days *and* years. Fellow workers mark our worth not once but over and again — a process which is obscured if we think of people suddenly sitting in judgement. Thoughtful appraisal is built one brick at a time. It comes out of a knowledge of our skills, past work, and personal qualities; our strengths as well as weaknesses; the achievements alongside the mistakes and messes. There's usually a history to it.

Of course, there are different sorts of histories. The story of a work group can be told according to the doings of leaders; their involvement in shaping its rules and structures, and the important events they were involved in. So, if power is a buck that finally stops, history becomes a record of steps upward or downwards. In a hierarchy, assessment comes to mean the event of being assessed by superiors (including promotion). The process of control narrows to when "somebody needed to be disciplined".

With this blinkered view, it isn't surprising if openness looks intimidating. Peer power could seem like the demand to take down those psychological walls round our desk and suddenly submit to a public inquiry. The fact that we *all* make our group's history is overshadowed or elbowed out by the sole inquiry of who came down to sort things out and when.

The team's history is essential in understanding the dispute with Lin Harwood. That was no sudden judgement from above. On the contrary, there was a marked continuity in their valuation and re-evaluation. Three years had given people great respect for her work. As a result, their re-assessments were also drawn out.

> *Ernie*: I knew Lin originally as a person who was a
> kind of source of inspiration; an exceptionally
> intelligent person who was constantly overflowing with
> ideas and things, and constantly stimulating. And had
> a knack of getting to the heart of the matter.

Trust soundly built was hardly going to be demolished overnight. As in many groups, a reversal in people's views meant that one or two supports fell away; a few more began to wobble and totter; and later, most of the rest shifted all at once. (For Sally Walker, who remained Lin's friend, it "escalated and became some sort of impossible thing to sort out".)

Feelings and Fairness

Collective teamwork involves recognising feelings as a part of working together. So what about the conflict between the claims of friendship, and a team's fair dealing? People at FSU weren't all close friends nor, on the whole, in and out of each other's lives outside work. Perhaps they were no closer than many work groups who don't see themselves as collective. But members assumed (even when they felt the team wasn't living up to its standards) that caring about and being concerned for those you work with, was an essential part of being a 'real' team. They expected to come to know, personally like or dislike, respect and often enjoy one another.

I don't want to idealise this. We've seen examples of times when people felt the team had not shown caring or concern. This was Sally's criticism of the team's response to Lin and, in a different way, when Ali Rhind brought her feelings and problems to the study day.

> *Sally Walker*: There had been a lot of angst and a lot of problems and a lot of pain over all that. And it wasn't really taken up within the Unit.

Not everyone was confident the group would always be able to handle, for instance, selfishness, prejudice, or jealousy. Pam Carter saw the dangers of trying to export bad feelings via a scapegoat, in a similar way that groups elsewhere dump feelings on the boss or 'the hierarchy'.

> *Pam*: Competitiveness, for instance, and a lot of feelings that are around that area — jealousy, anger — those kinds of things are actually hard to acknowledge and deal with.

Yet she was increasingly optimistic that self-management offered the potential for tackling this; bringing to the surface feelings that are present in any group. Such feelings can't be excluded, but nor should they be separated.

> *Pam*: Having no nominal leader; not pretending any at all to anybody — either inside, or to outside organisations — then you can get on with the job of accommodating those feelings within yourself or within the group.

Conclusion

This chapter began with Newcastle staff hearing an old challenge: 'You want power, but are you willing to accept responsibility?' In one way, I've turned the challenge round, asking whether agencies really want teams. Managers may favour a strong staff unit who are able to accept extra responsibilities, but will they be afraid of the more powerful group that's entailed?

Underlying discussions about power and control, there's often an assumption that this is 'dirty work'. It's implied that we want to keep our hands clean, either by staying as clear as possible, or scouring round for some neat, tidy procedures.

I've suggested that there is no such cleansing solution. The most apparently fair and neutral measurement of performance (e.g. a worker failing to complete a precisely defined task, or just not turning up on time) means that someone must raise and deal with it. Whether it comes to the boss or the work group, they have to choose what they say and with how much force. Which excuses will be acceptable? How much leeway will they give? Even doing nothing is a choice. Dirty job or not, a collectively working team cannot pass it on somewhere else, at least not without denying their own wish to self manage.

Shirley Forster thought the FSU team "more ruthless," and that, "you can waste an awful lot of time being sorry for people". But was this hard-hearted or hard-headed? What's likely to distinguish collective teams is not 'community justice' as a special feature, but their attempt to blend and balance those aspects of 'community control' that occur in *every* workplace.

When Lin Harwood spoke of "the right to be alienated," she was half joking. But only half, because collective teamwork has the serious aim of non-alienated work; a workplace where people can take pride in what they do and how they do it; where they respect their colleagues and themselves. I've presented a model where the aim is a series of open forums in which people acknowledge and own their power, and where communication is honest and clear. When there are problems of discipline and control, the conclusion is not that a collective team is failing in these aims, but that the aims can sometimes conflict.

The consequences of what a team like FSU does (or fails to do) arrive at the door of the worker concerned, the team as a whole, and crucially, their users. Trying to achieve fairness, and give people their due, still needs the question: who is fairness for? Teams cannot be solely concerned with each individual's work satisfaction, nor with the product of their work. Neither can the balance always come down on the side of community, friendship and a respect for colleagues as people with their own hopes and meanings.

Sixteen

Women and Men

Ernie Dobson: There have always been mainly women workers here. And there has been, by and large, an absence of some of the stereotypical things that you associate with ambitious men when they've got power — like being competitive and not being upfront. Certainly when we were talking about what would be lost if we had to have a Unit Organiser, at that time we couldn't conceive of having a Unit Organiser; and certainly beyond the pale and totally dysfunctional to this place would be to have a male Unit Organiser.

At this book's centre is a workgroup almost all of whom were women.[1] Just as important, many of them drew on experience and ideas of the Women's Movement. Neither feature is coincidental to the way the team developed — how it tried to work, and its move to self-management. In earlier chapters I've mentioned a number of gender linked issues. For instance, chapter ten looked at the rotation of tasks like cleaning and typing — 'unskilled women's work' in many teams. In chapter fifteen, when Lin Harwood and Chris Johnson debated informal power, they naturally reached for Jo Freeman's feminist pamphlet.

It's beyond the scope of the book to explore gender issues generally. But I want, briefly, to sketch some of the connections between the Unit's practice and wider feminist ideas.

"A Truly Feminist Influence"

The team wasn't entirely feminist. Between 1980 and 1983 there were explicit discussions about feminist ideas and practice. But, as Pam Carter said, "Not everybody was at the same point. Some people were more resistant to it". Men were never excluded, though some men excluded themselves. Pam mentioned "two blokes who weren't sympathetic, and basically they just got out".

In 1985, when Unit staff discussed this chapter, some of them queried whether gender was still a major issue. Angela Sewell, who'd joined three months before, thought the focus had shifted away from work with women. Parveen Akhtar commented:

> I haven't been very happy about being personally referred to as a feminist.

Two years earlier the feminist connection had been plain, with the Unit involved in national FSU's Women's Development Group. They contributed to a "Women's Issues" edition of FSU Quarterly[2]. Shirley Forster described the Pool Girls' Club; Ali Rhind wrote on the Women's Workshops; and Chris Johnson sketched the development of "Hardwork Cleaners", a women's co-op, urging FSU workers elsewhere to give co-ops help in setting up. Shirley introduced that Quarterly, writing:

> That we should be consciously anti-sexist; that we should provide services which positively discriminate for women (who form the bulk of the people we work with).

As we've seen, the Unit had worked specifically with women in a number of projects. However, this gradually wound down. Funding for the Women's Workshops ran until the end of 1984. Groupwork with women about health issues had ended. There was less involvement with the Pool Girls Club.

The shift was linked to staff changes. Between 1984 and 1986 several workers left who had not only been working with women, but tried to apply an explicitly feminist approach. Chris Johnson was one of the authors of an article on feminism and community work.[3] Pam Carter and Shirley Forster spelled out the influence of feminism in a paper they wrote in 1983 on the Unit's philosophy.

So had the tide ebbed? Chris and her co-authors stressed that they weren't writing for a female audience alone: "Feminist insights are of value to men as well."[4] While they endorsed the need for work with women, they also advocated a "truly feminist influence beyond the limited horizons of so-called women's issues".[5] Feminist ideas, they argued, applied far more widely — for instance, to how groups are structured and the social relations within them. Pam and Shirley agreed. They saw workers at the Unit sharing ideas, including those "drawn from sexism awareness and feminist ideology". For them too, the issues went much deeper than the views of particular staff or the content of particular projects.

What are these wider and deeper ideas, and how do they link with self-management? As a first step let's look at the relative positions of women and men as social services workers.

Reality Out There

Some readers may have thought that a social services team run mostly by women is no surprise. Aren't "social workers, like cats, traditionally feminine"?[6] But this is a myth. Ronald Walton, reviewing women's involvement in social work from 1860, found men persistently in control. As agencies became more hierarchical and bureaucratic, men took the bulk of managerial posts, becoming a "career elite".[7]

This matches Carole Satyamurti's research in a social services department before and after the Seebohm reorganisation of 1970. She observed, "the seizing of a career opportunity by a new generation of managerially orientated, mainly young, mainly male personnel".[8] A central feature of social services agencies is that women do most of the direct work with users, while managers are mostly men.[9] It's a picture which fits Ernie Dobson's comment at the beginning of this chapter.

> *Angela Sewell*: That's what reality out there is like. It's very male dominated.

Walton ends his book by arguing against "male rationalistic domination", which he links to extended formal hierarchies and "mechanical managerial and planning systems".[10] He is not simply criticising hierarchy and managerialism, but making an important point about the gender division. It marks a separation between what are often seen as two sides of social services work. On one side, is 'personal' work — tasks associated with nurturing, caring and comforting. On the other, are bureaucratic functions like rule-making, control and discipline. Dividing these between women and men corresponds to a particular view of what constitute feminine and masculine *qualities*. As we'll recognise, it also attempts to split the exercise of power from influence; men are to direct and control, while women maintain and support. Insofar as this is successful, it ensures that women's power must be covert and masked — for example, gossip rather than forthright comment.

Positive Discrimination

Viewed from the perspective of a collective team, it's clear that self-management tackles many of these problems. Having said that, it's also plain that most attempts to combat male predominance in the workplace pursue policies of *positive discrimination* rather than formal equality. One strategy is to open up higher posts to women and others discriminated against. Conventional hierarchy is not challenged; instead the aim is removing barriers to promotion. Variations of these policies have been adopted by many social services agencies (including national FSU).

Can such policies really achieve greater equality? The classic criticism is that while paying lip service to the idea, in reality they only mean an equal opportunity of becoming unequal. It's absurd to believe that *everybody* can have a higher status job.[11] The most we could expect is women and men having equal proportions of highly valued *and* undervalued work. For instance, in social services as now organised, non-sexist policies might mean that currently 'advantaged' groups would do more low status work. More men would work directly with children and old people.[12]

Another criticism asks what we mean by 'equality' when frequently, what's valued is not the work done, but *who* does it. The fact is, that while the relative status of work varies from culture to culture and at different times in history, the only entirely consistent feature is that *whatever* dominant groups choose to do is awarded higher status — and men are invariably dominant.[13] One example is the entry of women into clerical work earlier this century. For a time, women appeared to be gaining ground in a predominantly male area. But this turned out to signal lower grading and lower pay for jobs which men then largely vacated.[14]

Even where women are 'let in', and men don't desert their traditional areas, the change is often restricted to a token few. As the feminist, Jean Elshtain writes, token women:

> are readily assimilable into the ongoing system and may, ultimately, only widen the gap between those women who 'succeed' and the many who do not.[15]

Equality of Respect

How do such critiques take feminists towards collective working? Jean Elshtain, recognising the difficulties posed by hierarchy, does not call for equal rights or equality of opportunity. Her proposal is "*equality of respect and treatment* grounded in respect for persons". Aiming at *re-evaluation* of different kinds of work, formal equality is then built on the respect we have for each other. This notion is valuable in explaining why it's not enough just to have formal egalitarian 'ground rules', if we haven't succeeded in valuing anew the work people do.

In personal social services this would have implications well beyond the split between direct service workers and management. As we've seen at FSU, radical ideas about re-evaluating work bring out those less discussed tensions — between 'professional' staff and other workers like secretaries, child care staff, and so on. In a local authority team there's likely to be a gulf between fieldworkers, and home helps and aides. Not only are the latter sorts of workers undervalued as a rule, but in many cases their status corresponds to the low esteem given to particular *users* of services. Ancillary staff who work with old people and people with mental handicaps are a good example.[16] Demanding a reappraisal of work with these groups is a way of insisting that they too are *worth* more.

Respect and rights are joined in feminist writing from a wide range of perspectives. It's a view of women as co-operators, for whom each other's personal feelings and individual perceptions are valid and valued. The aim is respect for people's own accounts and the meaning they give to their social reality. For instance, Annie Hudson,[17] another ex-Newcastle FSU worker, writes of:

> feminism's concern with affirming each individual woman's right to define and choose how she wants to

live her life, even if those choices do not always concur
with those of a feminist social worker.

We'll see how this approach begins to bridge ideas about
women as workers, and as users. Shirley Forster and Pam
Carter linked together women's consciousness about sexism
with "ideas about raising the power and status of the people
we work with". They aimed at "raising people's conscious-
ness/self esteem; enabling people to speak for themselves".
There's an obvious interplay with the team's concern for honesty and accessible language. It's there too in how staff talked
together; in their openness and the space made and offered
for others to contribute views. If these things weren't always
achieved, at least they'd moved a long way towards a group
process stressing mutuality. Trying to achieve "equality of respect" is also a good way to explain why the Unit saw their
work with women and with ethnic minorities as of a piece.

Underlying these points is something else we'll find familiar
— this time from the discussion of co-learning in chapter thirteen. Ideas about respecting women's own accounts[18] imply a
particular explanation of how people learn and what it is they
know. For example, a central feminist project is enabling
women to build their own individual and collective story —
herstory. A vital feature of this project is that women are an
oppressed group whose accounts and meanings have been
lost or hidden, and replaced by those of men. Retrieving this
knowledge or building it afresh is seen as a collective process
for women together.[19]

There are obvious parallels with the framework of collective learning sketched earlier. Understanding that women's
accounts have been invalidated, the 'body of knowledge' no
longer appears neutral and detached. Instead its authority depends on the power of the men who authorise it. Similarly,
learning can't be filling empty vessels — women treating other women as objects — but needs an engagement in dialogue
as co-learners and co-teachers. "There are subjects", wrote
Paulo Freire, "who meet to name the world in order to transform it".[20] Alongside which we can put the feminist perspective of Sheila Rowbotham.

You are not only learning a new picture of how things are together, you are creating your own very important strength.[21]

Women Working Collectively

Even from this brief sketch, it will be plain why many women have looked to collective working as a means of pursuing feminist aims and avoiding discrimination. This book has drawn over and again from women's writing about working collectively, much of it based on Women's Movement experience. Indeed, there is no mystery that people trying to work together on a co-operative and equal basis should adopt and adapt a form of organisation which reflects those aims.[22] Feminist arguments don't stop at organisational practice which treats women justly — they advocate a women's practice that offers organisational justice.

We saw in Jo Freeman's proposals,[23] how women's groups in the 1970's often avoided formal leadership, aiming instead for direct democracy with recallable and accountable delegates. Some groups simply equated hierarchy with patriarchy.[24] Others criticised "the masculine ethic" of existing organisations.[25] Meredith Gould, reviewing these developments, found that even where hierarchy was reintroduced "women's organisations sought to minimise centralisation and formalisation".[26]

As at Newcastle, when women took jobs or became involved in other organisations, they brought their Movement experience and ideas with them. Where they could set up new agencies or change old ones, regularly there was a push towards non-hierarchical or explicitly collective forms. In Britain, both small commercial co-ops[27] and collective teams in social services are likely to have a large proportion of women members. Teams may set out or end up as women-only.[28]

The choice is mutual. Collective teams may prefer to hire women, and many women welcome the chance of a collective workplace.[29] Not all of this is due to feminist ideals. Women may have strictly practical reasons for joining a co-operative or collective group; they can see it first as a job.[30] After all, it does offer a small scale solution to many of the problems of discrimination. So, women whose experience in hierarchies is that talented women work under incompetent men,[31] will say how much they appreciate the chance to do challenging work that utilises and develops their skills. Denied access 'up into' management, self-management brings the same tasks and functions within reach of the whole work group. There is no need to put up with the status games which women in particular have found alienating.[32] Nor sexual harassment from bosses. (Two former FSU workers mentioned this occurring in a previous hierarchical workplace).

Collective teams are also likely to benefit women in other ways — for instance, by equalising pay and conditions. Many of the chores traditionally given to women workers may be revalued, if not shared out. And a sensitive view of family and other personal circumstances is likely.

> *Lin Harwood*: I liked working there, I did. I liked the clients. I mean, it got me down sometimes, but it was a really canny job; really good if you had kids and the kids were ill. There was no hassle. Working conditions there, I think, were really brilliant and I'll never have that again.

Personal and practical reasons for working in a place ('It suits me') don't negate principled ones. A feminist argument is that 'the personal' should be very much the business of organisations. So a workplace *should* be organised in a way that respects women workers as equals and empowers them. And it should be a pleasant, enriching place to work, too.

The feminist understanding dovetails with another theme of this book: the link between social relations within an agency, and between the agency and its users. When workers aim at more equal and kinder ways of working, that is both an end in itself, and a means of achieving other goals.[33] Working together collectively is part of the process of reaching other women and enabling *them* to become empowered.[34]

Outside Looking In

The sketch here is not meant to idealise feminist ways of organising. It aims at drawing out some of the links and parallels with the kind of collective teamwork described in this book. In particular, I've tried to show how FSU's ideas and practice — its approach to personal relations, co-working, co-learning, and empowerment — were strengthened by feminist principles and experience. There were divergences as well — not least because there isn't one single feminist viewpoint. In any case, the Unit didn't follow a feminist *line*.

Like the experience of collective teams, women's experience can be subtly marginalised, and seen as applying only to special circumstances: consciousness raising groups, for instance, or all-women co-ops. So Sheila Rowbotham is helpful when she points out that in Britain in the 1970's it was mainly the Women's Movement which carried "the concern to make the forms of relating inwardly democratic and co-operative". And these ideas are not just a characteristic of feminism, but "a radical rejection of bureaucracy and hierarchy in every sense".[35]

Perhaps more than any other chapter, this one is written from the outside looking in. There are dangers when men recount the doings of women's groups — and not just the obvious dangers. For example, some feminist writers identify masculine process as combative and competitive. They suggest that the quality of women's interaction — the discourse of women — is innately more open and co-operative.[36] Women naturally, "think of our ideas as gifts to the group — to all of us".[37] But doesn't this seem an all too convenient excuse for men not to try? And doesn't it somehow imply that working co-operatively is, or ought to be *easy* — ignoring the sheer slog that's often needed?

Women's Movement writers have sometimes made equally unhelpful suggestions about power. One idea is that the need for control and exercise of power can be avoided if only everyone is sufficiently open and sisterly. Or that conflict can always be explained as caused by outside forces. Both are surely recipes for women to 'fail' in facing disagreement and conflict of interest.

Because, all groups which work together meet intrinsic problems, whether involving members' skills and preferences, their personal qualities or lives outside. There are teams and there are times when there is mutual learning, support and honest criticism; and when people are prepared to admit they don't know or can't do something. But then there are the rifts and struggles. It's true that a work group may be prevented from becoming a team by what Ernie Dobson described as the, "*qualified* man who's got this kind of status and image to look up to". But women too, can find themselves in bitter and destructive disputes with colleagues. The fact is, unrealistic expectations of harmony are unhelpful for any team.

Let me finally, recall the issue raised in chapter ten about the 'ground rules' of collectives, and how they can seem like a fixed structure, especially for new members. For similar tensions are at work when women join co-ops and collectives. There's a danger that the lack of discrimination against women workers is taken for granted, while other reasons for collective working — feminist aims for social relations — are allowed to lapse. Parveen Akhtar's comment at FSU — that she wasn't happy being referred to as a feminist — suggests that *feminist* reasons for collective working need to be restated, renewed and 'owned' by new workers.

Seventeen

Community Control

Margaret Chiles: I think the principle of collective working is absolutely wonderful. But I do think that who you're accountable to is important. And the people that FSU should really be accountable to are the people who use FSU.

Chris Johnson: If one of our aims is to enable people to have more control over their lives, then it is a bit hypocritical not to allow them control over the services we provide.[1]

Far more often than the Unit used the term 'collective', they spoke about being *democratic*. Empowerment couldn't stop inside the team's office, insisted Margaret Chiles, and staff agreed. From the start of the changes I've described, their aims had always been wider than self-management. So while this is a book about democracy at work, it's also about a conception of self-management bound up with democracy-at-large: how practitioners enable users to become empowered.

The two aspects are not simply consistent in principle; they're inextricably tied together in practice.

Lilian White: We're working towards allowing people we work with to have more control over the services we're offering. And if we hand [self-management] back over, we give the power and control to a management structure that works against it.

Can workplace democracy in a social services agency (or any other) be extended to users and other local people? And if so, how? By advocating 'community control' Chris Johnson was re-asserting one of the main ideals of community work. But it has also been one of the characteristics of collective teams that they frequently aim at the involvement of service users in running agencies. This was especially true of those set up in the 1960's and early '70's, which experimented with open meetings. As I'll sketch briefly, such 'power to the people' initiatives often foundered. As did Newcastle's far more limited attempt to get users onto its local management committee.

In the first part of this chapter I'll outline what happened at FSU, showing the sort of committee they had, and how they tried to get users to join it. Then I'll explore some of the wider issues involved — issues faced by very many agencies concerned to involve users. Lastly, I'll suggest what collective working has to offer. This does not mean pulling a rabbit of participation from the hat of collective working. FSU and, no doubt, most other collective teams wouldn't offer themselves as a 'How to do it' model. As usual, the important lessons are not 'answers', but more fruitful questions. Readers will see that they are the same questions we've asked about the *internal* processes of collective teamwork.

Newcastle Unit's Committee

> *Margaret Chiles*: I didn't have an awful lot of faith, really, in their collective (if it was a genuinely democratic collective) if they hadn't actually managed to achieve something that they'd set out to achieve three years before, [1981] which was to get a real thriving management committee, made up of users.[2]

> *Ian Bynoe*: You're just a front, really, for a voluntary organisation. You know, they go for people who wear suits and are called solicitors and other things.

Like other Family Service Units, Newcastle had a local management committee.[3] Who were its members and what functions did it serve? At first glance, they hardly looked the sort of people who'd be pushing for user management. When Lilian White first joined FSU in 1980, she saw the committee as, "very much middle class white men in suits. I was absolutely terrified of them. Avoided it like the plague if I could". She had come across them previously, as an outsider.

> *Lilian*: An annual general meeting that I had somehow
> been invited to was at the Havelock, I remember —
> the local community centre. And I left absolutely
> furious. Because they had that woman in who was
> dressed ever so well and with ever so posh accent, who
> talked about depression in 'the inner city woman'. And
> being a single parent living in that area at that time, I
> was feeling very very upset. But also furious about be-
> ing part of that AGM.

The committee's membership gradually altered. As we saw in
chapter eight, the City Council no longer dominated, although it continued to nominate at least one person, in addition to the representative from social services. Also, staff set
out to recruit new members whose work or local involvement
linked with the Unit's.

Management committee members 1983/4/5 taking part in this
research, with their jobs at the time.[4]

Tony Boyd (Honorary Treasurer) .... Accountant
Ian Bynoe.. . Solicitor
Margaret Chiles... District Nurse
Monica Elliot.. . Worker with Newcastle
....Tenants' Federation
Pam Flynn... Adult Education Outreach
Tom Hammill..Social Work Lecturer,
.... Newcastle University
Alan Jackson (chair)................ ....Senior Social Worker
.... Newcastle Social Services
Shahin Orsborn........................ Deputy Head of a Newcastle
....Community school
Peter Stone...................................Assistant Director (community
.... services) Newcastle Social Services

Lilian: AGM's became more full. We stopped getting speakers in. They became more fun; much more of a social event. And much more of an opportunity to share the work we do. We tried to hook local people in to be more a part of the work we were doing.

Gradually over the years as well, our management committee's changed quite a lot. They're more people who are really in tune with the work we do. But are still very much the professional class.

National FSU seemed to envisage a professional committee. Its handbook advised that, "membership might include representatives from the field of social work, community relations, education, health, business, and law". During the study, Newcastle fulfilled this to the letter.

Was it, then, "just a front", as Ian Bynoe said? More accurate is to see it as an example of rules of deference. The Unit, at least implicitly, acknowledged that it operated in a hierarchical world of ranked position and status. It followed the grants game-plan where, especially for a grant giver, such a committee confers formal respectability. Like a variation on Descartes' maxim — 'We manage, therefore we are'. There was even a correct costume and way of behaving.

Ian: At the National Council Alan Jackson was there charming them with his Scots accent. I was there wearing my suit, and with my lardy-dah accent.

Both Ian Bynoe and Tony Boyd were part of a tradition of staff in commercial firms donating time to social services projects. For Tony, being honorary treasurer was a civic responsibility. Which didn't negate the political advantage to FSU, having a partner in a prominent firm of accountants take responsibility for the books.

Tony Boyd: I have two or three other honorary things. I think most of the partners have some.

Two Way Traffic

The committee may have been substantially professional, with enough suitable members (middle class white men in suits among them) to be wheeled out when the need arose. But it was also a good deal more. Plainly, it wasn't the usual decorative list of 'important' names that means little outside the pages of an annual report. But neither was it a line-up of supporters. 'You sit on my management committee and I'll sit on yours'; the set-up where grant-aided agencies resemble companies with interlocking directorships.

> *Peter Stone*: The committee feel a degree of comfort in actually not having a simply defined committee role, but are prepared to act in a number of ways. And are prepared to see themselves as a decision-making forum that the staff need, which can be independent when it wants to be but can, you know, be led at other times.

Even without the automatically weighty members (Peter himself and later, Les Roberts, representing social services) this was not a lightweight group. They were active interested people with their own expertise. If it helped the Unit to have them as part of its intelligence gathering and reconnaissance, the traffic was two-way. Other agencies working in the West End, found out what FSU was up to. As well as offering support, advice and encouragement, members could and did ask sharp awkward questions.

> *Shahin Orsborn*: In Newcastle there aren't many black people who have a kind of different perspective on race. I happen to be one. I think most of the people here tow the line that some people say — 'There's no race problem in Newcastle'.

> *Pam Flynn*: I went on it quite deliberately as a change agent. Because it was, like, church and establishment oriented do-good sort of junk.

They invited Margaret Chiles because of her local activity (and before she became a councillor).

> *Margaret*: I think probably they talked to other people. People like Lilian, who I knew from involvement with Woodcraft Folk. And I was fairly active in the trade union, 'cause I'm in the hospital branch of NUPE.

And I was a local person as well. You know, helping local people to get organised.

To summarise, I'm suggesting that members of FSU's committee met several important needs of the Unit. They were part of its legal and administrative framework. They gave it additional political channels — channels to the funding authority, to national FSU,[5] and elsewhere. Then, as involved practitioners, they provided criticism, support and information from outside the staff group. This overlapped with personal encouragement for individual workers.

This was the committee who supported joint staff management and who, with staff, wanted to involve users.

Users on the Committee

Discussions about local people coming on the management committee went back at least to 1978. In 1981, staff and existing members had a full debate. Like Margaret Chiles, Ernie Dobson and Lilian White argued that "a democratic system is obviously preferable". They wrote:

> In drawing a parallel with our work and our committee, a definite contradiction emerges. Local people, the very people we are providing a service for, have no official input into control, direction or management of this Unit.

They proposed a two-stage plan. At first, they should ask local groups to nominate members. Later, "a public meeting open to all residents in our area" could elect members by majority vote. As we saw, Chris Johnson held similar views. Her paper to the committee raised some of the problems.

> *Chris*: Who chooses the local people and how are they chosen? Should we choose? — I think not — or should local people choose their representatives themselves? Should they be consumers of our services or are any local people eligible? Should they be members of groups or can individuals be nominated in their own right?

We need to consider if the workings of this committee will need to be altered to accommodate local people. For example, the time may be hopelessly inconvenient — many women (who are the majority of people we work with) have to be at home cooking tea for husband and kids at 6 o'clock. The language we use — if we start talking in social work jargon it will be very alienating. The things we talk about — the people we talk/write about may be identifiable to local people on the committee. Will this alter the way we present our work etc? Support — local people may initially feel out of their depth, uncomfortable, bored, etc — how do we make sure the meetings are worth them coming to?

Groups, users and other local people were invited to join. A few came once or twice, but most didn't want to. My asking "Why not?", and criticism from committee members like Margaret, "touched on some of our raw edges", said Shirley Forster. Several users told me their reasons for turning down the invitation. Some disliked evening meetings, and walking home in the dark. Others felt they'd have little to contribute. For George Cross it was time.

> *George*: I've been involved in the area a lot. I'm on the [Elswick] Pool management committee. I'm on Elliot's support group. That was one of the reasons they wanted me as well. I've been using their minibus for years — and their facilities.

The committee, for its part, had tried to change. It made efforts to cut out jargon, and had experimented with the format of meetings — no longer held at 6pm.

> *Tom Hammill*: We actually have had, from time to time, different kinds of meetings where people broke up into small groups to discuss issues. I think we've been very flexible and ready to be creative to accommodate — get them in.

> *Pam Flynn*: We recognise meetings would need to be different, differently timed, and all those sort of things. Everybody understands that. And we had the AGM

that was in the form of a bit of a festival — come and see what the Unit does.

By the end of 1984, staff and committee members acknowledged the dispiriting reality. "We have made efforts; we haven't succeeded", said Pam Flynn. They agreed on a different strategy — "inviting users to discussions about work, without expecting them to come onto committee". These discussions began with a good response, especially from members of local tenants' associations, and issue based groups. Though, at those I went to, people wanted to raise local concerns rather than focus on the Unit's work as such.

Learning from Failure?

Some people at FSU saw this as a failure. They felt frustrated and a bit gloomy at not achieving user management, or even shifting the balance on the committee away from professionals. Margaret Chiles doubted whether the Unit could be democratic without formal accountability to users through its management structure. Alan Jackson saw informal meetings very much as second best. He hoped they would be only a stepping stone to complete involvement.

But not everyone shared these views. Interestingly, Lilian White and Ernie Dobson — two of the staff who'd been most committed to getting users on the committee — looked back and wondered whether the committee had turned out to be the wrong place to start the process. They saw the discussion groups, not simply as a means to an end, but valuable in themselves. Ernie argued that many users didn't see the Unit as an entity, but knew one or two bits of it.

Well, how should we judge FSU's efforts? That fact that some team members changed their minds may lead readers to think, wryly, 'They would, wouldn't they?' Indeed, why consider the experience of a team which fluffed it, when there are many examples of other grant-aided agencies which *do* have users on management bodies? Like FSU, they often begin with a 'professional' committee, and expand this to clients, and representatives of local groups.[6] Just as important are experiments such as Neighbourhood Councils, and user committees, or where elderly and disabled people have been involved in the running of their residential home.

But let's look at this more closely. Because, in fact, Lilian and Ernie weren't questioning the principle of user management, but the practice of *users on management committees*. The best way to see the difference is to imagine just the situation they'd set out to reach. Suppose there *had* been users on FSU's committee. Would that have constituted success — democratic accountability, or at least a necessary step on the way to it? There are a number of reasons for saying that, quite frequently, the answer might be 'No'. To explain why, let me broaden the discussion to the general issue of participation.

Public Participation

The rhetoric of participation is one part of the public services where no cuts have been made. But people advocate it for very different reasons.[7] Let's consider things from an agency's perspective. A wish to involve users in running services may be seen as a way of transferring power to those whose lives are directly affected. But participation is also supported for purposes which fall short of empowerment. For instance, there's an argument that people's involvement *enriches* them as individuals; or that it's *therapeutic*, because it increases their confidence and self-esteem. Equally, an agency can appreciate the benefits to *itself* of a degree of user participation. Tenants can help solve the problems of housing managers; trustee prisoners make it easier to run a jail.

So we need to look carefully at the approach people are taking. Quite often a useful test is their opinion of the institutions and systems which already exist. Do they see participation as a *supplement* to existing bodies and channels — a means of making the system work? Or do they accept the need for major changes and new initiatives, as a counterbalance to normally disabling and overpowering relations?

The difference is vital. Bodies like local councils, grant aided organisations and even government departments, often set out to encourage public consultation or participation. At their best, these initiatives welcome proposals *and* criticism, because agencies admit honestly that their services aren't always appropriate and relevant to people's needs. Participation schemes that 'bring people in' are an improvement on needs surveys and other devices which treat users and local people as objects to be measured. Agencies begin learning *with* users rather than learning *about* them.

But, at base, there may still be an assumption that our present institutions and structures *are* democratic. Isn't this shown by elected representatives, and public rights of information, as well as political parties and interest groups which all citizens can use? When things go wrong, aren't there formal procedures for complaint and redress? According to this view, problems in participation are often because people don't take the trouble or aren't assisted to use the channels which exist.

Clearly, there's a wide gulf between this, and acceptance of the need to democratise institutions; aiming at genuine power sharing. And even more removed is the realisation that, even in the short run, 'good' government and self-government are not alternatives.

> Effective dialogue between agency, users, workers and local people is not just a means of developing appropriate services, but of making services democratic. Services that are structured, planned and run democratically will reflect and change in accordance with people's own definitions of their needs and demands.[8]

The two approaches here can be summed up as a *politics of access*, and a *politics of empowerment*. The distinction isn't always this plain, and there's considerable overlap in practice. For instance, helping people to build confidence and realise they have rights they can pursue, is itself part of the empowering process.[9] Even so, those who agree on a programme of steps towards participation will often differ in their basic assumption. Is an agency concerned to 'get them in'? Or committed to sharing control, and empowerment?

Someone Else's Housekeeping?

Having taken the agency's point of view, now let's ask what would persuade us to get involved as users. Straight away, we need to make a distinction between the agency asking me to become a partner *on my case*, and an invitation to participate *in its management*.

Recall FSU's move from 'trust me and let me do it for you', to wanting to work *with* users. As Joan Smith put it, they tried to be "more open and honest in our working relationships with the people we were supposedly helping". But what they were being open *about* were those problems and troubles users brought. More exactly, the contents and 'themes' of the relationship were users' own issues and meanings. Sharing power involved, first of all, power as social workers or community workers, immediately affecting users' lives.

Now, it's one thing to invite users to become co-workers (or even co-managers) on the problems *they bring*, but why should they want to work with staff on the Unit's problems? To some extent, management is still *housekeeping* — concerned with the internal working of a place. Was it surprising if local people invited by FSU, wanted to discuss their own interests first?

After all, this was already an internal tension, with the secretaries and some of the part-timers choosing to sit-out joint management. Users, even more than staff, may see their own day to day concerns as quite enough. Let someone else deal with managing an agency.[10] Perhaps, like FSU's secretaries, they're content to leave things to people they trust. Or maybe they feel that since staff are paid for taking responsibility, they should get on and do it.

Collective working doesn't mean that everyone spends all their time running everything. But it does ask members of a work group to act as concerned citizens within a tiny democracy. With similar logic, we can argue (as FSU did), that users and other local people *ought* to be involved in controlling an agency which uses public resources, influences local policy, and exercises power affecting the lives of individuals outside its walls. What was right in principle was in their self-interest as well. But is this always the perception of an agency's users? As Pam Carter wrote of the 1981 survey:

> If problems and areas of work are identified, no matter how accurately, by statutory or voluntary agencies, the extent to which they can work with the community is limited if that perception is not shared by local people.

Even if perceptions are shared, agreement is needed both on what's wrong and what needs doing. (That's why it was "problems" *and* "areas of work".) Agencies may decide 'what's needed round here', and in the examples I've mentioned, that could be anything from adult education classes to more community spirit.[11] But it's hardly astonishing if local people ignore or dispute such views. And if they agree that what's needed is 'community control', they won't automatically assume that joining *our* committee is the way to get it.

Structures or Forums?

One response to these objections is to see them *strengthening* the case for users on management bodies. Precisely because users' can challenge the agency's views, is surely a good reason for 'getting them in'. This lay behind Alan Jackson's criticism of "middle class trendies coming in... to say what should be happening". Since the agency should be meeting users' needs, not its own, they ought to have a part in initiating issues and defining the problems.

But paradoxically, this takes us to one of the main reasons why user membership of a committee isn't automatically a 'success'. The point is, that while there's nothing wrong with the 'Why' of the argument, what's suspect is the 'How'. As I've said throughout this book, formal membership alone, whether of a committee or other body, tells us nothing about certain key social relations.[12] A concern to fill committees is never enough. There may be names on the notepaper and even bums on the seats, but are members working together, learning from each other, and sharing power? At the extreme, how many bodies have their token woman, disabled or black person, for window-dressing rather than a full partner?

The confusion that needs untangling here is the same one we've met over and again, when people try to alter organisations by changing *structures*. They jump from the need for a process (in this case, dialogue with users), to creating or adapting a structure (like a committee) as the solution. An odd thing is that, in other respects, criticism of bodies like management committees is often quite harsh.

The management committee can indeed seem more and more like a curiosity or antique: an organisational form which comes down to the present as a quaint survival from a world passed by — a world in which charity was charity and the local jumble sale still reigned supreme.[13]

But then, we're asked to draw a surprisingly tame conclusion, that the old curiosity shop should be refitted to sell new stock — including 'community control'. The problem is not limited to small grant-aided agencies. Assuming that 'making the system work', and empowering people are one and the same thing, constantly leads to solutions being sought within the organisational chart. User involvement is approached as if this framework was an unbreakable cage, with add-on participation becoming standard, whether in the personal social services, or in education, housing, or planning.

Let me be clear. I'm not proposing that we ignore or abandon rules and structures. But we should stop trying to use them to solve problems they don't address. Enabling and encouraging participation is a *civic* rather than an organisational problem. I realise that saying this may dismay many people — especially those who've had to fight their way through a constitutional crisis where fuzzy rules and poor structures seemed to play a big part. After you spend hours and months redrafting your rules, focussing precisely on structure and objectives, it will seem irritating to be told that the key goal is *not* the new structure, but the quality of group process.[14]

If readers have gone through such restructuring — for instance, hammering out a new constitution — then let me ask them two questions. First, how far is their satisfaction with a job well done, *actually* due to the new structure? Is that the 'tangible product'? Or might it be just as much the fact that they've learned a great deal with and about their fellow workers, their agency, and its overall work? In addition, haven't people had a chance to understand and *own* the new structure? (rather than have it handed down by the founding mothers and fathers).

Second, can they *continue* the process of change, gradually and organically? Or will they find themselves starting yet another exhausting (and urgent) redrafting in two or three years? People argue that democracy takes too much time.

And, of course, it will, if treated as 'solving' a crisis every few years. How would we feel about gardening if it always meant descending on a wilderness with pickaxe and shovel?

Rights and Power

There's a further challenge to what I've said. It links back to Chris Johnson's questions about which local people would join FSU's committee; would they be chosen, or have a right to stand for election? Put another way, the issue is not just about rules, but one of formal *rights*. Questions of access to a body like a committee may be couched in procedural terms — saying who may attend, speak and vote — but underneath, the substantive issue is who actually exercises power. So, is it ducking this to have a set-up, say, where users and local people may attend a discussion, but aren't part of the body with formal powers?

This is the classic situation, attacked by advocates of 'Citizen Control', where people are placed on *consultative* bodies which can be ignored when there's conflict. An agency can then welcome their *support* while deflecting their *criticism*.[15] Sherry Arnstein, in her "Ladder of Citizen Participation", considers "informing, consultation and placation" as tokenism. She describes how people are "placed on rubber stamp advisory boards for the express purpose of 'educating' them or engineering their support". Only "partnership, delegated power or citizen control", she urges, are true "degrees of citizen power".[16]

I'm not disputing the importance of these issues. It does matter whether people attend a body by right, or by grace and favour. And if someone is a 'representative', it's fair to ask who chose them and how. Further, there are vital questions about who controls an agency's resources — especially money. But saying we need "citizen control" not consultation, is actually restating the question, not offering a solution.

Consider the point made earlier in this book, that in *any* organisation, the operation of legal rules can't be separated from the reality of power relations — who's actually running the show. We need to be aware that, however useful as a means of gaining access to bodies, formal legal rights neither guarantee more open and equal relations, nor establish a *pro-*

cess which encourages all participants. Even the most careful-ly balanced constitution will be modified by judgements and power exercised in other forums.

So, someone having a seat on a body with *formal power* is no surety of a shift in the power balance. On the contrary, this may reproduce *exactly* the danger that advocates of citizen control warn against — outsiders are included in a committee simply to legitimate what would happen anyhow. Despite having formal rights, participants can again end up serving the interests of the already powerful.

Apathy and Incorporation

It's always tempting to begin with the familiar and visible — like someone who drops money down a dark alley, but then looks for it under a lamppost. Structures, procedures and even rights, seem a lot easier to deal with than the complexities of hidden power. Yet, as we've seen, this is a major challenge. Without examining open and hidden power and how they in-teract and interconnect, we're left with a series of apparently disconnected problems. Two examples are *apathy*, put for-ward to explain why people don't get involved; and *incorpora-tion*, as one of the dangers if they do.

When people are criticised for apathy, the charge is less a lack of feeling — in the sense of being uncaring or indifferent to public issues — as not tackling them with the means availa-ble. However, the revealing question about people's inactivity is not why they fail to join democratic bodies as good citizens, but why they stay away despite obvious individual *self-interest*.

In Jane Mansbridge's study of a New England Town Meeting,[17] she gives the plainest example: wealthy residents pushing through a tax change favouring themselves, when it would have only needed the poorer majority to turn up and vote against it. Mansbridge's explanation tallies with many of Newcastle's discussions. To some extent, people choose whether the 'benefits' of participation in a body outweigh the 'costs'. An evening meeting in Elswick had to fit in with other things, like putting children to bed, or maybe the counter at-traction of "Ladies' Darts Night". But there are other sorts of 'costs' too: overcoming our lack of confidence in public fo-rums, and fear about how others will see us. Margaret Chiles thought many users might feel as she once did about the management committee.

> *Margaret*: Years ago I wouldn't have had that
> confidence and I just wouldn't have gone back again.

Should someone's inaction or apparent unconcern be judged largely as a choice *they* make? Lip-service aside, in most workplaces and public agencies, democracy is rarely on the agenda. The fact that people take this for granted and don't even find it odd, is something which operates in the interests of the powerful. So why is it surprising when proposals for citizen participation meet suspicion or indifference?

If we don't have the 'habit of democracy', how much is this due to the covert or hidden power of others to *exclude* us? I don't mean that in FSU or other agencies, management committees decide 'in secret' to make users unwelcome. One characteristic of hidden power is that they don't have to. The game needn't be fixed for us to wonder if it's really worth playing; if the other players are too strong; or whether the "weight of the institution" makes the effort pointless. Organisations are not immovable, and neither are management committees always inflexible. But a healthy scepticism about power relations is justified.

With *incorporation*, lines of force no longer repel and exclude outsiders; they attract and capture. Individuals seem to become no more than 'satellites' of powerful agencies. One stock figure — virtually a stereotype in accounts of participation — is the user or local community activist who gets sucked in by an agency, losing touch with 'grassroots' opinion. Explanations for this often concentrate on the person's motives. Perhaps they just want to run things.[18] Or do they enjoy being on display as part of an agency's showcase? There can be cynicism (from both local people and practitioners) when a client volunteer uses their experience as a jumping-off point for a paid career. (Implying that 'real' members of a local community shouldn't want professional jobs.)[19]

Yet this makes it entirely an individual's fault. They are blamed for their bad faith, failure, or personal characteristics. The power relations involved remain disguised — despite similar relations existing in any number of situations where 'lay' people participate in public agencies. This happens when someone becomes a school governor, a magistrate, or a local councillor. In each case they find themselves in an institution with its own history and ways of doing things. Whatever their ambitions and aims, they meet a network of existing relationships pushing and influencing them.

In short, apathy and incorporation are not simply two kinds of silent acquiescence. There's more to it than choosing either to remain outside, letting 'them' get on with it; or, moving inside, lending legitimacy. Thinking instead of overt and covert power enables us to see that responsibility also lies elsewhere.

So are people who initiate participation ready to see others develop their own power? Can an agency's power be confronted by outsiders, and does it accept responsibility for it? It could be especially uncomfortable for a radical staff group, seeing itself building *alliances* with users and local people, to realise that *it too* may overpower — pulling people into its orbit rather than enabling them to pursue their own interests. What if the allies it courts have, or begin to gather, strength to push back? Will agency staff who welcomed their *support* now fear *control*, or will they realise that these are two inseparable parts of a dialogue?

Collective Teams and Community Control

At the start of this chapter I asked how workplace democracy could be extended outside. For advocates of citizen control, what I've written may seem discouraging — a description of obstacles to participation, rather than a path to achieve it. In fact, while I'm not starry eyed about what we can learn from the experience of collective teams, neither am I pessimistic.

Certainly, there are no guaranteed recipes — mix ingredients and watch democracy rise. Not every collective or co-operative group is a roaring success at keeping its own self-management healthy, let alone involving users and other local people. Nevertheless, a collective framework offers ways of reshaping and restating the questions we ask, and helping us recognise possible solutions.

Let me explain. I've proposed that understanding and learning from collective teams will help build and strengthen team working elsewhere. Central to that understanding are new ways of thinking about organisations and how people work (or fail to work) together. On one hand, that implies a critique of the assumptions usually made about: structures and rules; hierarchy and individual working; and the realities of power and power sharing. On the other, *collective working* provides a set of alternative goals which include: a shift in power; co-learning and judgement building; and valuing and sharing people's experience, skills, and personal qualities.

When it comes to 'community control', my proposal is simple: that we apply the same critique and adopt the same criteria. Successful collective working suggests what democratic social relations will look like elsewhere. It offers a guide for building and evaluating co-work in groups other than work groups. And that means forums which have, at least the aim of joint working — clubs, committees, even political parties or a local council.

It would need another book to explore this fully. But, in the remainder of the chapter, I'll illustrate it with a few of the themes discussed earlier. First, though, let's return briefly to those 1970's collective experiments in 'community management'.

1968 and All That

1968 was the year Newcastle FSU was plonked down on Elswick; its original brief essentially colonial. Elsewhere, the co-ops and collectives set up, then and later, frequently had an explicit commitment to some form of 'community control'. Not all such counter-cultural initiatives looked outwards; some were mainly concerned with members' own lives and personal relationships.[20] But a large number did aim at social change, especially when the new projects were social service agencies.

In one sense, this was part of the ambitious "openness" discussed in chapter fourteen.[21] At an early stage of collective running, the overriding need was seen as taking down barriers, and demystifying professional status and skills. It led to attempts to run agencies with open meetings, where people from a particular neighbourhood could attend and become involved. Involving the community was often seen as "a needed first step towards more comprehensive political democratisation and social change."[22]

In practice, there were serious problems. Here's Rosemary Taylor, describing the development of free clinics in the United States. She observed how most:

> agreed on a platform of community control. It was, after all, the hallmark of reform strategies in the late sixties. But community control has always been an ambiguous idea for policy-makers, political activists, and free-clinic organisers. Control by whom and over what? In the field of medicine it has meant, variously, control by patients, control by health workers (skilled and unskilled), and finally control by the potential consumer and the wider, amorphous 'community'.[23]

Collective teams in Britain followed a similar pattern. Looking back on the seventies, Charles Landry and others described the difficulty of trying to run, for instance, a radical magazine or a film collective, with open meetings.[24] A central issue was expertise. The need to get on with day to day tasks conflicted with always having to explain things to newcomers. Then, because much of the open discussion was on general policy, decisions were made by people who didn't have to do the work and weren't in touch with it. The outcome was that power was exercised elsewhere, and 'democratic' open meetings became a rubber stamp.

Readers will recognise the 'oppositional' stage of collective working, here taken outside a team's boundaries. The rejection of hierarchy brings a refusal to acknowledge very tangible differences in ability and expertise, commitment and power. There are unrealistic expectations of harmony; and the notion that equality requires everyone (including 'the community') spending time discussing everything.

Later schemes have been less ambitious. Health centres have set up patients' groups. Agencies like community law centres have developed 'reserved' places on their management for particular groups. Even so, it's important to see that the problems of open meetings won't be 'solved', since, in an exaggerated form, they are the inherent tensions of any collaborating group. And that applies to the gap between practitioners and 'lay' people on a traditional management committee.

Co-Learning

Are people ready to bridge these gaps by co-learning? We need to ask the same questions for groups *outside*, as we asked about learning and judgement building *inside* work teams. Groups face tensions arising from varying levels and different kinds of expertise. There's the challenge of integrating new-comers; will old hands be prepared to reopen debate on the old topics?[25] What about conflict between individual hopes and plans, and the needs of the group as a whole?

On a community body, the time and effort of joining in represent a practical 'cost' which shouldn't be ignored. Like a collective team in its early stages, there's often an initial peri-od when members are catching up and growing in their un-derstanding. There are more meetings and more discussions, simply because there's a lot of rapid new learning.

One reason why practitioners have an edge and often fill up committees, is that they are already familiar with the top-ics, and with being-on-a-committee as part of their day to day work. It's an entry stake that let's them join the game more readily.[26]

I don't mean that 'professional' members of committees always have it easy. We saw that within a work group, meas-urement of the time and effort given to meetings is often ob-scured. The same happens in other groups. Information may be power; it's also a large envelope full of papers that comes through the door just before you leave for work. Alan Jackson often put me up on my visits to Newcastle, and usually his post contained something from FSU — either national office or the Unit — adding to a daunting pile on the hall table. Col-lective working in a community group can't solve the problem of these 'costs' — including less obvious ones like dislocated family and social life. But it acknowledges them, and offers ways of spreading the burden and arranging for people to get support.

I should add that a metaphor of costs doesn't imply some market version of democracy — 'I owe you two hours of par-ticipation in your project in exchange for your involvement in mine'. What we're building here is *common wealth*; the pool-ing of people's knowledge, skills and experience. Included in the notion that local people *should* get involved, is the implication that they can see some possibility of common wealth worth investing time in.

Chapter thirteen offered a challenge to practitioners: owning their expertise and working to make it confrontable by users and other 'lay' people. That applies equally to practitioner's on committees. One reason they can acquire an 'oracle' status and be deferred to, is that they are assumed to *know*. (As if a lawyer, say, automatically knew the law, rather then having to work hard to give advice on new legislation).

There's a similar need to avoid patronising users and local people; putting them on a pedestal as those who *know what it's like round here*. For while their experience and knowledge is valid and important, it can also be restricted and partial. They may not realise what they know, or its value, until they begin discussion and listening to others. Co-learning is an invitation to put the pieces together, but it requires work and time from practitioners and non-practitioners alike.

Perhaps the vital question is whether people really want to learn from others — and to enter into a real dialogue. So, yes, committees may organise training sessions and perhaps even write briefing papers of some kind, for new members or one another. But this can leave many aspects untouched. Is there, for instance, space for people to think out loud, make mistakes and take risks?

> *Ernie Dobson*: This is a safe place for people to walk in and say, 'I'm fed up. I need to talk to you. I've got this problem and I don't know how to deal with it. I can't cope; give me some help here'.

Ernie was referring to FSU staff, but it's not a bad test to ask how far this is possible in all kinds of gatherings. Most of us are afraid of looking foolish in public; or in the semi-public setting of a work group or committee. Can we say, 'I don't know', and are there ways of helping us learn and find out?

Deference or Reference?

Whether different sorts of people feel comfortable in a particular forum — for example, because it's a safe place for them to speak up — is sometimes linked to *class*.[27] A common criticism is that middle class ways of conducting meetings can deter working class participants.

> *Margaret Chiles*: I have got sufficient confidence now to say, 'What does that mean?'. Years ago ... I'd have thought, 'It's way above my head'. And that is what worries me about the management committee. Because it puts — it excludes users without meaning to. Because it is full of people using jargon, academic and intellectual expressions and phraseology.

A number of studies explore social class within public participation, proposing, for example, that middle class people are more articulate, especially when used to 'rules of order'. In striving to achieve a consensus, they are said to suppress conflict and criticism — especially when it's blunt and working class. In contrast, meetings which successfully attract working class participants, are "much more open, informal and vocal".[28]

Without denying the importance of class, let me repeat the argument in chapter eleven, that traditional committee procedure is not neutral. Rather than challenging inequalities, it confirms and strengthens them. In other words, making meetings democratic is more complicated than appeals for informality and flexibility, or attacking middle class decorum.

Working class organisations, like tenants' associations or trade unions, have their share of alienating, authoritarian, *disabling* meetings, based on rules of deference. They too, may be chaired by someone ready to 'cut the cackle' and push business through. The alternative, enabling different people to speak and drawing out and giving confidence to the quiet ones, is seldom a feature of traditional meetings procedure. Being trapped by decision-making, instead of aiming for judgement building, is not a middle class monopoly.

The vital point is that *all* deferential behaviour hinders the kind of open discourse that's required. The alternative to an etiquette of "seemly and proper" behaviour which respects and defers to status, is not unseemly and improper. It's to respect and refer to knowledge and experience regardless of rank: 'Who knows?' rather than 'Who's who?'

I've described how a work group should give, and grow used to expecting, colleagues' *best criticism*. A similar phrase is 'loyal opposition'. The kernel of the idea is that we need and benefit from open dialogue when facts, opinions and plans can be tested and challenged. The same is true for community groups.

But like work groups, members of management committees and other bodies often prefer not to hear such criticism, for the very good reason that it can sting. This is especially true if it comes from those whose judgements we value. But, exactly for this reason, best criticism is the litmus test of participation in schemes for 'partnership' and involvement with users and local people.[29] Just as some people need to find the courage to speak, with others it's the courage to listen.

Invitation to Self-Management

There can't be a final flourish to this discussion — a rousing last chorus to end the show. But perhaps I should add a word about FSU's committee.

What I've written isn't an argument for the status quo. Margaret Chiles was right to assert that the Unit's principles meant working for democratically accountable services. But where she didn't go far enough, was by seeking and measuring change within the existing structures. Rights of open access to existing bodies can, it's true, be a strong antiseptic, but they will leave untouched the causes of the disease.

The disease, of course, is our increasingly undemocratic, closed, deferential society. Learning and working together is called 'cheating'. Power is hidden; and opposition focusses on blaming *them*, rather than taking responsibility for what we might change.

I've argued that a central aim for workers in a collective team is joining, supporting, and helping set up linked and overlapping networks. The result is likely to be diversity, rather than neat single structures. The perspective should be relations between individuals and groups in a series of forums.

As we've seen, the kind of formal legitimizing body that FSU's management committee provided, can be enlarged into a much more supportive and critical forum. In groups elsewhere it will also include groups of users and local people.

But this may not be the best approach in every case, (judged that is, by the criteria of genuine dialogue and co-working). Often, it will be more fruitful — both for participants and agency workers — to try out something small, limited and modest.[30] For example, rather than spending time and energy to pull one or two users onto a committee, we could offer space for a group of users to develop their own agendas, along their own timescale.[31]

Whether with local people, users, or fellow practitioners, the goal must be inviting the pull and push of their judgements and criticism, their alliances and collaboration — and offering ours. For the best guarantee of the accountability of one self-managing work group is the strength and health of other democratic self-managing groups which can form the jury of its peers.

Afterword

Spring 1988

In Spring 1988 I visited Newcastle once more. There had been
many changes at the Unit — most obviously in staff. Ernie,
Parveen, Elliot, the three secretaries and Carole Tate were the
only members of the 'old' team still there. Shirley had left to
have a baby — though she twice came back as a sessional
worker. Anne Davies was working in Newcastle Social
Services. Angela Sewell had taken a job in London. Pam Carter, was teaching social work at Newcastle Polytechnic, though
she was also on FSU's management committee.

Most staff hadn't been replaced. This was because the
City Council was trying to keep to the Government's spending
limits, and that meant major reductions in grant aid. (Though
FSU still had the largest single grant.) Ernie, as the most experienced worker, took a central part in negotiating with the
City. It had been, he said, "a real drain for us, constantly having to justify ourselves to the authority. That's a real drain of
energy." But, he added, it sharpened what I'd written about
grant aid.

> *Ernie*: What's happening now is that the Authority is
> attempting to develop a policy in a form which it can
> apply to evaluating grant aid. 'These are our criteria.
> To what extent do these organisations meet them? And
> how does it help us with our priorities?' They're at-
> tempting to do that now; at the stage of making initial
> statements. Once people get some feedback, you've ac-
> tually something clear and tightly drawn up, for the
> next twelve months.

The practical result was that they were down to four
fieldworkers. Nargis Khan had joined as an "advice/advocacy/
development" worker in November 1986. She now did group
as well as individual work. Diana Proctor was temporary stu-

dent unit organiser (halftime), with her job and half a secretary's post still funded by CCETSW.

The other major change was in the pattern of work. A big chunk of the service — direct work with families — had gone. The balance was now firmly towards community work. With Lilian going on her course, and Anne and Angela leaving, the Unit no longer provided a social casework service, and took no 'statutory' child care work. Parveen too, had moved further away from traditional group work.

There had been a corresponding shift within the student unit — a main factor in Angela's going. For both families and students, placements with a casework element required a minimum number of Unit staff doing family work. As well as resource people for the students, they were needed to respond to families on days students weren't there, and to pick up the work when they were back in college. Now, the student unit offered group and community work; and advice and advocacy placements.

Another change was in their use of the building. There was the sheer problem of running it with few staff. They no longer provided a drop-in service. But people did come in. And groups used it: community workers; the black youth workers' group; and a number of community groups.

> *Elliot*: Ideally we'd like to have more people come to the building and using it for whatever purpose. But it is a fact that we have changed the picture because of cuts. We can't have an open door policy. But there are more groups who are coming in. For example, there's Elswick minibus group.

I asked them about the previous interaction between casework and community work. Wasn't there a loss of creative tension? A risk from community work in isolation?

> *Elliot*: But isolation from whom? Because, for example, you have the community groups who are part of the West End Review. Community organisations, group workers and community workers are coming together; looking at issue based work. We're trying to adopt a collective approach: on race, for example; on privatisation; the new Housing Bill. I think we are

actually opening up, instead of being a patch based Unit.

Even so, if contact with community workers had increased, casework meetings with the local Social Services teams had ended.

Nargis: Liaison with Social Services has fizzled out for different reasons. Though we have been talking about starting it up again.

Ernie: We've been criticised the last year or two — and understandably — because we haven't been very good at communicating the detail of what we actually are doing. Where the links are weakest are with social services area teams.

But I think we've actually done more linking. I think it's got stronger. Where the strength is, is other community projects, places like the Asian Women's Centre, and with black groups.

What of their own committee, and attempts to get users either on support groups or in interest groups?

Ernie: The management committee's much more concerned with discussing the work. And that's quite useful. Also, instead of saying let's get some more users on the committee — (it wouldn't be difficult to get them, but whether you could keep them) — was to maybe recognise that informally there is a fair amount of day to day accountability to members of groups. So instead of taking that out, and plonking people individually into an alien situation — the management committee — why not have your accountability and your evaluation in the group? Why not formalise it?

Our thinking about that hasn't changed that much. But instead of people being, say, in support groups, we say to that person, 'Will you come and help us evaluate that piece of work', rather than workers do it?

As a small team they were vulnerable to absence. The months preceding my visit had been particularly bad, with both Elliot

and Nargis off with serious illness. After Lilian left they'd decided they could no longer send anyone to UO's meetings. But
they had taken part in other national initiatives like Equal
Opportunities training, and, in January 1987, FSU's national
management committee had formally reviewed and endorsed
the continuation of joint staff management.

What of the future? The problem of funding hung over
them. Lilian was hoping to come back, but there wasn't
enough money to fund five fieldworkers. Diana questioned
how far it was possible to have democratic management with
such a small number of staff. Running the place, and keeping
management and administration going, was hard work just by
itself. Yet deep down, they insisted, their aims and philosophy
had not changed: "Certain things of what we try to do are still
the same; assisting people to gain more control over their
lives."

★

So, because this is a very ordinary and everday story, there is
no happy ending; no ribbons neatly tied.

Surely, readers weren't hoping for anything else, were
they? Something different from the loose ends and frustrating
potentials of their own job? But could this book end otherwise?

> *Shirley:* I would hope that somebody would read it that
> would think, 'Well, at least some of this we could have
> a bash at in our workplace.'

Appendix One

HIERARCHY	OPPOSITIONAL PHASE	COLLECTIVE
Communication		
Legitimate communication is deferential; according to status and position, up and down lines of accountability	Rejection of hierarchical channels. "I'm one of the workers here. You speak to me".	Clear lateral rules of reference, eg. "X is dealing with this."
Space		
Space is allocated according to rank. For example, managers have individual protected areas. Senior staff have the right to intrude into the workspace of subordinates.	Explicit dismantling of barriers. "We all muck in together." Suspicions that personal space will become private. Tendency to noise, muddle and overcrowding. Informal barriers rebuilt, eg. with filing cabinets, and by staff working at home.	There is renegotiation of space as a common resource. For example, agreement about quiet rooms, and defined space for users. Different kinds of work have protected boundaries.
Power		
Managers must manage. Workers then enjoy the prestige of the victim, and can constantly blame "the hierarchy". Power exercised by subordinate staff is denied, and may take the form of gossip, office politics.	Unreal expectations of harmony. Notion that a need to discipline a colleague is a failure of collective working. The denial that power is exercised allows staff to avoid owning its informal use.	Acceptance of both group and individual power exercised openly. New procedures provide checks and balances. Criticism and support understood as inextricably linked.
Learning		
Training is regarded as a management function. Individual staff stress "my professional development".	Myth that everyone can do anything. Differences in ability and expertise are denied.	Individual and collective learning both recognised as legitimate. Also people learn from each other. There is respect for the knowledge of practitioners — Who knows? — rather than professional status — Who's Who.
Deciding		
Decisions are the prerogative of position. Formal process is top-down, with consultation as a privilege.	There's a tendency for everyone to decide everything together. Meeting time expands. Outsiders complain about "a talking shop".	Meetings streamlined. Extensive delegation, while authority rests with the group, which reviews its own and individuals' work.

Appendix two

Researching

Shirley Forster: I thought I knew nothing at all about research. But I did know lots of things, and a lot of them I've learnt from the process of being involved in this.

[You have] the right to say to the researcher, 'You don't make the rules of the research; I make the rules if you're gonna research me... First of all, your research has got to be useful to me if I'm gonna take part in it. I'm not just a sitting passenger; I've got the right to make up some of the questions. And I have the right to edit your material even if it means you leave out all the juicy bits that you're interested in'.[1]

In chapter one, I called my work with FSU *participatory research*; an attempt to work with them as co-investigators, rather than making them the 'object' of inquiry. I now want to look at this more closely. After all, if I was an honorary part-time researcher with the team, the questions I've asked about working collectively should be directed just as sharply at me.

For some readers this may appear odd. Shouldn't researchers control research? Inviting respondents to challenge and review it could seem like undermining scientific objectivity; even attacking 'academic freedom'. In Britain, till recently, most social science researchers would have taken this view. The dominant approach has sought to follow and match the physical sciences by presenting 'findings' supposedly reinforced by tightly drawn rules of method. There's been stress on measurement, and the separation and control of causal factors, with use of techniques such as sampling and control groups.

Fortunately, things have begun to change.[2] Researchers are increasingly ready to say publicly what many of them already admit in private — figures don't always tally, and illuminating results are due as much to luck, as rigorous design and closely observed procedures. Linked to this is their renewed willingness to speak about issues of power and influence involved. Who does research; how they do it; who pays for it; and what gets written up and used; these are all essentially political questions.[3]

There has also been a welcome debate — led by feminist writers — about the personal relations involved. For example, there's an understanding that, to people on the receiving end of a survey or questionnaire, distance and objectivity often feel like alienation and intrusion. Feminist scholars have urged researchers to stop treating people as data — response units. Instead, they suggest the alternative of reciprocity between researchers and researched.[4]

Other approaches try to achieve such a mutuality, using models like *co-operative inquiry*[5], *experiential analysis*[6], and *citizen research*.[7] Participatory research is one of this family.[8] Rather than describing each in detail, I'll sketch the important features they broadly share. They have many of the traits we've come to expect in collective and co-operative ways of working, especially when committed to empowerment.

Co-research *with* people begins by respecting and valuing their accounts and meanings; how they tell it and how they see it. Rather than becoming a 'sample' or 'experimental data', people's experience is frequently presented as 'life history', their story. And it's not just their experience which is vital, but their perception and understanding of that experience.[9]

The 'personal' is valued in another way, too. The involvement and enthusiasm of the researcher are no longer seen as weaknesses, but acknowledged as valid and legitimate. Rather than a dangerous bias or contamination to be avoided, personal involvement is recognised as "the condition under which people come to know each other and admit others to their lives".[10]

A central goal of co-research is *dialogue* — a living process with reciprocal sharing.[11] Researchers and participants together explain and mutually challenge emerging ideas and interpretations. This means, to a broad extent, involving those researched at each stage of the process: from initiation and negotiation, to the final conclusions — and in what happens in between.[12]

Clearly, this co-work is also *co-learning*, with the important feature that learning is not for the researcher alone. This leads to a concern with questions of knowledge — especially 'popular knowledge'. There's an explicit acceptance that power and politics determine who asks the questions; who controls the learning, and uses the knowledge.[13]

To make power confrontable, the researcher operates openly, with the knowledge and consent of participants. This excludes certain ways of working, like participant observers who hide their purpose from the people researched. In conventional research, whether to be overt or covert is seen as an ethical and practical question for the researcher. Is it right to lie to gain access? If you are honest, will people try to limit what you learn to what they want you to know?

Co-research includes observation, but it's a particular kind of *critical* observation. For example, with FSU, the aim wasn't simply openness, but presenting my observations to the people observed. For they, too, were observers — of their team, and of me and my work. They were asked to comment and criticise. 'This is what I think I'm seeing. Is that right? Is that how you see it? Where else should I look?' The moral and practical issues are not just those of researchers, but involve the people affected.

Alternative research approaches are generally sceptical of quantitative methods of inquiry, when they convert people's acts and ideas into data to be taken away and manipulated by the researcher.[14] Supposedly neutral technical tools, figures and tables, lines and boxes, gain a persuasive concrete existence of their own. Since what can't be counted is often discounted, the results may have little connection with the complexities they claim to measure.[15] While statistics and measurement have their place, a breakdown into isolated 'variables' can distort rather than make sense of a complex wholeness. Alternative approaches acknowledge the untidyness of judgement and knowledge building. This usually means a research process with complementary stages and cycles; divergence and convergence.[16] The messiness of speculation strengthens the rigour of analysis. The result won't always please an accountant, but it may convey something of the flavour, variety and vitality of the people involved.[17]

Participatory Research

I've labelled this study participatory research. How does it differ from other approaches, since, quite clearly, it shares many of their aims? Let me stress that I'm not talking about a single 'school' of practice; nor a rigid model. But to explain the difference, recall the question in chapter seventeen about why people are asked to participate.

If they have the choice, why would 'respondents' want to be involved in research? Aren't the shortcomings of traditional models excellent reasons why they should keep as far away as possible? After all, even some of the alternative approaches sometimes go no further than seeking collaboration as a way of producing better and more accurate findings — to improve "the quality and depth of the information given".[18] But better and more accurate for who? In other words, are researchers trying to 'bring people in' to what remains principally the practitioners' concern? And if participants other than researchers get something out of it, what is that benefit?

Participatory research is not neutral on these issues. It recognises that most research serves the powerful: governments over the governed; management over workers. So its goal is *democratic* as well as collaborative inquiry. This means the core issue is empowerment; not only people's involvement, but their *control*. It challenges inequality by supporting people in the creation of their own knowledge; strengthening their abilities and resources. Its rationale is their right to participate actively in processes affecting their lives.[19]

Writers on participatory research often see this link between research and action as its characteristic feature. Investigation, analysis, learning, and taking action, aren't separate and distinct, but an interrelated whole. Investigation may be initiated by outside researchers, but it should remain anchored in the issues of the community or workplace. Similarly, analysis, reflection and learning are for all participants. "We both know some things; neither or us knows everything. Working together we will both know more, and we will learn more about how to know."[20] Finally, we are talking about social as well as personal change; social action in addition to personal understanding.

It will be plain that the issues raised by participatory research recur in many other chapters. Quite simply, they're the problems and questions in any piece of collaborative work, whether it's the practicalities of co-learning and co-working, or who exercises power in a given setting. So where the earlier focus was on FSU's co-working with one another and with users and colleagues in other agencies, let's now look at my work *with* the team.

INITIATION AND CONTROL

Who Initiates?
Who Defines The Problem?
Who Pays?

CRITICAL CONTENT

What Is Studied?
Why?
By Whom?

COLLECTIVE ANALYSIS

How Is Information Gathered?
By Whom?
How Is Data Analysed?
By Whom?

LEARNING AND SKILLS DEVELOPED

What Is Learned?
Who Develops What Skills?

USES FOR ACTION

How Are Results Disseminated?
Who Uses Them?
How Are They Used?Who Benefits?[21]

Who Initiates? Whose Problem?

Calling chapter one *Scene Setting*, I had in mind the different
'actors' entering the story — each with their own ideas and
aims. Though my initial contact came from Tim Cook and
Janet Williams, the reasons they opened the door to the research differed from Newcastle's reasons for letting me in.
For Tim and Janet, the main 'problem' was Newcastle's request for Joint Staff Management, and the response of the rest
of FSU. While the Unit's concern was getting their scheme approved and making it work.

   The research became a small part of the negotiations on
joint management. An outside report suited the interests of
the national organisation and the Unit. This isn't to deny that
we all shared an interest in learning something about self-
management for its own sake. The book is evidence of that.

   What about me? From time to time I've briefly told readers about the person making these observations and judgements. Why did I get into this? Well, before researching, I
worked in hierarchies (first in law, and then social work)
whose failings were all too obvious. Could collective teams offer more? Like Newcastle's students, I'd wondered if it was
"pie in the sky". And felt that mixture of suspicion, increduli-
ty, and hope, with which outsiders often approach self-management. Going to Newcastle and other teams, I'd hoped their
story would help people to critically understand and, if they
chose, move towards democratic working.

   Of course, for the Unit, that was only part of their interest. They saw self-management as one of a series of changes,
and they wanted me to describe the picture as a whole. In addition, their principles and practice were centred on
empowerment; with collective working as an outcome of trying
to change their relations with users. That this should be a
participatory study, was my proposal. For people like Chris
Johnson and Ernie Dobson, co-research fitted the assumptions they made in their community work. Other workers may
have taken it on trust for a while.

   Parveen Akhtar: But you don't find that difficult? That
   it is inhibiting for you in terms of your views as
   researcher? Your perceptions of the situation may be
   very different to what we see or what we think.

Well, whose purposes shaped the book? Readers will make up their own minds.

Who Paid?

Orthodox research usually mentions funding with a ritual expression of gratitude to various bodies who've put up the cash. It's a tradition which separates the question 'Who pays?' from issues of control.

The cash for this study came from my savings; borrowing from friends; and salary of my partner, Zena Brabazon. The Department of Social Policy (DSP) at Cranfield Institute of Technology gave me a study grant of £3000, plus £1000 towards expenses. The Charities Aid Foundation gave National FSU a grant of £2,400, which paid my University fees (£1550), with the rest for research expenses. Newcastle Unit met a further £363 expenses. The book was published on a non-profit basis, with subscriptions and loans.

Much of the funding was in kind. From September 1985, Colin Fletcher, my supervisor at Cranfield, gave his advice and support 'unpaid'. People at FSU put me up and fed me when I stayed in Newcastle.

No strings were attached to any of this — aside from the obvious shoestring on which the whole thing was done. That *did* affect the work — for example, it meant transcribing and editing at the sitting-room table. But there was no exercise of control through cash. In particular, DSP specifically agreed to a research model which left respondents in control of their material. The Newcastle staff group could have vetoed the entire account.

Gathering Information

Readers have heard about interviews, discussions, reading and observation. However, a few explanatory points are needed, especially on what's missing.

The picture presented of the city and FSU's local area is skimpy, and relies on snapshots. Even so, I hope it gives some idea of the context of the Unit's work. At minimum, readers can weigh my impressions and judgements.

A shortcoming of the book is the lack of material from users of the Unit. I've referred to a small number of interviews

I carried out. One difficulty was that most users didn't wish to be tape recorded or quoted. But there was a more serious problem. As we saw in chapter seventeen, how an agency runs is often seen as someone else's housekeeping. The users I talked to regarded Unit management as an internal matter for the staff. They thought of FSU mainly through their own concerns — community or groupwork, or 'their' social worker.

> *Lilian White*: Because joint staff management isn't actually happening in the reception room where they could see, they [users] haven't actually perceived any difference in how we function together.

A third difficulty related to the 'package' of changes at the Unit and the length of time they'd been underway. Few users were in a position to compare 'then' and 'now'. Ernie made the point that formalising self-management had been a "catching up" with what was already going on.

> *Ernie Dobson*: There is a relationship between the way we're working and the way we're managing. And the way we're managing is catching up with the way we work. Then in fact, in terms of our users' experiences, there is no big change.

For all these reasons, plus my sheer lack of resources to enlarge the research into a full participatory study with users, the book doesn't explore how they viewed self-management.

Interviewing

Quotations are mostly from taped interviews, which were as central to the research as the book. They were very loosely structured, and open-ended. People introduced issues they considered important, as well as commenting on and maybe challenging the topics I raised. Interviews were during 1984 and 1985. There were forty-four in all, lasting from forty minutes to three hours. I gave each person a verbatim transcript for correction and alteration. Some people added written comments. Only Carol Tate asked me not to use her transcript. I'm sorry Carol's views are missing, but of course, I respected her decision.

People interviewed gave permission for workers to read their edited transcripts, which were kept in a folder at the Unit. Responses 'fed in' to subsequent interviews and discussions. We've seen staff refer to comments by Peter Stone, Kath Satoris, Blanche Callan, Evelyn Rae, and Yvonne Waters. Everyone queued to read Lin Harwood's long and very critical transcript. Though it may seem surprising, editorial control didn't lead to people censoring material, nor prettying it with soft focus. What you see is mostly what I got. Lin, for instance, hardly removed a word.

> *Lin Harwood*: We come to work, and we're all warts and scabs, and get up each other's noses.

In this, Newcastle matched other equally blunt collective teams I've researched with. In any case, the aim was to make people's meaning clear — not that every word uttered had to stand. They made changes to clarify a phrase, or take out bits where we'd strayed off the track and talked about things unconnected with the Unit.

As well as taped interviews, hundreds of conversations were not recorded. I might have been walking along the street with someone, chatting in the Unit, or in their home. People were generous with their time, and very patient. I remember, for example, Lilian White, late one evening, wearily discussing a long and tiring study day. And Alan Jackson, answering hard questions first thing in the morning. There's a lot less of Alan in this book than there ought to be. The reason is that most of our talking was at times — in the car, or over meals — when the tape recorder was off.[22]

Analysis and Writing Up

Unlike conventional research 'stages', participatory research makes no sharp distinction between data gathering and analysis. The point is not simply that they overlap, but PR has an explicit aim of linking the process and outcomes of the 'investigation'. Concretely, at Newcastle it meant that early on — from September 1984 — I began writing drafts and sketches for the Unit, showing the framework that seemed to be emerging.

I explained that these weren't formal reports, but "unfinished, hesitant . . . themes, speculations and more questions". I asked staff to debate, challenge and criticise what I'd written. Did they agree with my choice of topic, or how the writing was taking shape? Their tape-recorded comments influenced my subsequent reflection and writing. A similar paper for the management committee sketched the ideas developing. That too was: "an open set of notes... an attempt to invite your comment and criticism".

As well as enlisting people in the process, I asked them to begin thinking about the write up. A stroke of luck was that, shortly before, Fran Martin had researched with the Women's Workshops. FSU faced the difficulty in changing her report.

> *Shirley Forster*: I think it's just to do with knowing that once it's written down in the form of a draft, I'd feel it was very hard to comment on. That's my experience of Fran's draft of what the Workshop Report was gonna be. Which she checked out with us first. And what we all did was sit there and say, 'That's fine; that's what we want'.
>
> Because, I mean, she's done it and she's done a good job. But she's decided what should be in that, not us. So I'm just saying, if we really want this to be what we want to say, rather than what Alan wants to say, we have to decide that now, before Alan gets it half worked out. Because then we'll just let him. That might be what we want to do.

At their request, I produced an outline list of headings and sub-headings; "some kind of loose framework to hang things onto". "The stage before a draft", Angela Sewell called it.

> *Ernie Dobson*: I found [the outline] quite stimulating. What's astonishing to me is that you've managed to come up with so many areas. It gives a picture of something far more sophisticated than I actually envisaged the ... [drowned out by laughter from the rest of the team].

In response, they queried some of the issues I'd listed, and the weight given to them. For example, was there over-emphasis on work with women and the influence of feminism? This was when Parveen Akhtar said she hadn't been "very happy about being personally referred to as a feminist". The team as a whole thought race and anti-racism should be a stronger topic.

> *Angela Sewell*: I began to ask what did the Unit stand for, for me. And it was work around women, but also work around race. Somehow [the outline] swings the whole thing over much more to women and feminism than I experience the Unit. Working with black people, and the black workers here, that's much more enmeshed.

During 1985, I posted off chunks of draft to Newcastle and to Tim Cook and Janet Williams at national office. My visits to the Unit now included discussion on the drafts, and I've quoted some of their comments on *The Needs of Black People*, and *Grant Aid*. There were group and individual responses as well. Janet and Tim were invited to contribute to this continuing process of comment and alteration, but didn't do so. In summer 1985, Unit staff asked me to finish the draft.

> *Ernie Dobson*: I feel that I've given. We've spent some time in meetings, and being interviewed and that sort of thing. I more or less think I've said all I want to say. I think it's almost a bit of fine tuning at this stage. Much as ideally we ought to write this thing collectively, that's not on.

> *Lilian White*: I've felt very guilty for a long time, feeling as if we should be giving it time. And wanting to do that. But when it comes to the crunch, never ever being able to give as much time as I would like. It's trying to hit a happy medium really. Because I would have hated it if it had been just going in, writing the stuff up, and presenting things.

> *Elliot Yabantu*: I like this idea of our being involved in this process. We have been, and so have users and everybody around. My own feeling is that really, at this stage, we should hand it over to you to put it together

[general laughter]. What it is we have said to you; how we have seen our involvement. Then after you have done that, come back to us, and then we'll say, 'We didn't say this', or something like that. We'll begin to work with it. Otherwise there's a sense in which one could say, 'What the hell did we get him here for if we must leave what we're doing, come and be involved in the writing of this thing?'

Fresh material came out of a workshop with Lilian and Shirley, at FSU's National Conference in November 1985. This shaped chapter fifteen on power and control. Writing and rewriting went on into 1986, with the draft changing in response to comments and criticisms.

What had begun as a 'report' to FSU was turning into a book. Why was this? I thought that on almost any aspect, it would have been unsatisfactory to leave out the wider stage which so often made sense of the small dramas at Newcastle. The Unit's experience needed placing in context — and that meant exploring further than either I or FSU had originally imagined. Take chapter fourteen on space. Without referring to experience in other collective teams, and to boundaries, the significance of Newcastle's reorganisation of its building would have been lost. Similarly, the decision of the secretaries to opt out of self-management needed a discussion on collectives and the politics of work.

So the breadth and length of this book followed from the team's view that joint staff management shouldn't be seen as standing on its own. Rather it was part of a cluster of interlinked changes. The more I worked at the draft, and compared other research, the more accurate and important this claim seemed. For instance, when I first sat back to re-read the history in chapter two, it was quite plain that every major theme discussed in the remainder of the book was already there — in germinal form, at least.

In September 1986, a completed draft was sent to Newcastle, and to Janet Williams and Tim Cook (by then no longer FSU's director). Everyone who'd taken part was invited to read a copy, and a deadline was set for final comments and criticism.

The only people requesting substantial changes were Tim and Janet. Aside from correcting factual inaccuracies, they criticised the draft's clarity, balance and emphasis; expressing disagreement with many of the ideas and conclusions. They jointly insisted on deletions and alteration to their own quotations and in how their views were presented. They also requested important changes to some of the book's general arguments. I couldn't agree, since the research was with and for *the Unit*. Tim and Janet didn't take up my offer to include their criticisms in full.

For publication, Janet and Tim would have preferred something much shorter. Team members didn't mind the length, and they did like the extensive quotations. Ernie thought, "It's really important to actually print what people say". Shirley was pleased that they were shown as: "People who changed their minds; and didn't know what they were doing; and disagreed. It starts to look a bit more human, doesn't it?"

The team discussed which chapters needed shortening; the inclusion of drawings; and a brief update at the end. They were keen to see the book appear.

Shirley Forster: Yeah. We've a lot of time went into it. Stuff that, just to be getting your Ph.D. That's nothing.

Elliot Yabantu: That's the stage I'm interested in. Seeing the reaction of the people who see this and who make a critique of it and challenge the ideas.

Notes

Chapter One

1 In Comparison, during 1984/85 Newcastle Social Services Department employed around 2,200 staff, including some 200 social workers.
2 The agency's journal, *FSU Quarterly*, contains numerous examples. See also: Drew Reith (1981; pages 22-24).
3 Barclay Report (1982).
4 Peter Phillimore (1981).
5 *Clients' Rights* (1984) National Council for Voluntary Organisations.
6 *Family Involvement In The Social Work Process* (1982) FSU.
7 Drew Reith (1981; p.18).
8 FSU's National Council had one member elected from each local management committee; ten other members elected at the AGM; plus a chairperson and honorary officers. The National Management Committee (NMC) is technically a sub-committee of the National Council —in effect, its executive.
9 Newcastle was unionised before most other Units. Along with other grant-aided agencies in the city, staff joined the National Union of Public Employees. When FSU workers elsewhere later joined the Confederation of Health Service Employees, arrangements were made for Newcastle to send representatives to national COHSE meetings.
10 Philip G. Herbst (1976; 12) found autonomous workgroups were more likely when, "not tightly embedded in a bureaucratic hierarchic structure, but were some distance from central headquarters".
11 Janet Williams' report to the NMC favoured joint management.
12 In 1985, FSU's South London Unit discussed self-management during an "interregnum" between UOs; eventually deciding against it.
13 Benwell Community Project (1978b; 23).
14 Benwell Community Project (1978b; 51).
15 Benwell Community Project (1978a).
16 Jon Gower Davies (1972; 115).

17 Benwell Community Project (1978b; 87).
18 "The statistics about unemployment, poverty, poor housing, low educational qualifications and all the other indicators of social deprivation have been presented often enough. In Britain we now have a sad competition between different parts of the North as they try to attract attention to their plight by claiming to come top of the worst-hit league. Elsewhere one boasts about one's riches, the size of one's swimming pool, holidays in the Bahamas and ponies in the paddock; the industrial North is reduced to proclaiming its misery." F.F.Ridley (1985).
19 *City Profiles: Results from the 1981 Census* (1983), and *Social Audit 1979-84* (1985) both published by Newcastle upon Tyne City Council, Policy Services Unit.
20 For a fuller discussion see methods appendix.
21 Ann Oakley (1981; 30).
22 I asked people to check and if necessary alter transcripts *to make their meaning accurate and clear*. In transcribing and punctuating, I tried to follow the speaker's speech patterns; mostly those of North and North East England. Some Geordie (Tyneside) speakers chose to standardise: for example changing "wor" and "us" to "our" and "me"; or adding a plural 's' — often left out in speech. Staff read the transcript after approval by the person interviewed.
23 Shirley Forster and Pam Carter chose to receive chunks of draft as I wrote them. Other ex-workers and management committee members waited till the whole draft was ready.
24 So, collective working was both valued for its own sake, *and* as a condition or means of achieving the Unit's consciously pursued goals. In other words, their aims were both "value rational" and "instrumentally rational" — Max Weber (1968; 24-26). This contradicts the view taken by Joyce Rothschild-Whitt (1979; 510) who researched American human service collectives, and argued that they had, "explicitly rejected instrumentally rational social action in favour of value-rational behaviour".
25 Maria Brenton (1978; 289) advocating worker participation, suggested it was all the more appropriate for "people-centred" social services. She argued that enabling clients to develop self-reliance and autonomy are "core values inherent in social work", which "should also be seen to operate for agency employees themselves". By contrast, a directive, vertical command structure will either reinforce directiveness in staff, or frustrate their efforts. She also set out the educative effect as the values and structures of an agency — for both workers and users — either sensitise or erode personal autonomy.

There was: "the need for a continuity of principle. In other words, the social services organisation should embody the values it professes to promote".

26 Tim McMullen, head of Countesthorpe College, Leicestershire, concludes that: "a hierarchic, authoritarian 'head-dominated' management system is an impossible framework for a school in which the authority relationships have changed between student and staff." Quoted in Colin Fletcher, Maxine Caron and Wyn Williams (1985; 53). Colin Ward (1983; 106-113) discusses how different kinds of work relations in architects' offices affect their service.

27 Maxwell Jones (1968; 11) saw a democratic, egalitarian structure in a psychiatric hospital leading to both patients and staff becoming more responsible, open and aware. Oliver Sacks (1982) noted, with sadness, the opposite process in a hospital for sleeping sickness. "A strict administration has come into being, rigidly committed to 'efficiency' and rules; 'familiarity' with patients is strongly discouraged. Law and order have been ousting fellow-feeling and kinship; hierarchy separates the inmates from staff; and patients tend to feel they are 'inside', unreachably distant from the real world outside. There are, of course, gaps in this totalitarian structure, where *real* care and affection still maintain a foothold."

Chapter Two
1 See chapter nine.
2 Dave Holder and Mike Wardle (1981).
3 Paulo Freire (1972a; 1972b).
4 Joan Smith (1985).
5 Harry Marsh (1981).
6 Unit Organisers were assessed a year after appointment, and then every two years. Janet William's comment is from Joan Smith's 1981 assessment.
7 In 1983, Jean Tams, one of the users, took part in selecting Elliot Yabantu as community worker. "I was on the meetings, you know. And when they came for the job, I could interview myself, downstairs and say who I think. I picked Elliot; he was good."
8 Including her sister, Brenda White, worker at the Pool Girls' Club.
9 See chapter sixteen.
10 "And certainly at variance with the job description" — a note from Tim Cook and Janet Williams.
11 It's vital to include times when problems were not solved and the team didn't work harmoniously. I am grateful to former staff, Lin especially, for recalling painful events.

12 Lin Harwood, (1982); Fran Martin (1985).
13 See chapter fifteen.
14 The phrase 'Joint Staff Management' was intended to avoid fears associated with 'collective'.
15 To be funded out of the unspent UO's salary. In fact, a subsequent cut in grant aid swallowed up any surplus.
16 In contrast to the "explosion of idealism that often fuels the founding of co-operatives". Tom Clarke (1983).

Chapter Three
1 National Council of Voluntary Organisations (1984). In an article about the NCVO report, Tim Cook (1983) told a story of how "thirty years ago a Family Service Unit expressed grave concern that a number of the families with whom it worked were meeting together to compare the services they were receiving. The staff wondered whether anything could be done to prevent this".
2 See chapter seventeen.
3 Though I've suggested *reciprocal* influence, the examples so far are mostly in one direction — i.e. from the agency to its users. A body of writing describes one aspect of the reverse process — responses of human services agencies to the very real stress brought by users. Users' pain and anger is seen as provoking an organisational response, as well as a personal one from staff. Isabel Menzies (1970) suggested how hospital routine can be a defence against the intense emotions nurses were likely to feel in caring for patients. Rather than deal with their own anxiety, nurses increased it by insisting on inflexible rules.

This interpretation sometimes falls into the trap of viewing users as the source of *primary* anxiety, with the institution's response as secondary. Janet Mattinson and Ian Sinclair (1979) saw staff in a social work agency as simply absorbing and reflecting feelings which actually belonged to users. In other words, a sophisticated blame-the-client explanation.
4 A note from Tim Cook and Janet Williams: "In our recollection NMC members were open minded about the issue, but the presentation by Ian Bynoe was unclear and left many questions unanswered. It was the failure to provide supporting arguments — not the principle of not having a boss — which was the issue for the majority."
5 FSU Quarterly no.6, Winter 1974. Dave Holder also co-wrote (with Mike Wardle) the book on Bishop Auckland mentioned in chapter two.
6 Anarchist writing presents the issue — eg. Tony Gibson (1983).

7   "In the case of bureaucratic hierarchical organisations, an attempt to move out of this system may be perceived as going in the direction of the opposite, that is, a chaotic unstructured state." Philip Herbst (1976; 29).

8   The UO's group voted 11 to 8 in favour of a UO at Newcastle.

Chapter Four

1   The Seebohm Report (1968) led to the amalgamation of local authority Welfare, Mental Health and Children's Departments.

2   Colin Whittington (1975).

3   Barclay Report (1982).

4   The same is true in other services. "Teamwork and the closely associated idea of collaboration, has almost become a sine qua non of effective practice within the human service professions". Susan Lonsdale, Adrian Webb, and Thomas L. Briggs (1980; 1-2). They contrast the "widespread recognition that effective care requires teamwork, with the frustrating experience that such collaboration is rarely perfect and often quite absent".

5   Phyllida Parsloe (1981; 25).

6   There are encouraging exceptions. Colin Beech and Jeremy Grice (1984; 20) describe collaborative teamwork in a project with solvent abusers. Alan Kennelly, Angie Reagan, Richard Pope and Julie West (1988) give an example of collective caseworking.

7   Carole Satyamurti (1981; 45) — research 1970-72.

8   Satyamurti p.198.

9   Olive Stevenson and Phyllida Parsloe (1978; 312) — research 1974-1977.

10   Stevenson and Parsloe (1978; 308).

11   Parsloe (1981; 40-41).

12   Stevenson and Parsloe (1978; 126).

13   Parsloe (1981; 146).

14   Jim Black, Ric Bowl, Douglas Burns, Chas Critcher, Gordon Grant, and Dick Stockford (1983) — research 1978/1979.

15   E.L. Trist and K.W. Bamforth (1951) used the term "reactive individualism" to describe the response of coal miners whose work groups were fragmented by new working systems. "Whatever their personal wishes, men feel under pressure to be out for themselves, since the social structure in which they work denies them membership in any group that can legitimise interdependence".

16   Paul Corrigan and Peter Leonard (1978).

17   Steve Bolger, Paul Corrigan, Jan Docking, and Nick Frost (1981).

18 Mike Davis and Martin Cook (1981; 8).

19 Jeanette Mitchell, Donald Mackenzie, John Holloway, and Cynthia Cockburn (1980; 82).

20 And others — eg. Hilary Walker and Bill Beaumont (1981; 188): Bill Jordan (1976; 200).

21 Two exceptions describing practice are: Bill Bennett (1980); and Jennifer Joslin (1980).

22 "Seeing is a rather curious thing for the alternatives have existed all the time, so if we were not able to see them this is because they did not fit our logic and our theory of what ought to exist." Philip Herbst (1976; 16).

23 Tim Cook thought this seriously misrepresents what occurred with Newcastle. In his view: "Just as the Newcastle team was convinced that the national organisation (including National Office) was informed about the development so National Office (at least) was convinced that no such information had been forthcoming".

24 Centre for the Analysis of Social Policy, University of Bath (1987; 251).

25 Such problems are explainable as a "mismatch between organisations built on the pattern of vertical control, and tasks which require management of a network of horizontal dependencies... The outcome may be passive retreat into protective indifference at the bottom level and active involvement in chronic personal and departmental power conflicts at higher levels." Herbst (1976).

26 Herbst (1976; 17) calls this "the logic of bureaucratic hierarchical design", suggesting that, in the organisation garden, it classifies some things as flowers, and uproots others as weeds. We need, he says, "to go back to discover and confront the assumptions which have created the logic in which people can get themselves caught and which, seeing no choice, and often with the best of intentions, they feel impelled to impose on others".

27 Charles Handy (1980; 429).

28 Rensis Likert (1961; 115) warned that "an organisation takes a serious risk when it relies on a single pin or single linking process to tie the organisation together". He advocated instead, "multiple overlapping groups".

29 Stevenson and Parsloe (1978; 310).

30 Barclay Report (1982; 211). Whether as the Barclay Committee's "entrepreneurial figure" or the Unit Organisers' Group's "Lynchpin", the image is of team leader as initiator and prime cause of successful innovation. Donald Schon (1973; 211) gives an alternative view: that 'charismatic leaders', are more likely to be good salespeople than genuine innovators.

31 Both Joan and Lilian (who represented Newcastle at UO's meeting for two years) remarked how solitary some UOs seemed. Lilian thought that for many UOs, you "either blame your Assistant Director or you say it's your staff group. They do a lot of that!" Social relations and organisational forms were linked at their level too.

32 Subordinates can fall into similar traps. Richard Sennett (1980; 38) describes "idealised substitution" when, whatever the boss "is and does, the opposite is what they want".

33 Janet Williams disagreed. "It seemed to be blaming staff assessment for not being something it does not set out to be — assessment of team performance. The point of assessment of anyone, (UO or otherwise) is to appraise their individual performance not that of their colleagues". She added that FSU was planning to have regular Unit reviews which could take account of this.

34 Sometimes we are — eg. David Billis (1984).

35 The sporting classification seems to have originated in Adrian Webb and Martin Hobdell (1980; 101). It was taken up elsewhere, eg. by Chris Payne and Tony Scott (1982).

36 "Giving a talk on the subject of this book one of the queries raised was, 'Surely what you mean are flat hierarchies'. This, I think gives an indication of how difficult it can be to conceive of organisations which do not have a hierarchical structure". Herbst (1976; 1).

37 R.Meredith Belbin (1981).

38 See John Rowan (1976).

39 Scapegoating entails an interpretation of the pattern of a group's social relations by focussing on the attributes of one group member. Ironically, this is also true of studies of 'leadership'.

40 D. Katz and R.L. Kahn (1966).

41 Carole Satyamurti (1981; 132). A siege mentality may be signalled by talk of 'bombardment rates', 'front line', 'target population', and 'client impact'. Such imagery dovetails with a view of 'the hierarchy' as all those generals back at the chateau who are probably as dangerous as the clients.

42 Satyamurti (1981; 192).

43 Parsloe (1981; 144-148).

Chapter Five

1 Phyllida Parsloe (1981; 148).

2 Quoted by Joyce Rothschild-Whitt (1979; 513).

3 Drew Reith (1981).

4 Rothschild-Whitt (1979; 521).

5 Workers in a London collective working with elderly people,

held off criticising a colleague, explaining that, "Because we work collectively, she's actually our friend as much as a person we're working with". Alan Stanton (1983; 208).

6   Robert Jackall (1984; 119) felt a pervasive "familial emphasis" in a co-op running a specialist cheese store. "Even when workers do not get along with one another they feel committed to one another, just as blood family members feel they share the same fate". Jane Mansbridge (1983), found similar features at 'Helpline Crisis Centre'. However, Katharine Newman (1980) suggested that some collectives demanded *ritual* expression of loyalty and commitment.

7   "Started off at seven quid a week and free everything. Live together, work together and fuck together. There was no stopping." Collective founder member quoted in Stanton (1983; 224).

8   Newcastle had no sub-groups meeting after work. Researchers seem to ignore such groups, though they are a feature of many teams. "It was an important part of the day for me, I remember, going to the pub. The group, for a variety of reasons was important to a lot of people. (That's not true for everyone.) Like, meeting at half-past five, six, whenever, was quite a nice moment." Worker in social services team, quoted in Stanton (1983; 61).

9   Lucy Mair (1972; 73).

10   Philip Abrams and Andrew McCulloch (1976) suggest we have a culturally narrow view of friendship. Abrams (1986 ed. Martin Bulmer) explores the theme of 'social distance', arguing that in a workplace, as in our neighbourhood, we'd like to be able to call on people nearby, but nobody wants trouble from *bad* neighbours.

11   Interview transcripts were edited and approved by students, some not wishing to be identified by name.

12   "Amazing dealing with some outside groups... photocopier salesman *had* to put me down as 'Administration Manageress' on his form, for fear of upsetting his computer or something. He just could not, or maybe would not, accept the title 'worker'." Stanton (1983; 266).

13   Ken Edwards (1984) described an agency which became a collective. "It was surprising how keenly the loss of an overall Director was felt by some outside organisations and individuals. These either complained they had nobody to relate to, or did not know which of us to contact on particular issues, or persisted in seeing the former Director as somehow still 'in charge'. It therefore became imperative to acquaint everybody we dealt with in the outside world with our structure: who was responsible for what."

14 "Sometimes a number of people came in at more or less the same time, and a woman worried about her son missing from home, a public health inspector dropping in for a cup of coffee, the secretary of a local group making a phone call, and a Councillor, might find themselves sitting together in the same room... Sometimes residents managed to meet their local Councillor or M.P. informally — and some senior management staff or Councillors can get a clearer picture of events in the community directly from local residents. Such natural mixing of people may also enable some relaxation of status, class or race barriers." Fatma Dharamsi and others (1979; 186-187). And see chapter fourteen below.

15 "Marks of rank are insisted upon, and often deliberately elaborated and multiplied; we have found wide agreement among industrial managers with the suggestion that the floor space of offices, the appearance, comfort, and cost of furnishings, the size of desks, the number and colour of telephones, height of partitions, the appearance of one's name in the internal telephone list or on the door of one's office, are all matters which have become more and more closely associated with rank, more and more used as expressions of one's position in the hierarchy of status." Tom Burns and G.M. Stalker (1966; 149-150).

Burns and Stalker saw tension when formal hierarchies tried to operate lateral 'organic' communication. "The sheer difficulty of contriving the correct social stance and the effective social manner for use in different negotiations, the embarrassment of having so to contrive, and the personal affront attached to failure to achieve one's ends by these means, induced in managers a nervous preoccupation with the hazards of social navigation in the structure and with the relative validity of their own claims to authority, information, and technical expertise." (p.93)

"When my boss wants to make a call (one secretary said) he stands there holding the phone while I dial, then we both stand around waiting for the other person to come on the line." Jean Tepperman (1976; 40).

16 Christopher Hill (1975; 247) remarks that, in the 17th Century, "what seems to us the innocent eccentricity of refusing to remove the hat in the presence of social superiors, or to use the second person plural to them, confirmed conservative contemporaries in their suspicions". For Quaker influences and links with collective working, see Virginia Coover, Ellen Deacon, Charles Esser, and Christopher Moore (1981).

17 R. Brown and A. Gilman, (1972; 252).

18 Cheris Kramerae, Muriel Schulz, and William M. O'Bar ed. (1984).

19 Erving Goffman (1972; 31). And see Charles Derber (1983).
20 A London bookshop used to have a notice on its wall which read: "Please don't ask to see the manager as we are a collective".
21 L. Trist and K.W. Bamforth, (1951; 32) suggest the hierarchical alternative is: "competition, intrigue, unwillingness to put allegations to the test and the reserve of personal secrecy".

Chapter Six

1 "The Left avoids the idea of management by calling people 'coordinators' — as if the skill of management was merely that of stopping people bumping into each other." Charles Landry, David Morley, Russell Southwood, and Patrick Wright (1985; 32).
2 Fran Martin (1985).
3 Newcastle City Council later cut FSU's grant, so this surplus disappeared.
4 This makes an excellent rule of thumb for distinguishing reference and deference in any office.
5 Peter Bruggen, Barbara Brilliant, and Suzanne Ide (1982). See also Peter Bruggen and Charles O'Brian (1987).

Chapter Seven

1 Jim Black and others (1983).
2 Barclay Report (1982; 133).
3 Phyllida Parsloe (1981; 49).
4 Gill Dixon, Chris Johnson, Sue Leigh, and Nicky Turnbull (1982: 59).
5 Donald Schon (1973) argues the difficulty and sheer unhelpfulness of assuming we can discover what's happening 'out there'; diagnose the causes of those events; plan an intervention; and evaluate the results (chapter 7).
6 Ann Glampson, Tony Scott, and David N. Thomas (1975); Rodney Hedley (1985).
7 See methods appendix.
8 Peter Beresford and Suzy Croft (1986) criticise conventional needs assessment (p.290), and suggest how to change agendas (p.304).
9 Formerly Unit Organiser at Bishop Auckland FSU.
10 Black and others (1983; 225).
11 Black and others (1983; 237) quote Richard Crossman, then Social Services Minister, responding to Lord Seebohm who wanted to brief him on the 1968 report. "He told me in great secrecy what was to be the central recommendation of the re-

port. I didn't particularly want to know, but he told me it was going to be a demand for a reorganisation of social services."

12 Steve Bolger, Paul Corrigan, Jan Docking and Nick Frost (1981; 54).

13 "It is indeed ironic that systems planners and administrators, having failed in their efforts at integrating and co-ordinating services, have now passed this responsibility on to those workers with the least power in the organisational structure, i.e. the 'line worker'." Stephen M. Rose and Bruce L. Black (1986; 75).

14 "The debate so far has been narrow. In this it has been typical of social services more generally. The dominant voices have been those of white male academics and managers. Service users have not been involved. Most service workers and voluntary and community organisations have had little or no part to play in the initiation and discussion of the new policies". Beresford and Croft (1986; 289).

15 This feature — meeting the agencies' needs — occurs time and again. For example, South Birmingham FSU was set up after a working party from national FSU, local social services, police, housing and probation gave the area a "high ranking" on rent arrears, family problems, children at risk etc. "There was no attempt made to consult people in the locality on whether they wanted an FSU and, if so, what kind of services were needed." Penny Dobson (1987; 10).

16 A note from Pam Flynn: "FSU and others, including the informal training network that Ernie, Shirley and I co-founded, later went on to develop a critique of Racism Awareness Training. This was spurred by Sivanandan's attack in *Race & Class*." A. Sivanandan (1985). See also: Ernie Dobson (1985; 18).

17 Figures from Newcastle City Council (1983).

18 John Gower Davies (1972).

19 Charlotte Wright (1979).

20 One difficulty was the secretaries' absence from Unit discussions about race issues, e.g. in 1985 they stayed away from a study day. Because they hadn't taken a full part in the process, there were differences betwen them and fieldwork staff about FSU's approach, to Asian families and the families' reluctance to use almost exclusively white public service agencies.

21 Ivan Illich (1978).

Chapter Eight

1 In 1987/8 it became the largest, when Newcastle's grant to the Council of Voluntary Service was reduced.

2   In 1984/85, the City's grant to FSU was (round figures) £80,000. The Central Council for Education and Training in Social Work funded the student unit with £18,000. The Women's Work-shops received £16,000; and £6000 came from other sources. In 1987/88 the City's grant was £78,000; CCETSW £21,600; and other sources £5,000.

3   Stephen Hatch (1980; 35).

4   The Barclay Report (1982; 73) referred to "formal voluntary agencies: national or local bodies who employ paid professional staff". It extended its definition of the 'voluntary sector' to include "informal carers" — for instance people who are looking after elderly relatives. Such bids for merit by association indicate the ideology being presented.

5   Jim Black and others (1983; 236).

6   Hatch (1980; 130). Another question is how 'voluntary' an agency seems to its users. Barry Mason, from Islington FSU, wrote (1983; 23) that, "It is often the [professional] network that has a stronger interest in our working with a family than the family itself. Indeed, if it weren't for the power and status of the referrer many families would not choose to have us involved".

7   Roger Hadley and Stephen Hatch (1980).

8   Hatch (1980; 119).

9   A note from Janet Williams: "This does not make it clear that there never was any question of more than three years money. Ali's anger is understandable. FSU appears as more cavalier in its attitude to her livelihood than I think is true."

10 Donald Schon (1973; 212) argued that agencies are obliged to present an *experiment* (which is valuable even if it fails) as a *demonstration*, which must be seen as a success. The grant system, he says, imposes a rhetoric of inquiry, experiment and evidence; but a reality of political manoeuvre, the need for connection with the powerful, and justification for positions already taken.

11 Ralph M. Kramer (1981; 189) observed American agencies forced to present minor changes as "original breakthroughs to compete for funding". Jennie Sibley (1986; 39) shows statutory agencies in a similar position, putting up projects angled to catch new funds.

12 Bruce L.R. Smith and Douglas C. Hague (1971).

13 Barclay Report (1982; 81-84). Tim Cook was a member of that Committee.

14 Teresa Gorman, Barbara Robson, Bernard Sharpe, and Cyril Taylor (1985).

15 Benwell Community Project (1978b).

16 Hatch (1980; 92).

17 My thanks to Marie Hannah, a Unit student, who shared the work of checking these records.

18 Diana Leat (1986).

19 Duncan Scott and Paul Wilding ed. (1985). Tony Addy and Duncan Scott (1987).
20 Ken Worpole (1983; 31).
21 Owen Kelly (1984). See also Owen Kelly and Dermot Killip (1980).
22 In West Germany, co-operative and collective projects are supported by a voluntary titheing system. Richard MacFarlane and Bernd-Georg Spies (1985).

Chapter Nine
1   The Barclay Report (1982; 133) urged the distribution of work among a team "in such a way that the collective resources are available, when needed to all clients: a considerably more difficult operation than simply allocating one worker to one client".
2   Also called "Integrated Methods". These ideas were widely discussed and taught in British social work in the late 1970's.
3   Dave Holder and Mike Wardle (1981). With Marcia Tondel (1974), Dave Holder was co-author of the article *Team Leadership*, mentioned in chapter three. During the research with Newcastle, Mike Wardle was senior social worker at the nearby Crudas Park Social Services.
4   Holder and Wardle (1981; 46).
5   "   "   "   p.53.
6   "   "   "   p.138.
7   "   "   "   p.185.
8   "   "   "   p.188.
9   Shirley Forster (1985).
10 Holder and Wardle (1981; 62).
11 Ivan Illich (1977) used the concept *iatrogenesis* — doctors harming patients when trying to cure them — extending the term to other "disabling professions", social work included.
12 Harry Specht and Anne Vickery (1977).
13 Allen Pincus and Anne Minahan (1973).
14 Howard Goldstein (1973;17).
15 Goldstein (1973; 78).
16 Roger J. Evans (1978).
17 Anne Vickery (1977; 52).
18 Holder and Wardle (1981; 83).
19 "   "   "   p.58.

Chapter Ten
1   Tony Eccles (1981; 352) criticised similar attitudes within worker co-operatives. "The movement's apparent delusion that it owns the idea of co-operation and has some right to tell the rest of us if we have permission to apply the word."

2　"The word *collective* widely used in the co-operative movement, is derived from the leftist political tradition, particularly from the anarchist wing of pre-1939 Spain. An influential book conveying this tradition, and its terminology to American worker co-operatives was Sam Dolgoff (1974). The experience of Maoist China, often highly romanticised, was perhaps an even more important source for ideas about collectives." Robert Jackall and Joyce Crain (1984; 103).

Some of the anarchist links are shown by Gaston Leval (1975). Joyce Rothschild and J. Allen Whitt (1986), give a brief overview of these different origins, though, astonishingly, ignoring feminism.

3　Jane Mansbridge (1983; 21) noted "the establishment all over Western Europe and North America of thousands of New Left collectives — ranging from free schools, health clinics and law communes to women's centres, underground papers and food co-ops".

4　"The type of people attracted to co-operatives in the 1970's. A great many are from middle class educated backgrounds and are under 35. They are repelled by work in hierarchical large scale industry and want more control over their working life. Most use the term 'collective' to describe their type of co-operative." Jennifer Thornley (1981; 44).

5　"From the members of the commune downwards, the public service had to be done at *workmen's wages*. The vested interests and the representation allowances of the high dignitaries of State disappeared along with the high dignitaries themselves". Karl Marx (1968; 287).

6　Anthony P. Sager (1979; 136).

7　Sheila Rowbotham (1983; 94).

8　David Moberg (1979).

9　Alan Stanton (1983; 231).

10　This happened at the law centre where Ian Bynoe used to work.

11　Rosemary Taylor (1979; 17).

12　Women's Self-Help Network (1984).

13　Original member of Islington Bus Company, a community resource centre. Stanton (1983; 276).

14　A local authority may impose conditions on a public service agency. In a workers' co-op, it may be agencies offering finance. Mary Mellor, Janet Hannah and John Stirling (1988).

15　Job Evaluation is a classic technical/managerial sleight of hand. Since its entire rationale is *ranking* different jobs as a basis for pay differentials, it inevitably prescribes hierarchy — including for workplaces where none exists.

16　Francis Stevens (1983).

17 Researching a Californian 'Free Clinic' collective in the early 1970's, Joyce Rothschild and J.Allen Whitt (1986; 80) found members dismissive of admin work. One worker was quoted: "Fee-for-service will mean billing and billing means paperwork. But no one can be a full-time paper-pusher without starting to hate the job. It's not fair to lay that on anyone."

18 Rothschild and Whitt (1986) talk of "the occasional casualties of the job rotation system" (7-9 and 109-110). They described how a good photographer in a collective newspaper was rotated to become an unhappy and ineffective advertising seller, eventually leaving the paper altogether. Despite references to *now* and *at present*, the case studies quoted were in 1973-5.
In contrast: "People realised that this specialisation was not a 'defeat' for the collective process but an improvement in the structure of work... The structure allowed people to grow in the work they cared about most without being excluded from other things that were important to them." Karen Brandow and Jim McDonnell (1981; 37).

19 Phyllida Parsloe (1981; 148) suggests that working in a collective team may mean "the ability to adapt one's pace to that of others and to substitute collective success for individual achievement".

Chapter Eleven

1 "All units have regular (usually weekly) staff meetings. These are used to plan, co-ordinate and review services; to allocate new work; to develop proposals for consideration by the management committee; and to carry out routine and administrative business." Drew Reith (1981; 23). During 1983-86 Newcastle's management committee met every other month.

2 See David Billis (1984).

3 Linear thinking has even come up with a *mathematical* proof of the need for hierarchy. It begins by visualising co-ordination as lines joining points. Within a group, each additional member is viewed as adding a potential new link-line for *each* of the existing members. Linear thinkers conclude that because the numbers of links involved rapidly become unmanageable, the solution must be hierarchical supervision. This argument has at least three major flaws. It treats people's working relations as one dimensional. It ignores existing or potential lateral links within hierarchies. It assumes that direct democracy means everybody discussing everything with everyone else.

4 William A. Kraus (1981) reviewed a wide range of sources showing the elements and advantages of collaboration. He also told a story. "In the initial stages of research and data collection for this work it seemed appropriate to start with the library... The initial word on which a reference search was begun was *collaboration*. The catalogue said: 'Collaboration: see *Treason*'."

5 Abraham Maslow (1966) recommended "healthy scientists to enjoy not only the beauties of precision but also the pleasures of sloppiness, casualness and ambiguity. They are able to enjoy rationality and logic but are also able to be pleasantly crazy, wild or emotional. They are not afraid of hunches, intuitions or improbable ideas."

6 "Top management didn't know what we were talking about. How *could* they show their own weakness in discussing a proposition which they simply didn't understand? Would you?" Charles Handy (1981; 263).

7 Chris Argyris (1972) found this a major problem even in commercial firms which had moved towards a matrix structure.

8 Irving L. Janis (1972).

9 When people are worried about status, they often fear admitting their ignorance or mistakes. Christine Hallett and Olive Stevenson (1980) gave an example from a case conference on a possible child abuse. Not only had some participants failed to ask about things they hadn't understood during the conference, they evaded the point when the researchers asked them about it later.

10 Carole Satyamurti (1981; 109) found that social services "top level discussions tended to be overwhelmingly characterised by conflict avoidance, the avoidance of discussion of specifics, non-mentioning of names and so on, and tended to be confined to general principles and the airing of shared grievances against third parties".

11 Though this was hardly 'respect' for Ali, however supportive and sympathetic the team were trying to be. "Respect does not mean non-critical acceptance of what is said, but rather stands for the right of the person to share her/his perceptions or feelings and to have those perceptions and feelings taken seriously". Rose and Black (1986; 114)

12 Techniques which are useful in meetings of practitioners and users. Tony Gibson (1979) describes a "community planning exercise" involving residents, planners, community workers, councillors and police. "Each of the experts was labelled so that residents knew who did what. The rule was that if you wore a label you couldn't speak until you were spoken to by a resident." A large model of the area was used as focus for discussion, thereby minimising deference to 'the platform party', and status games needing eye contact.

13 Michel Avery, Brian Auvine, Barbara Streibel, and Lonnie Weiss (1981). Also, Karen Brandow, Jim McDonnell, (1981).

14 Chris Argyris and Donald Schon (1978).

15 Just as advice about teamworking often assumes the existence of a 'team', able to discuss and take the advice.

16 C. Northcote Parkinson (1958) calls this the 'Law of Triviality', explaining it as people spending time on small items they can grasp. On major complex issues which may involve large sums of money and expert technical knowledge, they keep quiet rather than lose face.

17 In hierarchical firms, the weakness of Joint Works Councils is sometimes illustrated by their preoccupation with 'teas, towels, and toilets'. However, Anna Pollert (1981; 188) studying a cigarette factory, suggested these "were precisely the final nooks and crannies of choice and decision which were still tangible. Everything else seemed sewn up".

18 Raymond Williams (1985; 104). He also argues for "an educated participatory democracy", not "merely *apparent* involvement in decision-making".

19 For a variant see: Harvey Sacks (1974).

20 Richard Macfarlane's (1986; 52) study of Suma Wholefoods Co-op took a similar view. "What are the implications for this reliance on consensus collective decision-making for Suma? Obviously the process is slow and time consuming. For example the decision to move warehouse involved general meeting discussions (and on-going research and discussion) lasting from December 1984 to July 1985." Yet Macfarlane's example is very odd. As he makes clear, the move meant the co-op leaving Leeds (after ten years in that city), with major implications for members' lives, wages, and the co-ops' transport facilities.

21 Joyce Rothschild-Whitt (1979; 519) describing case studies from 1973-75. She and J.Allen Whitt (1986; 64), repeat this criticism word for word, even though the *fieldwork* data on which they base their conclusion, remains that reported in the 1979 article.

22 John Case and Rosemary Taylor (1979).

23 Max Weber's analysis of bureaucracy as an ideal type, remains the starting point for much subsequent writing. H. Gerth and C. Wright Mills ed. (1970).

24 Loren Baritz (1965); Geoff Esland and Graeme Salaman (1980); C. Wright Mills (1979).

25 Jane Mansbridge (1983; 146).

26 Judy Wajcman (1983) described a co-operative of women shoe workers who had occupied their factory and set up a "highly democratic way of working" (p.55). "Everything is done together, every little thing" (p.50). Hierarchy was subsequently imposed from outside.

Mary Mellor and John Stirling (1984; 15) drew from co-op research to suggest: "The collective model does not presuppose that everyone stops work to gather around the table on every issue. Rather it supposes that a co-op develops organically to the level where a consensus emerges based on a common experi-

ence and understanding of the business such that anyone
would come to a similar conclusion if they were called upon to
make the decision".

27 Jim Black and others (1983; 129).

28 Dave Holder and Mike Wardle (1981; 129).

29 "We used the phrase *liberated time* not free time, and we meant it
in just the same sense as a WWII Tommy did when he 'liberated' a tin of corned beef from the cookhouse. We mean that
workers must decide that *they* are going to get some direct use of
the vast storehouse of ability (their own ability, for goodness
sake) which is daily placed at the disposal of employers." Mike
Hales (1980; 137).

30 Case and Taylor (1979; 7).

Chapter Twelve

1 Joyce Rothschild-Whitt (1979; 519).

2 "Only Executives make decisions. The first managerial skill is,
therefore, the making of effective decisions." Peter Drucker
(1974; 465).

3 Richard T. Pascale and Anthony Athos (1982).

4 Pascale and Athos, p.114.

5 Pascale and Athos, p.110.

6 Peter Drucker (1974; 467-470) saw the essence of Japanese decision making as defining the question. That meant inviting a
wide variety of dissenting opinions, and focussing on alternatives rather than on the 'right solution'. This built effective exe-
cution into the decision-making process.

7 This isn't to endorse the paternalistic nature of Japanese
companies, which also has its underside — a pool of casual 'periphery' workers who aren't included. Satoshi Kamata (1983).

8 Pascale and Athos (1982; 90).

9 Michel Avery, Brian Auvine, Barbara Streibel, and Lonnie
Weiss (1981), authors of *Building United Judgement*, subtitle their
book: *A Handbook for Consensus Decision Making*.

10 Jennifer Thornley (1981).

11 "The first few meetings he attended nearly drove him mad... As a
bank clerk and an active Labour Party worker in his spare time,
he was used to business-like procedures. The meanderings of
the Winstanley [tenants] Committee went against the grain. (I
found them pretty strange myself, at first.) But gradually an
underlying logic appears. What goes on, within the Committee
and outside it, is a powerful exercise in communication". Tony
Gibson (1979; 42). Beatrix Campbell (1984; 54) observed a similar meeting in a Housing Co-op.

Chapter Thirteen

1   Though as Mary Mellor, Janet Hannah, and John Stirling (1988) point out, "co-operatives that are, in theory, owned by the workforce can be effectively 'owned' by banks and local authorities which can severely compromise control by the workforce". (Chapter 3).

2   "Management have long been accustomed to representing their labour as a cost and recording it as such on their profit and loss account. This is another historical situation which is hard to justify logically, but which has had an unquantifiable impact on the way organisations are managed. Costs, after all, are something you minimise and would ideally like to dispense with. Substitute the word 'people' for costs and it is very easy to see how labour can be alienated once it becomes figures not individuals." Charles Handy (1981; 386).

3   Charles Landry and others (1985; 47).

4   Chris Argyris and Donald Schon (1978; 9).

5   Don Zimmerman (1971; 221).

6   Sheila Martel (1981; 2) an FSU assistant director, editing a book on supervision, wrote that individual supervision is: "limited if it is not combined with a team structure which is both stimulating and supportive. The opportunities for social workers to learn from each other are greatly enhanced in a team where active discussion and co-operation are encouraged." All but one of the book's contributors describe *individual* learning and supervision.

7   Joan Smith (1985).

8   Fran Martin (1985; 23).

9   Paulo Freire (1972a; 46).

10 Paulo Freire (1972a; 66).

11 "We trained hard, but it seemed every time we were beginning to form up into teams we would be reorganised. I was to learn later in life that we tend to meet any new situation by reorganising; and a wonderful method it can be for creating the illusion of progress while producing confusion, inefficiency, and demoralisation". Petronius Arbiter, 60 A.D., Quoted by William A. Kraus (1981; 99).

12 It could also mean keeping quiet about collective working and learning, in case this is seen as a threat by the world outside. Stanton (1984; 4).

13 Argyris and Schon (1978; 195) give an example from a consultancy with company executives. "Several mentioned the fear that to be open is to 'clobber' people. Others mentioned that their dilemma was that the organisation was managed by fear. The president interrupted and said: 'I don't think we run this company by fear and I don't think that you should have said that'. There was an excruciatingly lengthy silence of five seconds, and the vice-president replied: 'I still believe that we manage this company by fear and I agree with you that I should not

have said it!' [The president] 'Let me say that I see what I just did. I have been asking for openness and risk-taking, and clobber the first person that takes a risk. I'm sorry; it's not easy to hear such things'."

14 David L. Altheide and John M. Johnson (1980).

15 Mary Mifflin (1985).

16 Phyllida Parsloe (1981; 151).

17 Donald Schon (1973) chapter six.

18 Ivan Illich (1970 and 1978) argued that a major part of what schools teach is the 'need' for education and schools.

19 Carl Rogers (1978; 178-185) discusses problems faced by participants who return from a residential workshop.

20 "The teacher selecting objects of study knows them better than the students as the course begins but the teacher *re-learns* the objects through studying them with the students." Paulo Freire and Ira Shor (1987; 100).

21 Allan Brown (1984; 95).

22 Christine Hallett and Olive Stevenson (1980; 88).

23 Joyce Rothschild and J. Allen Whitt (1986) note that 70% of members in the five collectives they researched, listed "Learning for future career" as one of the positive features of their jobs (p.153). In addition, their research found "a tendency for the personnel of social movement organisations to flow back and forth among various movement organisations, government agencies, and professional schools" (p.129). However, they failed to see the significance of these 'helical' careers; making the misleading suggestion (p.84) that egalitarian agencies have "no hierarchy of positions and so there is no ladder to ascend". A teacher at Countesthorpe College, a democratic comprehensive school in Leicestershire, doubted whether trying to equalise salaries had affected staff careers. "Judging from the number of ex-Countesthorpe heads and deputies in Leicestershire, it doesn't seem to have been such a handicap". Libertarian Education (1986; 10 — unsigned article).

24 This is the educational version of the division mentioned several times previously. Eg. Jim Black and others (1983; 210-217).

25 Written for the Central Council for Education and Training in Social Work (CCETSW), which funded the student unit.

26 Adrian Webb and Martin Hobdell (1980; 106-107).

27 Mike Fisher (1983). See also Suzy Croft and Peter Beresford (1987; 26-27).

28 Donald Schon (1983).

29 Schon (1983; 241).

30 Schon (1983; 138).

31 Schon spells out a different "professional-client relationship", p.290-307.
32 "Additions to the law school curriculum like 'Law and the Poor' serve a useful function by making it crystal clear that the remainder of the curriculum deals with law and the rich." Stephen Wexler (1970; 1055). Wexler urged lawyers to reject the belief, "that poor people are unable to take care of themselves, let alone do work traditionally reserved for professionals". He also says some interesting things about the relationship between users and counter-professionals.
33 Jonathan Zeitlyn (1980).
34 *Community Action* magazine shows this development in Britain. For example, an unsigned article in February 1972 (p.26) called for local authority planners to become "bureaucratic guerrillas".
35 Donald Schon (1983; 342).
36 "Skill-sharing is often made more difficult simply because no-one can admit to having skills or knowing more than somebody else without putting themselves in an unfavourable and ideologically 'illegitimate' power relation over that person." Landry (1985; 46).

Chapter Fourteen

1 When friends of mine in a social services team phoned head office about rain coming through the roof, they were told there was no money left for maintenance. But they *could* have a new carpet, as that allocation was unspent.
2 The point isn't that all workers should become architects. But a dialogue with fellow practitioners is possible, along the lines suggested by Donald Schon in chapter thirteen. Otherwise teams find themselves blocked off from doing anything except complaining about their building after the event.
3 "Social workers had erected filing cabinet partitions in the open-plan office 'to symbolise their separation and secrecy'." Steve Platt (1986; 21).
4 "'Haven't you noticed that there's three distinct groups in this factory... We more or less decided to put our machines in these places'. Cindy was referring to her feeling that Olive and the machinists who sat with her stuck together. As did Pat and Brenda." Judy Wajcman (1983: 117-118).
5 Alvin Gouldner (1964)
6 Confirmed by two studies of the effects of mechanisation introduced to coal-mining. New methods led to the breakdown of teamwork, and the substitution of relationships marked by stress, uncertainty and hostility. E.L. Trist and K.W. Bamforth (1951. And see E.L. Trist, G.W. Higgin, H. Murray, and A.B. Pollack, (1963).

7 Tom Burns and G.M. Stalker (1961) compared 'organic' systems which respond to rapid change, and 'mechanistic' organisations which don't. One sign of the latter is that staff are "tethered" to a particular work area. "Production management . . . cannot bring itself to believe that a development engineer is doing the job he is paid for unless he is at a bench doing something with his hands; a draughtsman isn't doing his job unless he is at his drawing-board, drawing, and so on. Higher management in many firms are also worried when they find people moving about the works, when individuals they want are not 'in their place'." (171) By contrast, in an 'organic' firm: "Access to anyone was. . . physically simple and direct; it was easier to walk across to the laboratories' door, the office door, or the factory door and look about for the person one wanted."

8 For some feminists the division of space reflects and perpetuates 'women's work' and lack of power. Dale Spender (1980: 220) argues that women grant men "sustained and uninterrupted time to work". Lucy Mair (1972; 55) makes a similar point. "In the division of roles between the sexes much of the work that falls to men is not manual labour. It consists in a great deal of talking, and since the place for talking can be chosen for its amenities, the talkers may sit in the shade while the toilers stand or walk in the sun".

9 Newcastle's open door never meant totally open access. *Personal* space was always safeguarded — including interview rooms, and locked cupboards for valuables.

10 Fatma Dharamsi and others (1979; 186).

11 Stanton (1983; 212).

12 Jennifer Joslin (1980).

13 The practice later ceased running collectively. One doctor wanted higher pay, and some of the para-medical workers were sacked after a dispute. See: Anne Karpf (1981); Andrew Veitch (1983); Debbie Smith (1984); Barbara Briggs (1985).

14 In 1968, Lou Gottleib owned a ranch near San Francisco which had become a hippy commune. When charged with operating an organised camp in violation of State health regulations, he protested, "If they find any evidence of organisation here, I wish they would show it to me". Quoted in Rosabeth Moss Kanter (1973; 138).

15 "Another influence on the way teams function is the space they occupy and the way it is organised. Usually this is decided by headquarters staff... and they are thus prevented from controlling what is probably an extremely important factor in determining how they will work." Phyllida Parsloe (1981; 38).

16 "In many bureaucracies, clerks and other low-status office workers can normally be seen within a large office space while the

more powerful employees gradually disappear into asylums as they move up the ranks... The executive office is designed to serve the interest of the one who occupies it, functioning in many ways as a sanctuary from the demands of others." Charles Derber (1983; 81).

17 "In general, the higher the rank, the greater the size of all territories of the self and the greater the control across the boundaries." Erving Goffman (1971; 65). This includes *time* as well as space. For example, rules of deference determine who may be kept waiting, and whose summons overides the day's schedule.

18 Stanton (1983).

19 The removal of barriers — literal as well as metaphorical — is a recurring theme in numerous attempts to build participatory democracy. For instance, Stewart Wilson (1980; 120) head teacher of Sutton Centre Community School in Nottinghamshire, argued that: "The main job is to remove all the artificial barriers which have been created over the years in the world of education, for any school which has aspirations to be a real community school".

20 "Natural mixing of people may also enable some relaxation of status, class or race barriers." Fatma Dharamsi (1979; 187).

21 Val Millman (1986; 42) noted "demarcation of male and female territory" in schools, with "boys dominating the activities taking place in the classroom, the playground and on the sportsfield".

22 "You don't see many old people here. The reception is busy, active; a lot of energy buzzing around; lots of information. Things that young people can take in very quickly. The general atmosphere has that sort of orientation. I think that's quite off-putting. People feel a bit intimidated; it presents a certain image." Member of collective quoted in Stanton (1983; 256).

23 Other collective teams stress not wanting to appear "a bunch of hippies". This is more than a figure of speech. It relates to the 'counter-cultural' history of many collectives, which gave an oppositional meaning to 'informality'.

24 "The staff sit in three irregular but immutable circles in a row down the narrow length of the room. I tend to stand most of the time, but there is a circle to which most of the new staff clearly belong." Nicholas Otty (1972; 77).

25 Robert Frost (1914) from the poem *Mending Wall*.

26 "The adoption of a zimmer frame may represent a greater acquiescence to institutional norms, but, at the same time, the frame may be used to 'stake out' personal territory in public places such as lounges." Sheila M. Peace, Leonie A. Kellaher, and Diana M. Wilcocks (1982: 7).

Alan Roberts (1979) discusses the opposition of private and collective solutions to limited space (chapter ten).

Chapter Fifteen
1 Legally, staff were hired and fired by the national organisation, so Newcastle Unit had no formal authority to dismiss a worker.
2 Stephen Lukes (1974; 56).
3 Jo Freeman, (1982).
4 A view with a long and respectable anarchist history. Peter Kropotkin (1972) saw idleness as due to the absence of pleasant, useful work. See also: Vernon Richards (1983).
5 "How do you get people to work when there is no reward of labour, and especially how to get them to work strenuously?" "No reward of labour?" said Hammond gravely. "The reward of labour is *life*. Is that not good enough?" William Morris (1941).
6 Quoted in Stanton (1983).
7 I met a woman who'd been sacked from a London collective. Several years later, she still found it hard dealing with collective teams. "If there's a group of workers I just seize up. Although I'm quite friendly with all of them on an individual one-to-one thing. It's funny, but as soon as they're in a group I get terrified."
8 Joyce Rothschild-Whitt (1979; 513).
9 Charles Handy (1979).
10 Hans Gerth and C.Wright Mills ed. (1970).
11 Tom Burns and G.M. Stalker (1961; 120-121) found that 'mechanical' types of organisation had "a precise definition of rights and obligations". 'Organic' types had sanctions based instead on "a presumed community of interest with the rest of the working organisation."
12 Marshall Colman (1982; 57).
13 Charles Landry and others (1985; 12).
14 Newcastle's secretaries' feelings might be seen in this way, though they were explicit that there was no conflict of interest, and that they trusted the staff team to consider their interests.
15 "To the extent that a person or group consciously or unconsciously creates or reinforces barriers to the public airing of policy conflicts that person or group has power". Peter Bachrach and Morton S. Baratz (1970).
16 Lukes (1974: 24).
17 Lukes (1974: 38).
18 Lukes (1974: 9) gives the example of a how the *reputation* of a large corporation in a 'company town' was enough to inhibit action to prevent industrial pollution.
19 John Gaventa (1980).
20 Alvin Gouldner (1964).
21 Gouldner (1964; 53).

22   "   (1964; 165).
23   "   (1964; 173).
24   Stuart Henry (1983; 221).
25   Henry (1968; 184).
26   "   (1968; 186)
27   For example, the Hawthorne study highlighted 'rate restriction' among informal work groups, as a major management problem. Fritz J. Roethlisberger, and William J. Dickson (1939). The significance of this study is less in what it says, than the enormous body of writing it led to.
28   "Within the group are people I like, and some I don't like at all. And I tend to listen more sympathetically to the former. If I find myself on different sides of an issue with someone I like very much I'm actually in pain over that. When I disagree with someone I dislike intensely I might get a buzz out of the argument. But even people I dislike can be right." Quoted in Stanton (1983).
29   "Moreover the social reinforcement from worker peers that is integral to a collective organisation is antithetical to a capitalist organisation where workers are placed in direct competition with one another for employment, promotions and pay." Henry M. Levin (1984).
30   Richard Sennett (1980; 153).
31   "Mutual scapegoating is a self-perpetuating system, in which nothing is resolved and no one feels guilty. For all concerned to remain in collusion with such a system is a defence which allows each to make his anonymous contribution to the group mentality." E.L. Trist and K.W.Bamforth (1951; 32).
32   Isabel Menzies (1970; 16) describes the "collusive social redistribution of responsibility and irresponsibility" among hospital nursing staff.
33   "Even on wet days there's satisfaction of a kind, cursing the bosses' nine-till-five world as it sucks you towards it through the pissing rain; embracing dis-satisfaction and recognising it as the one obvious fact of existence". Mike Hales (1980; 31).
34   Janet Mattinson and Ian Sinclair (1979) suggest that the emotions and behaviour of clients, are "mirrored" by social workers. They give the example of a social worker's "fishwife display" . . . of "sputtering rage with a Homeless Family Unit". Rather than see this as the worker's own anger, it's interpreted as "secondary anxiety" representing the feelings of the client who has also lost control.
35   "Let's say I'm working at [job] and making $2 an hour and being pushed around by a lot of schmucky people I don't really like, whose political leaning make me quite ill, and let's say they make some comment and I retort, 'I don't like what you said'.

Well, I don't feel that I was threatened in that situation very much because I didn't have much to lose if they fired me. Whereas here [collective] I was so comfortable ... everyone's so nice and friendly and some people come up and give you a back rub . . . It's kind of intimidating to be in that position." Jane Mansbridge (1983; 159).

36 Just as the same peer relationships enable-a team to challenge a colleague who is *overworking*, as underworking.

37 Mary Parker Follett (1973).

Chapter Sixteen

1 Apart from male students, Ernie was the only man for 3 years. Letters were sometimes addressed to him as UO, apparently making the same assumption as a user who told me she had "expected the man to be the boss". Rosabeth Kanter (1975), called this "statistical discrimination", the idea that assuming something is 'normal' isn't the same as prejudice. (eg: one woman in an office of men *is* likely to be the secretary). Actually, the point is that hierarchical rules of deference. are usually sexist.

2 FSU Quarterly July 1983.

3 Gill Dixon and others (1982).

4 " " " " (1982; 70).

5 " " " " (1982; 59).

6 The mythmaker was Eileen Younghusband, quoted in Ronald Walton (1975).

7 Walton (1975; 235-238).

8 Carole Satyamurti (1981; 196).

9 David Howe (1986; 21). See also: Judy Hale (1983; 182). Hale observed that "an analysis of the hierarchical composition of the profession shows that the numerical representation of women is inversely proportional to the level of seniority".

10 Walton (1975; 263).

11 Janet Radcliffe Richards (1980).

12 For Janet Finch (1984) a non-sexist care policy would ensure that "women were no more likely than men to take on front-line caring for members of their own family".

13 Rayna Reiter ed. (1975).

14 Harry Braverman (1974; 296).

15 Jean Elshtain (1976; 8).

16 Suzy Croft (1986).

17 Annie Hudson (1985; 635-655).

18 Ann Oakley (1981).

19 Jean Baker Miller (1979).

20 Paulo Freire (1972a; 135). Carien Fritze (1982) linked Freire with a feminist approach.

21 Sheila Rowbotham (1983; 68).

22 Carole Ehrlich (1978) suggested common ground between feminist and anarchist ideas on organisation.

23 Jo Freeman (1982).

24 Meredith Gould (1980; 237).

25 Rosabeth Kanter (1975; 42).

26 Meredith Gould (1980: 242).

27 Jennifer Thornley (1981) noted feminist influence among the "new co-operators" of the 1960's in Britain. In the USA, Robert Jackall and Joyce Crain (1984) found that women were 61% of co-operators in small co-ops.

28 Eileen Cadman, Gail Chester, and Agnes Pivot (1981).

29 "Two men had offices of their own. A. had an office of his own first of all; in the middle room. S. in the back room on his own. And three women in the front office." "Classic, isn't it?"
"We don't have any men in our group. It's been all women for the past two years, and I would imagine that we will employ all women for the foreseeable future." Members of a collective working with old people, quoted in Stanton (1983).

30 "Women as a principle for some and a matter of survival for others." Comment on hiring policy at a Housing Advice collective. quoted in Stanton (1983).

31 Lane Tracey (1972).

32 Margaret Hennig and Anne Jardim, (1979).

33 "When women's groups strive to be participatory, co-operative, and non-hierarchic, they are a microcosm of a feminist vision of relationships in a non-sexist society. In work groups, political organisations — whatever associations women form — women must continue to pay attention to the *way* to organise, the *way* to relate to each other, the *way* to allocate tasks and share knowledge — and thus power — the *way* to make decisions. In other words, feminists focus steadily on the ends *in* the means." Joan Rothschild (1976; 17).

34 "We want eventually to be, and to help other women to be, in charge of their own lives; therefore, we must be in charge of our own movement, directly, not by remote control. This means that not only those with experience in politics, but all, must learn to take their own decisions, both political and personal." Women's Liberation Workshop Manifesto (1969).

35 Sheila Rowbotham (1983; 145).

36 Dale Spender (1980) — specially chapter 4.

37 Lee Jenkins and Cheris Kramer (1978; 67) criticise the reliance of social psychology on studies of predominantly male groups.

Chapter Seventeen

1 From a paper written for the Management committee in July 1981.

2 Other committee members spoke of "community" rather than user management, though users were not a fixed group, but a changing pool of individuals, families, and local groups.

3 Local committees were technically sub-committees of FSU's National Council.

4 Monica Elliot didn't have time for a transcribed interview. Another member was Mayor of Newcastle, Arthur Stabler, which prevented him taking an active part.

5 Alan Jackson represented the Unit at National Council.

6 This happened at South Birmingham FSU. See Martin Thomas (1986); South Birmingham FSU (1987).

7 Christine Hallett (1987).

8 Peter Beresford and Suzy Croft (1986; 302).

9 Another essential difference is that an empowerment approach always values people's own lives above the issue raised. However much a practitioner may be itching to take up a particular case, the choice whether to go ahead belongs to the client. The need is to help that person make a choice based on their own critical assessment, rather than passive acquiescence. Stephen M. Rose and Bruce L. Black (1986; 97-101).

10 "All I want to do is my job, and they want me to make decisions." Worker at Brent Community Transport, quoted in Stanton (1983).

11 Creating "community spirit" was part of the brief of Bishop Auckland FSU. Dave Holder and Mike Wardle (1981). Paul Fordham, Geoff Poulton and Lawrence Randle (1979; 22) were: "to increase the effective penetration of both responsible body and local authority adult education services."

12 Jeff Bishop and Paul Hoggett (1986; 101-102) studied groups ranging from fishing and collecting clubs to dance and sports groups. "We hardly encountered one organisation where the formal constitution and/or committee structure was not perfectly democratic. Yet if one went below the surface one discovered enormous variations... The official organisational structure tells you very little about the actual distribution of power".

13 Patrick Wright (1985).

14 Of course, new organisational forms *are* developed, but they're less important than the process involved and a qualitative change in people's *relations*. Philip Herbst (1976; 42) confirms this, from his experience of industrial participation schemes. The usual approach was to see the participation process as, "something temporary and dispensable, and what is of lasting value is the new system structure which has been evolved". Herbst insisted that the opposite is true. "The new characteristics of the process is the goal. The structures arrived at are tem-

porary . . . The more enduring characteristics at this stage lie in the quality of the developmental process".

15 "Channels of influence viewed from below are often no more than channels of support when viewed from above." Noel Boaden, Michael Goldsmith, William Hampton, and Peter Stringer (1982; 170)

16 Sherry Arnstein (1969; 216).

17 Jane Mansbridge (1983; 111) examined the costs and benefits for people participating (or not) in a Town Meeting where there was formal equality in a face-to-face direct democracy with real power. While it was open to all, there was a hidden entry price, varying from person to person. 'Costs' included arranging a babysitter, travel from an outlying farm, and a dislike of meetings and fear of speaking publicly. However this wasn't her whole explanation. "Working-class citizens in Selby avoid town meeting not only because they need the day's pay but also because their experience outside town meeting leads them to assume they will not be able to influence what goes on at the meeting".

18 C. Lesley Andrews (1979; 92).

19 Mary Mellor and John Stirling (1983) saw similar suspicions when workers tried to raise capital to set up a co-op. "If one person creates 30 jobs for others, he or she is praised for service to the community; if 30 workers decide to provide jobs for themselves they are treated in a far more circumspect way".

20 Andrew Rigby (1974; 122) found that even when commune members withdrew to a "counter-community", they saw themselves helping to change the world outside *by example*. Other groups were more direct. "Typically their aim is the encouragement of participatory democracy within local communities through encouraging local inhabitants to claim their right to decide and influence decisions that affect their own lives".

21 Raoul Vaneigem (1967) updated Plato's parable of the cave. During a struggle between lamp-owners and oil carriers, a hole is made in the wall, and light streams in. But people build windows rather than live in the *open*.

22 Michael Peter Smith (1980; 200).

23 Rosemary C.R.Taylor (1979; 22). Paul Starr (1979; 259) suggested the word 'community' was usually a code, meaning blacks, Hispanics, or low income white ethnics —the groups radicals wanted their organisations to serve.

24 Charles Landry and others (1985; 38).

25 "[Covent Garden] Forum discussions were often conducted on a relatively technical level and this was a major source of confusion for many of the non-professionals on the Forum, especially new members elected at the second and third elections who had

not undergone the educative experience of those who had been members since the Forum's inception". Peter Hain (1980; 146).

26 Many organisations (from community groups to political parties) deter people by upping the ante: putting pressure on participants to take on ever more responsibilities to stay 'in the game'.

27 "The Chairman may indeed be a genial fellow; there may well be flowers in the room, carpets on the floor, comfortable chairs and all the other paraphernalia which taken together enables us to declare that the bourgeois is at home. But it is his home; you are invited there and must behave on his terms". Zenon Bankowski and Geoff Mungham (1976: 26) describing efforts to make legal tribunals less formal, and "closer to the people".

28 Peter Hain (1980; 186). Jane Mansbridge (1983), makes similar observations. See also Tony Gibson (1979) specially chapter three.

29 "We are trying to allow people to express and experience themselves as people engaged in some type of struggle to know more about their world in order to act on it. Crucial to this effort is the capacity to express what one believes to be true, and to be respected for the communication." Rose and Black (1986; 114).

30 Beresford and Croft (1986) chapter eleven. Compare: Ali Mantle (1985).

31 Where there is a flourishing and *established* group of users on a management body, separate space may be needed by a group of new users, as yet unfamiliar with the rules.

Methods Appendix

1 Other than those of Lin Harwood and Janet Williams, quotations in this appendix are from Unit discussions of drafts, between September 1984 and December 1986.

2 Change signalled in three books: Colin Bell and Howard Newby ed. (1977); Helen Roberts ed. (1981); Colin Bell and Helen Roberts ed. (1984).

3 Many earlier critiques examine the political nature of social research. On the general issue, see: C. Wright Mills (1970). Loren Baritz (1960) argued that management and organisation studies have substantially served the interests of those who control. Ian Taylor, Paul Walton and Jock Young (1975) see most social science as, implicitly or explicitly, providing data about the powerless, to assist their control by "powerful agencies and political men" (p.24). "For radical researchers, the point about attempting to remain faithful to the researched population is that he has already taken sides; in the sense that he is concerned to feed back his results, not to the powerful, but to those most immediately and directly affected" (p.26).

4   Ann Oakley (1981; 30) and Janet Finch (1981; 70).
5   Peter Reason and John Heron (1986).
6   Shulamit Reinharz (1983).
7   Peter Beresford and Suzy Croft (1984).
8   Peter Reason and John Rowan (1981) edit an important collection of alternative research approaches.
9   Maria Mies (1983; 117); Hilary Graham (1981;104).
10 Ann Oakley (1981; 58).
11 Paulo Freire (1972); Paulo Freire and Ira Shor (1987).
12 John Heron (1981; 19).
13 Budd Hall (1981).
14 Critiques of these aspects of traditional research are found in Peter Reason and John Rowan ed (1981); Budd Hall, Arthur Gillette and Rajesh Tandon ed. (1982).
15 "Through our balanced cool appraisal there comes an undercurrent of hatred and horror about what traditional research does to those it studies, those who do the research, and about the dreadful rubbish that is sometimes put forward as scientific knowledge". So, 'new paradigm' research seeks "alternatives which would do justice to the humanness of all of those involved in the research endeavour". Reason and Rowan (1981; xi-xii).
16 See in particular John Rowan's helpful framework (1981; 93).
17 Barry McDonald and Rob Walker (1979; 185) criticise education case studies as "autocratic" or "bureaucratic", with problems seen as, "irritating obstructions to the scientist's pursuit of new knowledge".
18 Ann Oakley (1981; 50).
19 This summary draws heavily from Budd Hall (1982; 13) For a critique of participatory research, see: Tom Lovett, Chris Clarke and Avila Kilmurray (1983; 98), questioning what they see as its rejection of rationality and rigour.
20 Patricia Maguire (1987; 46).
21 Questions posed by the Participatory Research Network (1982; 42).
22 This isn't the only way to do participatory research. I used tools that were available and affordable. Other researchers use cartoons, photos, video and theatre.

BIBLIOGRAPHY

Unless otherwise stated, publication was in London.

Philip ABRAMS and Andrew McCULLOCH (1976) *Communes, Sociology and Society.* Cambridge University Press.

Tony ADDY and Duncan SCOTT (1987) *Fatal Impacts?: The MSC and Voluntary Action.* Manchester: William Temple Foundation.

David L. ALTHEIDE and John M. JOHNSON (1980) *Bureaucratic Propaganda.* Boston Massachusetts: Allyn and Bacon.

C. Lesley ANDREWS (1979) *Tenants and Town Hall.* HMSO.

Chris ARGYRIS (1972) *Today's Problems With Tomorrow's Organisations,* in John M. Thomas and Warren G. Bennis ed. *The Management of Change and Conflict.* Penguin.

Chris ARGYRIS and Donald SCHON (1978) *Organisational Learning: A Theory of Action Perspective.* Reading, Massachusetts: Addison-Wesley.

Sherry ARNSTEIN (1969) *A Ladder of Citizen Participation.* Journal of the American Institute of Planners, July, p.216.

Michel AVERY, Brian AUVINE, Barbara STREIBEL, and Lonnie WEISS (1981) *Building United Judgement: A Handbook for Consensus Decision Making.* Madison Wisconsin: The Centre for Conflict Resolution.

Peter BACHRACH and Morton S. BARATZ (1970) *Power and Poverty: Theory and Practice.* New York: Oxford University Press.

Zenon BANKOWSKI and Geoff MUNGHAM (1976) *Images of Law.* Routledge.

BARCLAY REPORT (1982) *Social Workers Their Role and Tasks.* Bedford Square.

Loren BARITZ (1965) *The Servants of Power: A History of the Use of Social Science in American Industry.* New York: Science Editions.

Colin BEECH and Jeremy GRICE (1984) *The Heart of the Matter.* Community Care February 16th.

R. Meredith BELBIN (1981) *Management Teams: Why They Succeed or Fail.* Heinemann.

Colin BELL and Howard NEWBY ed. (1977) *Doing Sociological Research.* Allen and Unwin.

Colin BELL and Helen ROBERTS ed. (1984) *Social Researching: Politics Problems, Practice.* Routledge.

Bill BENNETT (1980) *The Sub-office: A Team Approach to Local Authority Fieldwork Practice,* in *Radical Social Work and Practice,* ed. Mike Brake and Roy Bailey. Edward Arnold.

Benwell Community Project (1978a) *Private Housing and the Working Class.* Newcastle-upon-Tyne.

Benwell Community Project (1978b) *The Making of a Ruling Class: Two Centuries of Capital Development on Tyneside.* Newcastle-upon-Tyne.

Peter BERESFORD and Suzy CROFT (1986) *Whose Welfare: Private Care or Public Services?* Brighton: Lewis Cohen Urban Studies Centre.

Peter BERESFORD and Suzy CROFT (1984) *Patch and Participation — The Case for Citizen Research.* Social Work Today, 17th September.

David BILLIS (1984) *Welfare Bureaucracies.* Heinemann.

Jeff BISHOP and Paul HOGGETT (1986) *Organising Around Enthusiasms: Mutual Aid in Leisure.* Comedia.

Jim BLACK, Ric BOWL, Douglas BURNS, Chas CRITCHER, Gordon GRANT and Dick STOCKFORD (1983) *Social Work in Context: A Comparative Study of Three Social Services Teams.* Tavistock.

Noel BOADEN, Michael GOLDSMITH, William HAMPTON, and Peter STRINGER (1982) *Public Participation in Local Services.* Longman.

Steve BOLGER, Paul CORRIGAN, Jan DOCKING, and Nick FROST (1981) *Towards Socialist Welfare Work.* Macmillan.

Karen BRANDOW, Jim McDONNELL (1981, second edition) *No Bosses Here!: A Manual on Working Collectively and Co-operatively.* Philadelphia: New Society Publishers.

Harry BRAVERMAN (1974) *Labour and Monopoly Capitalism — The Degradation of Work in the Twentieth Century.* New York: Monthly Review Press.

Maria BRENTON (1978) *Worker Participation and the Social Service Agency.* Br. J. Social Work, vol 8.3, p.289-300.

Barbara BRIGGS (1985) *Abolishing a Medical Hierarchy: The Struggle for Socialist Health Care.* Critical Social Policy, 12, Spring. pp.83-88.

Allan BROWN (1984) *Consultation: An Aid to Successful Social Work.* Heinemann.

Roger BROWN and A. GILMAN (1972) *The Pronouns of Power and Solidarity,* in Pier Paolo Giglioli ed. *Language and Social Context.* Penguin.

Peter BRUGGEN, Barbara BRILLIANT, and Suzanne IDE (1982) *Secrets and Gossip: Staff Communication.* Bulletin of the Royal College of Psychiatrists, Vol.6, No.7, July, 117.

Peter BRUGGEN and Charles O'BRIAN (1987) *Helping Families: Systems, Residential and Agency Responsibility.* Faber.

Martin BULMER ed. (1986) *Neighbours: The Work of Philip Abrams.* Cambridge University Press.

Tom BURNS and G.M. STALKER (1966) *The Management of Innovation.* Tavistock.

Eileen CADMAN, Gail CHESTER, and Agnes PIVOT (1981) *Rolling Our Own: Women as Printers, Publishers and Distributors.* Minority Press Group.

Beatrix CAMPBELL (1984) *Wigan Pier Revisited: Poverty and Politics in the 80's.* Virago.

John CASE and Rosemary TAYLOR ed. (1979) *Co-ops, Communes and Collectives: Experiments in the 1960's and 1970's.* New York: Pantheon.

Centre for the Analysis of Social Policy (1987) *Review and Consolidation in Brent Social Services Department.* University of Bath.

Tom CLARKE (1983) *Contrasting Theories of Co-operative Production.* Centre for Research in Industrial Democracy, Glasgow University.

Marshall COLMAN (1982) *Continuous Excursions — Politics and Personal Life.* Pluto.

Community Action (1972) *Bureaucratic Guerrillas.* Unsigned article February p.26.

Tim COOK (1983) *Sauce for the Goose is Sauce for the Gander.* Community Care, June 2nd.

Virginia COOVER, Ellen DEACON, Charles ESSER, and Christopher MOORE (1981) *Resource Manual for a Living Revolution.* Philadelphia: New Society.

Paul CORRIGAN and Peter LEONARD (1978) *Social Work Practice Under Capitalism.* Macmillan.

Suzy CROFT (1986) *Women, Caring and the Recasting of Need — A Feminist Reappraisal.* Critical Social Policy, 16, p.23-39.

Suzy CROFT and Peter BERESFORD (1988) *Are We Really Listening?: The Client Speaks,* in Terry Philpot ed. *On Second Thoughts: Reassessments of the Literature of Social Work.* Reed Business/Community Care.

Jon Gower DAVIES (1972) *The Evangelistic Bureaucrat; A Study of a Planning Exercise in Newcastle upon Tyne.* Tavistock.

Mike DAVIS and Martin COOK (1981) *Prefiguring The Future.* The Chartist, No.83.

Charles DERBER (1983) *The Pursuit of Attention: Power and Individualism in Everyday Life.* New York: Oxford University Press.

Fatma DHARAMSI and others (1979) *Community Work and Caring for Children.* Ilkley: Owen Wells.

Gill DIXON, Chris JOHNSON, Sue LEIGH and Nicky TURNBULL (1982) *Feminist Perspectives and Practice,* in Gary Craig, Nick Derricourt and Martin Loney, ed. *Community Work and The State.* Routledge.

Ernie DOBSON (1985) *The Role of Racism Awareness Training in the Anti-Racist Struggle.* FSU Quarterly No.37, p.18.

Penny DOBSON (1987) *An Exercise in Consultation — Residents Decide the Future of a Social and Community Work Agency.* MSc Birmingham University.

Sam DOLGOFF (1974) *The Anarchist Collectives: Workers' Self-Management in the Spanish Revolution 1936-39.* Montreal: Black Rose.

Peter DRUCKER (1974) *Management: Tasks, Responsibilities, Practices.* Heinemann.

Tony ECCLES (1981) *Under New Management.* Pan.

Ken EDWARDS (1984) *Collective Working in a Small Non-Statutory Organisation.* Bulletin of the Management Development Unit of the NCVO.

Carole EHRLICH (1978) *Socialism, Anarchism and Feminism.* Black Bear/Research Group One.

Jean ELSHTAIN (1976) *Alternatives to Individualism.* Quest, Vol.II No.3, Winter 1976, p.8.

Geoff ESLAND and Graeme SALAMAN (1980) *The Politics of Work and Occupations.* Milton Keynes: The Open University.

Roger J. EVANS (1978) *Unitary Models of Practice and the Social Work Team,* in Rolf M. Olsen ed. *The Unitary Model: Its Implications for Social Work Theory and Practice.* Birmingham: British Association of Social Workers.

Family Service Units (1982) *Family Involvement In The Social Work Process.* Discussion Paper.

Family Service Units (1985) *Access To Records.* Policy Paper.

Janet FINCH (1981) *It's Great To Have Someone To Talk To: The Ethics and Politics of Interviewing Women,* in Helen Roberts ed. *Doing Feminist Research.* Routledge.

Janet FINCH (1984) *Community Care: Developing Non-Sexist Alternatives.* Critical Social Policy, 9, Spring 1984, pp.6-18.

Mike FISHER ed. (1983) *Speaking of Clients.* Community Care/Unit for Social Services Research, University of Sheffield.

Colin FLETCHER and Neil THOMPSON ed. (1980) *Issues in Community Education.* Falmer Press.

Colin FLETCHER, Maxine CARON and Wyn WILLIAMS (1985) *Schools On Trial: The Trials of Democratic Comprehensives.* Milton Keynes: Open University Press.

Pam FLYNN, Chris JOHNSON, Sue LIEBERMAN, and Hilary ARMSTRONG ed. (1986) *You're Learning All the Time.* Nottingham: Spokesman.

Mary Parker FOLLETT (1973) *Dynamic Administration: The Collected Essays of Mary Parker Follett,* ed. Elliot M. Fox and Lyndall F. Urwick. Pitman.

Paul FORDHAM, Geoff POULTON and Lawrence RANDLE (1979) *Learning Networks in Adult Education.* Routledge.

Shirley FORSTER (1983) *The Pool Girls' Club.* FSU Quarterly, No.30, p.12.

Shirley FORSTER (1985) *Taking Care.* FSU Quarterly No.35, p.2.

Jo FREEMAN (1982) *The Tyranny of Structurelessness.* Dark Star.

Paulo FREIRE (1972a) *Pedagogy of the Oppressed.* Penguin.

Paulo FREIRE (1972b) *Cultural Action for Freedom.* Penguin.

Paulo FREIRE and Ira SHOR (1987) *A Pedagogy for Liberation: Dialogues on Transforming Education.* Macmillan.

Carien FRITZE (1982) *Because I Speak Cockney They Think I'm Stupid: An Application of Paulo Freire's Concepts to Community Work With Women.* Newcastle-upon-Tyne: Association of Community Workers.

Robert FROST (1914) from the poem *Mending Wall,* in *North of Boston.* David Nutt.

John GAVENTA (1980) *Power and Powerlessness: Quiescence and Rebellion in an Appalachian Valley.* Oxford: Clarendon.

Tony GIBSON (1979) *People Power: Community and Work Groups in Action.* Penguin.

Tony GIBSON (1983) *Who Will Do The Dirty Work?* in *Why Work?* ed. Vernon Richards. Freedom Press.

Ann GLAMPSON, Tony SCOTT, David N. THOMAS (1975) *Guide to the Assessment of Community Needs and Resources.* National Institute for Social Work.

Erving GOFFMAN (1971) *Relations in Public.* Penguin.

Erving GOFFMAN (1972) *Encounters.* Penguin.

Howard GOLDSTEIN (1973) *Social Work Practice: A Unitary Approach* University of South Carolina Press.

Teresa GORMAN, Barbara ROBSON, Bernard SHARPE, and Cyril TAYLOR (1985) *Qualgos Just Grow: Political Bodies in Voluntary Clothing* Centre for Policy Studies.

Meredith GOULD (1980) *When Women Create an Organisation: The Ideological Imperatives of Feminism,* in D. Dunkerley and G. Salaman ed. *International Yearbook of Organisation Studies 1979* Routledge.

Alvin GOULDNER (1964) *Patterns of Industrial Bureaucracy.* Toronto: The Free Press.

Hilary GRAHAM (1981) *Surveying Through Stories,* in Helen Roberts ed. *Doing Feminist Research* Routledge.

Roger HADLEY and Stephen HATCH (1981) *Social Welfare and the Failure of the State.* Allen and Unwin.

Peter HAIN (1980) *Neighbourhood Participation.* Temple Smith.

Judy HALE (1983) *Feminism and Social Work Practice,* in Bill Jordan and Nigel Parton ed. *The Political Dimensions of Social Work.* Oxford: Blackwell.

Mike HALES (1980) *Living Thinkwork: Where Do Labour Processes Come From?* Conference of Socialist Economists.

Budd HALL (1981) *Participatory Research, Popular Knowledge and Power: A Personal Reflection.* Convergence Vol.14 No.3, 6-17.

Budd HALL, Arthur GILLETTE and Rajesh TANDON ed. (1982) *Creating Knowledge: A Monopoly?.* New Delhi: Society for Participatory Research in Asia.

Christine HALLETT and Olive STEVENSON (1980) *Child Abuse: Aspects of Interprofessional Co-operation.* Allen and Unwin.

Christine HALLETT (1987) *Critical Issues in Participation.* Newcastle-upon-Tyne: Association of Community Workers.

Charles HAMPDEN-TURNER (1971) *Radical Man.* Duckworth.

Charles HANDY (1979) *Gods of Management.* Pan

Charles HANDY (1981) *Understanding Organisations.* Penguin.

Lin HARWOOD (1982) *Groupwork with Isolated Women.* FSU Quarterly No.24.

Stephen HATCH (1980) *Outside the State: Voluntary Organisations in Three English Towns.* Croom Helm.

Rodney HEDLEY (1985) *Measuring Success: A Guide to Evaluation for Voluntary and Community Groups.* Advance.

Margaret HENNIG and Anne JARDIM (1979) *The Managerial Woman ·* Pan.

Stuart HENRY (1983) *Private Justice — Towards Integrated Theorising in the Sociology of Law.* Routledge.

John HERON (1981) *Philosophical Basis for a New Paradigm,* in Peter Reason and John Rowan ed. *Human Inquiry.* Chichester: John Wiley.

Philip G. HERBST (1976) *Alternatives To Hierarchies.* Leiden: Martinus Nijhoff.

Christopher HILL (1975) *The World Turned Upside Down: Radical Ideas During the English Revolution.* Penguin.

Dave HOLDER and Mike WARDLE (1981) *Teamwork and the Development of a Unitary Approach.* Routledge.

David HOWE (1986) *The Segregation of Women and Their Work in the Personal Social Services.* Critical Social Policy, Spring p.21.

Annie HUDSON (1985) *Feminism and Social Work: Resistance or Dialogue?* British Journal of Social Work 15, 635-655.

Ivan ILLICH (1970) *Deschooling Society.* Penguin.

Ivan ILLICH (1977) *Limits To Medicine.* Penguin.

Ivan ILLICH (1978) *Celebration of Awareness.* Penguin.

Ivan ILLICH (1978) *The Right to Useful Unemployment and Its Professional Enemies.* Marion Boyars.

Robert JACKALL (1984) *Paradoxes of Collective Work: A Study of the Cheeseboard. Berkeley, California,* in Robert Jackall and Henry M. Levin, ed. *Worker Co-operatives in America.* University of California Press.

Robert JACKALL and Joyce CRAIN (1984) *The Shape of The Small Worker Co-operative Movement,* in Robert Jackall and Henry M. Levin, ed. *Worker Co-operatives in America.* University of California Press.

Irving L. JANIS (1972) *Victims of Groupthink.* Boston: Houghton Mifflin.

Lee JENKINS and Cheris KRAMER (1978) *Small Group Process: Learning from Women.* Women's Studies International Quarterly. Vol.I p.67.

Chris JOHNSON (1983) *Hardwork Cleaners' Co-op.* FSU Quarterly, No.30, p.7.

Maxwell JONES (1968) *Beyond The Therapeutic Community.* New Haven and London: Yale University Press.

Maxwell JONES (1982) *The Process of Change.* Routledge.

Bill JORDAN (1976) *Freedom and the Welfare State.* Routledge.

Jennifer JOSLIN (1980) *Essex Road Team — A Community Based Team Adopts a Patch System,* in Roger Hadley and Morag McGrath ed. *Going Local: Neighbourhood Social Services.* Bedford Square.

Satoshi KAMATA (1983) *Japan in the Passing Lane: An Insider's Account of Life in a Japanese Auto Factory.* Allen and Unwin.

Rosabeth Moss KANTER (1973) *Communes — Creating and Managing the Collective Life.* New York: Harper and Row.

Rosabeth Moss KANTER (1975) *Women and the Structure of Organisations,* in *Another Voice: Feminist Perspectives on Social Life and Social Service.* ed. Marcia Millman and Rosabeth M. Kanter. New York: Anchor..

Anne KARPF (1981) *A Cure for the City?* City Limits, 30th October.

D. KATZ and R. L. KAHN (1966) *The Social Psychology of Organisations.* New York: John Wiley.

Owen KELLY (1984) *Community, Art and the State: Storming the Citadels.* Comedia.

Owen KELLY and Dermot KILLIP (1980) *Social Change and State Funding.* Association of Community Workers. Discussion Paper No.20.

Alan KENNELLY, Angie REAGAN, Richard POPE and Julie WEST (1988) *A Collective Challenge To Traditional Practices.* Social Work Today 3rd March p.16.

Ralph M. KRAMER (1981) *Voluntary Agencies in the Welfare State.* Berkeley: University of California Press.

Cheris KRAMERAE, Muriel SCHULZ, and William M. O'BAR ed. (1984) *Language and Power.* Sage.

William A. KRAUS (1981) *Collaboration in Organisations: Alternatives to Hierarchies.* New York: Human Sciences Press.

Peter KROPOTKIN (1972, original English edition 1906) *The Conquest of Bread.* Penguin.

Charles LANDRY, David MORLEY, Russell SOUTHWOOD, and Patrick WRIGHT (1985) *What a Way to Run a Railroad: An Analysis of Radical Failure.* Comedia.

Diana LEAT (1986) *The Price of Grant Aid.* New Society May 2nd.

Gaston LEVAL (1975) *Collectives in the Spanish Revolution,* ed. Vernon Richards. Freedom Press.

Henry M. LEVIN (1984) *Employment and Productivity of Producer Co-operatives*, in Robert M. Jackall and Henry M. Levin, *Worker Co-operatives in America.* University of California Press.

Libertarian Education (1986) *Countesthorpe College, Part of the Solution or Part of the Problem?* Unsigned article Spring 1986, p.10.

Rensis LIKERT (1961) *New Patterns in Management.* New York: McGraw-Hill.

Frank LINDENFELD and Joyce ROTHSCHILD-WHITT ed. (1982) *Workplace Democracy and Social Change.* Boston: Porter Sargent.

Tom LOVETT, Chris CLARKE and Avila KILMURRAY (1983) *Adult Education and Community Action.* Croom Helm.

Steven LUKES (1974) *Power: A Radical View.* Macmillan.

Barry MacDONALD and Rob WALKER (1979) *Case-study and the Social Philosophy of Educational Research*, in David Hamilton, David Jenkins, Christine King, Barry MacDonald and Malcolm Parlett ed. *Beyond The Numbers Game: A Reader in Educational Evaluation.* Macmillan.

Richard MacFARLANE (1987) *Collective Management Under Growth: A Case Study of Suma Wholefoods.* Milton Keynes: Open University, Co-operatives Research Unit.

Richard MacFARLANE and Bernd-Georg SPIES (1985) *Autonomy or Incorporation: The Case of the Alternative Movement in West Germany.* Tavistock Institute of Social Relations.

Patricia MAGUIRE (1987) *Doing Participatory Research: A Feminist Approach.* Amherst Massachusetts: Centre for International Education, University of Massachusetts.

Lucy MAIR (1972, 2nd Edition) *An Introduction to Social Anthropology.* Oxford University Press.

Jane J. MANSBRIDGE (1983) *Beyond Adversary Democracy.* University of Chicago Press.

Ali MANTLE (1985) *Popular Planning, Not in Practice: Confessions of a Community Worker.* Greenwich Employment Resource Unit.

Harry MARSH (1981) *The Agency: Its History and Its Clients*, in Joshua Miller and Tim Cook ed. *Direct Work With Families.* Bedford Square.

Sheila MARTEL ed. (1981) *Supervision and Team Support.* Bedford Square.

Fran MARTIN (1985) *Makes a Difference When You've Done Something — Not Just Hoovered the Floor.* Report to the DHSS on the Women's Workshop, 1981 to 1984, Newcastle FSU.

Karl MARX (1968) *The Civil War in France, from Marx and Engels: Selected Works.* Lawrence and Wishart.

Abraham MASLOW (1966) *The ·Psychology of Science.* New York: Harper and Row.

Barry MASON (1983) *The Family, the Social Worker and the Professional Network.* FSU Quarterly, No.29, p.23.

Janet MATTINSON and Ian SINCLAIR (1979) *Mate and Stalemate: Working With Marital Problems in a Social Services Department.* Oxford: Blackwell.

Mary MELLOR and John STIRLING (1984) *Worker Co-operatives — Self-exploitation or Self Realisation?* Paper presented at the British Sociological Society Conference, April 1984.

Mary MELLOR, Janet HANNAH and John STIRLING (1988) *Worker Co-operatives In Theory And Practice.* Milton Keynes: Open University Press.

Isabel E. P. MENZIES (1970)*The Functioning of Social Systems as a Defence Against Anxiety*. Tavistock.
Mary MIFFLIN (1985) *What I Have Got Out of Quality Circles*. Industrial Participation, No.588, p.28.
Jean Baker MILLER (1979) *Towards a New Psychology of Women*. Penguin.
Val MILLMAN (1986) *From Raising Awareness to Positive Action: Opportunities for Intervention*, in Pam Flynn, Chris Johnson, Sue Lieberman, and Hilary Armstrong ed. *You're Learning All The Time*. Spokesman.
C. WRIGHT MILLS (1979) *The Sociological Imagination*. Penguin.
Jeanette MITCHELL, Donald MACKENZIE, John HOLLOWAY, and Cynthia COCKBURN (1980) *In and Against the State*. Pluto.
David MOBERG (1979) *Experimenting With The Future: Alternative Institutions and American Socialism*, in *Co-ops, Communes, and Collectives* ed. John Case and Rosemary Taylor, New York: Pantheon.
William MORRIS (1941, originally 1890) *News from Nowhere*. Nelson.
National Council For Voluntary Organisations (1984) *Clients' Rights: Report of a Working Party*. Bedford Square.
Newcastle Upon Tyne City Council, Policy Services Unit (1983) *City Profiles: Results from the 1981 Census*.
Newcastle Upon Tyne City Council, Policy Services Unit (1985) *Social Audit 1979-84*.
Katharine NEWMAN (1980) *Incipient Bureaucracy: The Development of Hierarchies in Egalitarian Organisations*, in Gerald Britan and Ronald Cohen (1980) *Hierarchy and Society*. Philadelphia: Ishi.
Ann OAKLEY (1981) *Interviewing Women: a Contradiction in Terms*, in *Doing Feminist Research*, ed. Helen Roberts. Routledge.
Nicholas OTTY (1972) *Learner Teacher*. Penguin.
C. Northcote PARKINSON (1958) *Parkinson's Law*. Penguin Books.
Phyllida PARSLOE (1981) *Social Services Area Teams*. Allen & Unwin.
Richard T. PASCALE and Anthony ATHOS (1982) *The Art of Japanese Management*. Penguin.
Participatory Research Network (1982) *Participatory Research: An Introduction*. New Delhi: Society for Participatory Research in Asia.
Chris PAYNE and Tony SCOTT (1982) *Developing Supervision of Teams in Field and Residential Social Work*. National Institute for Social Work.
Sheila M. PEACE, Leonie A. KELLAHER, and Diana M. WILCOCKS (1982) *A Balanced Life?: A Consumer Study of Residential Life in One Hundred Old People's Homes*. School of Applied Social Studies, Polytechnic of North London.
Peter PHILLIMORE (1981) *Families Speaking: A Study of Fifty-one Families' Views of Social Work*. FSU.
Allen PINCUS and Anne MINAHAN (1973) *Social Work Practice*. Itaxa Illinois: Peacock.
Steve PLATT (1986) *Council Goes Local*. New Society, 30th May, p.21.
Anna POLLERT (1981) *Girls, Wives, Factory Lives*. Macmillan.
Peter REASON and John ROWAN ed. (1981) *Human Inquiry: A Sourcebook of New Paradigm Research*. Chichester: John Wiley.
Peter REASON and John HERON (1986) *Research With People: The Paradigm of Co-operative Experiential Inquiry*. Person-Centred Review, Vol.1, No.4, 1986, 456-476.

Shulamit REINHARZ (1983) *Experiential Analysis: A contribution to Feminist Research Methodology* in Gloria Bowles and Renate Duelli-Klein ed. *Theories of Women's Studies*. Routledge.

Rayna REITER ed. (1975) *Towards an Anthropology of Women*. New York: Monthly Review Press.

Drew REITH (1981) *The Agency: Its Organisation, Work Methods and Staffing*, in Joshua Miller and Tim Cook ed. *Direct Work with Families*. Bedford Square.

Ali RHIND (1983) *Elswick Women's Workshop Project*. FSU Quarterly No.30, p.59.

Janet Radcliffe RICHARDS (1980) *The Sceptical Feminist*. Penguin.

Vernon RICHARDS ed.(1983) *Why Work? Arguments for the Leisure Society.* Freedom Press.

F.F. RIDLEY (1985) *The Disaster That Won't Stop At Liverpool*. Guardian 17th September.

Andrew RIGBY (1974) *Alternative Realities: A Study of Communes.* Routledge.

Alan ROBERTS (1979) *The Self-Managing Environment*. Allison and Busby.

Fritz J. ROETHLISBERGER and William J. DICKSON (1939) *Management and the Worker*. Cambridge Massachusetts: Harvard.

Helen ROBERTS ed. (1981) *Doing Feminist Research*. Routledge.

Carl ROGERS (1978) *Personal Power*. Constable.

Stephen M. ROSE and Bruce L. BLACK (1986) *Advocacy and Empowerment: Mental Health Care in the Community*. Boston: Routledge.

Joan ROTHSCHILD (1976) *Taking Our Future Seriously*. Quest Vol II, no.3, Winter 1976, p.17.

Joyce ROTHSCHILD-WHITT (1976) *Problems of Democracy*. Working Papers for a New Society, Vol IV, No.3, Autumn, pp.41-45.

Joyce ROTHSCHILD-WHITT (1979) *The Collectivist Organisation: An Alternative to Rational Bureaucratic Models*. American Sociological Review Vol.44, August, p.509-527. Reprinted (with some changes) in Lindenfeld and Rothschild-Whitt (1982).

Joyce ROTHSCHILD and J. Allen WHITT (1986) *The Co-operative Workplace: Potentials and Dilemmas of Organisational Democracy and Participation*. Cambridge University Press.

John ROWAN (1976) *The Power of the Group*. Davis-Poynter.

John ROWAN (1981) *A Dialectical Paradigm For Research*, in Peter Reason and John Rowan ed. *Human Inquiry: A Sourcebook of New Paradigm Research*. Chichester: John Wiley.

Sheila ROWBOTHAM (1983) *Dreams and Dilemmas*. Virago.

Harvey SACKS (1974) *On the Analysability of Stories by Children*, in Roy Turner ed. *Ethnomethodology*. Penguin.

Oliver SACKS (1982) *Awakenings*. Picador.

Anthony P. SAGER (1979) *Radical Law: Three Collectives in Cambridge*, in John Case and Rosemary Taylor ed. *Co-ops, Communes and Collectives*. New York: Pantheon.

Carole SATYAMURTI (1981) *Occupational Survival: The Case of the Local Authority Social Worker*. Oxford: Basil Blackwell.

Donald SCHON (1973) *Beyond the Stable State: Public and Private Learning in a Changing Society*. Penguin.

Donald SCHON (1983) *The Reflective Practitioner: How Professionals Think in Action*. Temple Smith.

Duncan SCOTT and Paul WILDING ed. (1985) *What Price Voluntary Action?*. Manchester Council for Voluntary Service and the Department of Social Administration, University of Manchester.

Seebohm Report (1968) *Report of the Committee on Local Authority and Allied Personal Social Services*. CMnd 3703, HMSO.

Richard SENNETT (1980) *Authority*. Secker and Warburg.

Jennie SIBLEY (1986) *Planning in a Hierarchic Organisation*. Social Services Research, Vol: 15, No.2, p.39.

A. SIVANANDAN (1985) *RAT and the Degradation of Black Struggle*. Race and Class Vol XXVI No.4, Spring.

Bruce L.R. SMITH and Douglas C. HAGUE ed. (1971) *The Dilemma of Accountability in Modern Government: Independence Versus Control*. Macmillan.

Debbie SMITH (1984) *Doctoring Democracy*. Spare Rib No.142, May.

Joan SMITH (1985) *Growing Together: Innovatory Work with a Whole Family*. FSU.

Michael Peter SMITH (1980) *The City and Social Theory*. Oxford: Basil Blackwell.

SOUTH BIRMINGHAM FSU (1987) *Speaking For Ourselves: Residents Make Decisions*.

Harry SPECHT and Anne VICKERY (1977) *Integrating Social Work Methods*. Allen and Unwin.

Dale SPENDER (1980) *Man Made Language*. Routledge.

Alan STANTON (1983) *Collective Working in the Personal Social Services: a Study with Nine Agencies*. MSc. Cranfield Institute of Technology.

Paul STARR (1979) *The Phanton Community*, in John Case and Rosemary Taylor ed. (1979) *Co-ops, Connunes and Collectives:*Experiments in the 1960's and 1970's *New York:* Pantheon.

Francis STEVENS (1983) *Law Centre Staff Research Project*. Law Centres Federation.

Olive STEVENSON and Phyllida PARSLOE (1978) *Social Service Teams: The Practitioners' View*. HMSO.

Ian TAYLOR, Paul WALTON and Jock YOUNG (1975) *Critical Criminology*. Routledge.

Rosemary C.R. TAYLOR (1979) *Free Medicine*, in John Case and Rosemary Taylor ed. *Co-ops, Connunes and Collectives*. New York: Pantheon.

Jean TEPPERMAN (1976) *Not Servants, Not Machines: Office Workers Speak Out*. Boston: Beacon.

Martin THOMAS (1986) *Going Local*. FSU Quarterly, no.38.

Jennifer THORNLEY (1981) *Workers' Co-operatives — Jobs and Dreams*. Heinemann.

Marcia TONDEL and Dave HOLDER (1974) *Team Leadership*. FSU Quarterly no.6, 1974.

Lane TRACEY (1972) *Postscript to the Peter Principle*. Harvard Business Review, July-August, 65-71.

E.L. TRIST and K.W. BAMFORTH (1951) *Some Social and Psychological Consequences of the Longwall Method of Coal-Getting*. Human Relations, 1951, 4, 3-38.

E.L. TRIST, G.W. HIGGIN, H. MURRAY, and A.B. POLLACK (1963) *Organisational Choice*. Tavistock.

Raoul VANEIGEM (1967) *The Revolution of Everyday Life* (Not copyright; published in numerous editions.)

Andrew VEITCH (1983) *A Stimulating Dose of Utopia*. The Guardian 21st December.

Anne VICKERY (1977) *Social Work Practice: Divisions and Unifications*, in **Harry Specht and Anne Vickery ed.** *Integrating Social Work Methods*. Allen and Unwin.

Judy WAJCMAN (1983) *Women In Control*. Open University Press.

Ronald WALTON (1975) *Women in Social Work*. Routledge.

Colin WARD (1983) *Housing: An Anarchist Approach*. Freedom Books.

Adrian WEBB and Martin HOBDELL (1980) *Co-ordination and Teamwork*, in Susan Lonsdale, Adrian Webb, and T.L. Briggs ed. *Teamwork in the Personal Social Services and Health Care: British and American Perspectives*. Croom Helm.

Max WEBER (1968) *Economy and Society*. University of California Press.

Max WEBER (1970) ed. H. Gerth and C. Wright Mills, *Essays in Sociology* Routledge.

Stephen WEXLER (1970) *Practicing Law for Poor People*. Yale Law Journal, Vol.79, p.1049.

Colin WHITTINGTON (1975) *Organisational Research in Social Work*. British Journal of Social Work Vol.5, 59-74.

Raymond WILLIAMS (1985) *Towards 2000*. Penguin.

Stewart WILSON (1980) *The School and the Community*, in Colin Fletcher and Neil Thompson, *Issues in Community Education*. Falmer Press.

Women's Liberation Workshop (1969) *Manifesto*. Shrew, November—December.

Women's Self-Help Network (1984) *Why Operate Collectively?* Ptarmigan Press: Campbell River, British Columbia.

Ken WORPOLE (1983) *Laundered Ideologically*. Another Standard, April.

Charlotte WRIGHT (1979) *Pakistani Women in the West End of Newcastle*. Dissertation for B.Med. Science, Newcastle University.

Patrick WRIGHT (1985) NCVO Management Development Unit Bulletin, June.

Jonathan ZEITLYN (1980) *Print: How You Can Do It Yourself*. Interchange.

Don ZIMMERMAN (1971) *The Practicalities of Rule Use*, in Jack Douglas ed. *Understanding Everyday Life*. Routledge.

ACKNOWLEDGEMENTS

Books are never the sole work of the people named on the cover. That's particularly true for participatory research, and more so when a project has been years in the making.

My special thanks to the following people who were always more than generous in helping the book come to fruition: workers, users and committee members at Newcastle FSU; and Colin Fletcher at Cranfield Institute of Technology. When I began listing all the other people who'd contributed in any way, I realised there was just no space to include their names. Well, they know who they are, and will have to make do with a warm, general 'Thank You'.